The *Fin-de-Siècle* Scottish Revival

Edinburgh Critical Studies in Victorian Culture
Series Editor: Julian Wolfreys

Recent books in the series:

Rudyard Kipling's Fiction: Mapping Psychic Spaces
Lizzy Welby

The Decadent Image: The Poetry of Wilde, Symons and Dowson
Kostas Boyiopoulos

British India and Victorian Literary Culture
Máire ní Fhlathúin

Anthony Trollope's Late Style: Victorian Liberalism and Literary Form
Frederik Van Dam

Dark Paradise: Pacific Islands in the Nineteenth-Century British Imagination
Jenn Fuller

Twentieth-Century Victorian: Arthur Conan Doyle and the Strand Magazine*, 1891–1930*
Jonathan Cranfield

The Lyric Poem and Aestheticism: Forms of Modernity
Marion Thain

Gender, Technology and the New Woman
Lena Wånggren

Self-Harm in New Woman Writing
Alexandra Gray

Suffragist Artists in Partnership: Gender, Word and Image
Lucy Ella Rose

Victorian Liberalism and Material Culture: Synergies of Thought and Place
Kevin A. Morrison

The Victorian Male Body
Joanne-Ella Parsons and Ruth Heholt

Nineteenth-Century Settler Emigration in British Literature and Art
Fariha Shaikh

The Pre-Raphaelites and Orientalism
Eleonora Sasso

The Late-Victorian Little Magazine
Koenraad Claes

Coastal Cultures of the Long Nineteenth Century
Matthew Ingleby and Matt P. M. Kerr

Dickens and Demolition: Literary Afterlives and Mid-Nineteenth-Century Urban Development
Joanna Hofer-Robinson

Artful Experiments: Ways of Knowing in Victorian Literature and Science
Philipp Erchinger

Victorian Poetry and the Poetics of the Literary Periodical
Caley Ehnes

The Victorian Actress in the Novel and on the Stage
Renata Kobetts Miller

Dickens's Clowns: Charles Dickens, Joseph Grimaldi and the Pantomime of Life
Jonathan Buckmaster

Italian Politics and Nineteenth-Century British Literature and Culture
Patricia Cove

Cultural Encounters with the Arabian Nights in Nineteenth-Century Britain
Melissa Dickson

Novel Institutions: Anachronism, Irish Novels and Nineteenth-Century Realism
Mary L. Mullen

The Fin-de-Siècle *Scottish Revival: Romance, Decadence and Celtic Identity*
Michael Shaw

Forthcoming volumes:

Her Father's Name: Gender, Theatricality and Spiritualism in Florence Marryat's Fiction
Tatiana Kontou

The Sculptural Body in Victorian Literature: Encrypted Sexualities
Patricia Pulham

Olive Schreiner and the Politics of Print Culture, 1883–1920
Clare Gill

Victorian Auto/Biography: Problems in Genre and Subject
Amber Regis

Gissing, Shakespeare and the Life of Writing
Thomas Ue

The Aesthetics of Space in Nineteenth-Century British Literature, 1851–1908
Giles Whiteley

Women's Mobility in Henry James
Anna Despotopoulou

The Persian Presence in Victorian Poetry
Reza Taher-Kermani

Michael Field's Revisionary Poetics
Jill Ehnenn

Contested Liberalisms: Martineau, Dickens and the Victorian Press
Iain Crawford

Plotting Disability in the Nineteenth-Century Novel
Clare Walker Gore

The Americanisation of W. T. Stead
Helena Goodwyn

Literary Illusions: Performance Magic and Victorian Literature
Christopher Pittard

For a complete list of titles published visit the Edinburgh Critical Studies in Victorian Culture web page at www.edinburghuniversitypress.com/series/ECVC

Also available:
Victoriographies – A Journal of Nineteenth-Century Writing, 1790–1914, edited by Diane Piccitto and Patricia Pulham
ISSN: 2044–2416
www.eupjournals.com/vic

The *Fin-de-Siècle* Scottish Revival

Romance, Decadence and Celtic Identity

Michael Shaw

EDINBURGH
University Press

To the memory of my gran

Edinburgh University Press is one of the leading university presses in the UK. We publish academic books and journals in our selected subject areas across the humanities and social sciences, combining cutting-edge scholarship with high editorial and production values to produce academic works of lasting importance. For more information visit our website: edinburghuniversitypress.com

Edinburgh University Press Ltd
The Tun – Holyrood Road, 12(2f) Jackson's Entry, Edinburgh EH8 8PJ

First published in hardback by Edinburgh University Press 2020

Typeset in 11/13 Adobe Sabon by
IDSUK (DataConnection) Ltd, and
printed and bound by CPI Group (UK) Ltd, Croydon, CR0 4YY

A CIP record for this book is available from the British Library

ISBN 978 1 4744 3395 2 (hardback)
ISBN 978 1 4744 3396 9 (paperback)
ISBN 978 1 4744 3398 3 (webready PDF)
ISBN 978 1 4744 3397 6 (epub)

Contents

Illustrations

Figures

Plates

Series Editor's Preface

'Victorian' is a term, at once indicative of a strongly determined concept and an often notoriously vague notion, emptied of all meaningful content by the many journalistic misconceptions that persist about the inhabitants and cultures of the British Isles and Victoria's Empire in the nineteenth century. As such, it has become a by-word for the assumption of various, often contradictory habits of thought, belief, behaviour and perceptions. Victorian studies and studies in nineteenth-century literature and culture have, from their institutional inception, questioned narrowness of presumption, pushed at the limits of the nominal definition, and have sought to question the very grounds on which the unreflective perception of the so-called Victorian has been built; and so they continue to do. Victorian and nineteenth-century studies of literature and culture maintain a breadth and diversity of interest, of focus and inquiry, in an interrogative and intellectually open-minded and challenging manner, which are equal to the exploration and inquisitiveness of its subjects. Many of the questions asked by scholars and researchers of the innumerable productions of nineteenth-century society actively put into suspension the clichés and stereotypes of 'Victorianism', whether the approach has been sustained by historical, scientific, philosophical, empirical, ideological or theoretical concerns; indeed, it would be incorrect to assume that each of these approaches to the idea of the Victorian has been, or has remained, in the main exclusive, sealed off from the interests and engagements of other approaches. A vital interdisciplinarity has been pursued and embraced, for the most part, even as there has been contest and debate amongst Victorianists, pursued with as much fervour as the affirmative exploration between different disciplines and differing epistemologies put to work in the service of reading the nineteenth century.

Edinburgh Critical Studies in Victorian Culture aims to take up both the debates and the inventive approaches and departures from convention that studies in the nineteenth century have witnessed for the last half century at least. Aiming to maintain a 'Victorian' (in the most positive sense of that motif) spirit of inquiry, the series' purpose is to continue and augment the cross-fertilisation of interdisciplinary approaches, and to offer, in addition, a number of timely and untimely revisions of Victorian literature, culture, history and identity. At the same time, the series will ask questions concerning what has been missed or improperly received, misread, or not read at all, in order to present a multi-faceted and heterogeneous kaleidoscope of representations. Drawing on the most provocative, thoughtful and original research, the series will seek to prod at the notion of the 'Victorian', and in so doing, principally through theoretically and epistemologically sophisticated close readings of the historicity of literature and culture in the nineteenth century, to offer the reader provocative insights into a world that is at once overly familiar, and irreducibly different, other and strange. Working from original sources, primary documents and recent interdisciplinary theoretical models, Edinburgh Critical Studies in Victorian Culture seeks not simply to push at the boundaries of research in the nineteenth century, but also to inaugurate the persistent erasure and provisional, strategic redrawing of those borders.

Julian Wolfreys

Acknowledgements

There are few things as rewarding as acknowledging the generosity, advice and support of those who have made this book possible.

The research for this study was largely undertaken as a PhD student at the University of Glasgow, and my two supervisors went well beyond the call of duty in their dedication to the project. For their rigour, guidance and continuing support, I am deeply grateful to Murray Pittock and Christine Ferguson. My examiners Murdo Macdonald and Mary Ellis Gibson were meticulous with their comments and edits, and they gave me faith that the thesis could be adapted into a book. I am also indebted to Ruth Livesey and Anne Varty for encouraging me to undertake this project back in 2010.

To my friends who, whether they liked it not, sailed with me through the troughs of stress and the highs of discovery: thank you. You know who you are.

For their input – and patience – over the last few years, I express my thanks to the editorial team at Edinburgh University Press; I would also like to thank the various readers they approached who provided constructive, challenging, heartening feedback. Beyond the publishing house, I am indebted to the following colleagues for their encouragement, thoughts, and selfless offers to read draft chapters and proposals: Kirstie Blair, Koenraad Claes, Elizabeth Cumming, Bill Halloran, Tom Hulme, Nicola Kirkby, Sara Lyons, Catriona Macdonald, Wendy Parkins, Jamie Reid-Baxter, and Derek Ryan.

The unsung heroes of academic research are the world's librarians and archivists. I am particularly indebted to the expertise and dependable efficiency of staff at the following institutions: Archive Services and Special Collections, University of Strathclyde; Beinecke Library of Rare Book and Manuscripts, Yale University; Broughton House and Garden (NTS); Glasgow Museums; Glasgow School of Art; The Hunterian, University of Glasgow; The Library and Museum of Freemasonry; National Library of Scotland; RCAHMS; and Special Collections, University of Glasgow Library.

Several institutions have financially supported this research, as well as the book's production costs. For their generosity, my thanks go to the Arts and Humanities Research Council; the Faculty of Arts and Humanities, University of Stirling; the School of English, University of Kent; the School of Critical Studies, University of Glasgow; and the Beinecke Rare Book & Manuscript Library, Yale University. The support of The Strathmartine Trust towards this publication is gratefully acknowledged. For kindly allowing me to reproduce the many images that feature in this book, I am thankful to the British Museum; City of Edinburgh Museums & Galleries; Dundee Art Galleries and Museums; Edinburgh University Library; Glasgow Museums and Libraries; Heidelberg University Library; The Hunterian, University of Glasgow; Historic Environment Scotland; MAK – Austrian Museum of Applied Arts; National Galleries of Scotland; National Library of Scotland; University of Dundee Museum Services; University of Glasgow Library; University of St Andrews Library; University of Strathclyde Library; and the Victoria & Albert Museum.

Defining the precise origin of a book is ultimately a futile task, but I suspect this one wouldn't have been written without those Mockintosh mirrors, Jacobite legends and precarious towers of Penguin Popular Classics that I was surrounded by in childhood. For their support then and now, my greatest thanks go to my family.

Introduction

In 1895, Victor Branford, a former student of Edinburgh University who would go on to co-found the Sociological Society in 1903, wrote a review of a magazine that had lately been published in the Lawnmarket of Edinburgh's Old Town, a place that was 'until recently inhabited too much by prostitutes and thieves'.[1] This magazine was *The Evergreen*, a 'northern seasonal' published by the town planner and sociologist Patrick Geddes, which reflected Geddes's broader interest in reviving Edinburgh's Old Town and transforming it into an artistic centre. The magazine fused literature and art with scientific and sociological essays, and it was widely applauded for its handsome design, inviting comparisons with other *fin-de-siècle* magazines, including *The Yellow Book*. As Branford quipped, it was 'a fine art production from what was one of the filthiest and most degraded slums of Europe'.[2] But *The Evergreen* and Geddes were not simply interested in contributing to the revitalisation of Edinburgh's Old Town. In his assessment of *The Evergreen*'s aims, Branford makes reference to the magazine's namesake, Allan Ramsay's *Evergreen* (1724), a collection of poetry that hoped to arouse interest in medieval and early modern Scottish literature, in the wake of the 1707 Acts of Union. Branford believed that Geddes's *Evergreen* was equally keen to defend and reanimate Scottish culture and traditions:

> In 1724 Allan Ramsay published his *Evergreen*, desiring thereby to stimulate the return to local and national tradition and living nature. [. . .]
>
> Amongst the 'local and national' traditions which patriotic Scotsmen are to-day trying to revive and keep alive, the present *Evergreen* specially concerns itself with those connected with Scottish nationalism, Celtic literature and art, and the old Continental sympathies of Scotland (more particularly the 'ancient league with France'). [. . .] In the incipient Celtic Renascence, Ireland has played a much more conspicuous part

> than Scotland. But the writings of Miss Fiona Macleod are gradually disclosing to the British public quite another Scotland than that with which the lowland writers have familiarized them. And it is generally overlooked, too, that in Art the Glasgow School, in consideration of its local origin and its emphasis on colour and decorative treatment of subject, may be counted congenitally part of the Celtic Renascence. To many, the most hopeless quest will seem the endeavour to restore Edinburgh to its position as a culture capital, and to make Scotland again a power (of culture) in Europe, as it was in recent, in medieval, and most of all in ancient times. Yet who knows?[3]

Branford here identifies several key features and objectives of Geddes's community and *The Evergreen* magazine. He highlights Geddes's desire to rehabilitate Scotland's position as an international cultural power, by reanimating its European connections, including the Franco-Scottish alliance. In making these points, Branford is quick to caution that those in Geddes's circle were not defined by an anti-Union sentiment, despite their connections to 'Scottish nationalism'; they were primarily concerned with developing a revival movement that was firmly 'of culture', seeking to assert Scotland's nationhood and its international presence through cultural means. A defining feature of this movement, in Branford's assessment, was its enthusiasm for Celtic literature, mythologies and art – a passion that he finds reflected in the art of the Glasgow School, a reference to the pioneering circle of artists in Glasgow that encompassed Charles Rennie Mackintosh, Margaret Macdonald, the Glasgow Girls and the Glasgow Boys. In its desire to defend and revitalise Scottish literature and art, and its valorising of Celtic culture, Branford casts this movement as directly comparable with the Irish Revival (a more politically nationalist cultural movement headed by such figures as William Butler Yeats, Lady Gregory and J. M. Synge), and characterises it as a key voice in the wider 'Celtic Renascence'. In Branford's framing, a national movement analogous to the Irish Revival, with international ambitions, took hold across Scotland at the *fin de siècle*, of which *The Evergreen* was one of its notable products.

Branford was not the only contemporary critic to detect a concern with cultural defence and revivalism in *fin-de-siècle* Scotland. Writing in 1913, one of the first literary critics of the 1890s, Holbrook Jackson, identified a 'Scottish movement', analogous to the Irish Literary Revival, that centred on Geddes, which he characterised as an effective revival.[4] Author and playwright Israel Zangwill asserted the existence of a *fin-de-siècle* 'Scotch School', which he applauded for trying to 'emancipate itself from the intellectual thralldom of

London'.[5] Reflecting on the 1890s, Lewis Mumford, a collaborator of Geddes, wrote on the 'artistic and literary revival in Edinburgh and Glasgow, which was dimmed only by the profounder Irish revival of O'Grady, A. E. and Yeats'.[6] The author Neil Munro also noted that 'we are having a Scots revival in literature' in one of his letters to William Blackwood in 1894.[7] And in the words of Elizabeth Sharp – editor of *Lyra Celtica*, a collection of poetry published by Patrick Geddes and Colleagues – Geddes's projects intended to 'arrest the tremendous centralising power of the metropolis of London' and to 'restore to Scotland something of its old pre-eminence in the world of thought'.[8] As these various quotations illustrate, contemporary critics and witnesses of cultural developments in 1890s Scotland detected a palpable desire to challenge the centralisation of culture and intellectualism to London and a conviction to reassert Scotland's distinctive cultural presence internationally.

Despite contemporary critics identifying a concern with cultural defence and revival in *fin-de-siècle* Scotland, there has been no sustained consideration of it since. As Murray Pittock and Isla Jack have neatly summarised, while the Irish Revival's 'Scottish equivalent seemed almost as important' in the late Victorian period, it 'remains sadly neglected today'.[9] Although Kurt Wittig noted that Scottish literature was 'heaving again' in this period,[10] and Roderick Watson has more recently identified 'stirrings' of cultural confidence in the 1890s, such comments are often brief observations in studies on broader periods.[11] The most substantial considerations of Scottish nationality in relation to *fin-de-siècle* culture to date are John Morrison's chapter on the Celtic Revival in his book, *Painting the Nation: Identity and Nationalism in Scottish Painting, 1800–1920* (2003), and Douglas Gifford's 2015 essay, 'From Celtic Revival to Scottish Renaissance?'. Although the latter is primarily concerned with revealing the health and vitality of Scottish culture c.1870–1920, tacitly challenging Tom Nairn's view that there was little Scottish literature 'worth attention from 1880 to 1920',[12] Gifford's essay also usefully identifies similarities between Scottish and Irish culture at the *fin de siècle*, as well as continuities between Scottish literature of the *fin de siècle* and the 'Scottish Renaissance' of the 1920s. His polemic calls on critics of Scottish literature to revisit 'our cultural maps of the 1870–1920 period', which, he thinks, urgently require reconsideration.[13]

In highlighting the need for critics to focus on *fin-de-siècle* Scotland's ties to Irish developments as well as the Scottish Renaissance of the 1920s, Gifford's essay implicitly works against a common assumption in Scottish literary criticism that Scotland developed a cultural revival comparable to Ireland's only in the 1920s, with the emergence of such writers as Hugh MacDiarmid and Edwin Muir. For instance, when comparing late Victorian Scotland to Ireland, Glenda Norquay writes that a 'project of Celtic revivalism in Scotland' was not only absent but also 'prevented' by a relative lack of academic interest in Scotland's Celtic inheritance, noting that Robert Louis Stevenson's 'espousal of Celtic' was a rare exception.[14] Alongside such understandings of absent Celtic revivalism, several literary scholars have also framed the *fin de siècle* as marking a weak point for Scottish nationality and culture. Associating 1890s literature with an anti-national and anti-international insularity, Margery Palmer McCulloch writes that, by the Second World War, Scottish modernist texts had travelled far from 'kailyaird parochialism in the late nineteenth century'.[15] Until recently the Kailyard – a term often associated with the 1890s writings of J. M. Barrie, S. R. Crockett and Ian Maclaren that were set in small Scottish towns – has tended to underpin characterisations of 1890s Scottish literature, breeding blanket generalisations that frame 1890s Scottish culture and identity in terms of the parochial and the anti-national. This was particularly apparent in the criticism of the 1960s through to the 1980s. Echoing Ian Campbell's view that the late nineteenth century suffered from a 'diluted national consciousness',[16] Gillian Shepherd argues that Kailyard writers 'sought to thwart a national consciousness that might have been' – a quotation that suggests Scotland was lacking a national consciousness in this period. Expanding on this claim, Shepherd starkly refers to Kailyard novelists as proponents of 'national infanticide'.[17] More nuanced understandings of the Kailyard have since been put forward by Andrew Nash, who shows that Kailyard literature was concerned not simply with locality but also with a defence of Scottish nationality: in Nash's framing, certain Kailyard texts attempted to correct English characterisations of Scottish identity, and he also rightly notes that the parochial and the national need not be mutually exclusive paradigms in Scotland, through highlighting the broader literary tradition of portraying 'rural and humble life as representative of Scottish national identity'.[18] Nevertheless, the association of the Scottish *fin de siècle* with an infirm, or even deceased, national consciousness continues to be endorsed; Cairns Craig, for instance, has recently claimed that Scotland was 'effectively dead' before the Scottish Renaissance of the 1920s.[19]

Building on Gifford, Morrison, Pittock and Jack, this book presents the first sustained consideration of *fin-de-siècle* Scottish revivalism, which hopes to revise several of the misunderstandings of the period that have taken hold, and to reveal the complexity of *fin-de-siècle* Scottish culture. By assessing a range of literature and art from across Scotland c.1880–1914, these chapters unearth and analyse the Scottish Revival that the likes of Branford, Zangwill, Jackson, Sharp, Defries and Munro identified. I demonstrate here that several writers and artists were discontented with what they perceived to be the increasing marginality of Scottish identities, cultures and traditions in this period, which fuelled a concerted effort to defend and revive Scottish literature and art, anticipating several twentieth-century developments. This revivalism can be found in neglected texts and artworks of the era, and also in key canonical works that have not been considered in relation to pertinent constitutional and cultural contexts, such as those of Robert Louis Stevenson, Arthur Conan Doyle, Violet Jacob and Charles Rennie Mackintosh. But although this book reveals that a number of figures across the nation desired to develop cultural revivalism in Scotland, it does not portray that desire as uniform or cohesive in shape. Not only was the nature of the Scottish Revival contested and complex, but also individual promoters were inconsistent on the issue, much like several Irish revivalists.

Beyond uncovering the concern with revivalism in Scotland, and revealing the similarities (and tensions) between the Scottish and Irish Revivals, this book also explores the significant role that dissident *fin-de-siècle* styles and ideas played in supporting the Scottish Revival. In their turn to traditional Scottish culture, including Celtic crafts and mythologies, Scottish revivalists participated in a broader interrogation of *fin-de-siècle* modernity and 'civilisation' that was found across Europe, and they often looked to wider European cultural developments to fuel their revival. As in other European nations, Scottish revivalists engaged in decadent neo-paganism, occultism, neo-Jacobitism, *japonisme* and mysticism to fuel their attempts to define the nation and revive aspects of its culture. In shedding light on the decadent, symbolist and international dimensions of cultural revivalism in Scotland, this book hopes to add several new perspectives to critical understandings of Scotland's *fin de siècle*, a period that Craig believes remains one of the least well understood in Scottish cultural history.[20]

Cultural Revivals in *Fin-de-Siècle* Europe

The understanding of the term 'cultural revival' that I adopt in this study builds on John Hutchinson's theory of cultural nationalism. In his essay 'Cultural Nationalism and Moral Regeneration', Hutchinson juxtaposes the concept of cultural nationalism with that of political nationalism. Political nationalism, he writes, is an endeavour that seeks 'to secure a representative state for [a] community', and it is this ambition for statehood that distinguishes political nationalism from cultural nationalism. For Hutchinson, cultural nationalism is not necessarily concerned with attaining statehood: its focus is on defining, 're-unit[ing]' and regenerating a national community, and highlighting its distinctive development, 'oppos[ing] assimilation of the community to any universal model of development'.[21] While Hutchinson juxtaposes this cultural nationalist aim to build a stronger sense of nationality against political nationalism, he is nevertheless keen to stress that they are not mutually exclusive concepts. Cultural and political nationalists are 'different, even competing' groups, but cultural nationalists, he writes, 'are often driven into state politics to defend the cultural autonomy of the nation'.[22]

Like Hutchinson's definition of cultural nationalism, cultural revivalism refers to attempts to define and unify a national community through cultural apparatus, without necessarily arguing for statehood. But cultural revivalism is distinguished by its particular emphasis. Cultural revivals, such as the *fin-de-siècle* Scottish Revival, prioritise the recovery (or appropriation) of past cultural formations and traditions to bind and define the nation, and to resist the nation's assimilation. As we shall see, these movements – defined by returning to folklore, mythologies, histories and traditional crafts – at times placed themselves in opposition to industrial modernity but, equally, they were not always antithetical to modernity. Several *fin-de-siècle* cultural revivalists were concerned with reconciling modernity with the continuance of tradition to define and unify the national self.

Across *fin-de-siècle* Europe, such cultural revival movements were ubiquitous, developing distinctive accents in each nation. As Michelle Facos identifies, revival movements, concerned with the 'survival of native traditions and values', 'thrived in much of Europe – in Scandinavia as well as in Ireland, Belgium, Hungary, Poland and Russia'.[23] Facos argues that these movements were partly concerned with rejecting the dominance of industrial capitalism in the late nineteenth century, which was felt to be uprooting peoples, while Neil Kent proposes an additional explanation for their rise: they responded to anxieties about mounting centralisation and cultural homogeneity across Europe.[24] This concern with cultural homogeneity was reflected in the Young Belgium movement, which I discuss in Chapter 2, whose writers hoped to defend their nation's literary culture from increasing centralisation of artistic life to Paris.

To safeguard their particular cultures, Facos demonstrates that several European revivalists turned to romantic nationalism, which 'tended to be expressed in the form of durable "master narratives" containing an origin myth, historical heroes, ongoing antagonists, [. . .] nostalgia for a lost golden age, and the promise of an imminent revival', according to Richard Marsden.[25] Like the romantics before them, several revivalists also valorised the lifestyle of the peasantry, 'whose links with primordial times continued unbroken in forests and villages', which made them 'sacred protectors' of national cultures.[26] Eric Hobsbawm illustrates that such 'invented traditions' were 'mass produced' throughout Europe between 1870 and 1914 in order to stimulate greater cohesion within groups,[27] and literature and art became key tools for distributing these traditions. Various European artists and writers created works to advance their nation's cultural revival, a striking number of which reveal a debt to a contemporary art movement that prioritised the mystical and spiritual over realism – symbolism. Facos writes that symbolism's focus on realities beyond the material was in step with the 'biomystical link between a landscape and its inhabitants' that several revivalists developed,[28] and she illustrates the clear convergence of cultural revivalism and symbolism in several Swedish revivalist artworks, including those of Richard Bergh, who turned to mythology, folklore and the mystical for artistic inspiration.

Sweden's *fin-de-siècle* revival provides an example of a nationalism that was not politically nationalist, by Hutchinson's definition, as Sweden was already in possession of statehood. But several cultural revival movements in Europe ran alongside, and intersected with, political nationalist campaigns. Certain Irish revivalists, such as W. B. Yeats, embody this intersection, in looking to Celtic mythology to revive awareness of Irish tradition while finding themselves drawn into debates on political nationalism.[29] Similarly, at the time of the Russification of Finland (a Russian policy intended to weaken Finland's political autonomy at the *fin de siècle*), Akseli Gallen-Kallela led Finland's turn to mythology to bolster the nation's artistic and cultural identity. Gallen-Kallela was especially influenced by Finland's national epic, *Kalevala*, which informed several of his works, including the *Aino Myth* triptych (1891).

As in Ireland and Finland, cultural revivalism in *fin-de-siècle* Scotland developed alongside growing anxieties over the nation's constitutional position, with a number of Scots articulating their concern that Scottish nationality and the nation's political autonomy were being undermined by increasing centralisation towards London. Although there was very little interest in 'secur[ing] a representative state' for the Scottish nation amongst *fin-de-siècle* cultural revivalists, several critiqued the constitutional make-up of the United Kingdom, and certain figures actively campaigned to obtain some of the apparatus of statehood for Scotland, including a national legislature, through agitating for Home Rule. In order to understand the distinctive nature of the Scottish Revival fully, we must address the political contexts and anxieties that it developed against and, at times, directly spoke to.

Constitutional Discontents and Scottish Home Rule

In his study on Scottish national identity c.1830–60, *Unionist Nationalism*, Graeme Morton demonstrates that mid-nineteenth-century Scotland was broadly content with its constitutional position within the United Kingdom, on account of the fact that Scotland was largely self-governing. Morton highlights that, in this period, the British state's capacities were so limited that there was minimal intervention in Scottish affairs and, consequently, the Scottish bourgeoisie were free to govern Scotland through its various institutions, such as the church, law, education, the periodical press and municipal government. In Morton's framing, 'it was anathema to contemporary thought to campaign for a Westminster-style Scottish state' because the Scottish bourgeoisie 'had all the power it needed to govern its own society'.[30] In this period, rather than being antagonistic, Morton stresses that the Union and Scottish liberty were perceived as mutually supportive concepts – a phenomenon that he defines as 'unionist nationalism'. We find this unionist nationalism throughout Scottish culture in the mid-nineteenth century, but it is perhaps best embodied by Joseph Noel Paton's design for the National Memorial of the War of Independence (1859). This memorial design consisted of a large Celtic cross, adorned with various statues and *bas-reliefs* at its base, one of which depicted 'The Union'. Here, on a monument that commemorates the military efforts of Wallace and Bruce, the Union is simultaneously celebrated through a depiction of two female symbols of Scotland and England joining hands 'as Independent Powers'.[31] The expression of Scottish national liberty and history is in no way portrayed as compromised by Union here: instead, the Scottish wars of independence are portrayed as facilitating an equal partnership, one in which Scotland can still express and commemorate its autonomy.[32]

The sense of Scotland's continuing freedom within Union is reflected in mid-Victorian Scottish political poetry. Kirstie Blair's examination of the ways Scottish periodical poetry engaged with nineteenth-century European nationalist movements reveals that Scots saw their nation as a model for European nations hoping to achieve national liberation, rather than as a nation that also needed to be liberated. Blair identifies an array of poems from the periodical press that demonstrate Scots' sympathy for Kossuth's and Garibaldi's campaigns in Poland and Italy to illustrate this point. Scots portrayed their nation as 'Land of freedom', 'whaur Freedom's standard never fell', 'ever famed for thy beauty and freedom'.[33] The poets that Blair identifies saw Scotland as a beacon of freedom and liberation in the mid-nineteenth century, a nation that had achieved its liberation in the fourteenth century, which had continued despite the Union. As late as 1884, in poetry written during the Reform Bill agitation, we find Scottish political poets referencing 'the stern independence o' Scotland'.[34] Such lines illustrate that not only did many Scots think of their nation as free in the nineteenth century, but also there was still space in the public imagination to conceive Scotland as an independent nation.

But even amidst the expressions of Scottish freedom and independence within Union in the mid-nineteenth century, there were nascent signs of Scottish discontent with the United Kingdom's constitutional dynamics. In 1853, the National Association for the Vindication of Scottish Rights was established, with an initial meeting in Edinburgh 'crowded to excess, many hundreds besides having failed to obtain admission'.[35] The association was primarily concerned with the under-representation of Scottish affairs in Westminster, and, to help remedy this discontent, the association proposed that '"the office for Secretary of State for Scotland be restored"'[36] and that there should be increased Scottish parliamentary representation in Westminster.[37] Michael Keating rightly notes that the association was 'firmly within the unionist tradition, asking for more consideration for Scottish issues at Westminster and in Whitehall',[38] but it is important to stress that, for some in the Association, their goals were not limited to increasing Scotland's presence in parliament and government. One attendee, at an even larger Glasgow meeting, called for a 'Scottish assembly', an idea echoed by Glasgow's *The Commonwealth* newspaper, which argued that the establishment of a Scottish Secretary, along with increased representation in Westminster, would 'do much; but they will not do all' and that the 'full remedy' was a 'parliament'.[39]

As we move into the later nineteenth century, several of the tensions that some Scots felt within the Union grew. A number of historians have noted that the nature of the Union changed in the late

Victorian period. For instance, Alvin Jackson notes that 'for Scotland, the massive growth of the civil service in the later 19th century was essentially the growth of the union'.[40] A growing state and growing centralisation, Jackson argues, led to the feeling that Scotland's freedom was increasingly compromised and, consequently, according to Morton, unionist nationalism 'died out' at the *fin de siècle*, to be replaced by an identity that was 'more Scottish than British'.[41] We similarly find a concerted effort to defend and expand Scotland's civic state at the *fin de siècle*, reflected in the proliferation of new national institutions, including the Scottish Text Society (1882), Royal Scottish Geographical Society (1884), Scottish History Society (1886), Scottish National Portrait Gallery (1889), Scottish Mountaineering Club (1889), Scottish Football League (1890), Royal Scottish National Orchestra (1891), Scottish Council for Women's Trades (1895) and Scottish Trade Union Congress (1897). Richard Finlay argues that these institutions bore the mark of Scottish 'cultural defensiveness': they attempted to 'create a cultural apparatus which would reinforce notions about Scotland's distinctive national identity'.[42] Similarly, Christopher Whatley has demonstrated that the many civic memorials that were erected in late Victorian Scotland reflected a 'renewed sense of national consciousness'.[43]

These concerns over Scotland's constitutional position, and a growing desire to defend the nation and its autonomy, are reflected in the formation of a further association, which hoped to enact the most radical reform to the Anglo-Scottish Union since its establishment in 1707 – the Scottish Home Rule Association (SHRA). Although London-based concessions, such as the restoration of the Scottish Office and the Secretary of Scotland, were made in 1885 to assuage anxieties over the rise of 'insolent centralization', as John Stuart Blackie, Chairman of the SHRA, put it,[44] they were felt to be insufficient. Thus, in 1886, the SHRA was formed with the primary aim of re-establishing a Scottish legislature in Edinburgh, through either devolution or federation. Through this proposal, many in the Association hoped to reduce Westminster's capacities chiefly to matters of empire (making it an 'Imperial Parliament'). Colin Kidd suggests that the SHRA's existence was, 'if anything, a symptom of creative imperialism',[45] implying that Scottish Home Rule was primarily conceived to ease the pressures on a Westminster parliament overburdened with imperial affairs. But, while Scottish Home Rulers certainly sold the wider advantages that Home Rule might bring to the Empire, discontents with the Union and a desire to defend Scotland's interests were very clearly (and sometimes strongly) sounded. Adding nuance to Kidd's claim that the Union was uncontested in this period – 'part of the wallpaper in Scottish political life'[46] – Whatley rightly stresses that 'we should not assume that the wallpaper was to everyone's taste', and he highlights the fact that Home Rule became a 'powerful movement' in late Victorian and Edwardian Scotland as a consequence.[47] Very few Scots questioned the presence of *a* union in the late nineteenth century, but there was growing discontent with the form of *the* Union.

Evidence that Scottish Home Rule became a 'powerful movement', rather than one defined by 'feebleness' (as Tom Nairn characterised it), is reflected in its longevity and its increasing momentum between 1886 and 1914.[48] Critiquing the idea that the SHRA was a mere 'parrot cry' of Irish discontents, Reginald Coupland argues that 'if Scottish nationalism [. . .] had been only a pale reflection of Irish nationalism, it would probably have faded away in the course of that bleak Conservative decade [1895–1906]'.[49] The Scottish Home Rule movement certainly went through its peaks and troughs between 1886 and 1914 but the issue did not subside over those three decades: Scottish Home Rule motions were carried in the House of Commons from 1893 onwards, which were supported by a clear majority of Scottish MPs, and these efforts led to two bills that were carried by significant majorities on their first readings across the whole of the House of Commons (in 1908 and 1911), and one that passed its second reading (1913) before being rejected in the House of Lords. With the support of the Liberal-backing Young Scots' Society, as well as a body of pamphlet literature and various Home Rule periodicals – including *The Scots Magazine and British Federalist* (1893–4),[50] Theodore Napier's *The Fiery Cross* (1901–12), Charles Waddie's *The Scottish Nationalist: A Monthly Political and Literary Journal Devoted to the National Life of Scotland* (1903), John Wilson's *The Scottish Patriot* (1903–6) and T. D. Wanliss's *The Thistle* (1909–18) – Home Rule 'came seriously close to dominating Scottish politics before the outbreak of war in 1914'.[51]

In addition to its longevity, Scottish Home Rule was also a broad movement, even in its infancy, as SHRA membership records reveal. The association is often characterised as a primarily Liberal cause, which it was, but it also attracted a colourful range of figures from across the political spectrum, many of whom became prominent figures in British politics. Britain's first Labour Prime Minister, Ramsay Macdonald, its first socialist MP, Robert Bontine Cunninghame Graham, and his co-founder of the Scottish Labour Party, Keir Hardie, were all Vice-Presidents of the SHRA. An early President was

Gavin Brown Clark, who founded the Land Restoration League and successfully stood as a Crofters' Party candidate in the 1885 General Election, taking the Caithness seat from the Liberals. John Crichton-Stuart (third Marquess of Bute), the aristocrat renowned for his architectural patronage and collaborations with William Burges, was a further enthusiast. Bute wrote on the topic of Home Rule in several publications, including *The Scottish Review*, a pro-Home Rule magazine, which its editor, William Metcalfe, hoped would 'protest against the idea that London is the centre of Scottish life'.[52] Metcalfe even proposed to Bute that the magazine could become the organ of a Scottish 'National Party' in 1889.[53] While fronted by men, the movement also attracted prominent women, including Lady Florence Dixie, a war correspondent, author, champion of women's rights, and aunt of Lord Alfred 'Bosie' Douglas.

John Ferguson, an Irish Home Ruler who emigrated to Glasgow, was a further early Vice-President of the SHRA. His membership might suggest intimate co-operation between the two Home Rule movements but the SHRA's response to Irish Home Rule was defined by a deep and complex ambivalence. While sympathy and solidarity were expressed towards the Irish, several Scottish Home Rulers also felt that the Irish question was being prioritised over Scotland's concerns, as Naomi Lloyd-Jones has thoroughly demonstrated.[54] As a consequence, a number of Scottish Home Rulers were openly derogatory. Belittling Ireland, Blackie proposed that Home Rule should be granted to the 'sober-minded sensible nation first'.[55]

The Irish question's most significant influence on Scottish Home Rule was that Gladstone's Home Rule proposals in the mid-1880s were felt to shift Scotland's constitutional position and escalate its assimilation into a unified British nationality. An early SHRA election poster reveals Scottish anxieties around the proposed changes to the Union, in light of Irish Home Rule (Fig. i.1). The poster identifies several Scottish discontents with the Union, mostly financial, but a striking warning is also issued to the voters regarding the proposals to establish an Irish assembly and remove all Irish representatives from Westminster: 'Beware of dividing the United Kingdom into only two Kingdoms: Britain and Ireland. SCOTTISH NATIONALITY WOULD BE LOST.' The poster undoubtedly tries to stir a sense of fear amongst the electorate, but to dismiss the quotation as mere scare-mongering would ignore the very real threat that such proposals for Irish Home Rule posed to a key concept that had helped ensure the stability of the Anglo-Scottish Union throughout the nineteenth century: three-kingdom unionism.

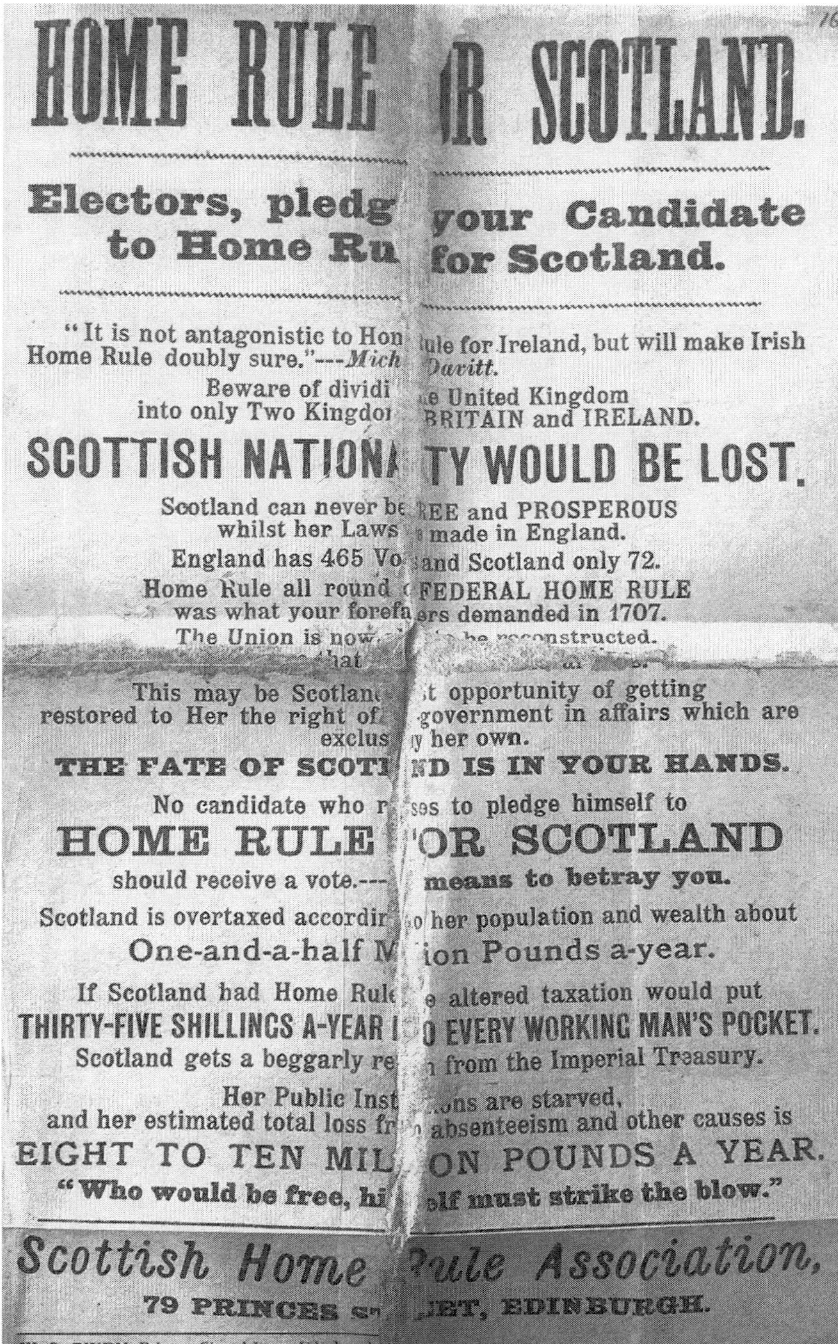

Figure i.1 Home Rule for Scotland election poster (c.1886–92). With thanks to the National Library of Scotland.

Three-kingdom unionism was the dominant conception of the United Kingdom in the nineteenth century, which foregrounded the state's composition of three distinctive parts, the Kingdoms of England, Ireland and Scotland. Unlike the 'four-nation' understanding of the British state that gained traction in the twentieth century, the United Kingdom was widely understood as being composed of three kingdoms, despite the fact that they were all, technically, one kingdom – the United Kingdom of Great Britain and Ireland (a seeming contradiction that reflects the ambiguity of the Acts of Union 1707, which simultaneously created a single kingdom and also implied the continuing existence of different kingdoms).[56] In the nineteenth century, several newspapers divided their news reports into three different sections, corresponding to each of these 'kingdoms', and national campaigns tended to highlight the three-kingdom composition of the United Kingdom: during the 1832 Reform Bill demonstrations, for instance, processions were often headed by the flags of the three respective kingdoms. Internationally, the United Kingdom was also referred to as the 'three kingdoms': commenting on the Edith Lanchester scandal in 1895,[57] *The New York Times* noted that the affair would 'rivet the attention of the three kingdoms'.[58]

It is easy to see why three-kingdom unionism was an appealing paradigm to defenders of Scottish identity: considering that Scotland was the smallest of the three kingdoms, it elevated Scotland's position to that of an equal with Ireland and England. But, crucially, three-kingdom unionism also recognised the continuing national distinctiveness of each 'kingdom' within the union, and implied that the state was an alliance of three peoples, rather than one assimilated, 'British' entity. It was this understanding of the United Kingdom that was felt to be under threat in the late nineteenth century from the proposals for an Irish assembly, as the SHRA poster demonstrates. Home Rulers worried that the creation of an Irish assembly, with representatives sitting in Ireland rather than Westminster, would create an alternative paradigm – not a three-kingdom state but a British and Irish state, where Scotland's distinctive national presence would be absorbed into 'Britain'. Connected to this issue, Scottish Home Rulers were also concerned that, without Irish members, Westminster parliaments would be more unbalanced: rather than being checked by both Irish and Scottish representatives, England's dominance over Scotland would increase. Waddie wrote to *The Scotsman* that the 1886 proposal for Irish Home Rule would amount to 'national assimilation'.[59] These anxieties reveal the deeply complex relationship between Irish Home Rule and Scottish Home Rule.

To some extent, the Irish Home Rule campaigns provided a model for Scots, but Gladstone's proposals for Irish Home Rule were also felt to threaten Scotland's constitutional position and nationality, which further fuelled the desire for Scottish Home Rule.

The extent of the SHRA's members' discontent with Scotland's constitutional position at the *fin de siècle* is reflected in the fact that they courted anti-Union rhetoric and imagery. Kidd is right to note that some SHRA figures 'insisted' on their commitment to unionism,[60] but others strongly attacked the 1707 Union. Crichton-Stuart, for instance, wrote on the 'evils of Union' in an essay published by the SHRA,[61] while Blackie noted that the 1707 Union was not a union, 'for a Union implies the separate existence of two bodies acting together in fair partnership'.[62] Like many others in the SHRA, Blackie mourned the fact that the federal union proposed by Fletcher of Saltoun in the early eighteenth century had not been adopted. The visual statements of the SHRA reflect these attacks on the 1707 Union and suggest an even more marked dissidence. The SHRA's heraldry in 1891 (Fig. i.2), for instance, adopts the coat of arms of pre-Union Scotland, which forms a visual attack not only on the 1707 Union specifically but on any union altogether. The use of Scotland's pre-Union heraldry was not limited to the SHRA's pamphlets either – it can also be found in the form of a large *bas-relief* above

Figure i.2 Heraldry of the Scottish Home Rule Association (1891). With thanks to the National Library of Scotland.

the entrance of J. M. Dick Peddie's National Bank of Scotland building on St Vincent Street, Glasgow (1898–1900). While the iconography of pre-Union Scotland was being distributed, some writings by SHRA associates also toy with the concept of Scottish independence. One early Vice-President of the SHRA, the Gaelic language activist Stuart Erskine, or Ruaraidh Erskine of Mar, flirts with the notion of an independent Scottish state in his article, 'The Independency of Scotland' (1892). Distinguishing between Home Rule and independence, and citing Poland's oppression by Russia, Erskine states that 'the right of Scotland to independence is the natural consequence of her right to exist'.[63] Similarly, in 1902, *The Fiery Cross* printed an article calling for the 'Repeal of the Unions'.[64] Evidently, Scottish discontent with the constitution was not always couched within proud unionism at the *fin de siècle.*

Discontent with Scotland's constitutional position was not simply expressed by those in the Home Rule Association. A larger-scale expression of constitutional discontent was voiced in 1898, when 'it seemed to some that the Scottish nation was under challenge'.[65] This discontent was rooted in the ubiquitous use of the word 'England' when referring to Britain. By no means a new issue, the problem escalated at the *fin de siècle* with the growth of the state and the rise of English nationalism. D. G. Boyce argues that, with the emergence of an increasingly centralised British nation-state, England was 'the shaper of that unified nation's identity'. As a consequence, Boyce contends, 'the concept of Britishness that was being evolved in the late-nineteenth century was quintessentially English, based on English power, institutions and political necessity'.[66] Scottish resistance to the perceived anglicisation of the British state was reflected in a petition to Queen Victoria in 1898, organised by Napier, which was signed by 104,647 Scots, objecting to the use of 'England' when referring to Britain.[67] This discontent further escalated in 1902 with Edward VII's coronation. A number of Scots felt that Edward's title was a further example of Englishness fusing with Britishness, as there had never been a King Edward of Great Britain or the United Kingdom before. Among the responses to this problem, a series of 'Scotch patriotic medals' were made to dissociate Britishness from Englishness. One such medal styled the king as 'Edward I of Britain' and proclaimed that 'Our Army, Navy / Flag, Parl't & King / All Are / British not English', distilling the various complaints that were raised in Wanliss's book, *The Bars to British Unity* (1885), a 'protest against the Anglifying of the Scottish people'.[68] Such medals, and

Wanliss's book, were far from anti-unionist; if anything, they reveal Scots' concerns that unionism was being lost and that Scotland was becoming assimilated into England, or a heavily anglicised Britain. But they do none the less demonstrate increasingly vocal discontent with the way the Union was changing and a desire to defend what many felt to be Scotland's increasingly compromised nationality. If Scots broadly felt themselves to be free and independent within the Union in the middle of the nineteenth century, this was increasingly less the case by the *fin de siècle*.

Cultural Revivalism in Scotland

Home Rulers relied on cultural apparatus to advance their cause – embodied in Charles Waddie's collection of propaganda poems, *Scotia's Darling Seat: A Home Rule Sermon and other poems* (1890) – and they were keen to recruit key cultural figures to the SHRA. One figure they approached was the town planner, sociologist and publisher of *The Evergreen*, Patrick Geddes. Responding to an invitation to join the SHRA, Geddes reveals his tacit support for Scottish Home Rule, demonstrating one instance of cultural revivalism intersecting with constitutional politics in *fin-de-siècle* Scotland. Although Geddes declines the invitation to join the SHRA, expressing his broader disinterest in parliamentary politics, his 'total dissent from contemporary political methods', he adds:

> I believe I can do best service to the cause by working at the realities of the Scots Renascence. I believe [that] all the peers and members can do nothing real or permanent until the literary, the academic, the social, the industry movement of Renascence floats them on. [. . .] I must wait until I see the members of the home rule association furthering Scottish literature, work for Scotch Universities, Scottish art, Scottish industries of a very greater extent before I could join them.[69]

Far from opposing the principle of Home Rule, Geddes here stresses that a cultural revival must anticipate and underpin Scottish Home Rule, and he imagines himself as helping to further that cause through 'working at [. . .] the Scots Renascence' – reviving the health of Scottish literature, art and history. Beyond this letter, Geddes's writings reveal that he shared Scottish Home Rulers' deep discontent with the United Kingdom's constitutional arrangements. He was vigorously opposed to political centralisation in London, preferring civic and regional autonomy. He stated:

> at present we have 'the provinces' all bowing to Westminster, whence they are granted doles; so their best people leave for London. They send their money to Westminster, which [. . .] is returned to some of them in the alluring form of 'a grant'. But why not use this money themselves in the first place?

According to Lewis Mumford, Geddes was also known to speak of 'the imbecility of the cockney', when referring to parliamentarians.[70] Geddes's conviction about devolution and regionalism was not limited to Anglo-Scottish relations – he believed in a wider process of decentralisation away from Westminster – but his strong critique of the concentration of power in London nevertheless echoes the views of several Home Rulers, including Blackie. As with those of the Home Rule associates, Geddes's statements were by no means anti-Union – at one point, he declared his commitment to 'the larger responsibilities of united nationality' – but they do point to his discontent with constitutional dynamics in the United Kingdom.[71] It was his belief in countering centralisation, as well as his desire to reanimate Scottish culture, that led Geddes to develop his concept of the 'Scots Renascence' – one of the central expressions of Scottish cultural revivalism at the *fin de siècle*.

In 'The Scots Renascence' (1895), an essay that closes the first issue of *The Evergreen*, Geddes elaborates his theory of cultural revivalism. Here, he provides an assessment of Scottish culture, identifying both the 'depressing' state of Scottish nationality (134) and the emergent buds of revival. The essay opens with an account of Blackie's funeral, where Geddes speaks of the Celtic scholar and Home Ruler as 'the leader of nationality', and describes the Scots as 'a Renascent – ever renascent – unconquerably renascent people' (132). But, despite this hopeful initial statement, Geddes goes on to describe the neglect of Scottish history and culture in his age. He argues that there has never been 'so large a proportion of Scotsmen conscientiously educating their children outside every main element of that local and popular culture, that racial aptitude and national tradition, upon which full effectiveness at home, and even individual success elsewhere, have always depended' (133). He laments that Scottish history 'has become well-nigh unknown among us', citing the 'utter forgetfulness' of people with regard to William Wallace's ally, John de Graham, who the town of Grahamston is named after, and complaining that the 'education we boast of [. . .] steadily falls behind that of other European countries' (pp. 134, 138–9). While noting the greatness of Robert Louis Stevenson, who had also recently died, Geddes fears that Scottish literature too is 'disappear[ing]', noting that 'the vacant place of native literature [is] supplied with twaddle and garbage in varying proportion, settled by the fluctuation of newsagents' imports' (134). In the midst of such neglect of Scottish tradition, history and literature, Geddes expresses his anxiety over the 'spoiling of what might be good Scots to make indifferent Englishmen' (133), echoing Blackie's concerns over Scottish anglicisation in the Victorian period. Geddes's bleak assessment of Scottish culture here resembles Hugh MacDiarmid's 'over-determined impulse for Renaissance' in the 1920s[72]: by dismissing his own or recent generations' culture, he adds greater urgency to his proposals.

But Geddes does not purely dismiss his contemporary culture; he also highlights signs of cultural awakening. For instance, he notes the rebirth of art in 'our Western inferno of industry' (135) – a reference to the Glasgow School – along with his appreciation of the emerging 'literature of locality', citing J. M. Barrie as a contributor to this movement (137). He also identifies a 'renascent' Scottish architecture and the 'resuscitation of Old Edinburgh' (135), which he sees as a marker of renewing care for Scottish history and tradition. Indeed, it is knowledge of, and rootedness in, tradition that Geddes believes will nurture a 'mightier literature' and culture more broadly (137). 'The Scots Renascence' closes with an implied recommendation that Scots should increasingly turn to Celtic art, literature and tradition to nourish the national culture, equating 'our Scottish' with 'our Celtic Renascence' (139). In equating Scottish culture with Celtic culture, Geddes was at times guilty of 'a rather undiscriminating homogenization of Scotland's self-image',[73] but, at other times, he was attentive to the plurality of Scottish culture and of Scottish Celticism itself. For instance, several of his projects reflect his conviction that Scotland was home to two differing Celtic traditions: a Fingalian Highland Celtic tradition and an Arthurian Lowland Celticism, which I examine in Chapter 5.

To overcome the perceived processes of centralisation and anglicisation, and to nourish awareness of Scottish history and culture, Geddes designed an array of projects, several of which are discussed in detail in this book. His cultural centre and museum, the Outlook Tower in Edinburgh, was designed, as has been noted, 'to recreate an active centre and so arrest the tremendous centralising power of the metropolis of London', and from this base in the Lawnmarket of Edinburgh he designed various projects underpinned by cultural revivalism. He planned a mural sequence of Scottish heroes (discussed in Chapter 3); published a series of Celtic Revival texts, including *The Evergreen* and the Celtic Library; produced historical pageants that highlighted Celtic contributions to art and culture; and helped design Scottish national institutions, including the Scottish National Zoological Park and a National Institute of Geography.[74] Commenting on such efforts, Israel Zangwill praised Geddes's resistance to the 'centripetal force', as well as his desire to 'range [Edinburgh] again amongst the capitals of culture'.[75] Geddes's 'Scots Renascence', as a theory and a collection of initiatives, was undoubtedly the most extensive example of cultural revivalism in *fin-de-siècle* Scotland, which drew the attention of individuals from across the globe.

But late Victorian cultural revivalism was by no means limited to Geddes and his projects, as Branford was attentive to. In the 'Western inferno', Glasgow, Charles Rennie Mackintosh was calling for architecture to be 'more national',[76] and his work, and that of the Glasgow School more widely, demonstrates interest in Celtic design traditions and the Scottish architectural vernacular, which I explore in detail in Chapter 2. Given Mackintosh's and others' rootedness in Scottish tradition, and their fusing of that tradition with modernity, it is unsurprising that Geddes was highly appreciative of the work undertaken in Glasgow and proposed inviting the Glasgow School of Art into 'our artistic movement'.[77] Not only did Geddes describe Mackintosh's Glasgow School of Art building as 'one of the most important buildings in Europe',[78] but he organised a tour of the partially completed building, led by Mackintosh, to coincide with the 1901 International Exhibition in Glasgow.[79] The kinship between the East and West Coast revivalists is further reflected in the contribution of Glasgow artists, such as E. A. Hornel, to *The Evergreen*, and it culminated in a collaboration between Geddes and Mackintosh: between the 1910s and 1920s, Geddes commissioned Mackintosh to design arcades for a town planning effort in Lucknow, India, as well as a war memorial (the designs for which are housed in the Hunterian Art Gallery, Glasgow).[80] Rather than being 'little related', there were many similarities between cultural developments in Scottish cities, as well as active collaboration between them, as this book explores more fully.[81]

Glasgow was also the main site of cultural nationalism in theatre, where Scottish developments were explicitly modelled on a key institution of the Irish Revival – the Abbey Theatre in Dublin. In 1908, the Scottish actor, playwright and founder of the Glasgow Men's League for Women's Suffrage, Graham Moffat, established the Scottish National Players in Glasgow to 'follow the example of the Irish National players at the Abbey Theatre, Dublin, and to provide something similar for Scotland'.[82] The Irish influence was also evident in the Scottish Repertory Theatre (1909–14), which was established by Alfred Wareing, who had managed the Abbey Company and previously brought Abbey Theatre dramas to Scotland in 1907. Wareing had four aims for the Scottish Repertory, the final of which was to encourage the development of 'purely Scottish drama [. . .] for the production of plays national in character, written by Scottish men and women of letters'.[83] Although the Scottish Repertory Theatre broadly failed to nurture new Scottish theatrical talents, it did produce a number of dramas by Scottish playwrights, including several by J. M. Barrie, Robert Louis Stevenson and Neil Munro (who was a director of the Scottish Playgoers Company). The Scottish Repertory also brought a wealth of European dramatic talent to Scotland. From its base at Glasgow's Royalty,[84] the Repertory was the first theatre in the United Kingdom to stage Anton Chekhov, with its production of *The Seagull* in 1909,[85] while works by Maurice Maeterlinck, Henrik Ibsen and George Bernard Shaw were also staged. Perhaps alluding to their common endeavours, the Scottish Repertory produced a six-night run of Irish revivalist plays in 1912, including Yeats and Lady Gregory's *Cathleen ni Houlihan*. Beyond its cultural nationalist aims, the Repertory had socio-political significance in Glasgow: as Helen Corr notes, its productions of plays by Shaw and Ibsen inspired one of Glasgow's most influential radicals and suffragettes, Helen Crawfurd.[86]

Beyond literature, art and theatre, cultural revivalism was also evident amongst Scottish musicians and language activists. Alongside the formation of the national orchestra, Scotland's folk revival of the late nineteenth and early twentieth centuries, which built on renewed interest in the collection of folk ballads, saw the rise of such composers as Alexander Mackenzie, Hamish MacCunn and Learmont Drysdale, who produced arrangements of traditional Scottish songs.[87] Marjory Kennedy Fraser, closely connected to Geddes's circle, recorded and adapted various traditional songs in her *Songs of the Hebrides* volumes (from 1909), featuring lyrics in Gaelic and English. The preservation of Gaelic hymns and literature was primarily advanced by a contributor to *The Evergreen*, Alexander Carmichael, best known for his collection of Gaelic folklore, *Carmina Gadelica*, while Gaelic language activism was furthered by various figures, including the editor of *The Highlander*, John Murdoch, and Ruaraidh Erskine, who published the radical Gaelic language magazine, *Guth na Bliadhna*, between 1904 and 1925. Douglas Hyde, an Irish Gaelic revivalist who would go on to become the first President of Ireland in 1938, noted that the Gaelic Revival in Scotland was 'much healthier and more vigorous' than in Ireland,[88] and, challenging the notion that Scots simply mimicked Irish developments, James Hunter argues that Scots forged 'the link between Gaelic revivalism and nationalism' before revivalists in Ireland did.[89] These Gaelic Revival efforts were complemented by attempts to defend the Scots language: for instance, in his preface on *Scottish Vernacular Literature* (1898), T. F. Henderson calls for a revival of the study of literature written in Scots.[90] The growing demand to consider Scottish literature as a distinct discipline to English literature – evidenced by St Andrews University changing its syllabus wording from 'English Literature' to 'English and Scottish Literature' in 1897,[91] and the formation of a Chair in Scottish History and Literature at Glasgow in 1913 – permitted greater scholarly attention be devoted to literature written in Scots.

While all of these figures were united in reviving Scottish artistic traditions or awareness of Scottish cultural history, they were not all natural bedfellows. There was disagreement and competition over the forms that revivalism should take. For instance, the novelist and playwright Neil Munro found the Celtic revivalism of Geddes's circle to be inauthentic. He wrote:

> This so-called Celtic Revival in Edinburgh is a rather curious thing. It is engineered very largely, I think, by people of no Celtic pedigree, and perhaps the only Celtic scholar in it is Mr Alexander Carmichael.[92]

Positioning himself in opposition to the supposed inauthenticity of Edinburgh's revivalists, Munro, from Inveraray, cast himself as the reliable revivalist of Celtic culture, 'expound[ing] the genuine Highland character and direct[ing] attention to the illimitable stores of romance and poetry still lying in the old glens'.[93] As I outline in Chapter 1, Andrew Lang criticised the Geddesian renascence in similar terms. Such tensions reveal that cultural revivalism in Scotland was not only pervasive at the *fin de siècle* but polyvocal, existing in a range of contested, competing forms.

Decadence and Revival

Rather than providing an exhaustive study of the various forms of cultural revivalism that developed in late Victorian and Edwardian Scotland, this book instead examines Scottish cultural revivalism through a particular lens. In his short essay, 'Scotland and Decadence',

Stuart Kelly provides the only focused assessment of Scotland's relationship to *fin-de-siècle* decadence to date, concluding that there was very little relationship to comment on. According to Kelly, Scotland failed to nourish a decadent writer, artist or thinker around the 1890s, and he also suggests that Scotland and decadence are 'oxymoronic'. Drawing on reductive stereotypes of life in Victorian Scotland, where 'restraint and gravity became the cardinal virtues', Kelly argues that it was impossible for the excessiveness, indulgence and 'fecklessness' of decadence to take root.[94] In Kelly's framing, Scotland was a fundamentally anti-decadent space, resistant to the decadent sensibility. Since Kelly, critics have offered more nuanced readings of the period: in his essay on late Victorian Scotland, Tom Hubbard identifies several symbolist and decadent tropes in Scottish art and literature, provocatively describing John Gourlay in George Douglas Brown's *The House with the Green Shutters* (1901) as 'the most decadent of decadents'.[95] But Hubbard ultimately concludes that Scotland 'was innocent of Max Nordau's charges of "degeneration"',[96] invoking Nordau's influential theory that the *fin-de-siècle* art was 'degenerate', prioritising immorality, irrationality and mysticism. In contrast to these understandings that portray Scotland as free from either decadence or degeneration, I demonstrate in this book that cultural revivalist literature and art were often underpinned by *fin-de-siècle* dissidence. Not only were Scottish revivalists inspired by the styles and ideas of decadent writers, artists and thinkers across Europe, and influenced those abroad, but their work embodied several of the features of 'degeneration' that Nordau outlined. *Fin-de-siècle* decadence and symbolism, I contend, played vital roles in supporting and defining Scottish cultural revivalism.

Decadence and degeneration are closely related terms. Decadence, a term that 'derives from the Latin *decadēre*, a "falling down" or "falling away"',[97] was often used as a derogatory label in the late Victorian period to critique people, ideas or groups that were felt to be working 'against the grain' of industrial, scientific, moral and commercial progress. 'Decadents' were characterised as 'over-civilised' or as actively attempting to undermine Victorian civilisation and progress through their valorisation of past ages, be they Ancient Greece or the Caroline era.[98] Indeed, figures associated with decadence (several of whom subversively adopted the derogatory label) were known to participate in 'neo', or revival, movements that celebrated ideas or concepts that were privileged in previous eras, including the new hedonism, new paganism, the Occult Revival, neo-Catholicism and the Jacobite Revival. On account of its adherents' ambivalence towards modernity and their willed returns to the past, decadence, like Nordau's degeneration, was felt to be the 'enemy of progress'.[99] Instead of endorsing the stadialist notion that societies gradually improve through a series of developmental stages, several decadent writers countered that 'historical crescendo predicted by the believers in progress' by arguing that industry, commerce and rationalism embodied cultural decline.[100]

In their revivalist attempts to reanimate supposedly better ages or ideas from the past, many figures associated with decadence came into rhetorical proximity to cultural revivalists. George Moore was one decadent figure who, when mourning the 'deadened conformity' of late Victorian life, lamented the loss of 'national' traditions, noting that 'the kilt is going or gone in the Highlands'.[101] For Moore, the preservation of national traditions was an important means of staving off the unbridled advance of 'progress'. In contrast to the increasingly dominant critical view that decadence was essentially 'anti-national',[102] this book reminds us that, alongside the cosmopolitan facets of decadence, there were numerous instances when decadence and cultural (and political) nationalism intersected at the *fin de siècle*. Indeed, another Irishman, one of the most emblematic figures of decadence, Oscar Wilde, very explicitly styled himself as an Irish nationalist on his American tour, declaring that 'we in Ireland are fighting for the principle of autonomy against empire, for independence against centralisation'.[103] With Wilde and Moore, we see the capacity for decadence and nationalism to co-habit. If decadence indicates 'the individuation of parts', a theory that Regenia Gagnier explores in detail by building on claims by Paul Bourget, Havelock Ellis and Friedrich Nietzsche that literary decadence represented the triumph of individuation (the breakdown of the whole to the part), it is unsurprising that cultural revivalism and decadence overlapped on several occasions. Like decadent individuation, national revival movements, such as the Irish Revival, hoped to differentiate, to individuate, their nation from a larger entity or 'whole'.[104] The decadent counter-culture and cultural nationalisms were by no means mutually exclusive.

The intersection of cultural revivalism and decadence was no less apparent in Scotland. As I demonstrate throughout this book, in their attempts to revive traditions and critique stadialist understandings of historical progress, Scottish revivalists frequently performed decadent styles and participated in movements that the likes of Nordau would class as 'degenerate', including neo-paganism, occultism, *japonisme* and neo-Jacobitism, to stimulate their cultural revival. *The*

Evergreen alone provides a clear example of this, as a Scottish revivalist magazine that featured many decadent facets, including 'Scoto-Beardsleyan' illustrations that were clearly inspired by *The Yellow Book*.[105] Throughout the magazine, we witness cultural revivalists' concern with paganism, neo-Jacobitism, occultism, neo-Catholicism and Japan. These features led one critic for *The Glasgow Herald* to refer to *The Evergreen* as a 'neo-Catholic, purified-pagan' magazine, an assessment that I elaborate on in Chapters 3 and 4, while *The Scotsman* described it as a 'sort of Scottish "Yellow Book"'.[106] As this quotation suggests, *The Evergreen* was not straightforwardly decadent, if any *fin-de-siècle* text was. The publisher, Geddes, was himself inconsistent in his evaluations of decadence, as I reveal in Chapter 3, and this ambivalence underpins the wider 'ferment of decadence and anti-decadence' in the magazine.[107] Nevertheless, there were clear decadent facets to *The Evergreen* that underpinned and defined much *fin-de-siècle* Scottish revivalist art and literature.

Even *The Evergreen's* London-based counterpart, *The Yellow Book*, was a site for expressing Scottish cultural nationalism. This is especially marked in D. Y. Cameron's illustrations for the front cover and spine of the eighth issue of *The Yellow Book*. By this point, following the scandal of the Wilde trial in 1895, *The Yellow Book*'s editors tried to distance the magazine from London's culture of decadence, and contributions from further afield were actively solicited. This context most clearly informs the eighth issue, where the Glasgow School provides all of the visual art decorations, including the front cover. This cover design explicitly highlights the Scottish contribution, as well as the Glasgow-specific emphasis, through the emblems that are depicted: alongside the thistle that appears on the spine of this volume, Cameron's front cover includes the four symbols of Glasgow's heraldry in a shield: the tree, bird, fish and bell (Fig. i.3). Flanking this shield sit a unicorn on the left and a lion on the right, alluding to the Scottish styling of union heraldry. As such, the iconography here is unionist, but there is an element of national resistance to this design too. The most telling feature of the cover is the boat in the background, which features a lion rampant flag (the Scottish royal standard) flying at its stern. This feature forms a visual riposte to the standardised back cover design of *The Yellow Book* from the sixth issue onwards, which presents the bow of a very similar ship, decorated with an English bulldog. By imagining the stern of the ship with a Scottish flag, Cameron not only writes Scotland visually into the culture of decadence but asserts Scotland's distinctive presence in the Union too.

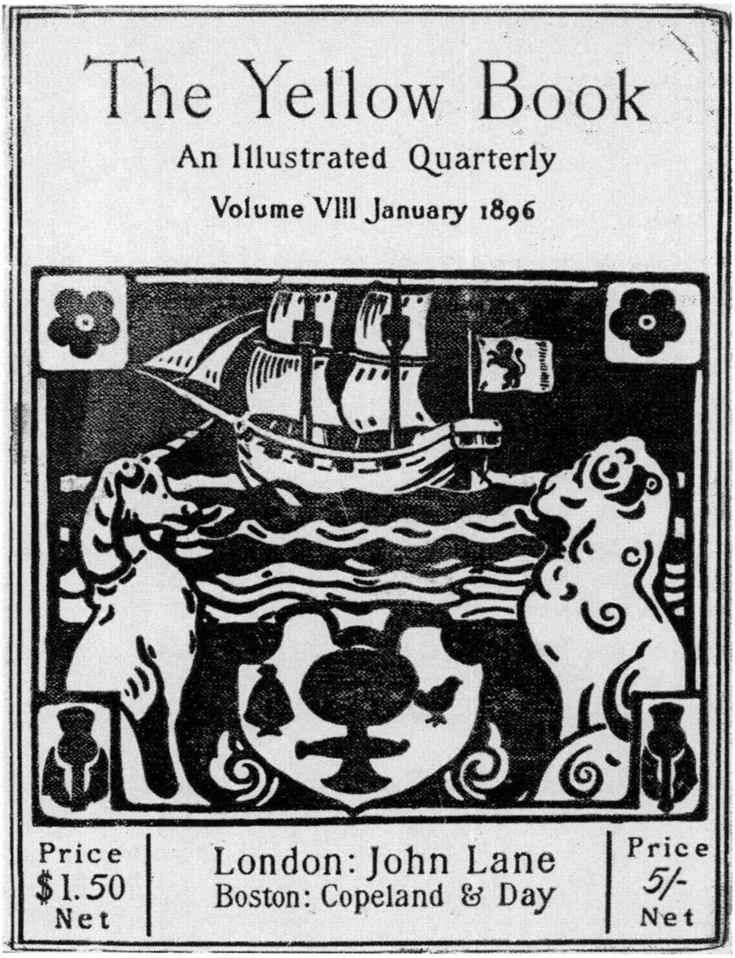

Figure i.3 D. Y. Cameron, front cover design for *The Yellow Book*, 8 (1896). University of Glasgow Library, Special Collections.

The place where Scottish cultural revivalism and decadence most commonly intersected was the Celtic Revival – a loose movement consisting of a range of initiatives concerned with Celtic myth, literature, art, languages and music at the *fin de siècle*. Many figures associated with *fin-de-siècle* decadence were involved in the Celtic Revival, such as W. B. Yeats, who was one of the leading lights of Irish Celticism and also a member of the Rhymers' Club in London, a poetry club that attracted numerous decadent figures, including Ernest Dowson, Lionel Johnson, Arthur Symons, Oscar Wilde and John Gray (several of whom were also from Ireland or Wales). For the poet Edward

Thomas, Celticism was, at its root, decadent: he labelled 'these lovers of the Celt a class of "decadents", not unrelated to Mallarmé', on account of their mutual love of the impractical, their resistance to the mercantile and their concern with what William Sharp termed 'the beauty of beauty'.[108] But, while Thomas is right to note that there were common features that bound several Celtic revivalists to decadence, it is also important to note how amorphous the Celtic Revival was. Although there were attempts to bring Celtic revivalists from across the United Kingdom and Brittany together through such initiatives as the Pan-Celtic Congress meetings, the third of which was held in Edinburgh in 1907,[109] divisions and polyvocality defined Celtic revivalism. Not only were there tensions between the differing nations' styles of Celtic revivalism (Irish revivalists were keen to distance themselves from some developments in Scotland, and vice versa, as I explore in Chapter 3), but also there were tensions amongst Celtic revivalists within particular nations. For instance, as some Celtic revivalists in Scotland embraced Matthew Arnold's presentation of the Celt as intuitive, feminine and politically ineffectual – a paradigm discussed in greater detail in Chapters 1 and 3 – others complicated this understanding.

Due to the amorphous nature of *fin-de-siècle* Celticism, it has come to occupy a contested space in understandings of national identity on the British Isles. As Daniel Williams argues:

> From one perspective Celticism is a product of English epistemological mastery and political domination, an internal form of Orientalism in which the feminine, superstitious, and poetic Celt could be easily accommodated as a junior partner in the British Imperial adventure. From another, Celticism offers a radical reconceptualization of national identities within the British Isles, fostering new avenues of dialogue and artistic and political collaboration.[110]

The first part of this quotation builds on Joep Leersen's view that Celticism was 'imposed from outside' on to the Celtic nations, by the likes of Ernest Renan and Arnold. Renan and Arnold, despite finding admirable qualities amongst 'the Celts', ultimately portray 'Saxons' as 'the agents of history', and only allow the Celts the opportunity 'to contribute their sensuality, femininity and natural magic' to Saxon progress. In Renan's and Arnold's paradigms, Williams contends, the Celt is 'invited to assimilate'.[111] But alongside these assimilationist valences, Williams also identifies more disruptive aspects of Celticism. Certainly in Ireland, Celtic identity was weaponised as a key tool for cultural and military resistance, and some Irish revivalists relied on Arnold's stress on Celtic separation and otherness to do so. For Williams, Yeats's embrace of Arnoldian notions of the Celt provides an example of 'the ways in which a colonised author appropriates the stereotypes ascribed to his people by an imperial power and turns them into positive attributes'.[112] This endeavour to recast supposedly backward, 'Celtic' traits – such as superstition and mysticism – into markers of civility and authority was also evident in Scotland, as I illustrate in Chapters 2 and 4. While we find evidence of Arnoldian Celticism being deployed to accommodate Scotland, I demonstrate here that the Scottish turn towards the Celt, like its turn towards decadence, also nourished a resistance to assimilation and an assertion of Scotland's cultural difference.

To illustrate and examine the development of Scottish cultural revivalism, and the ways it relied on dissident *fin-de-siècle* movements that critiqued 'civilisation', I begin by exploring the work of Robert Louis Stevenson, and the Scottish romance revivalists more widely. Chapter 1 argues that several of Stevenson's works were both proto-Celtic revivalist and proto-decadent in their critique of civilisation, and that the adventure romance genre was an important cultural apparatus for interrogating Victorian Scottish society's supposed divisions and for promoting greater national cohesion. The second chapter unlocks how internationally attuned Scottish revivalist writers and artists were, looking to other nations and traditions to inspire their revival of Scottish myths, crafts and literatures. I focus here on two international connections that Scottish revivalists were particularly keen to develop, one with the decadent and symbolist writers of Young Belgium and the other with Japan. I also demonstrate the ways in which these connections helped form a cross-border counter-hegemony that sought to resist the marginalisation of traditional cultures or smaller nations.

A central facet of *fin-de-siècle* cultural revivalism across Europe was myth-making, and Chapter 3 examines the ways in which Celtic and Mediterranean paganisms were embraced and appropriated by Scottish cultural revivalists in order to fashion mythological origins and a collection of heroes to help bind the nation. This chapter also reveals the ways in which resistance to neo-paganism and cultural revivalism were voiced in Scotland, focusing on the work of John Davidson. Allied to neo-paganism was the Occult Revival, which several Scottish revivalists participated in, as I demonstrate in Chapter 4. Occultism's proximity to neo-Catholicism and neo-Jacobitism made it especially attractive to Scottish cultural revivalists, who often associated pre-Reformation Scotland with healthier days of Scottish nationality. Not only did cultural revivalists participate in the Golden Dawn and the Theosophical Society, but some attempted to create an equivalent occult order to Yeats's Celtic Mysteries in Edinburgh.

The final chapter examines a lesser-studied aspect of *fin-de-siècle* theatre – the Pageantry Revival. I demonstrate that a range of Scottish cultural revivalists embraced these processional, dramatic displays of history to distribute the particular myths of descent that they had created in their fiction and art to wider audiences. Through their turns to various aspects of Scotland's past, and their participation in decadence and symbolism, the figures considered in this study mounted a 'proto-modernist critique of civilisation', which, they felt, was devaluing tradition and compromising their cultures and identities.[113]

Notes

1. Branford, 'Old Edinburgh and the *Evergreen*': 88.
2. Ibid.: 89.
3. Ibid.: 90.
4. Holbrook Jackson, pp. 40–1.
5. (Cited in) Defries, p. 315.
6. (Cited in) Defries, p. 7.
7. (Cited in) Lendrum, p. 60.
8. Elizabeth A. Sharp, *William Sharp*, p. 249.
9. Pittock and Jack, p. 338.
10. Wittig, p. 257.
11. Watson, p. 75.
12. Nairn, p. 113.
13. Gifford, pp. 216, 234.
14. Norquay, 'Squandering Names': 118.
15. McCulloch, *Scottish Modernism*, p. 206.
16. Campbell, p. 126.
17. Shepherd, pp. 310, 317.
18. Nash, pp. 17, 23.
19. Craig, 'The Case for Culture': 19.
20. Craig, 'Arcades', p. 15.
21. Hutchinson, p. 123.
22. Ibid., pp. 122, 125.
23. Facos, pp. 2–3.
24. Kent, p. 76.
25. Marsden, p. 17.
26. Facos, p. 4.
27. See Hobsbawm, 'Mass-Producing Traditions'.

28. Facos, p. 5.
29. For more on Yeats's nationalism, see Nally, Howe and Gonne.
30. Morton, *Unionist Nationalism*, p. 56.
31. For more on this design, see Smailes: 95–101.
32. For more on memorials and unionist nationalism, see Coleman, pp. 39–87; Morton, *Unionist Nationalism*, pp. 181–4.
33. (Cited in) Blair: 77, 84, 87.
34. Ad Rem, ll. 17–18.
35. 'Justice to Scotland': 712.
36. Ibid.
37. (Cited in) 'The Union with England and Scottish Nationality': 96.
38. Michael Keating, p. 42.
39. 'The Union with England and Scottish Nationality': 98.
40. Alvin Jackson, p. 174.
41. Morton, *Unionist Nationalism*, p. 188.
42. Finlay, p. 43.
43. Whatley, p. 101.
44. (Cited in) Kennedy, p. 216.
45. Kidd, *Union and Unionisms*, p. 278.
46. Ibid.: p. 24.
47. Whatley, p. 16.
48. Nairn, p. 95.
49. Coupland, p. 303.
50. Throughout 1894, *The Scots Magazine* (1739–) published *The British Federalist* in each issue.
51. Finlay, p. 52.
52. (Cited in) Hannah, p. 169.
53. (Cited in) 'The Scottish Review, 1882–1900', p. 788.
54. Lloyd-Jones: 866–71.
55. (Cited in) Kennedy, p. 213.
56. Pittock, 'Scottish Sovereignty': 13–14.
57. The socialist and feminist Edith Lanchester was incarcerated in a lunatic asylum for intending to enter into a 'free love union' with her Irish, working-class lover.
58. (Cited in) Rubinstein.
59. (Cited in) Lloyd-Jones: 869.
60. Kidd, *Union and Unionisms*, p. 277.
61. Crichton-Stuart, p. 10.
62. Blackie, *The Union of 1707*, p. 2.
63. Erskine: 100.
64. 'Scotland and Ireland': 5.
65. Morton, 'Scotland is Britain': 127.
66. Boyce, '"The Marginal Britons"', p. 234.
67. Morton, 'Scotland is Britain': 128.
68. (Cited in) Wanliss, p. 2.

69. Letter from Patrick Geddes to Mr Campbell, 1 November 1895 [National Library of Scotland: MS 10508A].
70. (Cited in) Defries, pp. 4, 221.
71. Geddes, 'The Scots Renascence': 133.
72. Carruthers, Goldie and Renfrew, p. 16.
73. Carruthers, *Scottish Literature*, p. 9.
74. Plan for a National Institute of Geography, 1902 [Archives and Special Collections, University of Strathclyde: T-GED 22/1/British Isles/Scotland/539/1].
75. Zangwill: 232.
76. Mackintosh, 'Untitled Paper on Architecture', p. 196.
77. Notes by Patrick Geddes for a lecture to the Celtic Society, 1897 [Archives and Special Collections, University of Strathclyde: T-GED 5/2/9].
78. Patrick Geddes, 'Aesthetics – on the Utilitarian Contempt, Indifference and Distrust of Aesthetics' [Archives and Special Collections, University of Strathclyde: T-GED 5/3/70].
79. Welter: 318.
80. For more on this commission and Anna Geddes's friendship with Margaret Macdonald, see Welter.
81. Hardie, p. 110.
82. (Cited in) Brown, *History as Theatrical Metaphor*, p. 77.
83. (Cited in) Ibid.
84. The Royalty Theatre was situated on Sauchiehall Street in Glasgow; Charles Rennie Mackintosh designed a street canopy for the Repertory Theatre, although it is not known if this commission was ever executed.
85. Brown, *Scottish Theatre*, p. 134.
86. Corr, 'Crawfurd, Helen (1877–1954)'.
87. For a consideration of Scottish nationality in relation to music hall entertainment, see Maloney, pp. 158–82.
88. (Cited in) Hunter: 182–3.
89. Ibid.: 182
90. T. F. Henderson, p. iv.
91. Crawford, 'Scottish Literature and English Studies', p. 229.
92. (Cited in) Lendrum, p. 65.
93. Ibid., pp. 59–60.
94. Kelly, pp. 54–5.
95. Hubbard, p. 276.
96. Ibid., p. 262.
97. Murray and Hall, p. 1.
98. Symons, *The Symbolist Movement*, p. 180.
99. Nordau, p. 560.
100. Burton, p. 50.
101. Moore, p. 142.

102. Potolsky, p. 54.
103. Hofer and Scharnhorst, pp. 159–60.
104. Gagnier, *Individualism, Decadence and Globalization*, p. 21
105. 'Some Illustrated Books', p. 13.
106. 'The Evergreen', *Glasgow Herald*, p. 11; 'The Evergreen: A Northern Seasonal', p. 6.
107. Nicholson: 65.
108. Thomas, pp. 11–12; William Sharp, 'Introduction', p. xlvi.
109. Geddes imagines *The Evergreen* contributing to a broader Celtic Revival in 'The Scots Renascence': 137; for more on pan-Celticism, see Daniel G. Williams, pp. 80–1.
110. Daniel G. Williams, pp. 81–2.
111. Ibid., p. 72.
112. Ibid., p. 73.
113. Carruthers, *Scottish Literature*, p. 9.

Chapter 1

The Scottish Romance Revival

In one of the key essays of *fin-de-siècle* Scottish cultural revivalism, Patrick Geddes's 'The Scots Renascence', published in the first volume of *The Evergreen* in 1895, Geddes calls for a revival of the nation's cultural health and collective national identification with Celtic literature, arts and tradition. As archetypal role models for this revival of nationality, Geddes selects and equates two figures that are rarely considered together by contemporary critics: Robert Louis Stevenson and John Stuart Blackie. These figures had died within three months of each other – Stevenson in December 1894 and Blackie in March 1895 – which prompts Geddes to reflect on their funerals, in Samoa and Edinburgh respectively, and to evaluate their contributions to Scottish life:

> From this pageant of Edinburgh it is but one step in thought to that solitary Samoan hill, up which dusky chiefs and clansmen, henceforth also brethren of ours, as he of theirs, were so lately bearing our other greatest dead – the foremost son of Edinburgh and Scotland. The leader of nationality in ripest age, the leader of literature in fullest prime, have alike left us. Each was in his own way 'Ultimus Scotorum'; each in his own way the link with our best days of nationality and genius.[1]

In this quotation, Geddes treads a fine line between revivalism and twilight. On the one hand, Blackie and Stevenson are portrayed as the leaders of nationality, ripe and full. The admirable contribution these two figures have made to the health of Scottish nationality, in Geddes's eyes, is their full engagement with Scottish history, along with their endeavours to place Scottish culture in dialogue with the wider world; both refused to submit to the 'fool's paradise' of 'narrower' nationality (134). Their ability to unify Scotland is also highlighted by Geddes, reflected in the lexis he adopts to describe the 'tens of thousands' at Blackie's funeral, with such words as 'uniting', 'merged', 'communion', 'multitude', 'chorus' and 'interpulsating' (pp. 131–2). But, alongside these evocations of the health of Scottish nationality, embodied by these two figures, Geddes also implies that Scotland has lost its greatest defenders. They were not only surviving links with Scotland's greatest days, but also 'Ultimus Scotorum' – the last of old Scotland.[2] Geddes's response to their deaths is a call to action; he feels the need to foster cultural revivalism to continue their legacy and, as Blackie and Stevenson did, recover 'our best days of nationality and genius'. Although they may be dead, Geddes implies that, through Stevenson and Blackie's examples, Scottish nationality can revive, like 'the little mound of heather, opening into bloom' on Blackie's coffin (132).

Despite Geddes's deep appreciation for Stevenson's writing and his intention to publish a volume of his work,[3] Stevenson's work and the broader culture of adventure romance fiction written by Scots in this period are very seldom considered in relation to Geddes's projects or the wider interest in *fin-de-siècle* Scottish cultural revivalism. Indeed, even though the Scottish writers of the Romance Revival – including Stevenson, Arthur Conan Doyle, Andrew Lang, J. M. Barrie, Violet Jacob and John Buchan – all wrote on Scotland and many formed friendships with each other, there has yet to be a sustained consideration of them as a loose, vibrant group, responding to Scottish (among other) contexts. This chapter demonstrates that these writers' representations of Scottish nationality bore several similarities, and that they all contributed to advancing Scottish cultural revivalism (albeit in differing ways). Each of the figures examined here not only helped lay the ground for greater national cohesion in Scotland, through interrogating the commonplace nineteenth-century notion of Scotland as a nation divided between Highland Celts and Lowland Saxons, but several of their romance writings also portray Scottish culture as threatened, and mock or defy attempts to assimilate Scottish culture into British or English culture. In doing so, several of these texts were concerned with defending Scottish cultural distinctiveness. We also find *fin-de-siècle* critiques of nineteenth-century narratives of historical progress and 'civilisation' in these writings, especially in Stevenson's, which hoped to reclaim the role of tradition and resist the spread of cultural uniformity. Cairns Craig has argued that Scottish romance fiction often emerges in periods when there is a refusal to 'submit to historical amelioration', and, in the fiction of the Scottish Romance Revival, this interrogation of 'improvement' is very clearly apparent.[4]

The Late Victorian Romance Revival

The Romance Revival of the *fin de siècle* was an international phenomenon that manifested in a variety of forms. Historical romances, fantasy romances, science fiction romances, gothic romances, imperial romances and the adventure romance (which this chapter will focus on) were all popular forms of literature in this period. Anna Vaninskaya is right to note that attempting to offer a concise definition of this multifarious genre is an 'ultimately futile exercise', but a clearer sense of the genre as a whole, and adventure romance particularly, can be achieved through considering the ways that practitioners of the genre, and its critics, characterised it.[5]

Aesthetically, the term 'romance' is most helpfully understood in a dialogic relationship with its nineteenth-century counterpart, realism. Rather than being a neatly defined genre in itself, romance often refers to texts that resisted or critiqued English realism and French naturalism. One of the most popular romance writers of the period, Ouida, the pseudonym of Maria Louise Ramé, reflected on the relationship between realism and romance in her non-fiction work. In 'Romance and Realism' (1883), for instance, she mounts a rhetorical attack on realism, writing that 'the *éternellement vrai* is as real as the *infiniment petit*'. In Ouida's eyes, the lofty and the remarkable are just as real as the ordinary, minor, mundane subjects that were often associated with the nineteenth-century realist genre. Continuing her critique of realism, she writes: 'what I object to is the limitation of realism in fiction to what is commonplace, tedious, and bald – to the habit, in a word, of insisting that the potato is real and that the passion-flower is not'.[6] Here, she challenges the opponents of romance, who see it as a lesser genre because it represents that which is not lifelike, by asserting that romance *is* truthful; romance simply focuses on alternative forms of reality – the extraordinary and the unknown.

When defining the romance genre in Britain, Ouida stresses that its refusal of the commonplace often leads writers to represent spaces and nations that are unfamiliar to the readership, moving into unknown territories that are frequently outside of Britain. This facet of romance writing clearly appealed to Ouida, as she was keen to liberate herself and her writing from aspects of British culture and tradition. For instance, when comparing romance to realism, she writes that the Genoese lover 'is every whit as "real" as the British prig [. . .] or the British philistine', revealing her exhaustion with certain British cultural expectations.[7] Beyond Ouida, various other romance writers were drawn to the genre for its capacity to reject or critique aspects of British culture that they were tired of. For instance, H. Rider Haggard's scathing attack on the 'accursed' Naturalistic school,[8] 'About Fiction' (1887), asserts that adventure romance fiction offers a break from English conventionalism, writing that 'English life is surrounded by conventionalism, and English fiction has come to reflect the conventionalism, not the life'.[9] Similarly, in his essay, 'A Gossip on Romance' (1882), Stevenson critiques his English readership, who, he believes, are more interested in familiar, insignificant details than extraordinary incident: 'English people of the present day are apt, I know not why, to look somewhat down on incident, and reserve their admiration for the clink of teaspoons and the accents of the curate.'[10] For Haggard, Stevenson and Ouida, romance is characterised as a means of both escaping aspects of English or British culture and critiquing it.

The desire to escape England or Britain and to encounter the unfamiliar abroad was informed by the high imperialism of the *fin de siècle*, defined by increased imperial expansion as well as heightened competition between the major empires. The expanding British Empire provided the setting for many adventure romance novels, a reviving form that had been popularised in the early nineteenth century by Walter Scott. Haggard's fictions, especially *She* and *King Solomon's Mines*, reflect romance writers' interest in conducting imperial anthropology – encountering, defining and interpreting the 'other' abroad. Although Haggard's work is underpinned by several imperialist and racist discourses, he is keen to stress that the romance genre presents a means of bridging the gap between the 'civilised' coloniser and the 'barbarian' colonial subject in 'About Fiction'. Romance, for Haggard, was a genre that could disrupt perceived divisions between nations and cultures.[11] Andrew Lang went further on this topic: he argued that romance appealed to the 'ancestral barbarism of our natures',[12] and, as such, he believed the genre revealed the barbarism that lies within all societies and people. Lang even uncouples the binary between realism and romance, suggesting that the division is a simply a reflection of the Victorians' inability to confront the fact that they were simultaneously civilised and barbarous.[13] The *fin-de-siècle* adventure romance genre both endorsed and complicated the narratives that sustained the British Empire.

Romance was also distinguished from realism in terms of gender. Elaine Showalter, for instance, argues that the romance genre was a male response to the female hegemony of the three-volume novel,[14] a position that is supported by the fact that romance novels were characterised by some as 'boys' books',[15] while several of them endorse misogynistic discourses, as Anne McClintock reveals in her reading of Sheba's Breasts in *King Solomon's Mines* (1885).[16] Andrew Lang also authenticated the connection between romance and masculinity, by characterising the genre as a healthy retort to 'unmanly' naturalism.[17] However, the idea that romance novels, and adventure romances specifically, were an exclusively male domain is problematic. Stevenson's *Catriona* (1893), for instance, was written for male and female readers, as the final chapter, addressed to a boy and girl,[18] reveals. Furthermore, Marie Corelli, like Ouida, was a hugely successful romance novelist in the late nineteenth century. Several *fin-de-siècle* romance texts may have been directed at men, but the genre nevertheless appealed to female audiences and writers too.

Given that these late Victorian adventure romances tended to involve border crossings, both political and cultural, within the framework of empire, the Romance Revival, as a genre, was unsurprisingly embraced by several cultural revivalists, who were similarly reflecting on cultural and political borders, and negotiating the power dynamics between differing nations and cultures. Nicholas Daly has demonstrated that romance fiction directly engaged with Irish nationalism, noting that Stoker's *The Snake's Pass* (1890) reflects the romance genre's 'considerable importance for the Irish cultural nationalist project'.[19] The capacity for romance novels to contribute to cultural nationalism was no less apparent in *fin-de-siècle* Scotland.

Even a cursory consideration of the above features demonstrates that *fin-de-siècle* romance novels offered useful tropes to support Scottish cultural revivalism. The genre, in Lang's eyes, helped challenge the civilised–barbarous binary, which many Scottish revivalists hoped to do to demonstrate that Celtic culture (which was often considered less 'civilised' than Saxon culture in the nineteenth century) was not opposed to modernity or inferior to it. The romance genre, in some writers' hands, also helped revive a sense of manliness, which was key to some cultural revivalists, such as Blackie, and the genre was often concerned with the processes of defining national identity (where peoples confront 'spectres of *themselves*' abroad).[20] Furthermore, for some romance writers, the genre helped resist aspects of 'English' or British culture, as well as its cultural hegemony. In a number of *fin-de-siècle* Scottish romances, each of these features is present and, taken together, they helped advance the cultural revival that was often rooted in defending Scottish nationality and questioning internal divisions.

Celt and Saxon in Victorian Scotland

A key facet of the Scottish cultural revival, and several Scottish romance writings, was the desire to nurture more national cohesion by interrogating the notion that Scotland was ethnically divided between Highland Celts and Lowland Saxons (or Teutons). Interest in this Celt–Saxon paradigm was by no means limited to Scotland in Victorian Britain: several Victorians, most notably Matthew Arnold, located, defined and evaluated these ethnicities in a manner that often endorsed their differences and, consequently, authenticated racial divisions within the United Kingdom. Despite announcing his desire to stimulate more mutual sympathy between the two races and to establish a chair of Celtic at Oxford, Arnold's *On the Study of Celtic Literature* (1867) nevertheless validates the stereotypes that underpinned Celt–Saxon divisions. His essay styles the Celt as sensual, feminine, spiritual, and ineffectual in politics – traits juxtaposed against the factual, masculine and rational Saxon.[21] Although Arnold does not see the Celt as inferior in every sense, arguing that the 'Philistinism' of England's 'Saxon nature' would benefit from incorporating several Celtic traits – a proposal that Daniel Williams characterises as Celtic contributionism – he nevertheless portrays the two groups as distinct races with some key, opposing characteristics.[22] The enduring understanding of ethnic division within the United Kingdom, which Arnold emboldened, had its implications for every nation, but its influence on Scotland and Scottish nationality were particularly strong as it was felt to divide Scotland in half, between its supposedly Celtic Highlands and Saxon Lowlands. As a consequence, *fin-de-siècle* cultural revivalists were keen to address and challenge these contexts and divisions, which had developed over two centuries.

Robert J. C. Young argues that the strength of the Celt–Saxon dichotomy in the British Isles was largely a result of developments at the end of the seventeenth century. Young demonstrates that, prior to the Glorious Revolution of 1688 and the arrival of a Hanoverian king, the ethnicity of England was broadly styled as 'Celtic', rooted in Arthurian legacy. But after 1688, this encoding gave way to

> an alternative Whig history, which stressed the nation's English Protestant identity and its Saxon constitutional freedoms. Protestantism was always (ahistorically) Saxon and English. The Arthur who had united the diverse inhabitants of Britain was replaced by an identification with the Saxon English Alfred.[23]

Consequently, Young argues, over the course of the eighteenth century, the non-Saxon inheritance of England was displaced in order to develop a 'Saxonist purity', rooted in the characteristics of the British peoples outlined by Tacitus (primarily love of liberty and self-reliance), helping to distance England from Catholicism.[24]

This embracing of Anglo-Saxonism in England over the long eighteenth century had important implications for Scotland. In his article 'Teutonist Ethnology and Scottish Nationalist Inhibition, 1780–1880', Colin Kidd demonstrates that, as a result of the Acts of Union 1707 and the Jacobite rebellions, various Scottish Enlightenment figures attempted to highlight the supposed Germanic ethnicity of the Scottish Lowlands as a means of integrating Scotland into the English 'economic and imperialist core' and distancing themselves from dissenting Jacobites.[25] This involved developing an image of an underlying Germanic racial heritage in the Lowlands, and, as had occurred in England, it also necessitated marginalising the 'Celtic' features of Scotland. In doing so, Scottish Saxonism became markedly territorialised: the growing Lowland population (home to Scotland's main industrial centres) was cast by some Enlightenment figures as Germanic, and the declining Highland population was Celtic. David Hume and William Robertson were particularly influential in developing this model: Murray Pittock argues that they created 'a division between the "Germanic" Lowlands (forward-looking, commercial, liberty-loving, and British) and the "Celtic" Highlands (backward, rebellious, violent, and indolent)'.[26] John Pinkerton was equally committed to this ethnic divide; he portrayed the Celtic Highlanders as 'a race incapable of labour' in 1789,[27] while casting Lowland Scots as capable of conceding to 'English improvements'.[28] Pittock writes that this racial dynamic not only helped build up a greater sense of British unity, but 'happily also divided Scottish identity and thus undermined Scottish nationality',[29] a point that is echoed by Kidd, who claims that the Celtic–Saxon divide 'diluted the ethnocentric element which was such an important feature of nineteenth-century nationalisms'.[30] It should be noted that some figures who have been associated with the Scottish Enlightenment tried to recover the 'noble' features of the Celtic 'savage', including James Macpherson and James Beattie,[31] but attempts 'to break that will to unity', so key to national identity formation, were clearly performed during Scotland's age of Enlightenment.[32] The Scottish Lowland identity was defined in opposition to its Highland counterpart (one supportive of economic liberalism, the other hostile to it), creating a collective identity dynamic founded on a binary opposition within the nation that encouraged hostility and hierarchy.

The cultural application of the Highland–Lowland ethnic divide was rarely as resilient as some Enlightenment theorists might have hoped. Instead, we often find ambivalent portrayals of this paradigm in Scottish literature. Even Lowland unionists, such as Walter Scott, could complicate the model that they appeared to support, both advancing and resisting the Celt–Saxon binary. Scott replays, with some amendments, the racial territorialising of several Scottish Enlightenment figures in his 'Introductory Remarks on Popular Poetry' (1830), which was appended to *The Minstrelsy of the Scottish Border*. He writes:

> Excepting, therefore, the provinces of Berwickshire and the Lothians, which were chiefly inhabited by an Anglo-Saxon population, the whole of Scotland was peopled by different tribes of the same aboriginal [Celtic] race.[33]

Here, we find a typical example of Scott's anxiety about the Enlightenment model: he concedes that there was Germanic penetration into Scotland but he reduces it to the Lothians and Berwick. When compared to Hume's claim that 'all the lowlands' were Saxon, Scottish Saxonism is more restricted in Scott's framing.[34] Furthermore, Scott's constraining of the Saxon presence in Scotland allows him to claim that, otherwise, the 'whole' of Scotland is Celtic, invoking the language of common nationhood. And while Scott acknowledges the superiority of the Anglo-Saxon language, he does not pass judgement on the Celts maintaining their music, customs and dynasty.[35] Albeit endorsing racial difference and Saxon superiority, Scott nevertheless expresses respect for the image of the Celtic race that he constructs.

These complications in 'Introductory Remarks on Popular Poetry' are also central to Scott's fiction. For example, in 'The Two Drovers', from *Chronicles of the Canongate* (1827), Scott presents a Highlander (Robin Oig MacCombich) who is at odds with Saxon culture – embodied by his act of killing an Englishman, Harry Wakefield. MacCombich's revenge is characterised by the judge as an act of 'wild untutored justice',[36] but the audience in the court also interprets it as a 'false idea of honour rather than as flowing from a heart naturally savage' (234). The Highlander may have acted wildly, but there is justice and honour at the core of his act, and thus the story problematises the association of the Celt with savagery. Highlanders are also portrayed in the story as displaying 'patient endurance and active exertion' (203), countering Pinkerton's assessment of the Celts as indolent. Furthermore, Wakefield, the Englishman, is described as 'irascible' (211), a trait more akin to stereotypical images of the hot-tempered Celt than the rational Saxon. Scott complicates the marginalising of Highland culture further by authenticating the Highland spaewife's prediction that there will be a disaster if Robin goes to England, after seeing 'Saxon blood' on his hands at the beginning of the story (209). Rather than being discarded as irrational, Celtic foresight is legitimised in 'The Two Drovers'. Through playfully invoking and subverting Scotland's supposed ethnic divide, Scott presents his readership with a binary that he himself is keen to problematise.

Scott also complicated the Celt–Saxon binary through his work to bring Highlandism to the Lowlands and to project Highlandism as Scotland's national image. His most notable endeavour in this regard was his presentation of George IV to Edinburgh in 1822, where the Hanoverian King was dressed in pseudo-Jacobite garb in an attempt to reconcile Scotland's dynastic divisions. By bringing tropes associated with Jacobitism and Highland clanship to Edinburgh, Scott attempted to establish a distinct Scottish sphere, and promote cohesion within the nation through common identification with emblems of (a heavily appropriated, even imaginary) Highland culture. Further into the nineteenth century, Queen Victoria's love of the Highlands and the establishment of Balmoral Castle, opened in 1856, helped diffuse Highlandism further. The more material presence of Highland culture in the Lowlands was also advanced in this period by particular socio-economic developments, such as the substantial migration of Highlanders to Scotland's Lowland industrial cities. This migration led to the publication of Highland magazines in the Lowlands, such as *The Celtic Monthly: A Magazine for Highlanders*, increasing Lowland contact with Highland people and culture.[37]

But although the Celt–Saxon binary was being problematised and there was increasing enthusiasm for Highlandism, the divide nevertheless persisted well into the Victorian period, and, in some cases, it was marked and vitriolic. Indeed, many Lowland Scots in the Victorian period privileged their apparent Saxon ethnicity over their shared Scottish nationality with Highlanders. This was an observation made by the land reformer, John Murdoch, who noted that some in Scotland identified more with those in England than 'their own countrymen north of the Forth'.[38] Scots could be vehemently anti-Celt, which was especially apparent in their writings on the Irish. Thomas Carlyle strongly identified with Saxonism and was particularly hostile to the Celtic race, especially Irish people – referring to them as 'sanspotatoe' and 'ultra-savage'.[39] Despite Carlyle opposing laissez-faire industrialism, which was often associated with the Saxon race, Donald M. MacRaild argues that Carlyle was a key figure in fostering negative associations with the Celt in Victorian Britain.[40] Like Carlyle, who considered the merits of 'exterminat[ing]' the Irish,[41] the Scottish anatomist, Robert Knox, contemplated how best to 'dispose' of the Celts across the United Kingdom in *The Races of Men* (1850), and argued that the Celts of Ireland were 'the source of all evil'.[42] According to Stephanie Barczewski, few were satisfied with the idea of the United Kingdom as a mixed-race nation in the second half of the nineteenth century, a discontent that was fuelled by Irish immigration, which often led to racist attacks on the Celts.[43]

While this anti-Celt rhetoric was mainly aimed at the Irish, it was also pointedly directed at Highlanders. Large sections of the Lowland Scottish print media were intent on identifying with Saxonism and marginalising the Highlands further. In her doctoral thesis, '"Contempt, Sympathy and Romance": Lowland Perceptions of the Highlands and the Clearances during the Famine Years, 1845–1855', Krisztina Fenyô exposes the deeply racist portrayals of the Highlander in the Lowland Scottish press. As in Ireland, several Scots blamed the famine and Clearances on the racial indolence of the Celtic Highland inhabitants, who were incapable of adapting to industrious 'Anglo-Saxon' culture, rather than on unfair and dysfunctional land policy or landlordism. For instance, it was argued in *The Scotsman* that

> it is a fact that morally and intellectually they [the Highlanders] are an inferior race to the Lowland Saxon – and that before they can in a civilised age be put in a condition to provide for themselves and not to be throwing themselves on the charity of the hard-working Lowlander, the race must be improved by a Lowland intermixture.[44]

Such expressions of eugenic thinking, reflecting the views of Knox, reveal the extent of ethnic divisions in Victorian Scotland. Several Lowlanders celebrated the supremacy of the Anglo-Saxon at this time: 'the higher capabilities of the Anglo-Saxon' were heralded in such titles as the *Fifeshire Journal*.[45]

The magnitude of this divide is reflected in the few but striking comments that reveal that both the Highlanders and the Lowlanders were imagining themselves as having different nationalities and even referring to their two territories as different nations. As Fenyô summarises, it was believed by some in the Lowlands that charity

> no more belonged to the Highlanders than to "the Hill Collies", or the subjects of "Queen Pomare", in other words Scottish Gaels were just as alien, or foreign a people to the Scottish Lowlanders as some Asian or other far away, and presumably inferior, people.[46]

These beliefs reflected the views of Charles Trevelyan, of the Highland and Island Emigration Society, who stated that Germans were 'less foreign to us than the Irish or Scotch Celt'.[47] The implication here is that the Scottish Highlands are not only foreign to the Lowlands but *more* foreign than other European countries. Fenyô qualifies that such expressions were extreme and that charity schemes were later organised by the likes of Donald Ross for victims of the Highland famine, but ethnic hostility was certainly apparent.[48] Furthermore, it was not simply a case of the Lowlanders marginalising the Highlanders through this rhetoric but, in turn, the Highlanders could imagine themselves as a different nation. The Highland Society, for instance, was keen to 'preserve the nationality of the Highlands'[49] and its national traditions. Scotland, in these framings, was a multi-national space, occupied by differing and alien Celtic and Saxon cultures.

The persisting understanding of Scotland's divided ethnicity posed a problem for those hoping to nurture a greater sense of cohesiveness in the nation, especially Scottish cultural revivalists. To promote more unity, this ethnic fissure had to be interrogated. As I demonstrate here and in the following chapters, there was no clear consensus amongst cultural revivalists on how to achieve this: some Scottish cultural revivalists questioned whether Celt and Saxon identities were so distinct and separate in Scotland, thus laying the ground for more commonality, but others tried to promote common identification, and a Scottish *ethnie* (discussed in Chapter 3), through developing a national Celticism, purging Scotland of its supposed Lowland Saxonism. Through these two means, and others, cultural revivalists hoped to challenge enduring divisions within the nation.

A key mid-Victorian attempt to challenge the binary between the Lowlands and the Highlands was the Wallace Monument on the Abbey Craig in Stirling, the historic town known as the 'gateway to the Highlands'. This project (initiated in the 1850s and completed only in 1869), which Geddes would go on to applaud, was supported by the National Association for the Vindication of Scottish Rights, and it was designed to help unify Scotland through promoting common identification with one of Scotland's national heroes, William Wallace.[50] The project's motivation to unite the nation is revealed in the commentaries on the meetings to arrange the funding, design and location of the monument. *The Glasgow Herald* reported on an early meeting and quoted the following declaration by the Earl of Elgin, who led the committee:

> The proposal to rear a National Monument to Sir William Wallace, this patriot hero of Scotland, must commend itself to the feelings of every Scottish heart. Movements for the carrying out of such an enterprise

> have previously been attempted, but have failed, owing, it is supposed to the want of combined efforts, and differences of opinion respecting an appropriate site. The originators of the present movement have resolved to obviate these difficulties by a general appeal to the whole country, and by definitely fixing the site on the Abbey Craig, near Stirling, overlooking the battlefield of Stirling, the theatre of the hero's greatest victory, and which was followed by his recognition as Guardian of the Kingdom.[51]

It is noteworthy here that national consensus was desired above all, and the location of Stirling was believed to be the best means of bringing this about. Geographically, Stirling united Highlander and Lowlander; as one contemporary commentator noted, when discussing the proposed monument,

> the ancient castle has held and assailed [. . .] and defied the ravages of time and war, linking the memories of a hundred generations, as the rock on which it stands links the two halfs of Scotland, and forms a place of strength in that narrow neck of the union.[52]

By choosing this locale, which linked both parties in the Scottish 'union' (the Highlands and Lowlands), the committee hoped to stimulate the 'whole country' in a 'combined effort' that was felt to be lacking previously. And through its attempt to 'preserve in Scotland something of a separate national existence',[53] the monument also heighted a sense of unity – promoting national identification with a 'historic state', as Hobsbawm defines it.[54]

Increased national unity was also encouraged through the monument's initial design, which 'othered' England and fashioned the image of a common foe. The original accepted design by Joseph Noel Paton, who designed the Memorial of the War of Independence, discussed in the Introduction, took the form of a galvanised iron statue, titled *Lion and Typhon* (Fig. 1.1).[55] Noel Paton's Wallace Monument design is an allegory of Wallace (and Scotland more broadly, given that the nation's royal standard features a lion rampant) overcoming Typhon, a deadly monster representative of tyranny. Unsurprisingly, objections were raised that it stirred too great an anti-English feeling, although it was later admired by Noel Paton's fellow Pre-Raphaelites, Holman Hunt and Dante Gabriel Rossetti.[56] Despite its eventual rejection, the design's initial selection suggests that the monument project hoped to increase national unity through an expression of cultural resistance, asserting Scotland's nationhood in defiance of assimilation. Like Paton's Memorial of

Figure 1.1 Sir Joseph Noel Paton, *Lion and Typhon*, initially selected design for the Wallace Monument, Stirling (c.1859). National Galleries of Scotland. Purchased 2001.

the Wars of Independence, this monument highlights the necessity of Scottish resistance to incorporation for meaningful unionism to exist – Wallace and Bruce's armies *had* to overcome England for there to be a union – but it also reveals that Scottish revivalists were keen to maintain the image of a common foe to promote national cohesion.

Moving towards the *fin de siècle,* we find that cultural revivalists were increasingly keen to resist the Celt–Saxon divide in Scotland to stimulate more national unity. A figure of continuity between the Wallace Monument and the *fin-de-siècle* cultural revival was John Stuart Blackie, who would go on to become president of the SHRA. When the foundation stone of the Wallace Monument was laid in 1861, Blackie delivered a speech on Scottish literature, which was 'a trumpet-blast of warning to his nation and defiance to its enemies'.[57] Blackie would become one of the most vocal advocates of Scottish traditions, cultures and languages. When responding to the idea that it was 'vulgar' to sing native songs, Blackie stated, 'I'll tell you what is vulgar: to pretend to be what you are not,'[58] a statement that anticipates a lecture by Douglas Hyde,[59] titled 'The Necessity for De-Anglicising Ireland' (1892), where Hyde outlines the 'folly of neglecting what is Irish'.[60] Blackie supported 'native' forms and resisted 'every pretty French conceit or whiff of Metropolitan sentiment that may be blown across the Border'.[61] Expressing deep anxieties about an encroaching 'disease of Anglification' and the creation of a 'Northern province of England called Scotland',[62] Blackie felt that Scotland was subject to a 'denationalising process', which he hoped to counter.[63] And this interest in cultural defence is reflected in his passion for Scottish political autonomy; as Chairman of the SHRA, Blackie would write works that drew from anti-Union rhetoric. In his long poem, *A Song of Heroes* (1890), which invokes Robert Burns, Blackie scorned those who 'sold / Scotland's grace and Scotland's honour / For a bag of English gold'.[64]

Alongside defending Scottish traditions and its political autonomy, Blackie also championed the interrogation of the Highland–Lowland divide and promoted increased Lowland appreciation for Celtic culture. In the 1880s, in response to the Land Wars in the Highlands – an agrarian conflict between crofters lacking secure tenancy and their landlords and the government, contemporaneous with the Irish Land League movements[65] – Blackie wrote *The Scottish Highlanders and the Land Laws* (1885). In the book, he conflates the land problem with political centralisation, asserting that Highland crofters were victims of a society where 'uniformity is the law, mechanism the method, and monotony the product'.[66] He directly challenges those who attempted to marginalise Highlanders and Highland culture, stating that they are not, and were not, 'semi savage'. Instead, Blackie turns his fire on 'Saxon civilization' and illustrates the 'barbarity of this policy of desolation'.[67] Blackie flips the language of the Enlightenment stadialism here: it is the more commercial, industrialised culture that exhibits 'barbarity' in his eyes, not the Celts. Blackie also critiques the English for their tendency 'to depreciate the Scot' and, in turn, he denounces Scots for 'look[ing] down upon the Celt'.[68] But Blackie was not entirely anti-Saxon: denouncing racial purism, he believed Scottish nationality benefited from its mixture of Celtic, Saxon and Scandinavian races.[69] In portraying the national genome as mixed, Blackie attempted to lay the grounds for more mutual identification within Scotland: no Scot was purely Celtic, Saxon or Norse. Blackie also successfully contributed to the revival of the study of Celtic and Gaelic culture in Edinburgh and, according to Stuart Wallace, almost single-handedly established the first Celtic chair in a Scottish university in 1882.[70] He aimed to reverse the relegation of Celtic culture, which he found 'disgraceful to the national character',[71] by elevating its status in the heart of Scotland's capital.

The Land Wars, which Blackie wrote on, were important events in the history of the Celt–Saxon divide. Via the land question of the later nineteenth century, and especially around the time of the Napier Commission (1883–4), Lowland Scots were taking a greater interest in Highland affairs. It became clearer that the problems in the Highlands were not generated by the Celts' ethnic 'indolence' but by 'the premature application of advanced commercial law'.[72] W. F. Skene's *Celtic Scotland* (1876–80), which demonstrated the pre-existence of an alternative social model in the Highlands in which land was shared and tenant rights were enshrined, played a key role in the Lowland reappraising of Highland culture.[73] Dewey argues that the primitive communism outlined by Skene appealed to the '"thinking Scotsmen"' of the age, who were 'peculiarly susceptible to the suggestion that advanced industrial societies, characterized by the self-maximizing economic individualism, were ethically inferior to earlier, more communal, forms of social organization'.[74] The idea certainly appealed to Blackie, who celebrated the democratic, 'mutual interdependence' of Highland clanship.[75] Lowland Scotland's interest in Highland affairs in the 1880s is also reflected in the formation of the Scottish Land Restoration League, which provided a broader forum for Highland land reform discussions beyond the Highland Land League. Increased connectivity also laid the ground for greater interaction between Lowlanders and the Highlands. If the Caledonian Railways main line between Glasgow and London (which opened in 1848) bound Lowland Scotland more closely into the British state,[76] the opening of the West Highland Railway in 1894 and expanded infrastructure on the Highland main line increased accessibility and cultural contact between the Highlands and Lowlands.

Blackie was by no means the only cultural figure in this period who hoped to generate more cohesion between Highlanders and Lowlanders. In the vein of Blackie, who Geddes commended for strengthening Scottish nationality, several *fin-de-siècle* cultural revivalists felt the need to interrogate the notion of Scotland as ethnically divided to promote greater mutual identification within the nation. As noted in the Introduction, several figures connected to Geddes's Outlook Tower community challenged the supposed inferiority or backwardness of Highland and Celtic Scotland. In the succeeding sections of this chapter, I argue that the *fin-de-siècle* Scottish Romance Revival was consistent with these dimensions of Scottish cultural revivalism.

Indeed, through reviving a literary form that focused on Highland–Lowland divides – the Jacobite adventure romance – this genre of *fin-de-siècle* Scottish writing was particularly well equipped to interrogate and negotiate the understanding of the nation as racially divided and to reveal greater connection. These features of the Scottish Romance Revival are most clearly evident in the work of another figure that Geddes championed in 'The Scots Renascence', Robert Louis Stevenson.

Robert Louis Stevenson: Interrogating Fault Lines

According to Stuart Wallace, Geddes's attempt to link Blackie's ideas with Stevenson's is 'the oddest feature' of 'The Scots Renascence'.[77] Wallace presumably makes this judgement on account of Stevenson's tendency to avoid Blackie's classes at Edinburgh University as part of his 'highly rational system of truantry'.[78] But although Stevenson avoided Blackie's teaching, I argue here that several facets of *fin-de-siècle* cultural revivalism are common in their works. While a body of criticism has addressed Stevenson's presentation of Scottish nationhood and history,[79] considerations of Stevenson's life and work in relation to the movement of cultural revivalism in Scotland are broadly absent. Indeed, rather than embodying facets of Scottish cultural revivalism, several critics have characterised Stevenson's writings as elegiac expressions of 'national tragedy',[80] a point echoed in framings of *Kidnapped* (1886) as a 'bleak novel' that presents Scotland as a 'divided' nation.[81] Here, I propose an alternative reading of Stevenson's writings, which is activated by considering his work in the context of Scotland's emerging cultural revival. Rather than presenting bleak and tragic divisions that stubbornly persist in Scotland, several of Stevenson's fictional writings interrogate and attempt to reconcile the cultural and ethnic divides that they invoke – a desire Stevenson also voices in several of his essays and letters. Although Stevenson was by no means consistent in his portrayals of Scotland or his interest in cultural revivalism, I argue that, amongst his competing views and representations, we find two important threads of *fin-de-siècle* Scottish cultural revivalism in his work: an intermittent but defiant Celticism that encodes Scotland as a 'Celtic' nation and asserts Scottish cultural and historical difference to England, and a more sustained interest in presenting the shared features of Highlanders and Lowlanders, to interrogate the nation's supposed racial divide and promote greater national cohesion.

Stevenson's concern with Scottish cultural defence is revealed most stridently in a letter he wrote to a fellow Scottish writer, S. R. Crockett, in 1888. Stevenson had previously received a letter from Crockett, in which the latter had referred to Scotland as 'N.B.' (North Britain), a styling of Scotland that remained common in Victorian correspondence. Stevenson's response to his new correspondent was vehement. Writing from his home in Saranac Lake, New York, Stevenson wrote: 'Don't put "N.B." in your paper; put *Scotland* and be done with it. Alas, that I should be stabbed in the house of my friends! The name of my native land is not *North Britain*, whatever may be the name of yours'.[82] Stevenson here vigorously asserts his defence of Scotland's distinctive national status and resists the notion of an assimilated Britain, making assertions that would not be strange on Blackie's tongue. Crockett, no doubt disconcerted with the fury he had elicited, responded by agreeing with Stevenson, observing that 'N.B.' implies that 'Scotland was a conquest kintra'.[83] Stevenson's defiance of a common practice that he saw as accommodating Scotland reveals how intense his defence of Scotland could be. As he confessed in a letter to J. M. Barrie, who he described as a fellow 'Scotty Scot', Stevenson's 'Scotchness' was at times 'erisypelitous' – akin to an acute, infectious disease, the strength of which is evident in his letter to Crockett. But Stevenson also acknowledged that his 'Scotchness' was intermittent.[84] Indeed, in several of Stevenson's writings, especially those from his earlier career, we find him identifying himself not only as British, but as an 'Englishman'.[85] In any consideration of Stevenson's presentation of Scotland and Scottish cultural defence, his own 'intermittency' towards Scotland should be acknowledged, but amongst the complex range of positions Stevenson endorses, his defence of Scotland and his connections to Scottish cultural revivalism are clear.

The threads of cultural revivalism in Stevenson's writings are most clearly evident from the late 1880s and 1890s. During this period, we can trace Stevenson's resistance to the theory that Lowland Scotland was ethnically Saxon. In several essays and letters, Stevenson interrogates the idea that Lowland Scots were not Celtic. In one letter to his cousin Bob, Stevenson identifies the 'Anglo-Saxon heresy' of supposing that Lowland Scots are Saxon: he argues that there was very little Saxon penetration into Scotland, asserting that 'they super-imposed their language, they scarce modified the race [. . .]. The Saxons didn't come.'[86] In one of his later letters to the American artist W. H. Low, Stevenson similarly wrote that 'practically the whole of Scotland is Celtic', and he mocks 'the Low-German lot'.[87]

As Julia Reid summarises, 'this affirmation of Celticism' disputes the understanding 'that Scotland's Lowland population was ethnically closer to its English neighbours than to its Highland compatriots'.[88] In doing so, Stevenson not only casts Scotland as ethnically unified, but also challenges the supposed superiority or advancement of the Saxon race. Stevenson's attempt to discredit the association of the Scottish Lowlands with Saxonism here is consistent with several *fin-de-siècle* Celtic revivalists, such as Geddes, who frequently identified Edinburgh with Celticism,[89] and – like Blackie – Stevenson also explicitly endorses the views of W. F. Skene, author of *Celtic Scotland* (1876), in his letter to Low.

Like cultural revivalists, Stevenson was also a harsh critic of 'civilisation' – commercial, industrial modernity that styled itself in opposition to traditional cultures. This is evident from his earliest writings to his late writings in Samoa. In *Travels with a Donkey in the Cévennes* (1879), Stevenson instructs that we need to come down off the 'feather-bed of civilization', while, in a letter to Elizabeth Fairchild, he states that 'our civilization is a hollow fraud'.[90] Joseph Farrell has demonstrated that Stevenson's planned book on the South Seas was envisioned as an interrogation of Western 'civilisation' and its ignorance of the East.[91] Indeed, Stevenson believed that the process of 'debarbarisation' in the South Seas was truly one of 'decivilisation',[92] replacing traditional cultures with something inferior, which echoes Blackie's view that there was often more civility in traditional cultures than in industrial, 'civilised' ones. Stevenson's defence of native Samoan culture here is prescient for this study, as he found several telling parallels between the treatment of Highland Scots and Polynesians;[93] as Roslyn Jolly notes, 'the structural clash between ancient barbarism and modern civilization [. . .] was at the heart of Stevenson's conception of both Scots and Samoan history'.[94] He also found cultural equivalences between the two, believing Samoa to be a 'pre-Roman Empire' culture, just as he described much of Scotland's culture.[95] Stevenson's defence of Samoan culture echoes the Scottish cultural revivalism that took various forms across his works.

Although Stevenson does not appear to have voiced opinions on Scottish Home Rule, he certainly had views on Irish Home Rule and other constitutional matters relevant to Scotland. Like Blackie, Stevenson was planning a history of the Scottish Highlands, which grew out of his projected plan to write a history on 'Scotland and the Union'. He wrote to W. E. Henley in 1880 that he was 'reading hard for my work on "The Transformation of the Scottish Highlands"',[96] which would focus on 'the attempt to suppress the Highlands'.[97]

Although these projects were not realised in Stevenson's lifetime, his posthumously published essay 'Confessions of a Unionist' reveals his preoccupation with British constitutional and cultural tensions.[98] Stevenson ultimately uses the essay to align himself with the unionist cause, but the unionism Stevenson puts forward is highly provisional, and he even acknowledges his history of supporting Irish Home Rule. He writes that he had 'been in favour of home rule for Ireland ten or a dozen years before Mr Gladstone', before going on to explain that he now finds himself in 'the camp of Union' as a consequence of unacceptable violence amongst Irish nationalists.[99] Indeed, in 1887, Stevenson had written to Anne Jenkin – the wife of Professor Fleeming Jenkin, who Stevenson had written a biography on – proposing to go to Ireland to help on the Curtin farm, which was believed to have been boycotted and attacked by supporters of Parnell and the Land League. But even in that letter, Stevenson stressed his opposition to violence rather than his commitment to unionism, noting that 'the cause of England in Ireland is not worth supporting'.[100] The unionist that emerges in Stevenson's essay is far from committed. Having previously written in defence of self-government during the Boer War, in his 'Protest on Behalf of Boer Independence' (1881), Stevenson reveals his openness to Home Rule in principle.

Besides demonstrating his interest in constitutional questions on the British Isles, Stevenson also uses 'Confessions of a Unionist' to critique several aspects of government, in a manner akin to many Scottish cultural revivalists. While focusing on Ireland, Stevenson also comments on the Highlands of Scotland. He reveals his opposition to landlordism, and he blames the problems in the Highlands and Ireland on English 'indifference'.[101] Stevenson also considers the Irish situation through a comparison with Scotland, lamenting that the Irish 'have suffered many of the injustices' of the Highlanders.[102] One of the injustices Stevenson was particularly sensitive to was the Highland Clearances, which he described as 'inhuman'.[103] Furthermore, he critiques Westminster's surrender to what he interprets as the bullying tactics of Irish Home Rulers – 'what sheep they are in England [. . .] you have no idea in what disarmed, unwieldy helplessness we lie at the mercy of parliamentary obstruction and agrarian brutality'[104] – and he contrasts this English sheepishness with Americans, who have a preferable 'semi-barbarous self-reliance'.[105] In his defence of the Highlands and his critique of Westminster governance, we find further affinities between Stevenson's political positioning and several cultural revivalists in Scotland.

Stevenson's interrogation of what Menikoff terms 'roseate progressivism' in both 'Confessions of a Unionist' and his South Sea writings loosely aligns him with the emergent culture of decadence that was deeply suspicious of industrial modernity and often found value and valour in traditional cultures, as discussed in this book's Introduction.[106] Stuart Kelly has noted that the closest Scotland came to producing a 'Caledonian Huysmans' was Stevenson,[107] and while it is debatable whether Stevenson was the most decadent Scottish figure of the *fin de siècle* or not, there are certainly various connections that can be drawn between Stevenson and decadence. Farrell has perceptively defined Stevenson as a 'dissident from the bourgeois world',[108] which neatly summarises his proto-decadent sensibility. His appearance alone conformed to the decadent image. From an early age, Stevenson was known for sporting idiosyncratic clothing, not unlike that adopted by aesthetes such as Oscar Wilde; he was often simply referred to as 'Velvet Jacket' in Edinburgh.[109] A fellow Edinburgh resident tells us that he was also described by local boys as 'hauf a laddie, hauf a lassie, hauf a yellow yite',[110] and this portrayal of his androgynous, gaunt physique provides further parallels between his appearance and *fin-de-siècle* decadence. Besides these visual, associations, Stevenson's connections with prostitutes in Edinburgh and his desire to be more sexually frank – confessing that he imagined the character of Countess von Rosen in *Prince Otto* as a 'fuckstress' – demonstrated a disrespect for sexual propriety that was commensurate with several writers and artists associated with decadence.[111]

But it was not simply Stevenson's appearance and lifestyle that had ties to decadence; his artistic theory and philosophy also resonated with those of several decadent writers. Despite being remarkably productive throughout his career, Stevenson was keen to extol the virtues of idleness and critique the hegemonic Victorian conception of industriousness, resembling many decadent writings that denounce industry, often in favour of lethargy. This aspect of Stevenson's writing is most explicitly voiced in his essay 'An Apology for Idlers' (1877),[112] where he characterises those who are deprived of idleness as 'dead-alive, hackneyed people', lacking 'a strong sense of personal identity'.[113] And in terms of artistic style, Stevenson was a fellow advocate of 'art for art's sake', which he expresses in his manifesto-like rebuke to Henry James's defence of realism, 'A Humble Remonstrance' (1884). Here, Stevenson argues that art is independent of life, 'self-contained', and that it cannot recreate or 'compete with' life:

> To 'compete with life,' whose sun we cannot look upon, whose passions and diseases waste and slay us – to compete with the flavour of wine,

> the beauty of the dawn, the scorching of fire, the bitterness of death and separation – here is, indeed, a projected escalade of heaven; here are, indeed, labours for a Hercules in a dress coat, armed with a pen and a dictionary to depict the passions, armed with a tube of superior flake-white to paint the portrait of the insufferable sun.[114]

Indulging in aesthetic and rhetorical excess, Stevenson argues that true verisimilitude is as an impossible art and that writers should abandon their quest to represent life faithfully. Stevenson illustrates that art stands independent of life: 'Life is monstrous, infinite, illogical, abrupt and poignant; a work of art, in comparison, is neat, finite, self-contained, rational, flowing and emasculate.'[115] Anticipating Wilde's statement that art 'develops purely on her own lines',[116] Stevenson here defines his artistic philosophy in terms that are far from foreign to Théophile Gautier's dictum '*l'art pour l'art*'. Unsurprisingly, Stevenson was deeply admired by writers of decadence, including Wilde, Gide and Mallarmé; Wilde even asked for several Stevenson texts, including *Treasure Island*, to be brought to him while imprisoned in Reading Gaol. Kirsten Macleod notes that Dowson, Symons, Machen, Davidson and Yeats were also drawn to Stevenson's work.[117] While received wisdom often pits popular adventure romances against decadence,[118] both genres created a space to resist realism and critique forms of industrial, mercantile modernity that were styled as superior to traditional cultures – a critique that became a key component of Scottish cultural revivalism.

Stevenson's essays and letters reveal the ways in which his writing spoke to and reflected Scottish cultural revivalism, and we also find these trends in his romance fiction. The dominant cultural revivalist feature of his romances is the way he represents the relationship between Highlanders and Lowlanders in Scotland, often interrogating their supposed ethnic and cultural foreignness. Like Blackie, Stevenson acknowledged that the Highland–Lowland division inhibited a sense of national cohesiveness in Scotland. He articulates this view in 'The Scot Abroad', a chapter from *The Silverado Squatters* (1883), a chronicle of his life and travels in California. In this chapter, Stevenson includes a quotation from 'The Canadian Boat-Song' (1829), a poem that first appeared in *Blackwood's Magazine* as part of a series of sketches, 'Noctes Ambrosianae', in 1829:

> From the dim shieling on the misty island
>   Mountains divide us, and a world of seas;
> Yet still our hearts are true, our hearts are Highland,
>   And we, in dreams, behold the Hebrides.[119]

The speaker of this poem identifies themself as an emigrant Highlander, who remembers the Hebrides from Canada. What is striking about Stevenson's quoting of this poem is that, following his transcription of these four lines, he includes an additional line: 'And, Highland and Lowland, all our hearts are Scotch'.[120] By including this additional line, Stevenson modifies the poem: rather than purely focusing on the Highlands, he stresses the Scots' shared nationality and the commonality between Highlanders and Lowlanders. This sense of Highland–Lowland cohesion is elaborated on throughout 'The Scot Abroad'. In this chapter, Stevenson acknowledges how pluralistic collective identity is in Victorian Scotland, and how it breeds a sense of alienation between peoples within the nation:

> Countless local patriotisms and prejudices [. . .] part us among ourselves more widely than the extreme east and west of that great continent of America. When I am at home, I feel a man from Glasgow to be something like a rival, a man from Barra to be more than half a foreigner. Yet let us meet in some far country, and, whether we hail from the braes of Manor or the braes of Mar, some ready-made affection joins us on the instant.[121]

This quotation adds further evidence to Fenyô's argument that some Lowland Scots saw the Highlanders as a foreign people in the Victorian period. But Stevenson here acknowledges that, when abroad, their shared nationality is felt and their common bonds are activated. By quoting from 'The Canadian Boat-Song' and adding his additional line to it, Stevenson recognises the sense of division that has taken root in Scotland, but also reveals his interest in reconciling Highland and Lowland cultures under the banner of one Scottish nationality. It is this attempt to reconcile cultures within Scotland and build a sense of Scottish nationality, while acknowledging how deep national divisions are, that Stevenson continues to pursue in several of his adventure romances, including *Kidnapped* and *Catriona*.

Criticism on *Kidnapped* frequently identifies the Highland–Lowland divide as a central concern of the novel, but little space in critical discourse has been devoted to Stevenson's interest in overcoming this divide. Instead, critics have tended to highlight the impossibility of reconciliation in Stevenson's work. Reid argues that Stevenson presents 'Scotland as an irreconcilably divided nation',[122] while Alison Lumsden believes that 'Scott's apparent aesthetics of reconciliation' give way 'to one of Stevensonian division'.[123] Countering these claims, Donald McFarlan has noted that we need to be careful over accepting 'an over-simplistic duality'.[124] But he nevertheless highlights that Stevenson presents us with a nation of 'conflicting and contradictory strands of history',[125] a view consistent with the notion that Scottish literature is often defined by duelling polarities – the 'Caledonian Antisyzygy', as Gregory Smith termed it in 1919. These readings of Stevenson's novels rightly stress that Scotland's internal divisions are key concerns, but what they underestimate is the ways in which Stevenson attempts to rupture these divides that he invokes, and the ways in which he hopes to promote more mutual identification between the Highlander and Lowlander in his romance fiction.

Throughout *Kidnapped*, we find evidence of Stevenson invoking and interrogating the Highland–Lowland divide. Commenting on the two protagonists, David Balfour and Alan Breck Stewart, in a letter to J. M. Barrie, Stevenson wrote:

> I gave my Lowlander a Gaelic name, and even commented on the fact in the text; yet almost all critics recognised in David and Alan a Saxon and a Celt. I know not about England; in Scotland at least, where Gaelic was spoken in Fife little over the century ago, and in Galloway not much earlier, I deny that there exists such a thing as a pure Saxon, and I think it more questionable if there be such a thing as a pure Celt.[126]

In contrast to Stevenson's letter to W. H. Low, where he attempts to portray the whole of Scotland as Celtic and minimise Scotland's Saxon presence, here he portrays Scotland as a nation of racially mixed people. Nevertheless, these two positions that Stevenson puts forward serve a similar end: they both aim to weaken the argument that Scotland is ethnically divided. Despite his conscious effort to subvert the Highland–Lowland divide in *Kidnapped*, Stevenson tells Barrie that critics fell into what he termed 'the trap' of assuming that his characters embodied the Highland–Lowland divide, rather than problematised it.

Beyond the naming of Balfour, *Kidnapped* destabilises the notion of Scotland as ethnically divided in a variety of other ways. David Morris has argued that Stevenson uses *Kidnapped* and *Catriona* to question the juxtaposing stereotypes of Highlander and Lowlander that were often rehearsed in the nineteenth century; he writes of *Kidnapped*, 'there is nothing of the melancholy of the Gael. Nor do we have any representative of the unmethodical and procrastinating Highlander.'[127] For Morris, Stevenson dismantles assumptions about Highland culture, and we find repeated evidence of him interrogating binaristic traits of Highlander and Lowlander throughout the novel, primarily via David's experiences of Highland life. For instance, when David enters the Highlands and utters, '"if these are the wild Highlanders, I would wish my own folk wilder"',[128] he not only questions the idea that the Highlanders are less civil and more barbarous than Lowlanders, but he even inverts the established identity dichotomy by suggesting that the Lowlander is more savage than the Highlander. David articulates a similar thought later in the novel: 'we ourselves might take a lesson by these wild Highlanders' (113). David also explicitly attacks the notion that the Highlands and Lowlands constitute different countries. In response to Alan's Highland rebuff, 'as if this was your country!', David states, 'It's all Scotland' (114). Rather than experiencing complete 'disconnection' from the Highlands,[129] David often tries to highlight the commonalities between Highlanders and Lowlanders, and question the ways in which they have been stereotyped, much like Stevenson did through his supplementary line to 'The Canadian Boat-Song'. In this context, it is noteworthy that there are no references in the entirety of *Kidnapped* to 'Celtic', 'Celt', 'Saxon', 'Teuton' or 'Anglo-Saxon'. Unlike many of Scott's novels, which draw upon these terms, Stevenson purges the lexis of an ethnic paradigm that was felt to divide Scotland from his novel.

Certainly, there are moments in the text when the Highland–Lowland cultural fault line becomes reinscribed. David does long for 'tunes of my own south country' (132) and there is also discussion of him being on the 'wrong side of the Highland Line' (170). However, what that Highland line really separates is again interrogated in the penultimate chapter, when Alan proposes to David's uncle Ebenezer, who arranged his kidnapping and had tried to kill David, that he must pay Alan to take David, or David will be killed:

> 'Troth, sir,' said Alan, 'I ask for nothing but plain dealing. In two words: do ye want the lad killed or kept?'
> 'O, sirs!' cried Ebenezer. 'O, sirs, me! that's no kind of language!'
> 'Killed or kept?' repeated Alan.
> 'O keepit, keepit!' wailed my uncle. [. . .] 'I never had naething to do with onything morally wrong; and I'm no gaun to pleasure a wild Hielandman.'
> 'Ye're unco scrupulous,' sneered Alan.
> 'I'm a man o' principle,' said Ebenezer simply; 'and if I have to pay for it, I'll have to pay for it.' (198)

The confused heteroglossia is revealing here. Although Ebenezer invokes the divide between Highlander and Lowlander by calling Alan a 'wild Hielandman', Stevenson simultaneously disrupts it. While the Highlander, Alan, broadly uses Standard English and the Lowlander, Ebenezer, uses Scots, the pair then switch idioms at the end of the quotation: Alan states 'ye're unco scrupulous' and Ebenezer speaks in Standard English. Stevenson mischievously swaps these two characters' idioms around in order to interrogate their supposed division. The reader recognises that they are not as opposing as they think they are. Furthermore, it is the Lowlander, Ebenezer, who conforms more closely to the image of the lawless Highlander in the text: he betrays hospitality, sells David into slavery and tries to kill him by deception, not face to face, thus defying Highland codes of honour. The fact that the villain of the text is a Lowlander also helps to disrupt Lowland claims of superiority over the Highlanders. Stevenson goes out of his way to remind the reader repeatedly of how problematic the Highland–Lowland cultural fault line is. Stevenson's characters may insist on their cultural differences, but he encourages us as readers to acknowledge their affinities and how little they, as individuals, correspond to their respective types. By mocking several of his characters who assert their foreignness to each other, and revealing greater affinities between Highlanders and Lowlanders, Stevenson lays the ground for greater mutual identification across Scotland in *Kidnapped*.

Beyond challenging the Highland–Lowland binary that undermines a common sense of nationality in Scotland, Stevenson's romances are also keen to acknowledge Scotland's civic and cultural distinctions, and to distance Scotland from an assimilated British or English identity. These concerns of Stevenson's were made clear in his letter to S. R. Crockett but we also find them in his essays and romances, including 'The Foreigner at Home' and *Catriona*.

In his essay, 'The Foreigner at Home' (1882), Stevenson takes issue with the ignorance of the English about Scottish law, history, religion and education,[130] and seeks to demonstrate that, despite 'political aggregation' (171), Scottish nationality has persisted. Challenging the notion that Lowlanders have more in common with English people than Highlanders, Stevenson instead endorses the strength of Highland–Lowland connections and Scottish nationality:

> The Lowlander feels himself the sentimental countryman of the Highlander. When they meet abroad, they fall upon each other's necks in spirit; even at home there is a kind of clannish intimacy in their talk. But from his compatriot in the south the Lowlander stands consciously apart [. . .] his eyes are not at home in an English landscape or with English houses; his ear continues to remark the English speech; and even though his tongue acquire the Southern knack, he will still have a strong Scotch accent of the mind. (171)

Stevenson here tries to recast collective identity dynamics in Scotland. Rather than foregrounding a binary opposition between Highlander and Lowlander, Stevenson shifts this binary to Scotland and England, where England is cast as the 'other'. Identifying an external 'other' allows Stevenson to build a unified image of the Scottish self by juxtaposing the 'Scotch accent of the mind' against the image of the English mindset that he constructs. For instance, he identifies a relative lack of egalitarianism in England, when compared to Scotland: '[In England] the dull, neglected peasant, sunk in matter, insolent, gross and servile, makes a startling contrast with our own long-legged, long-headed, thoughtful, Bible-quoting ploughman' (167). The poor of Scotland are presented as educated and nourished, in comparison to the more degraded presentation of the poor in England that Stevenson offers. Stevenson's various depictions of Scotland in 'The Foreigner at Home' are certainly idealised, complemented by denigrating representations of England, but what these passages reveal is Stevenson's attempt to reconfigure communal identity relations in Scotland. The Highland and Lowland 'foreigners' he mourns in 'The Scot Abroad' are here portrayed as reconciled into a broader Scottish nationality. The foreigner in this essay is English. In a bid to resist any further 'aggregation' that could 'supplant' Scottish culture, Stevenson promotes a more unified national self in 'The Foreigner at Home', one that sees the 'other' outside, rather than within.[131]

The views that Stevenson espouses in 'The Foreigner at Home' are reflected in the representations he offers in *Catriona*. The novel is another example of a situation where Highlanders and Lowlanders end up 'in the pot together'.[132] The Highland–Lowland cultural fault line is invoked early on: Highlanders are portrayed as 'barbarians' that must be 'civilized' by the Lowland Whigs (34), who (with typical Stevensonian irony) are intent on convicting a man regardless of the evidence against him. Like *Kidnapped*, Highland and Lowland stereotypes are inverted to challenge the supposed divide – the Lothians, for example, are portrayed as 'rough' and 'wild' (111) – and the relationship between the two protagonists also embodies reunification. The lovers, Catriona and David, who represent Highland and Lowland cultures respectively, grow closer, especially while in Holland. However, the more Catriona identifies with her father, James More – who expresses 'contempt' for Lowlanders and the English language (229) – the more difference between them is created and they struggle to come together. It is only after Catriona turns against her father that she and David reconcile at Dunkirk. The context of their reconciliation and marriage reveals Stevenson's interest in binding Highlander and Lowlanders through their opposition to an 'other' – England:

> 'I have nothing left to give or to take back,' said she. 'I was all yours from the first day, if you would have had a gift of me!' she said.
>
> This was on the summit of a brae; the place was windy and conspicuous, we were to be seen there from the English ship; but I kneeled before her in the sand, and embraced her knees, and burst into that storm of weeping that I thought it must have broken me. (258)

It is with the threat of England in the background, and their common opposition to it, that Catriona and David unite. We also learn that Catriona's father has betrayed Alan; the quasi-villain of the novel turns out to be complicit with the English. Consequently, Catriona pledges herself to Alpin and tells her father to 'begone' (264); it is a highly similar ending to *Kidnapped*'s, where Ebenezer (who is anti-Highland, as opposed to James, who is anti-Lowland) is overcome. The Scots become reconciled at the end of the novel, embodied by Bohaldie's statement in the final pages that 'it's an ill bird that fouls his own nest, and we are all Scots folk and all Hieland', a view to which the characters 'were all agreed, save perhaps Alan' (267). Against this reconciliation, the divisions between Scotland and England are stressed, with Alan stating 'here's a Scots boot for your English hurdies!' (262) to a feigning Englishman. The novel closes with a sense of national unity, one where Lowlanders are even content to identify across the Highland–Lowland fault line with the Highlands, the territory and culture that was less incorporated into Britain. While Bohaldie's statement partially endorses the Highland–Lowland division, it also exhibits an attempt to overcome that division that was still live in Scottish society.

Stevenson not only exposes the problems with the Highland–Lowland binary and seeks to reunify Scotland – like Blackie and other revivalists in the period – but he very carefully attempts to disrupt the stadial historiography that, according to Kidd, helped to entrench divisions within Scotland. This project is particularly evident in two of Stevenson's other novels that are primarily set in Scotland: *The Master of Ballantrae* (1889) and *Weir of Hermiston* (1896). The beginning of *Ballantrae* can interpreted as a pointed critique of Enlightenment stadialism, which posited that societies gradually move from a 'backward', traditional, pre-industrial state to a commercial, modern, civil condition. The novel opens as a Jacobite romance in which Henry and James toss a coin to decide which one will support the Stuarts and which one the Hanoverians, thereby preserving their family's power in the event of victory or defeat for the Jacobites. Focusing on this sequence, Pittock has argued that

> While Henry and Mackellar represent Whig modernity and the Master the Jacobite past, it is they who are the more superstitious, brutal, and racist. [. . .] Progress, as a historical phenomenon, is vitiated; and a repeated metaphor of tossing a coin in the narrative, signifies not only the doubleness of the brothers and the Scottish character, but also the fact that there are two sides to every story, that virtues in the past are lost in journeying to the future.[133]

The fact that the entire plot rests on the tossing of a coin also disrupts the idea of history as linear teleology, as it presents historical events as the result of chance, rather than a determined process. As Maureen Martin notes, *Ballantrae* encourages the reader to recognise the 'deeply flawed narratives of Scottish identity', which is furthered through the novel's use of competing manuscripts that encourage us to be sceptical of the historical narratives with which we are presented.[134]

In contrast to *Kidnapped*, *Ballantrae* is less directly concerned with Scotland's Highland–Lowland binary; instead, it focuses on the divided loyalty to the Hanoverians and the Jacobites in Scotland. Nevertheless, the futility of this division and its impact on Scottish identity is, again, increasingly exposed throughout the novel as both brothers grow to loathe one another and, quite literally, battle between themselves. Their names, Henry and James, emphasise this: they refer to the dynastic split of the Tudors and Stuarts. Brothers, sharing a wealth of ties, become opposed and eventually die as a cause of this split. Over the course of the novel, the two also forget their country: James, for instance, is described as someone who 'withdrew himself from his own country-folk', almost immediately after the coin tossing, instead finding kinship with the Irish.[135]

Although the novel moves from national to imperial romance, it continues to comment on the Scottish predicament and the issue of stadialism, as the imperial territories abroad are often correlated to Scotland. Albany, New York, for instance, is where the novel concludes and its name has clear ties to Scotland: Albany was so named to honour James VII of Scotland, who was Duke of Albany, the territory north of the River Forth, which 'bridles the wild Hielandman'.[136] Albany was also once a dukedom for the heir of the King of Scots and it became a Jacobite peerage, held by Charlotte Stuart – the illegitimate daughter of Charles Edward Stuart. Like the Highlanders in Scotland's 'Albany', the native American inhabitants in Albany,

New York, are often styled as barbaric and primitive: we are told that it is a 'savage country' (193) and, earlier in the novel, there is a discussion of a 'line' that separates the civilised from the savages (54). There is a subtle link between the 'primitive' North Americans and the Jacobites: James, we are told, prefers the company of these 'savage men' to 'traitors' (196). The North American section of the novel holds up a mirror to Scotland.

Sir William Johnson, the renowned Irish diplomat and Indian officer in America who established trade links between New York merchants and native Americans, features in these latter sections of the novel. As Fintan O'Toole demonstrates, Johnson became immersed in native American cultures and styled himself 'not as a white settler and trader, but as a Mohawk war chief'.[137] His mission is compared to the Jacobite–Hanoverian (and Highland–Lowland) divide in *Ballantrae*, further associating the Jacobites with native Americans, such as when Mackellar notes, '[Johnson's] standing with the painted braves may be compared to that of my Lord President Culloden among the chiefs of our own Highlanders at the 'Forty Five' (207). Johnson's attempts at 'pacifying the frontier'[138] in America become an allegory for Scotland and Stevenson's own quest to bring the nation together. Although the novel finishes with both brothers dying, Mackellar's new-found respect for James (evident in his gravestone inscriptions) shows that he achieves a more balanced perspective, subduing the division and hatred he felt in the earlier part of the novel. The old antagonism weakens as Sir William continues his work in diplomacy and reconciliation. It is perhaps no surprise that a character named Pinkerton, sharing a name with the Enlightenment stadialist, John Pinkerton, is briefly brought in at the end, only to be killed and 'buried hard' (205).

Challenges to the notions of linear progress and stadialism are also central to *Weir of Hermiston*, written in the South Seas. *Weir* is concerned with the relationship of the individual to ancestry, and the ways in which familial and national ancestries overlap. Archie experiences a pronounced conflict with his father, Lord Hermiston – a character inspired by the eighteenth-century judge notorious for presiding over the unjust trial Thomas Muir, Lord Braxfield. Archie cannot recognise the dignity in his father that others see; when Lord Glenalmond states of Archie's father, 'he has all the Roman virtues: Cato and Brutus were such; I think a son's heart might well be proud of such an ancestry of one,'[139] Archie bitterly replies: 'I would sooner he were a plaided herd' (16). This hostility to his father and his legal views reflects Archie's dislocation from eighteenth-century Scotland.

As a consequence of spurning his supposed ancestral glory, a Sartrean nausea overcomes Archie and he struggles to find a meaning for his existence in a world surrounded by others who seem to possess the 'essential self' (70). This is evident in a passage following the sentencing of Duncan Jopp by Archie's father, when Archie passes Holyrood:

> He saw Holyrood in a dream, remembrance of its romance awoke in him and faded; he had a vision of the old radiant stories, of Queen Mary and Prince Charlie, of the hooded stag, of the splendour and crime, the velvet and bright iron of the past; and dismissed them with a cry of pain. [. . .] 'This is my father,' he said. 'I draw my life from him; the flesh upon my bones is his, the bread I am fed with is the wages of these horrors.' He recalled his mother, and ground his forehead in the earth. He thought of flight, and where was he to flee to? of other lives, but was there any life worth living in this den of savage and jeering animals? (21)

Archie's father's views reflect a broader culture of corruption in the capital of eighteenth-century Scotland, which Archie hopes to divorce himself from. His remembrance of the pre-Enlightenment national past as 'radiant' with 'splendour' is juxtaposed with the current state of the nation. The capital is portrayed as a 'den' of 'animals' that celebrate the capital punishment advocated by John Calvin, another grievance Archie has with his contemporary Scotland (28–9). Through these presentations, Stevenson confronts the locus of the Scottish Enlightenment and its stadialist thinkers: not only is Enlightenment Edinburgh portrayed as animalistic without reprieve, subverting stadialist portrayals of the Lowlands as the civilised part of Scotland, but, in Archie's eyes, Edinburgh has degraded from previous ages. Archie's longing to identify with a national, heroic past is a direct challenge to his father and the supposed superiority of eighteenth-century Lowland modernity.

Archie's struggle with narratives of improvement is complemented by the fact that the 'aboriginal memory' (62), which Penny Fielding discusses in detail in *Writing and Orality*,[140] is represented as an integral part of Scottish national identity in *Weir*:

> for that is the mark of the Scot of all classes: that he stands in an attitude towards the past unthinkable to most Englishmen, and remembers and cherishes the memory of his forebears, good or bad; and there burns alive in him a sense of identity with the dead even to the twentieth generation. (46)

The Scottish nationality portrayed in *Weir* is rooted in its ancestry, and remembering its ancestry – a feature that Archie struggles with, as it binds his father more closely to him. However, this 'aboriginal memory' also allows Archie and other characters not only to acknowledge but to experience, identify with and re-enter other pasts, which again challenge teleological understandings of history. Like Stevenson's earlier romances, *Weir of Hermiston* is not a narrative that validates stereotypical nineteenth-century portrayals of Lowlanders or stadialist phases. Instead, he uses his novels to question and reject these concepts that were felt to divide Scotland, in the hope of generating more mutual identification 'between [. . .] natures so antipathetic' (24).

What Stevenson's interest in interrogating the Highland–Lowland divide, uniting the two groups through the construction of external others, and in the questioning of teleological narratives of history reveal is the ways in which his romances, along with his essays and letters, reflect and embody various strands of *fin-de-siècle* Scottish cultural revivalism. In his resistance to the marginalisation of the Highlands, Stevenson exhibits a proto-Celtic revivalism – a position that is substantiated by his deep appreciation of Yeats's Celtic Revival poem, 'The Lake of Innisfree', over which, he told Yeats, he had 'fallen into slavery'.[141] Although Stevenson's amorphous ideas contradict themselves at times – he also writes without distress on the prospect of 'the euthanasia of ancient nations', for instance[142] – it is clear that he was engaged in, and contributed to, the developing culture of revivalism and cultural defence in *fin-de-siècle* Scotland. The fact that Geddes compares Stevenson to Blackie, and planned to publish a volume on Stevenson in the Spring of 1895, is unsurprising in this context. Rather than presenting an irreconcilably divided nation, Stevenson, like Geddes, was concerned with unifying the nation and defending its history and cultural distinctiveness, which the romance genre, in its capacity to traverse cultures and examine the relationship of the present to history, supported.

Arthur Conan Doyle and the Celts

> Stevenson's last year at Edinburgh University must have just about coincided with my first one, and Barrie must also have been in that grey old nest of learning about the year 1876. Strange to think that I probably brushed elbows with both of them in the crowded portal.[143]

This quotation from Arthur Conan Doyle's autobiography, *Memories and Adventures*, presents the creator of Sherlock Holmes fondly considering a scenario where he, Stevenson and Barrie – three of the leading figures of the *fin-de-siècle* Scottish Romance Revival – might have unknowingly been in each other's company in Edinburgh. Although the three figures never did meet together, they all had close relationships. Conan Doyle and Barrie not only collaborated to produce the libretto for their opera flop, *Jane Annie* (1893), an experience that prompted Barrie to write a Sherlock Holmes parody, 'The Adventure of the Two Collaborators' (published in 1923), but also played together on Barrie's cricketing team, the 'Allahakbarries'. In the 1890s, both Barrie and Conan Doyle also forged correspondences with Stevenson while he was based in the South Seas, and the deep friendship that developed between Barrie and Stevenson led Barrie to play an active role in campaigning for a monument to Stevenson in Edinburgh (which resulted in the St Giles' Cathedral *bas-relief*). In Conan Doyle's letters to Samoa, he conveyed his deep respect for Stevenson, closing one letter by stating, 'my hearty thanks for all the pleasure which you have given me during my lifetime – more than any other living man has done'.[144] Like Barrie, Conan Doyle also planned to visit Stevenson in Samoa, and he was asked to complete one of Stevenson's unfinished novels, *St Ives*, but he 'did not feel equal to the task'.[145] Conan Doyle's admiration for, and correspondence with, Stevenson and Barrie reveal how closely knit key Scottish romance revivalists were, even as oceans separated them.

But Conan Doyle and Stevenson (along with other Scottish romance revivalists) were connected not simply through their friendships and admiration, but also through the shared styles and concerns in their romance writings, one of which was their cultural revivalism. While criticism has neglected to consider Stevenson in the context of Scottish cultural revivalism, Conan Doyle has been read as actively ignoring Scottish concerns and his Scottish nationality altogether. Gerard Carruthers, for instance, has tentatively argued that Conan Doyle, as a British imperialist, 'erases' much of his Scottish identity, an identity 'which seems to matter little to him'.[146] It is true that Conan Doyle often privileged his adopted English identity over his Scottish nationality and Irish lineage, and he was, unlike Stevenson, a vocal enthusiast of Anglo-Saxonhood too. But Scottish cultural revivalism is nevertheless present in several of his writings. As with Stevenson, there are inconsistencies in Conan Doyle's treatments of Scotland, and his enthusiasm for the Saxon race complicates his relationship to Celtic revivalism further, but certain anxieties that permeate the writings of Scottish cultural revivalism are nevertheless evident in his work and demonstrate the complexity of his constitutional thinking.

To understand how Scottish cultural defence and British imperialism could co-habit for Conan Doyle, his writings on the Irish question are revealing. Like Stevenson, Conan Doyle decided to intervene in this public debate, but while Stevenson withdrew his support for Irish Home Rule in the late 1880s, Conan Doyle found himself converting to the cause in the twentieth century. Having previously stood as a Liberal Unionist candidate in Edinburgh Central (1900) and the Hawick Burghs seat (1906), Conan Doyle declared his support for Irish Home Rule in the early 1910s, and he explained the reasoning for his conversion across a range of newspaper articles. It was the 'apparently complete success' of Home Rule in South Africa, along with his concern over the anti-imperial sentiments of Irish nationalists, that prompted his conversion.[147] In a letter to the *Belfast Evening Telegraph* in 1911, explaining his support for Home Rule, Conan Doyle stated:

> A solid loyal Ireland is the one thing which the Empire needs to make it impregnable, and I believe that the men of the North will have a patriotism so broad and enlightened that they will understand this, and will sacrifice for the moment their racial and religious feelings in the conviction that by so doing they are truly serving the Empire.[148]

Here, Conan Doyle expresses the view that internal national unity was needed to facilitate cooperation across the Empire. A broader imperial whole needed unified subordinate parts, and he believed that Home Rule would help quell nationalist hostility to Britain and ensure greater imperial unity. For Conan Doyle, like many of the Scottish Home Rulers discussed in this book's Introduction, Home Rule and imperialism were mutually supportive concepts.

Conan Doyle's views would have been influenced by his close friendship with the Irish nationalist, Roger Casement. Casement, knighted by George V in 1911 but executed just five years later for his participation in the Easter Rising, had convinced Conan Doyle of the atrocious treatment of Congolese natives by King Leopold II's administration in the Belgian Congo, where Casement had worked.[149] Between 1910 and 1912, during the period that Conan Doyle declared his support for Home Rule, they became close friends, and even attended a theatre adaptation of Conan Doyle's 'The Adventure of the Speckled Band' together in 1910. Although Conan Doyle was opposed to Casement's participation in the Easter Rising, he nevertheless organised a petition to the Prime Minister against his execution (signed by William Archer, G. K. Chesterton,

James G. Frazer and Israel Zangwill, among many others). Even when evidence of Casement's homosexual offences were circulated, and public support for his case weakened as a result, Conan Doyle refused to withdraw his petition. Conan Doyle despised Casement's involvement in the Easter Rising, but he believed that the 'disgust[ing]' news of his execution would 'be exploited by every enemy of England from Dublin to San Francisco' and undermine the British Empire further.[150] A strong empire was one of Conan Doyle's priorities, and Home Rule became, in his eyes, a means of securing it.

In terms of race and culture, Celtic revivalism and Scottish cultural defence were certainly not Conan Doyle's top priorities. If anything, his energies were mainly invested in promoting Anglo-Saxonhood in the 1890s. In 1892, he expressed his hope that an Anglo-Saxon empire might soon be formed, by uniting 'England' with America, in order to 'civilise' the world: 'the Anglo-Saxon will swing the sword of justice over the whole world [. . .] America and England joined in their common Anglo-Saxonhood, with their common blood, will rule the world.'[151] When writing of America to Stevenson, he expressed similar Saxon supremacist views: 'my favourite dream is the possibility of our all being reunited again [. . .]. What a majestic and symmetrical people we should make!'[152] These views reflected wider 'imaginings of a new Englishness leading to a universally concocted, trans-Atlantically aligned, linguistic–racial federalism' at the *fin de siècle*.[153] But while Conan Doyle appears to be devoted to the cause of England and Anglo-Saxonism, concerns with both Scottish and Celtic revivalism are nevertheless evident in his work.

Conan Doyle's portrayals of the Celt are seldom consistent, and several of them conform to the Arnoldian conception of the Celt as irrational, intuitive and emotive. For instance, in the second Sherlock Holmes novel, *The Sign of Four* (1890), Holmes tells Watson of his encounter with a fellow detective in France, François Le Villard. Holmes admires some of Le Villard's skills but believes he is deficient in others: 'he has all the Celtic power of quick intuition, but he is deficient in the wide range of exact knowledge which is essential to the higher developments of his art'.[154] Arnold's distinction between the intuitive Celt and the factual Saxon is evident in Holmes's thinking here: while Holmes does not discount Le Villard's 'Celtic power[s]', he implies that they would benefit from being fused with exactitude and facts (which Arnold associated with the Saxon). As such, Holmes articulates (and partly embodies)[155] the Arnoldian ideal: grafting the best 'Celtic' features on to the Saxon race. The Celts also feature in another Holmes story, 'The Mystery of The Devil's Foot' (1910), where Holmes's pursuit of the murderer, Sterndale, runs alongside his research on 'neolithic' man,[156] as well as his readings on 'Celtic speech' (281), and the appeal he finds in 'forgotten nations' (242). The story invites the reader to compare simian Sterndale with the 'prehistoric strife' (242) of the Celtic territory (Cornwall) he seeks revenge in, and, in doing so, the story subtly portrays a Celtic space as closer to a barbaric, 'lawless' society (280), although this association is complicated at the conclusion of the story when Holmes expresses his empathy for Sterndale. When we turn to his short stories set in Scotland, the threatening mysteriousness of the 'Celtic nations' is also evident, such as in 'John Barrington Cowles' (1884). In this tale, Miss Northcott, a mesmerist with a '"vampire soul behind a pretty face"',[157] leads her Edinburgh suitors to their death, laughing when her fiancé, Mr Reeves, dies (34). It is also suggested that Northcott is responsible for Cowles's death: he disappears after being led to a vision of her and is never seen again. It is no surprise that Northcott's name includes 'north': like Thomas Millie Dow's *The Kelpie* (1895) and *Sirens of the North* (1895), which associate shape-shifting *femmes fatales* with Scotland, Conan Doyle further connects Scotland with supernaturalism through this *femme fatale*'s name. Scotland and the Celtic territories, in several of Conan Doyle's works, are presented as the preserves of supernaturalism, locales of otherness.

While these representations are not dissimilar to the denigrating nineteenth-century portrayals of the Celt as irrational and incapable of adapting to modernity, it is important to bear in mind how highly Conan Doyle valued the supernatural, becoming a spiritualist and writing *The History of Spiritualism* (1926) later in life. And these are not the only portrayals that Conan Doyle offers of the Scots and the Celts. Certain Conan Doyle romances are less concerned with fusing stereotypical Celtic and Saxon features and instead pit Scottish and Celtic identities against English ones. In *The Lost World* (1912), for instance, English identity is marginalised and both the Scottish and Irish characters dominate and show their dexterity in leading the Empire, while in *The Mystery of Cloomber* (1888) Conan Doyle critiques the arrogance and ignorance of Englishmen towards Scottish culture, resisting assimilationist strategies, while also valorising the Scots' research capabilities and ability to grasp the value of the immaterial.

The Mystery of Cloomber presents Conan Doyle's most striking attempt to resist the undermining of Scottish nationality and the marginalisation of Scottish culture. Conan Doyle raises the novel's concern with Scottish nationality and English or British cultural assimilationism early on. The narrator, Forthergill West, a graduate in Law from St Andrews, is introduced to the new tenant of Cloomber Hall, in the south west of Scotland, General Heatherstone. Heatherstone is surprised at West's complexion:

> 'Good heavens, McNeil!' [Heatherstone] cried, in the same quivering voice as before, 'the fellow's as brown as chocolate. He's not an Englishman. You're not an Englishman – you, sir?
>
> 'I'm a Scotchman, born and bred,' said I, with an inclination to laugh, which was only checked by my new acquaintance's obvious terror.
>
> 'A Scotchman, eh?' said he, with a sigh of relief. 'It's all one nowadays'.[158]

Heatherstone's casual assimilationism, seeing Scots as simply Englishmen, is foregrounded here as it plays a crucial role in the novel: it is Heatherstone's inability to recognise and respect the distinctiveness of both Scotland and Eastern cultures that proves to be his ruin.

The novel concerns three Buddhist priests from India who arrive in Scotland to seek revenge on Heatherstone, who formerly worked for the Indian Army and killed an arch-adept of the Buddhist priesthood. The disrespect of British imperialists towards oriental cultures is a key theme of the novel, and Conan Doyle goes to great lengths to draw equivalences between the Scots and the Orient. The darker skin of West here initially suggests his otherness, but once the three Buddhists arrive in Wigtownshire, following the shipwreck of the Glasgow-bound Indian ship, these comparisons become more pointed. For instance, Ram Singh, the main priest, wears a 'rough-spun tweed travelling suit' (86), which West finds incongruous. The Buddhists are also keen to defend Scotland. When Heatherstone continues to identify the South West of Scotland as part of England, and Captain Meadows describes it as a 'hole', they are corrected by the Buddhists: 'I think you must be wrong in considering this to be a barbarous locality' (74). The Scots and the Buddhists defend each other from Heatherstone, who attacks them. Their affinity is also signalled by Singh, who informs West's father, a specialist in oriental culture in Edinburgh, that 'your Eastern studies will have a lasting effect upon the knowledge and literature of your own country' (85). In turn, West's father describes oriental countries as his 'Eastern neighbours' (89). There is a marked affection between the Buddhists and the Scots, and this affection is juxtaposed with the Heatherstones, who identify with England and fail to respect either Scottish or Buddhist culture. When West, after denouncing science, advises us to 'look to the East, from which all great movements come' (126) in the final paragraphs of the novel, he subtly invokes the often-misquoted line attributed to Voltaire: 'we look to Scotland for all our ideas of civilisation'.[159] West's statement not only helps bind Scotland and the East together, but also demonstrates this Scot's understanding of the advantages of Eastern philosophies that are not limited to scientific empiricism – a view that was in tune with Conan Doyle's own desire to authenticate the spiritual world.[160]

The novel's concern with defending Eastern beliefs runs parallel with defending Scotland. It is Heatherstone's ignorance of oriental customs that is to blame for him killing the arch-adept Ghoolab Shah, who was 'about to attain a height of occult knowledge which would have brought man one step nearer to his Creator' (111), and his ignorance of Scottish customs reflects it. Heatherstone's final words highlight the novel's central preoccupations: 'My sad experience may show him [Dr Easterling of Stranraer] that I spoke truth when I said that there was much knowledge in the world which has never found its way to England' (116). Heatherstone acknowledges his ignorance in this statement but he still refers to Scotland as England. And his son is no different. After his father's disappearance, his son states, 'we shall see what the laws of England have to say upon it' (122), ignorant of Scotland's independent legal system. The narrator never explicitly corrects the Heatherstones' ignorance but Conan Doyle's word choice is knowingly ironic: for instance, a few pages after Heatherstone's son's statement, West uses the word 'corroborates' (124), thus invoking Scots law and reminding the reader of Heatherstone's son's ignorance. In doing this, Conan Doyle invites us to acknowledge and mock the Heatherstones' ignorance of and disrespect for both Scotland and Buddhism. It is the Wests who are best able to grasp and understand Eastern cultures and this ability is portrayed as potentially enriching to Scotland – a trait that should be defended.

Conan Doyle's defence of the image of Scottish nationality that he constructs in *The Mystery of Cloomber* also informs his later quest romance, *The Lost World* (1912), where there is not only resistance to the marginalising of the Scots (and the Irish) but a clear attempt to centre them at the heart of the imperial capital and to decentre England. Colin Milton has argued that *The Lost World* celebrates 'a composite identity which is "Britishness"',[161] but, while Conan Doyle is interested in the relationship between English, Irish and Scottish identities in this text, his presentation of national identity dynamics is more complex than this quotation suggests. The novel, serialised in 1912 after Conan Doyle had converted to the cause of

Irish Home Rule, reveals the author's interest in raising the status of the Celtic nations and their imperial capacities, as well as in challenging the stadialist historiography that Stevenson and Blackie had found so damaging to Scottish nationality.

The beginning of *The Lost World* is striking for its representation of non-English people, considering that it is set in London. McArdle, whose Scottish phrasing is parodied, mourns the lack of romance in the world, now that all the gaps in the map have been filled.[162] The narrator, Malone, an Irishman who seeks adventure (9), possesses an 'Irish imagination which makes the unknown and the untried more terrible than they are' (79). Professor Challenger, the protagonist of the novel, is, like McArdle, Scottish. Born in Largs and educated at Largs Academy, followed by Edinburgh University (15), Challenger expresses condemnation of 'the British hog' (26). Conan Doyle also had a Scot pose as Challenger for the photographic illustrations that were included in *The Strand* serialisation – himself (Fig. 1.2). Beyond the main characters, Malone relates an encounter with a lady at the beginning of the novel, who is 'more French than English in her type' (24). The reader is placed in a peculiarly un-English London.

E. D. Malone, "Daily Gazette." Prof. Summerlee, F.R.S. Prof. G. E. Challenger, F.R.S., F.R.G.S. Lord John Roxton.
THE MEMBERS OF THE EXPLORING PARTY.
Copyright. From a Photograph by William Ransford.

Figure 1.2 Photographic illustration for *The Lost World*, in *The Strand Magazine*, 43 (1912): 487.

The novel is not without its English characters but even they appear strangely un-English too. When the opportunity arises to define or express English identity, Conan Doyle often subverts or decentres it. Professor Murray, who has the 'common fault of most Englishmen of being inaudible' (61), not only is faint but also has a surname that clearly nods to Scotland. Such use of surnames to complicate identity is also apparent with Professor Summerlee. Although he is described as the Londoners' representative on the quest (71), the closest affiliation to the name in the period was Summerlee Ironworks in Coatbridge, Scotland. But the character who most clearly subverts and decentres English identity is Lord John Roxton. Roxton is initially described as the 'essence of the English country gentleman' (77), but various aspects of his representation stand at odds to this. For instance, it is widely agreed that Roxton is based on Conan Doyle's Irish friend, Roger Casement.[163] Casement's action against slavery in Peru and his work with the Putumayo Indians are clearly referenced in Roxton's speech, where he proudly narrates his attacks on Peruvian slave-drivers, including 'Pedro Lopez, the king of them all, that I killed in the backwater of the Putomayo River' (82). Furthermore, the Congo, which Casement famously defended, is referenced in the text (92). The fact that Malone's full name, Edward Dunn Malone, bears a strong similarity to that of the Irish journalist who worked with Casement, Edmund Dene Morel, also invites us to view Casement as a model for Roxton.[164]

And Casement is not the only source for Roxton: Cedric Watts has convincingly noted that Roxton is also based on R. B. Cunninghame Graham.[165] Cunninghame Graham was the United Kingdom's first socialist MP, a defender of Highland crofters during the Land War, a participant in the Bloody Sunday (1887) protest and a leading supporter of Scottish Home Rule, who would go on to become the first President of the Scottish National Party in 1934. Cunninghame Graham was also a romance revivalist himself and, like Stevenson, rejected the supposed superiority of 'industrial progress and creeping civilisation';[166] his ironically titled collection of short stories, *Progress* (1905), aimed to expose the brutalism of 'the great cause of progress', especially in imperial territories.[167] Like Cunninghame Graham, who spent time in South America, Roxton wears a 'South American poncho' (197) and is compared to Don Quixote (227). Cunninghame Graham so closely resembled Don Quixote that he was used as a model for etchings of the character, executed by William Strang, and he was also referred to as Don Roberto and 'Don Quixote' by many acquaintances, including Arthur Symons.[168] The fact that Conan Doyle bases his quintessentially English Roxton on leaders of the

Irish and Scottish Home Rule campaigns, seeking political autonomy from England, cannot be coincidental. While Conan Doyle expressed his enthusiasm for Anglo-Saxonhood in other writings, in this text Englishness is decentred. The fact that Roxton plans to move to Scotland (77) and describes an Indian as a 'bonnie boy' (236) substantiates this reading: Conan Doyle consciously subverts the Englishness of the apparently 'quintessential' English character.

The end of *The Lost World* is striking for the manner in which it continues this decentring of England. The trial to ascertain the validity of the explorers' claims delivers a final verdict, by Dr Illingworth of Edinburgh, of 'not proven' (295). This was (and is) known as the 'Scottish verdict', and it applied only in Scottish courts, not the London setting Conan Doyle places the characters in at the end of the novel. The confusion in the audience following the verdict highlights the strange and distinctive Scottish voice, and Scottish system, that occupy London here. As in *Cloomber*, the Scots legal system is invoked at the end of the text, but in *The Lost World* Conan Doyle does it to project Scotland into the heart of the imperial capital. The Scots and the Irish, in this representation, occupy the centre of the Empire and imperial management, and England instead is marginalised. If those from the 'Celtic nations' needed to absorb Saxon features in Conan Doyle's earlier work, there is little reliance on the Saxon here. In constructing this representation, Conan Doyle vindicates the capacities of the Celtic nations and their ability to manage the Empire. In this context, his invocation of Casement and Cunninghame Graham may have been executed not simply to decentre England and reclaim the Celtic nations; Conan Doyle, a recent convert to the Home Rule cause, subtly endorses the Scots' and Irish's capacity to govern successfully, as well as lead the Empire.

Much like Stevenson, Conan Doyle also uses *The Lost World* to interrogate stadialist historiography, as well as the Highland–Lowland divide. The novel is especially concerned with problematising Edwardian cultural and racial hierarchies: London (and Europe more widely) are at times portrayed as no better than, and even inferior to, the 'savage' Amazonians. In geography, the Amazon rainforest is correlated to Europe: its size is like Europe, stretching from Scotland to Constantinople (83), and the plateau is the size of the 'average English county' (194). Challenger, true to his name, also challenges the supposed inferiority of the natives: he applauds their 'primitive common sense' (186) and expects them to be as intelligent as the Londoners they have left behind, stating that Cucama Indians have 'mental powers hardly superior to the average Londoner' (39).

Conan Doyle is keen to highlight similarities rather than differences between this 'lost world' and modern, civilised Europe. He also achieves this end through his portrayal of the protagonist. Challenger may be a Lowland Scottish professional but he also has an 'elephantine sense of humour',[169] and he is compared to a 'bull-frog' (38), a 'monstrous beetle (88) and even to the ape-man (232): he is the 'missing link' (194) between apes and humans. Challenger can move from being the 'highest product of modern civilization to the most desperate savage in South America' (232). He is further evidence of the connection between Europe and the 'lost world', between supposedly civilised and barbarous cultures. Furthermore, the fact that the Lowland professional takes on the simian features that were often associated with the Celt (especially Irish Celts) in this period shows Conan Doyle's interest in critiquing the racial divide between the supposedly Celtic Highlanders and Saxon Lowlanders too. Like Stevenson, Conan Doyle disrupts established binaries and questions the idea that 'barbarous' or 'savage' cultures are all that different from, or inferior to, European ones. The characters want to 'get out of this horrible country and back once more to civilization' (259), but we are left pondering what clearly distinguishes their civilisation from the Amazonians.

As such, *The Mystery of Cloomber* and *The Lost World* demonstrate Conan Doyle's participation in Scottish cultural revivalism. *Cloomber*'s interest in resisting the dismissal of Scottish cultural distinctiveness and its highlighting of the nation's superior capabilities, coupled with *The Lost World*'s decentring of England to highlight the Celtic nations' ability to govern and manage the imperial capital, and the novel's disruption of teleological historiography, speak to Conan Doyle's interest in defending Scottish identity. While the Empire was a prevalent concern for Conan Doyle, and other writings were concerned with Anglo-Saxonhood, these writings demonstrate the variety and complexity of his œuvre.

Lang, Barrie, Jacob and Buchan

The facets of cultural revivalism that are found in the work of Stevenson and Conan Doyle are also evident in the works of various other Scottish Romance Revival writers of the *fin de siècle*. Across the works of Andrew Lang, J. M. Barrie, Violet Jacob and John Buchan, we also find representations of Highlanders and Lowlanders reconciled through common identification with Scottish nationality, as well as interrogations of modernity and attempts to recover marginalised identities. The brief survey of their writings that follows does not hope to provide an exhaustive account of their works' engagement with Scottish cultural revivalism, but to demonstrate how pervasive the Scottish Romance Revival was, and to indicate some of the elements of cultural revivalism that appear.

Andrew Lang may not seem a natural figure to include alongside *fin-de-siècle* Scottish cultural revivalists, considering his scathing attack on 'The Celtic Renascence' in *Blackwood's* in 1897. There, he identifies the Arnoldian Celticism of 'Fiona Macleod', amongst others, and attacks what he feels are its glamourised appropriations of Highland life. He also challenges William Sharp's attempts to find 'the Celtic element' in the writings of major English and Lowland authors, noting that 'when we bring race into literary criticism, we dally with that unlovely fluent enchantress, Popular Science'. As a remedy to this form of Celticism, Lang called for more writings in the vein of Neil Munro's more 'knowledge[able]' tales of Highland life, which make it 'live again'.[170] Lang firmly associates Celtic culture with the Highlands, and thus finds the attempts to unlock a Lowland Celticism anachronistic, but his qualification over Munro here is also telling. Lang was not opposed to looking to the Highlands and reviving its culture and history; he simply advocated an alternative approach to the one he finds in Sharp's writings. And it is this alternative revivalism that Lang performs in his short stories, where he is keen to reappraise both the Highlander and the Jacobite, and to challenge the notion that they have not contributed to modernity.

Julia Reid has demonstrated that Lang was deeply invested in the Romance Revival.[171] In his essay 'Realism and Romance' (1887), Lang defends the presence of romance in a world of modernity: 'there is still room for romance, and love of romance, in civilized human nature'.[172] Lang, who believed that 'we are all savages under our white skins',[173] appreciated romance's ability to question 'civilised' modernity. As Elsa Richardson writes, such claims demonstrate Lang's anthropological concern with questioning teleological orderings of historical development.[174] Lang's stories that focus on Scottish history, particularly his Stuart tales, are equally preoccupied with dismantling teleological accounts of historical progress, which had often rendered the Celt and Jacobite as belonging to a barbarous historical stage. These Stuart romances were anthologised posthumously in 1928 as *Tartan Tales*, edited by Bertha L. Gunterman, but the stories included are best considered in the context of Lang's original anthologies, as their internationalism reveals some of his key concerns. *The Red True Story Book* (1895) is one of these collections, featuring stories set in various nations, and contains 'Prince Charlie's War', representing the conflict between the Hanoverian government and the Jacobites. Typical of Lang's collections, the story is preceded by a very similar tale, 'The Death of Hacon the Good', concerning the attempts made by Gunnhilda and her sons to recover the throne of Norway. This placement encourages the reader to consider the Young Pretender's challenge for the throne in relation to Norwegian folklore. In 'Prince Charlie's War', Lang traces part of the history of the Jacobite rebellion and, in the final paragraph, following the Battle of Culloden, he suggests that aspects of Jacobitism have continued and that it is not a past 'stage':

> But it was not the end of the romance of the Highland clans. Crushed down, scattered, and cruelly treated as these were in the years that followed Culloden, nothing could break their fiery spirit nor kill their native aptitude for war. In the service of that very government which had dealt so harshly with them, they were to play a part in the world's history, wider, nobler, and not less romantic than that of fiercely faithful adherents to a dying cause. [. . .] And there may be other pages of this heroic history of the Highland regiments that our children and our children's children shall read with proud emotion in days that are to be.[175]

Here, Lang outlines his respect for the achievements of the Highland clans. Strikingly, Lang notes that the descendants of Jacobites have played a great role 'in the world's history', detailing the many territories where they have conducted their 'imperishable deeds'. Rather than styling the Jacobites as an impediment to imperial expansion, Highland militarist and imperial successes are connected to Jacobite loyalty here, a theme that is also evident in other texts in this period, including A. C. MacDonell's *Lays of the Heather* (1896). Much as in Stevenson's and Conan Doyle's works, Lang's story disrupts stadialist representations of the Jacobite Highlander: Jacobitism is reclaimed from barbarity, and its global influence and the achievements of its descendants are stressed. In Lang's hands, the Highlands are placed within, and speak to, an international context; the images of parochial backwardness are challenged.

In presenting this image of the Highlands and the Jacobites, 'Prince Charlie's War' reflects Lang's wider historiographical project, which, as Catriona Macdonald has demonstrated, was partly defined by 'disrupting distinctions between whig and jacobite'.[176] In challenging this historical divide, and in his attempt to reclaim the position of Highland culture, Lang's work bears similarities to that of Stevenson, who he formed a lengthy correspondence with,[177] and also to Conan Doyle, who acknowledged his debt to Lang for the 'first real opening' in his career.[178] Despite Lang's restriction of the Celtic race to the Highlands in 'The Celtic Renascence', which distances him especially from Stevenson, there are nevertheless common cultural revivalist traits in Lang's writings.

While J. M. Barrie had a close friendship with both Stevenson and Conan Doyle, his relationship with Lang was less intimate, although they did exchange letters. Barrie also published a satirical article in *The Scots Observer*, titled 'Mr. Plagiary Lang', under the pseudonym 'A Woman of Letters' – which was followed by response from 'Not a Man of Letters, But a Man who Reads' that was almost certainly written by Barrie too – where Barrie mocks those who failed to recognise the fact that Lang's book *Old Friends* (1890) was a series of parodies.[179] A parodist himself, Barrie engaged with a range of different genres during his career, and wrote several Romance Revival texts. While he is receiving increased critical attention, following advances made by R. D. S. Jack, Andrew Nash and Valentina Bold,[180] Barrie's work, like that of Conan Doyle, is yet to be considered in the context Scottish cultural revivalism. Indeed, Cairns Craig has argued that Barrie's work, in making us confront pasts and alternative realities that do not provide solutions to problems, *reverses* the process of revivalism.[181] While there is truth in this statement, there are nevertheless ties between Scottish cultural revivalism and Barrie's writings, which Geddes may well have been attuned to as he had Barrie in mind as a potential contributor to *The Evergreen*.[182] In several of Barrie's plays and his final novella, 'Farewell Miss Julie Logan', we find Barrie challenging the marginalisation, and repression, of both Scottish culture and history.

The Admirable Crichton (1902), a comedy of manners that inverts various social norms and hierarchies – much like Oscar Wilde's *The Importance of Being Earnest* (1895), to which Barrie's play continually nods – presents the audience with a servant (named after the Scottish polymath, James Crichton) who is deeply committed to the class system, alongside an affluent coterie who are radicals that demand more equality. In the second act, the characters become shipwrecked on an island, where Crichton proves to be the most adept figure, and he reaches the top of the social hierarchy there, becoming 'regal'.[183] However, when the characters return to England, Crichton goes back to his servant role and his dexterity on the island is ignored in Ernest's account of the adventure. Despite this slight, Crichton will still not 'listen to a word against England'.[184] In Crichton, we encounter a figure that reigns in the territories of adventure romance, much like Challenger, but his skills are ignored and erased in domestic England. The entire play is a series of jokes that blatantly invert stereotypes, but if we are to associate Crichton with Scotland, as the title and his ironic love for England suggest, Barrie appears to be throwing a spotlight on the ways in which aristocratic English society ignores (and takes credit for) the aptitude of those around them, be they lower-class or Scottish. The play is primarily concerned with class, but Barrie nevertheless leaves the door open to consider the play in the context of Anglo-Scottish relations.

Several of Barrie's other plays are more explicitly concerned with Anglo-Scottish relations, such as *What Every Woman Knows* (1908), in which the first half is set in Scotland and the second half in London. A battle is set up in the text between the Scottish protagonist, Maggie, and the English rival for her husband's affections, Lady Sibyl. The play mocks stereotypical features associated with both the Scots and the English but, ultimately, it is Maggie's Scottish practicality that rises above Sibyl's English grace, embodied by the following discussion between the two women:

> Maggie: Now's the time, Lady Sibyl, for you to have one of your inspiring ideas.
> Sibyl: (ever ready) Yes, yes – but what?[185]

In their battle, Maggie is victorious: she proves her savviness in being able to advance John's political reputation, further the women's movement[186] and finally win John back from Sibyl. Barrie again exhibits his interest in mocking aristocratic English society and demonstrating the dexterity of a Scot.

Some of these concerns are also touched on in Barrie's later play, *Mary Rose* (1920). The title of the play itself alludes to conflict between the Scots and the English as it is a reference to the Mary Rose ship that transported English troops to Newcastle in preparation for the Battle of Flodden. The play is largely set on the Western Isles, which Mary Rose had visited as a child. In adulthood, Mary and her husband Simon return to a Hebridean island and listen to the boatman's story of a young girl who vanished there. Simon mocks the boatman and his 'Highland stories': 'you and your bogies and wraiths, you man of the mists'.[187] But, like the Highland spaewife's prophecy in Scott's 'The Two Drovers', Cameron's story of the missing girl is authenticated when Mary goes missing for a second time. Her parents try to leave it in 'the past', as does Simon, who states 'let's forget all about it', but Mary Rose returns as a ghost, seeking her child.[188] In *Mary Rose*, the characters, who are encoded as English, can never be free of the Hebrides; they can never resign Celtic culture to the past. Barrie would return to this theme a decade later in his late novella, *Farewell, Miss Julie Logan* (1932), a post-Freudian Jacobite romance where ghostly Jacobite 'strangers' come back to honour and feed those they left behind. Despite his best efforts and support from Dr John, the narrator, Adam Yestreen, cannot purge the memory of his encounter with one of these 'papist' ghosts,[189] Julie Logan, who he dropped into a burn. In Barrie's swan song, characters can never be free of the past, and repressed Scotland continually returns.

Violet Jacob, Barrie's fellow resident of Angus, also penned romance fiction, and her best-known historical adventure, *Flemington* (1911), reflects the Scottish Romance Revival's interrogation of the nation's historical divides, primarily its split Jacobite–Hanoverian loyalties. The novel focuses on Archie Flemington, a government informant who descends from Jacobites but was raised by his passionately Whig grandmother. Flemington is employed to spy on the House of Balnillo, where the Jacobite, David Logie, lives. But, after becoming acquainted with Balnillo, Flemington develops affection for Logie and refuses to betray him. Flemington fails to adhere to the strict divides in eighteenth-century Scottish society and experiences fondness for both Logie and his grandmother. As Wattie, a fellow distributor of letters, puts it to Captain Callander: '*Flemington'll no let ye get him!* He's dancin' wi' George, but he's takin' the tune frae Chairlie [. . .]. There's mony hae done the same afore an' 'll dae it yet!'[190] Flemington attempts to inhabit a space where he can both identify with, and distance himself from, two opposing political causes in Scotland; he refuses to take a clear side in this historical dispute. Even Madame Flemington, who is fiercely anti-Jacobite in the first two books, becomes a more complex figure by the third book: the daughter of a Jacobite, she eventually expresses a degree of sympathy with the cause. Through *Flemington*, Jacob reveals her interest in muddying Scotland's sharp historic divides and revealing more complexity and connection between supposedly opposing camps.

In a letter to Jacob, John Buchan described *Flemington* as 'the best Scots romance since *The Master of Ballantrae*. The art of it is astounding,' a degree of appreciation that is unsurprising, considering that his own romance writing exhibits consistencies with both Jacob's and Stevenson's.[191] Buchan, who, like Stevenson, was not removed from the culture of *fin-de-siècle* dissidence (contributing to *The Yellow Book*, publishing *Scholar Gipsies* (1896) with John Lane, and visiting the studios of Margaret and Frances Macdonald),[192] also shared Stevenson's concern with the 'coalescing of the Highlanders and the Lowlanders'.[193] In his 1927 speech 'Highland and Lowland', Buchan stated that there was very little difference between these two identities: 'every part of Scotland is more or less of a racial mixture'.[194] For Buchan, the 'question of Celtic and Saxon' was irrelevant, and he believed that a 'unifying literature' and identification with common landscapes could help bring the two peoples together.[195]

These concerns are reflected in Buchan's short stories. In 'The Earlier Affection', from *Grey Weather* (1899), Buchan – like Jacob, Lang and Stevenson – addresses the Jacobite troubles. The story begins with an Englishman, Townshend, who ventures into the Highlands seeking his cousin, Ewan, who is wanted by the redcoats. There, Townshend comes into contact with five merchants, one of whom, Graham, speaks out against the Highlanders: '"What have your Hielands done," he cries, "for the wellbeing of this land?"'[196] Together, they find Ewan but the merchants have no intention to fight for him; the Deacon states, '"Are we to dip our hands in bluid to please a Hieland Jaicobite?" (140). Ewan implores: '"But ye are Scots folk [. . .] ye will never see a countryman fall into the hands of redcoat English soldiers"' (140). When Ewan speaks Gaelic, which goes 'to their heart's core' (142), the merchants come to support his cause. Although Graham is initially reluctant, following the battle with the redcoats they all express their 'triumph' and Graham calls Ewan his 'blood-brother' (144). While the merchants believe that they will have to head to the seashore and a '"kinder land"' (145) following the battle, a theme that Buchan revisits in *Witch Wood* (1927), this 1890s story nevertheless presents previously antagonistic Lowlanders embracing the 'Highland' cause and a Scottish identity.[197] As in *John MacNab* (1926), where the Highlanders who initially assert that 'there's no reason why we should continue to exist'[198] progressively grow more confident, Buchan exhibits his interest in reversing the marginalisation of Highland communities and in reconciling them into a broader Scottish nationality.

'The Earlier Affection' is also consistent with Stevenson's fiction in that internal Scottish unity is achieved through reinforcing the image of a threatening, external 'other' – the 'redcoat English soldiers'. The story reflects Buchan's own perspective: despite being a Scottish Unionist Party politician, he believed that the various national cultures within the Union should be nourished and distinguished.[199] He would even go on to state that 'every true Scotsman and Scotswoman should be a Scottish Nationalist'.[200] Indeed, it is difficult to understand why Robert Crawford refers to Buchan as 'the last British writer' and considers him in opposition to the 'Scottish nationalist MacDiarmid'.[201] For Buchan, unionism and Scottish nationalism could, and did, co-habit, and 'The Earlier Affection' reveals his interest in *fin-de-siècle* Scottish nation-building.

Buchan's imperial romances also reflect his concern with Scottish nationality as well as his interest in teleological historiography. In *Prester John* (1910), Buchan initially sets the colonists and the native Africans in opposition to each other. However, towards the end of the text, Crawfurd, the narrator, increasingly finds South Africa akin to Scotland (as Buchan did himself)[202]: the narrator compares South Africa to Kirkcaple,[203] the landscape becomes 'homelike' (185), and he develops a Scots vocabulary in South Africa (234). Crawfurd, who proves adept in imperial territories, projects Scotland into South Africa and also nourishes his Scottish nationality there. The conflation is underscored by the erection of a monument to Laputa, the leader of the African uprising, in Edinburgh at the novel's conclusion (271). The 'savage' Laputa is increasingly viewed as noble, especially after burying Crawfurd's 'brave dog' (199), but it equally remains the case that the 'white man's duty' (264) is to overthrow him and make sure he, who resists the 'bitterness' of civilisation, does not 'put the clock back' (202). There may be some respect for Laputa, who believed in defending 'Africa for the Africans' (97–8), and the novel does attempt to complicate the divide between supposedly savage and civilised cultures, but *Prester John* also validates that same divide by portraying Laputa's culture as backward and a threat to imperial progress. As such, Buchan's work reveals a complexity found in several imperialist Scottish Romance Revival texts, challenging teleological understandings of historical ordering to reclaim Highland culture, while endorsing this same conception of historical progress to justify intervention and colonisation abroad. While nineteenth-century Scottish writing was often sceptical of 'its eighteenth-century inheritance of the virtues of stadial history',[204] some *fin-de-siècle* writers could simultaneously sanction these virtues.

The sampling of texts considered in this chapter reveals as many differences and dissonances between *fin-de-siècle* Scottish romance revivalists as it does consistencies and continuities. On the topic of Celtic identity, for instance, various competing understandings are presented: we find attempts to unlock a Lowland Celticism and, thereby, style the whole of Scotland as Celtic in Stevenson's work, but we also discover attempts to portray Scots as a racial mix of Celts and Saxons in both Stevenson and Buchan. There is also evidence of 'Celtic contributionism' in Conan Doyle's work, where the best features of Celtic culture should be cherry-picked and grafted on to Saxon culture, and there are also figures, such as Lang, who at times confine Celtic identity and culture to the Highlands and Islands, demanding a Celtic Revival focus on the writings and traditions of those territories. But amidst the various differences between the Romance writers explored here, we also find common features that distinguish the Scottish Romance Revival, features that reveal the ways in which these figures participated in Scottish cultural revivalism. In their attempts to challenge deep-rooted divides within Scotland and interrogate or complicate teleological accounts of historical progress, these writers provide representations that promote greater mutual identification within Scotland. Indeed, for the likes of Stevenson and Buchan, this promotion of mutual identification within Scotland was a conscious project to help bind the nation.

These attempts to interrogate teleological accounts of history, to question the supposed civility and superiority of modernity as well as the marginalisation of the Highlands, and to promote greater unity within Scotland, are common traits of *fin-de-siècle* Scottish cultural revivalism, which are found in literature and art beyond the Romance Revival. In the chapters that follow, we witness how these aims and objectives led Scottish cultural revivalists more deeply into the realm of *fin-de-siècle* decadence, which was equally concerned with questioning the superiority of mercantile, industrial modernity. Across the Scottish cultural revival, we frequently find Celticism and decadence intersecting, via neo-paganism, neo-Catholicism, occultism and even *japonisme*, in a bid to define and defend the nation's cultures and traditions, and to nurture a greater sense of national unity.

Notes

1. Geddes, 'The Scots Renascence': 132–3.
2. As Murray Pittock demonstrates, the term 'ultime Scotorum' was used to describe the Jacobite, Graham of Claverhouse, Viscount Dundee in Archibald Pitcarine's elegy for him; see Pittock, *Poetry and Jacobite Politics*, p. 151.
3. Rough notes by Patrick Geddes relating to *The Evergreen* c.1895–6 [Archives and Special Collections, University of Strathclyde: T-GED 8/1/3].
4. Craig, *Out of History*, p. 44.
5. Vaninskaya: 57.
6. Ouida, 'Romance and Realism', in *Frescoes*, pp. 303, 306.

7. Ibid., p. 303.
8. Haggard, 'About Fiction': 176.
9. Ibid.: 178–9.
10. Robert Louis Stevenson, *The Lantern-Bearers*, p. 176.
11. Haggard, 'About Fiction': 172.
12. Lang, 'Realism and Romance': 689.
13. Ibid.: 690.
14. Showalter, pp. 76–7.
15. Lang, 'Realism and Romance': 690.
16. Haggard, *King Solomon's Mines*, p. 22.
17. Lang, 'Realism and Romance': 688.
18. Robert Louis Stevenson, *Catriona*, p. 269.
19. Daly, p. 78.
20. Fraser, p. 36.
21. Several of these traits of the Celt echoed Ernest Renan's *The Poetry of the Celtic Races* (1857), especially the femininity of the Celt.
22. Arnold, *On the Study of Celtic Literature*, pp. 8–9; Daniel G. Williams, p. 73.
23. Young, p. 16.
24. Ibid., pp. 17–18.
25. Kidd, 'Teutonist Ethnology': 67.
26. Pittock, *Scottish and Irish Romanticism*, p. 64.
27. Pinkerton, I, p. 28.
28. Ibid., p. 359.
29. Pittock, *Scottish and Irish Romanticism*, p. 64.
30. Kidd, 'Teutonist Ethnology': 46.
31. Carruthers, 'The Invention of Scottish Literature', p. 108.
32. Fanon, p. 128.
33. Scott, *The Minstrelsy*, I, p. 28.
34. Hume, I, p. 23.
35. Scott, *The Minstrelsy*, I, p. 30.
36. Scott, *Chronicles of the Canongate*, p. 239.
37. Michael Keating, p. 41.
38. Kidd, 'Teutonist Ethnology': 67.
39. (Cited in) Young, pp. 28–30.
40. MacRaild: 67–85.
41. Carlyle, p. 29.
42. (Cited in) Young, p. 83.
43. Barczewski, pp. 151–3.
44. 'Inquiry', p. 3.
45. (Cited in) Fenyô, pp. 85–6.
46. Fenyô, p. 110.
47. (Cited in) Devine, p. 251.
48. Fenyô, p. 234.
49. 'The Highland Society', p. 2.
50. Hanham, p. 77.

51. 'The Wallace Monument', *Glasgow Herald*, p. 4.
52. 'The Wallace Monument', *The Aberdeen Journal*, p. 8.
53. 'The Wallace Monument', *The London Reader*: 4.
54. Hobsbawm, *Nations and Nationalism,* p. 75.
55. For more on this design, see Smailes.
56. Halkett: 3.
57. Kennedy, p. 207.
58. (cited in) Ibid., p. 210.
59. Hyde was an Irish revivalist who would become the first President of Ireland in 1938.
60. Hyde, p. 42.
61. (Cited in) Kennedy, p. 211.
62. (Cited in) Ibid.
63. Blackie, *Essays*, pp. 222–3.
64. Blackie, *A Song of Heroes*, p. 111.
65. For more on collaborations between the two movements, see Hunter. For a detailed discussion on the Scottish Land Leagues and their relationship to Ireland's, see Newby.
66. Blackie, *The Scottish Highlanders*, p. 93.
67. Ibid., pp. 51–4.
68. Ibid., p. 4.
69. Blackie, *Essays*, p. 173.
70. Wallace, p. 272.
71. Blackie, 'The Highland Crofters': 607.
72. Dewey: 41.
73. Ibid.: 43.
74. Ibid.: 54.
75. Blackie, *Essays*, p. 188.
76. Alvin Jackson, p. 148.
77. Wallace, p. 316.
78. Robert Louis Stevenson, *Memories and Portraits*, p. 32; Stevenson does note Blackie's 'human geniality' as a professor, though in 'The Foreigner at Home' – see Robert Louis Stevenson, *The Lantern-Bearers*, p. 169.
79. Key studies for analyses of Stevenson and Scotland include Lumsden; Reid, *Robert Louis Stevenson*; and Menikoff.
80. Lumsden, p. 72.
81. Reid, *Robert Louis Stevenson*, pp. 131–2.
82. Robert Louis Stevenson, *The Letters*, VI, p. 156 (c.10 April 1888).
83. Letter from S. R. Crockett to Robert Louis Stevenson [Beinecke Library, Yale University: Gen MSS 664/11/288] (23 April 1888).
84. Robert Louis Stevenson, *The Letters*, VII, p. 238 (c.18 February 1892).
85. Robert Louis Stevenson, *The Lantern-Bearers*, p. 26.
86. Robert Louis Stevenson, *The Letters*, VIII, pp. 363–4 (c.9 September 1894).
87. Robert Louis Stevenson, *The Letters*, VIII, p. 235 (15 January 1894).
88. Reid, *Robert Louis Stevenson*, p. 158.

89. Geddes, 'The Scots Renascence': 131.
90. Robert Louis Stevenson; *Travels with a Donkey*, p. 63; Robert Louis Stevenson, *The Letters*, VI, p. 420 (c.1 September 1890).
91. Farrell, pp. 73, 76.
92. (cited in) Ibid., p. 183.
93. Ibid., p. 80.
94. Jolly, p. 75.
95. See Farrell, pp. 127–8, 155.
96. Robert Louis Stevenson, *The Letters*, III, p. 148 (21 December 1880).
97. Robert Louis Stevenson, *The Letters*, III, p. 139 (12 December 1880).
98. 'Confessions of a Unionist' was a response to Grant Allen's criticism of the presentation of the Irish in *The Dynamiter*, written c.1887.
99. Robert Louis Stevenson, *The Lantern-Bearers*, p. 238.
100. See Robert Louis Stevenson, *The Letters*, V, p. 392 (15 April 1887).
101. Robert Louis Stevenson, *The Lantern-Bearers*, pp. 238, 242.
102. Robert Louis Stevenson, *The Letters*, III, p. 145 (21 December 1880).
103. Robert Louis Stevenson, *The Letters*, III, p. 149 (December 1880).
104. Robert Louis Stevenson, *The Lantern-Bearers*, p. 243.
105. Robert Louis Stevenson, *The Lantern-Bearers*, p. 243.
106. Menikoff, p. 3.
107. Kelly, p. 57.
108. Farrell, pp. 43–4.
109. Ibid., p. 77.
110. Mrs Miller, p. 159.
111. Robert Louis Stevenson, *The Letters*, IV, p. 115 (May 1883).
112. For more on Stevenson and idleness, see Arata, 'Stevenson, Morris, and the Value of Idleness', pp. 3–12.
113. Robert Louis Stevenson, *The Lantern-Bearers*, p. 39.
114. Ibid., pp. 194–5.
115. Ibid., p. 195.
116. Wilde, *Plays, Prose Writings and Poems*, p. 93.
117. Macleod, p. 50.
118. Ibid., p. 49.
119. Robert Louis Stevenson, *The Silverado Squatters*, p. 65.
120. Ibid.
121. Ibid., pp. 61–2.
122. Reid, *Robert Louis Stevenson*, p. 132.
123. Lumsden, p. 73.
124. McFarlan, p. ix.
125. Ibid., p. xii.
126. Robert Louis Stevenson, *The Letters*, VII, pp. 238–9 (c.18 February 1892).
127. David B. Morris, pp. 127–8.
128. Robert Louis Stevenson, *Kidnapped*, p. 91.
129. Calder, p. 129.
130. Robert Louis Stevenson, *The Lantern-Bearers*, p. 165.

131. In 'The Foreigner at Home', Stevenson argues that England's understanding of its neighbours resembles American missionaries who know nothing of the religions they wish to 'supplant' (Robert Louis Stevenson, *The Lantern-Bearers*, p. 164).
132. Robert Louis Stevenson, *Catriona*, p. 19.
133. Pittock, 'Sir Walter Scott', p. 289.
134. Martin, p. 127.
135. Robert Louis Stevenson, *The Master of Ballantrae*, p. 6.
136. Robert Louis Stevenson, *Kidnapped*, p. 171.
137. O'Toole, p. 77.
138. Ibid., p. 352.
139. Robert Louis Stevenson, *Weir*, pp. 15–16.
140. Fielding, p. 185.
141. Robert Louis Stevenson, *The Letters*, VIII, p. 262 (14 April 1894); Juliet Dusinberre rightly points out that the first line of 'The Lake Isle of Innisfree' is clearly taken from Stevenson's poem, 'Travel', which appears in *Garden of Verses* (Dusinberre, p. 313).
142. Robert Louis Stevenson, *The Silverado Squatters*, p. 44.
143. Conan Doyle, *Memories and Adventures*, p. 260.
144. Letter from Arthur Conan Doyle to Robert Louis Stevenson [Beinecke Library, Yale University. Reference: GEN MSS 664/12/304] (30 May 1893).
145. Conan Doyle, *Memories and Adventures*, p. 261.
146. Carruthers, *Scottish Literature*, p. 122.
147. 'Conan Doyle and Home Rule'; Conan Doyle, 'Home Rule'.
148. (Cited in) Lellenberg, p. 579.
149. Conan Doyle would go on to write *The Crime of the Congo* (1909) in response to these atrocities.
150. Letter from Arthur Conan Doyle to [unknown], in *The Arthur Conan Doyle Encyclopedia*, available at <https://www.arthur-conan-doyle.com/index.php?title=Letter_about_Roger_Casement%27s_sentence_(29_june_1916)> (last accessed 12 August 2018) (29 June 1916).
151. (Cited in) Blathwayt: 51.
152. Letter from Arthur Conan Doyle to Robert Louis Stevenson [Beinecke Library, Yale University. Reference: GEN MSS 664/12/304] (12 January 1894).
153. Colls, p. 49.
154. Conan Doyle, *The Sign of Four*, p. 8.
155. It is worth noting here that Conan Doyle confirmed to Stevenson that Holmes was partly inspired by their Edinburgh professor, Joseph Bell.
156. Conan Doyle, *His Last Bow*, p. 256.
157. Conan Doyle, *The Edinburgh Stories*, p. 36.
158. Conan Doyle, *The Mystery of Cloomber*, p. 9. I have restored 'Scotchman' in this quotation, which appears in the first edition.
159. For a discussion on this quote, see Goudsward, p. 221 n. 42.

160. Fraser, p. 15.
161. Milton, p. 299.
162. Conan Doyle, *The Lost World*, pp. 14–15.
163. Lellenberg, p. 578.
164. Stashower, p. 322.
165. Watts, p. xviii.
166. John Walker, p. 4.
167. Cunninghame Graham, p. 61.
168. (Cited in) Watts and Davies, p. 256.
169. Conan Doyle, *The Poison Belt*, pp. 15–16.
170. Lang, 'The Celtic Renascence': 191.
171. See Reid, '"King Romance" in *Longman's Magazine*'.
172. Lang, 'Realism and Romance': 692.
173. Lang, *In the Wrong Paradise*, p. v.
174. Richardson, p. 159.
175. Lang, *The Red True Story Book*, pp. 322–3.
176. Catriona Macdonald: 218.
177. Lang's letters to Stevenson are anthologised in Demoor (ed.), *Dear Stevenson*.
178. Conan Doyle, *Memories and Adventures*, p. 77.
179. Barrie, 'Mr. Plagiary Lang': 97–8.
180. See Jack, *The Road to Neverland*, and Bold and Nash (eds), *Gateway to the Modern*.
181. Craig, *The Wealth of the Nation*, pp. 160–3.
182. Evergreen Business Committee Scroll Minute Book, 1895 [Archives and Special Collections, University of Strathclyde: T-GED 8/1/1].
183. Barrie, *Peter Pan and Other Plays*, p. 55.
184. Ibid., p. 71.
185. Ibid., p. 201.
186. Barrie was also a vocal supporter of the women's movement; for more information, see Jack, 'Barrie and the Extreme Heroine', pp. 137–8.
187. Barrie, *Peter Pan*, pp. 223, 274.
188. Ibid., pp. 261, 285.
189. Barrie, *Farewell Miss Julie Logan*, p. 299.
190. Jacob, p. 475.
191. Letter from John Buchan to Violet Jacob [National Library of Scotland: MS 27416/4] (31 December 1911).
192. Howarth, p. 40.
193. Henshaw: 4.
194. John Buchan, 'Highland and Lowland', unpublished speech delivered on 26 January 1927 and 18 February 1928 [National Library of Scotland: Acc. 9058/5/1].
195. Ibid.
196. Buchan, *Grey Weather*, p. 131.

197. *Witch Wood* (1927) similarly presents Scotland as an unkind land for the Scots, ending with two pro-Covenant defenders of Scotland – the captain of Montrose's army and the protagonist, Semphill – leaving Scotland.
198. Buchan, *John MacNab*, p. 125.
199. Henshaw: 18.
200. (Cited in) Paul H. Scott, p. 187.
201. Crawford, 'Dedefining Scotland', p. 100.
202. Henshaw: 6–7.
203. Buchan, *Prester John*, p. 169.
204. Craig, *The Wealth of the Nation*, p. 138.

Chapter 2

The Belgian Revival and *Japonisme* in Scotland

While cultural and political tensions were growing across the Irish Sea and north of the Anglo-Scottish border, a further fraught cultural frontier on the British Isles at the *fin de siècle* was the English Channel. There was palpable anxiety around the 1890s that Britain's imperial might, and its civilising mission, were being undermined by the cultural *malaise* of decadence that was infiltrating from France. Perhaps the best visual embodiment of this anxiety is Edward T. Reed's *Britannia à la Beardsley* (Fig. 2.1), published in *Punch's Almanack* in 1895. Here, in a style imitative of Aubrey Beardsley, Britannia is presented seated at the English Channel, indicated by the white cliffs of Dover in the background. But this is no patriotic vision of Britain. The goddess takes on a grotesque form, with leering eyebrows, dark hair and a flamboyant crown adorned with snakes. In other contexts, snakes on crowns represent wisdom, but these malevolent snakes signify a threat. Not only does the image undermine traditional representations of Britannia but it also encompasses many non-British features: the pierrot costumes of the dog and Punch point to France, the dark hair of both Britannia and her passant lion (typically synonymous with England) suggest a southern European other, and the Beardsley-inspired style points to Japan. Tellingly, Britannia's shield includes the design of the United Kingdom's union flag but the crosses are thorny and menacing. The suggestion here is that, via the likes of Beardsley and the decadence he embodies, Britain (a very Anglocentric Britain) is degenerating: its capacity to embody civilisation and progress is falling away. This conviction was consistent with a wider anxiety that the British Empire itself was experiencing its own demise, equivalent to the fall of the Roman Empire.[1] In Reed's illustration, decadence is the enemy, a sickness that allows traits of the 'other' to cross the cultural Channel and 'undermin[e] British nationalism'.[2]

Figure 2.1 Edward T. Reed, *Britannia à la Beardsley*, in *Punch's Almanack*, January (1895): 9.

But not all of those who sought to defend their national culture on the British Isles were so anxious about cross-cultural pollination with 'the other' or imperial rivals. Many of those interested in defending and asserting Scottish identity, for instance, were actively building cultural ties beyond the white cliffs. Scotland's French connection provides the most obvious example. Patrick Geddes, who wanted to activate Scottish 'international initiatives of collaboration',[3] was particularly keen to nurture the 'old continental sympathies of Scotland',[4] especially Franco-Scottish connections, which he did through various endeavours.[5] Most notably, he founded the Franco-Scottish Society in 1895, which was a cultural equivalent to the Auld Alliance of 1296–1560 that was designed to deter English invasion; Andrew Lang was among its notable members. By attempting to reanimate a cross-cultural bond that had once supported Scotland's resistance to political incorporation into England, the society helped Scotland reassert its international presence, its 'continuing independence from England'.[6] This friendship through a common foe was encapsulated in a drawing by Scotland's leading symbolist painter, John Duncan, which was issued to each attendee at the first joint meeting of the society at the New Sorbonne, Paris. The drawing represents Joan of Arc (burned at the stake by pro-English forces in Rouen in 1430) with her Scots Army flying a saltire – a subject suggested by Lang.[7] In 1896, Duncan adapted the subject into a painting, *Jehanne d'Arc et sa Garde Ecossaise* (Fig. 2.2), and the drawing also appeared in *The Evergreen*, a magazine that appropriately celebrated Franco-Scottish connections. By looking to other nations, especially nations that

Figure 2.2 John Duncan, *Jehanne d'Arc et sa Garde Ecossaise* (1896). City Art Centre (City of Edinburgh Museums & Galleries).

many in England were trying to style as Britain's antagonists, Scots could assert their difference from, and rupture, the Anglocentric imaginings of Britain that they were concerned with around the *fin de siècle*.

While the Franco-Scottish connection has been well documented, there were other important cultural contacts that nourished the Scottish Revival and reveal its particular nature. This chapter is concerned with the ways in which cross-cultural pollination and solidarity between Scotland and other nations, especially those that were felt to be on the margins, advanced Scottish cultural revivalism, resembling developments in Ireland. Luke Gibbons has argued that many cultural revivalists in Ireland looked to and identified with cultures that were represented as being less 'civilised', particularly those in 'the Orient'. Citing Stanley Mitchell, he states that '"connections of dissimilars"' developed in the nineteenth century between cultures 'outside the dominant ideologies of imperial civility'. Such cultures on the margins could be 'yoked together' to create a 'violent proximity' to challenge the hegemony of the stadialist conception of history, which assumed that less industrialised cultures were insular and backward.[8] By forming ranks with other cultures and demonstrating their internationalism, such communities defended themselves against the stadialist critiques that marginalised them. As Gibbons writes, through creating 'transnational affiliations or solidarities', 'the power of the centre' could be denied.[9]

Although Scotland was an 'advanced', industrial, imperial nation in this period, its national revival movement often involved identifying with, and recovering, Celtic culture and identity, which were widely portrayed as marginal and antithetical to modernity in the nineteenth century. Consequently, variations of these 'connections of dissimilars' were also designed in *fin-de-siècle* Scotland. Several of those who wanted to defend and assert Scottish nationality looked abroad and identified with cultures that were felt to be out of kilter with industrial and commercial modernity, or cultures that purposefully rejected and subverted notions of stadialist history. In the very ways that Gibbons outlines, Scottish writers and artists 'yoked' aspects of supposedly less civilised culture into their own work to celebrate the value of traditional cultures. These other nations also provided models of national revivalism to inform and inspire Scotland's revival.

In this chapter, I examine two international connections that several *fin-de-siècle* figures bred to help them question, undermine or problematise the stadialist ideas that were felt to marginalise Scottish and Celtic voices, as we encountered in Chapter 1. These two connections were with cultures that were reviled by some nineteenth-century figures committed to progress: Maeterlinck's circle in Belgium and traditional Japanese culture. In his study, *Degeneration*, the arch-stadialist and Zionist leader Max Nordau argued that Maeterlinck's work was defined by 'utterly childish idiotically-incoherent' decadent mysticism, and he also labelled *japonisme*, and a wider interest in oriental decoration, as one of the symptoms of the degenerate man.[10] No doubt he had the *japonaiserie*-collecting protagonist of Joris-Karl Huysmans's *À rebours*, Des Esseintes, in mind when making this judgement. For certain figures, enthusiasm for both Maeterlinck's circle and *japonisme* was characteristic of the *fin-de-siècle malaise*, which certain Scottish figures were keen to channel subversively.

I have chosen to focus on Scotland's 'transnational solidarities' with Maeterlinck's circle and Japan not because they were the only such connections that Scottish revivalists hoped to develop, but because they are particularly telling. Maeterlinck's circle, or La Jeune Belgique, formed a movement at the *fin de siècle* to reassert their Belgian nationality, which they felt (much like several Scots) was compromised by increasing cultural homogenisation and centralisation to Paris (or, in Scotland's case, London). This was certainly how it was seen by William Sharp, a man better known for his Celtic Revival writings under the pseudonym 'Fiona Macleod', which I discuss in Chapter 3. Sharp's translations and analyses of the work of Maeterlinck's circle led him to the view that Scotland should model its efforts on the Belgian movement, and it came to inspire much of his own fiction. Like the Belgians, who, according to Sharp, celebrated their supposed 'barbarity' to authenticate their difference from France and reclaim the sophistication of traditional cultures, Sharp injects their 'new barbarism' into his own writing, to proclaim confidently the dissident 'otherness' of an increasingly Celticised Scottish identity and to demonstrate its internationalism.

But although Belgium provided a fitting model for Scotland in various ways, the Japanese connection proved far more popular. Throughout Scotland, artists and writers turned to Japan and frequently did so to 'orientalise' Scotland and celebrate the values of traditional culture. While there were similarities between these two bonds, the Japan connection differed from the Belgian friendship in one key way: Scotland was building various imperial ties with Japan in this period, and the Japan connection helped Scottish cultural revivalists assert Scotland's industrialism and imperialism. This is one of the key distinctions that can be drawn between Scotland

and Ireland in the period: Scottish cultural revivalists hoped to define and defend Scotland by distancing the nation from an assimilated British identity, but very rarely in a way that challenged the Empire or the Union. While some in Ireland hoped to end the Union and Ireland's participation in the Empire, the Scottish project was defined by 'defence, not defiance' – the motto of a contemporary Scottish Home Ruler, Thomas Drummond Wanliss – which stressed that the Scottish Revival was not interested in resisting the Empire or a union. Japan allowed Scottish cultural nationalists to express and reconcile two (sometimes conflicting) aspects of Scottish cultural defence: undermining stadialist narratives of 'progress' while still celebrating the nation's 'advanced' industrial, imperial modernity.[11]

By discussing these two telling connections, the nature of the Scottish Revival at the *fin de siècle* becomes clear. Although Scottish writers and artists were at times unashamedly decadent in their attacks on industrial modernity, their focus was on challenging the supposed superiority of modern culture and its antagonism to 'the past', or traditional culture. Broadly, Scottish revivalism was not opposed to modernity itself but to a particular form of modernity that necessitated a movement *away* from traditional national or ethnic cultures.

Through examining these two cross-cultural ties at the *fin de siècle*, this chapter helps us reconsider some of the more outlandish characterisations of late nineteenth-century Scotland that emerged in the twentieth century. Several figures, notably Hugh MacDiarmid, argued that this period in Scottish literature was defined by parochialism and sentimentality, exhibiting little regard for international contexts and culture. By examining the 'affective communities' that Scots built with cultures abroad,[12] I prove here that MacDiarmid's and others' claims are deeply problematic, and that many of the international connections built by late Victorian writers anticipated modernist developments. By understanding the internationalism of *fin-de-siècle* Scottish literature, we can begin to reveal some of the lost continuities between nineteenth- and twentieth-century Scottish writers.

The New Barbarism

> 'Your civilisation is your disease, my barbarism is my restoration to health.' (Paul Gauguin)[13]

As we saw in the Introduction, decadent literature and art, like the Scottish Revival, frequently involved celebrating the value of traditional or supposedly less commercial and industrialised culture. While stadialists derided decadence as the 'enemy of progress',[14] many writers and artists embraced this supposed 'relapse into barbarism'.[15] Gauguin's statement above is a stark example of how vigorously figures that were critical of utilitarianism, as well as forms of modernity that ignored the past, embraced the idea of barbarism at the *fin de siècle*. Some decadents may have been 'urban, introspective, individuated, enervated', but the decadent was not always 'the opposite of the primitive, or Noble Savage'.[16] Often, decadence involved not only embracing 'barbarism' but also looking to supposedly primitive or savage cultures abroad and valorising their lifestyles.

One of the first decadent texts reveals that cross-cultural identification with, and celebration of, 'barbarous' peoples was a key component of decadence: Charles Baudelaire's 'Further Notes on Edgar Poe' (1857). Baudelaire's essay is remarkable for at times subtly, and at times outspokenly, challenging stadialist understandings of historical development. The essay also reveals that decadence did, at times, involve sympathising with either colonised peoples or other cultures believed to belong to an earlier historical 'stage'. Building affective communities or transnational solidarities was a key component of Baudelaire's rhetorical attack on progress and his defence of decadence.

'Further Notes on Edgar Poe' questions the idea that the 'literature of the decadence' is unhealthy or degenerate.[17] Instead, the essay tries to expose the inferiority of enlightened, 'civilised' culture and demonstrate the sophistication of the supposed savage. At the beginning of the essay, Baudelaire takes on those academic critics who complain about the 'literature of the decadence'. He mocks them, not only for their 'flatulent yawn[s]' (93), but because *their* taste is too base to understand the literature that they scorn. Responding to their complaint, he writes:

> Whenever I hear this anathema thundering in the air [. . .] I am invariably seized with a desire to reply, 'Do you take me for a barbarian like yourselves? Do you really think me capable of taking my pleasures as drearily as you do?' (93)

Here, Baudelaire styles the tastes of the 'academic' (94) critic as barbaric. This was a trope that would become common by the *fin de siècle*: representing the supposedly 'civilised' as the true degenerates. Baudelaire heralds Poe as the corrective to this dreary culture; Poe is 'the writer who, in the *Colloquy of Monos and Una*, discharges torrents of scorn and disgust upon democracy, progress and *civilization*' (95). Baudelaire casts Poe as the emblem of a new type of literature, one that resists some of the hegemonic concepts of the nineteenth century. In the vein of Schopenhauer,[18] Baudelaire offers a direct challenge to the idea of stadialist progress and expresses his utter disdain of it.

To counter 'civilisation', Baudelaire celebrates the sophistication of 'primitive' peoples, whose cultures were often the victims of imperial, civilising missions. He heralds the 'true greatness of the idle races!' that are sheltered from 'material perfection' (94). Undoubtedly reductive and patronising in his representation of 'primitive' peoples as simple and 'childlike' (100), Baudelaire nevertheless attempts to reclaim the sophistication of these traits in order to destabilise the civilised–savage binary. For Baudelaire, the 'savage' is more sophisticated than the supposedly enlightened. In making this argument, Baudelaire borrows from the tradition of the 'noble savage', a term coined by Dryden and often associated with Rousseau. However, Baudelaire goes further than Rousseau, who believed that modernity should not be entirely rejected but should incorporate some honourable traits of the 'savage'.[19] Baudelaire expresses his support for displacing 'civilised' culture altogether, by performing a willed return to a pre-Enlightenment, 'barbarous' state. He champions the 'primeval tendency', 'a primitive, irresistible force' found in 'nation[s] lacking all the ingenious inventions which dispense the individual of heroism' (96, 99). This difference marks one of the broad breaks between the romantics and the decadents: the degree to which they questioned 'civilisation'. There was a marked 'intensification' of the critique by the second half of the nineteenth century.[20] For Baudelaire, 'primitive' cultures are preferable to the race of 'bourgeois mediocrity' (101), which is embodied by 'the ethics of the shop-counter', 'an age dedicated to materialism' (100) – a critique that would later be replayed by Arthur Symons, who called merchants and money-makers 'the degenerates of civilisation'.[21]

The hypocrisy of so-called 'civilised' culture, which Baudelaire and Symons attack, was frequently confronted at the *fin de siècle*. E. von Baumgarten's illustration *Civilisation* (Fig. 2.3), for the German magazine *Jugend*, provides an arresting visual representation of the perceived hypocrisy. The image reminds the viewer that 'civilisation' comes at the cost of widespread injury and destruction to many, while the fair-haired, 'civilised' beneficiaries casually ignore these repercussions: civility is simply a veneer that masks the effects of 'progress'.

Figure 2.3 E. von Baumgarten, '*Civilisation*', in *Jugend*, 1.25 (1896): 407. Heidelberg University Library CC-BY-SA-3.0.

Despite Baudelaire's sympathy with the colonial subject and 'savage' races, it is unlikely that his comments were intended to be read as an attack on imperialism. Nevertheless, there are ties between the culture of decadence and post-colonialism. Baudelaire's belief in displacing 'civilised' culture and returning to the savage reflects the views of several postcolonial theorists. Jean-Paul Sartre argues that, to overcome their oppressor, the colonial subject has to return to their pre-colonial history, to their 'lost innocence', in order to reject their settler's occupation. In this 'triumph of barbarism',[22] the native becomes what 'the white man wants [them] to be' – a race opposed to 'progress'. But, in doing so, Frantz Fanon writes, the native learns that 'there was nothing to be ashamed of in the past, but rather dignity, glory and solemnity'.[23] This 'triumph of barbarism' was a feature shared by the discourses of decadence and imperial resistance, and these concepts could draw strength from each other.

The decadent solidarity with traditional cultures abroad was not limited to Baudelaire; several dissenting writers at the *fin de siècle* were keen to challenge the hegemony of 'civilised' culture by celebrating the 'other' abroad. In Oscar Wilde's 'The Decay of Lying', for instance, Vivian identifies more with the art of the Orient than the 'degraded race' he is surrounded by,[24] a comment I elaborate on in the 'Celtic *Japonisme*' section of this chapter. Edward Carpenter's rhetorical attack on imperialism lampoons the way the 'diseases of "civilization"' were used to 'destroy and defile' sophisticated, indigenous cultures throughout the world, specifying the Amazonians, the Pacific islanders and the Kafir, among many others.[25] In William Morris's lecture on 'The Art of Beauty', the Arts and Crafts designer adopts a more decadent tone than usual when attacking the 'Century of Commerce': he states that he would rather be 'living in a tent in the Persian desert' than put up with 'modern civilisation'.[26] Decadent writers did not always attempt 'to fortify the rigid boundaries of the self and British society against the barbarians at the gates';[27] at times, they reached out to the 'barbarous' and those abroad. Cross-cultural identifications with the primitive or foreign 'other', which several Scottish revivalists also performed, were not uncommon in *fin-de-siècle* decadent texts.

Because *fin-de-siècle* Scottish literature is often characterised as insular and sentimental, explorations of the Scottish interest in the 'new barbarism', and in nurturing 'affective communities' abroad, has been neglected. But such attempts to develop transnational solidarities to question or refute notions of 'civilisation' that styled traditional cultures as backward were key to the Scottish Revival, and they were often in the vein of Baudelaire. Through an association with the Belgian Revival, some of whose affiliates embraced the 'new barbarism', certain Scottish cultural revivalists hoped to lend strength to their resistance to stadialism, building a counter-hegemonic community that heralded the 'triumph of barbarism'.

William Sharp and La Jeune Belgique

If the *fin-de-siècle* Belgian cultural revival is ever considered in the context of Scottish literature, it is through Hugh MacDiarmid's writings.[28] In the first volume of the *Scottish Chapbook*, from August 1922, MacDiarmid asserts his belief that Belgium can provide a model for stimulating a Scottish cultural revival. He writes:

> What Belgium did, Scotland can do. Literary Scotland, like Belgium, is a country of mixed nationality. Instead of two languages, Flemish and French, we have Braid Scots, Gaelic and English. Let the exponents of these three sections in Scottish Literature to-day make common cause as the young Belgian writers [. . .] did in *La Jeune Belgique* and elsewhere, and the next decade or two will see a Scottish Renascence as swift and irresistible as was the Belgian Revival between 1880 and 1910.[29]

This quotation appears in the first volume of the *Chapbook*, the same volume in which MacDiarmid critiques the Celtic Revival and Scottish literature of the 1890s. He writes that 'for several generations Scottish Literature has neither seen nor heard nor understood what was taking place around it [. . .] Scottish writers have been terrified even to appear inconstant to established conventions'.[30] He sees William Sharp, the Celtic revivalist who contributed to (and managed) *The Evergreen* and Patrick Geddes and Colleagues' Celtic Library, as the embodiment of this tendency: Sharp was an exponent of 'Old Romance' Scotland that suffocated Scottish cultural revivalism.[31] But, as is increasingly being recognised by critics, MacDiarmid was unfairly dismissive of the previous generation of writers, on account of his 'over-determined impulse for Renaissance'[32]: the previous generation had to be portrayed as particularly weak for MacDiarmid to foreground his and his contemporaries' innovation and originality.[33] This tendency is clearly apparent in the comments above on Sharp and Belgium because it was Sharp, the supposed inhibitor of a true Scottish Revival, who pioneered the idea of using La Jeune Belgique as a model for a Scottish national revival thirty years before MacDiarmid. Indeed, via Sharp, Scotland played a crucial role in receiving and interpreting Belgian Revival writing – an example of *fin-de-siècle* Scotland's internationalism that stands at odds with MacDiarmid's reductive assessment of the nation's literature.

At the core of Belgium's literary culture in the late nineteenth century was Maurice Maeterlinck, a Fleming who wrote in French. Maeterlinck became one of the key symbolist writers in *fin-de-siècle* Europe, and his efforts earned him the Nobel Prize for Literature in 1911. He took great interest in mysticism – later writing *The Great Secret*, which Geddes read – and this interest informed his plays. Many of his short, minimalist dramas focus on characters who are forced to confront 'the unknown', 'a monstrous, invisible, fatal power', and the nausea that results.[34] The Sartrean concerns of Maeterlinck's plays meant that he was a key antecedent for what is often termed the 'Theatre of the Absurd' in the twentieth century,[35] and many parallels can be drawn between the likes of Maeterlinck's *The Blind* and Samuel Beckett's *Waiting for Godot*, in both style and philosophical concern.

But Maeterlinck was not the only influential literary product of Belgium in this period. Several other figures contributed to a magazine, *La Jeune Belgique*, which was established by Max Waller in 1881, following a merger of two student magazines: *La Jeune Revue littéraire* and *La Semaine des étudiants*. Some of the Belgian writers who found a voice in the magazine, besides Maeterlinck, were Charles van Lerberghe and Auguste Jenart – figures who are now obscure outside of Belgium. The magazine led writers to investigate 'what made their culture and literature different from France'; indeed, the very first editorial, when commenting on the youth of Belgium, demonstrated the desire to defend Belgian culture in the face of France's domination:[36]

> Qu'ils montrent qu'il y a une Jeune Belgique comme il y a une Jeune France, et qu'avec nous ils prennent pour devise: Soyons nous.[37]

> They show that there is a Young Belgium as there is a Young France, and like us they take the motto: Let's be ourselves.

This cultural nationalist dimension of *La Jeune Belgique* did not lead to insularity, though; the magazine featured many avant-garde French writers alongside young Belgian writers, such as Stéphane Mallarmé and Paul Verlaine.

It did not take long for the writings of Maeterlinck's circle to enter the English language: several writers and critics in the 1890s were reading, translating and reviewing their works. Gérard Harry, Maeterlinck's friend, provided some of the first published translations of Maeterlinck from 1890 onwards for Heinemann, including *The Intruder*, a play originally performed in 1891 as part of a benefit for the impoverished Verlaine and Gauguin. Following Harry, the English playwright, Alfred Sutro, and the Scottish critic, William Archer, translated Maeterlinck's works, and it was their translations that were used for Gowans and Grey's edition of *Three Plays by Maurice Maeterlinck* (1911), which reproduced the *Three Little Dramas for Marionettes* (1894). Laurence Alma-Tadema, daughter of the painter, would also release translations in 1914. Across the Atlantic, Richard Hovey translated a great many of Maeterlinck's works in the 1890s, which were published as part of Stone and Kimball's Green Tree Library – the first series in 1894, the second in 1896. Translations of *The Blind*, *Princess Maleine* and *The Seven Princesses* also appeared in the American poetry magazine *Poet-Lore* (August/September 1894), while Erving Wimslow translated *Princess Maleine* too. With these published translations came performances (several of which were in Scotland, as I detail below), along with discussion and criticism: Archer wrote the first article in English on Maeterlinck in 1891, 'A Pessimist Playwright', for *The Fortnightly Review*, followed by Hall Caine's introduction to Harry's English translation of *La Princess Maleine* and *The Intruder* (1892), which Oscar Wilde was originally asked to do.[38] Like Yeats after him, Wilde held Maeterlinck's works in high regard, and he and Maeterlinck even dined together in May 1898, following his prison sentence in Reading Gaol.

But a figure almost unanimously ignored in considerations of the reception of Maeterlinck's circle across the British Isles, despite penning numerous essays and translations on the Belgian Revival, is William Sharp. Critical considerations of Sharp focus almost solely on his popular writings under the guise of 'Fiona Macleod', but his life before 'Fiona' and the many works he wrote under his own name and other pseudonyms deserve critical attention. Indeed, his 'pre-Fiona' work was seen as significant in his own time: Richard Hovey, for instance, described Sharp's drama collection *Vistas*, along with Wilde's *Salomé*, as key examples of symbolism in the British Isles, in his essay 'Modern Symbolism and Maurice Maeterlinck'.

Sharp was clearly a dissident figure from an early age. Directly after abandoning his degree at Glasgow University, he joined a tour of the Highlands with travelling gypsies, and this love of the Highlands and unconventional communities came to define his career. It was his introduction to Dante Gabriel Rossetti in 1881 (with thanks to Sir Joseph Noel Paton, who had worked for his father's textile business in Paisley) that stimulated his career in writing. Sharp wrote the first book on Rossetti, *Dante Gabriel Rossetti: A Record and a Study* (1882), before becoming an art critic for *The Glasgow Herald* and quickly finding himself enmeshed in the *fin-de-siècle* cultural network, meeting Swinburne, Pater and Morris, among many others. He published several collections of poetry consistent with Pre-Raphaelitism and then, later in the 1890s, he would go on to write *The Pagan Review* and his Celtic Revival 'Fiona' works, which bred a fascinating, if rocky, friendship with Yeats.[39]

But one of the most significant contributions that Sharp made to cultural life in Scotland, and the United Kingdom more widely, was his study of the Belgian avant-garde. Sharp's desire to disseminate knowledge about the Belgian Revival is witnessed in the number of essays he wrote on the subject: 'A Note on the Belgian Renascence', two essays titled 'La Jeune Belgique', a biographical and critical essay titled 'Maeterlinck', a reflection on 'Ruysbroeck and Maeterlinck', and a review of Gérard Harry's production of *Princess Maleine* and *The Intruder* in *The Academy* (16 March 1892). Sharp's letters from 1892 reveal that he was also planning to write a book on French and Belgian writers. Furthermore, Sharp translated works by these dramatists: the most interesting ones (Maeterlinck's masterpiece, *Les Aveugles* and Auguste Jenart's *Le Barbare*) were never published but his translation of *The Night-Comers*, by Charles van Lerberghe, accompanied by an introductory note on the Belgian Revival, appears in the second volume of *The Evergreen*. It is not coincidental that Geddes intended to distribute *The Evergreen* in Brussels: members of Geddes's circle clearly wanted to foster connections with Belgium.[40] *The Glasgow Herald*, reflecting on Sharp's contribution to *The Evergreen*, noted that he was doing 'good service in opening what is practically a new field for readers in this country'.[41]

Sharp prided himself on being the first major critic and enthusiast of the Belgian Revival. In a letter to Catharine Janvier, the American artist and translator who he befriended, Sharp stated that the Belgian Revival was 'a subject wherein I am (I suppose) the only specialist among English men of letters'.[42] He dismissed the 'inadequate' work of his rivals, Archer and Caine, finding them unfamiliar with the scope of the Belgian Literary Revival.[43] Certainly, Sharp's articles do demonstrate a wider knowledge of the field, but it is crucial to note that his knowledge was not gained without support. Edith Rinder is now, regrettably, best known for being the muse behind Sharp's 'Fiona Macleod' identity but she produced many significant works of her own. She was closely connected to Geddes's Celtic Revival circle in Edinburgh, and her major contribution to this community was her collection of Breton Romances and folk tales for the Celtic Library, *The Shadow of Arvor* (1896). But she also translated several Belgian Revival texts that were compiled and published as *The Massacre of the Innocents: And Other Tales* (1895), after receiving consent from Maeterlinck.[44] It is highly likely that Sharp and Rinder would have assisted each other in their efforts.

So why did Sharp take such a keen interest in the Belgian Revival? Part of the explanation lies in his belief that Belgium offered Scotland a model of cultural revivalism and, consequently, he was keen to channel characteristics of the Belgian Revival into Scotland. While Sharp did at times represent Celtic civilisation as an 'exhausted society in decline',[45] discussed in more detail in Chapter 3, in several of his works, a resistance to the cultural marginalisation of Celtic culture at the hands of 'civilisation' can be traced. He wrote on the importance of maintaining diverse 'national ideals' across Britain and spoke out against the so-called 'civilising factor', as well as 'bastard utilitarianism', in the hope of recovering 'the old barbaric emotion' of the Celts.[46] Given these quotations, it is unsurprising that Yeats believed that 'Macleod' held 'the keys to the gates of the primeval world, which shut behind more successful races, when they plunged into material progress'.[47] Like Geddes, Sharp also expressed his exasperation about metropolitan culture, writing that 'London is so overwhelming provincial, because it is the centre towards which the provincial mind gravitates.'[48] Together, Sharp and Geddes hoped to turn cultural attention away from London to Edinburgh, through Sharp's proposal to publish a fortnightly magazine, *Celtic World*, and then *The Evergreen*.[49] Defying the centre, defying forms of 'civilisation' that saw the past as inferior or backward, is a key dimension of several 'Macleod' writings – one that is often overlooked.

This desire to confront the metropole and utilitarianism deeply informs Sharp's enthusiasm for Belgian culture, as he believed that the Belgians were also challenging their cultural marginalisation. This becomes most apparent when his article, 'A Note on the Belgian Renascence' (1895), which reviews Rinder's anthology, *The Massacre of the Innocents: And Other Tales*, is considered. Here, Sharp describes the characteristics of the Belgian Revival:

> A group of writers, all young in heart and mind, if not youthful in point of age, cohered in a common bond: the bond of a national, independent, original literature. The whip of Baudelaire, if it had lashed some into servility, had strung others into revolt. It was not now a question of the Franco-Belgian, but of the Belgian.[50]

While Baudelaire was keen to celebrate his constructed image of the marginalised 'savage' in 'Further Notes on Edgar Poe', he was also known to mock and marginalise France's neighbouring country, Belgium, for its supposed savagery. Indeed, one of Baudelaire's alternative titles for his volume, *Pauvre Belgique*, was 'Une Capitale de Singes' – A Capital of Apes.[51] Sharp notes that Baudelaire expressed contempt for Belgium's 'slavish' culture,[52] while, more widely in France, Belgians were increasingly considered 'barbarian' in the late nineteenth century. These tensions led many in Belgium to focus their cultural revival, as we have seen, on 'withstand[ing] Paris'.[53]

What is revealing in Sharp's article is that he frequently compares the position of the Belgians to the Scots and the Irish. Although Belgian revivalists were trying to distance themselves from France by recovering their more 'Teutonic side', while Scottish revivalists built bonds with France and resisted Germanic conceptions of Lowland Scotland – as we encountered in Chapter 1 – there were telling similarities nevertheless.[54] Sharp notes that Scotland, Belgium and Ireland all neighboured a far larger country, which fostered power dynamics that led to their cultures being marginalised or demeaned. Londoners, Sharp argues, were guilty of using the same patronising tone towards

Scotland and Ireland as Parisians adopted towards Belgium: 'As the Londoner smiles when he hears "the provincial" (whether from Edinburgh or Dublin or the darkest of the lost shires) speak of "society", so the Parisian man of letters condescended towards any new Belgian poet or novelist.'[55] Sharp's use of tense is significant here: while the Paris-centric force is referred to in the past tense, the London-centric force is in the present tense. This suggests that, while Belgium has managed to defy its marginalisation, the Irish and Scots still have work to do. Sharp regrets the fact that 'Celtic Irish and Celtic Scots obscured rather than obtruded their Celticism, partly out of persecution or active annoyance, partly out of weakness and folly, but mainly because of a perverse utilitarian instinct'.[56] The Belgian Renascence's ability to reclaim and reassert Belgium's nationality, while still using the French language, provided Sharp with a model for how Scotland and Ireland could also overcome that 'perverse utilitarian instinct' to assimilate, while still using English.

Belgium was also a useful model for the likes of Sharp because, unlike many other nations in the late nineteenth century that were pursuing political independence, Belgium was already independent and was simply seeking cultural autonomy, definition and respect. A Scots–Belgian connection would help support the Scottish Revival's aims of cultural and political defence, without invoking anti-Union or anti-imperial rhetoric. The fact that Belgium, like Japan, was nurturing a nascent empire is also important: both Scotland and Belgium shared the position of being small, imperial countries, so Belgium was an apt nation to identify with. Furthermore, Scotland had once had very close connections to Flanders: not only had there been significant historic migration between the two territories but there was a conservator of Scottish privileges in Flanders in the fifteenth century.[57] In numerous ways, Belgium was an ideal country with which to style a cultural 'affective community'.

Sharp's theorising on the ways that Belgium could provide a model for a Scottish Revival deeply informed his own literary practice. His fictional writings reflect his desire to establish a cultural friendship between Scotland and Belgium, through injecting Belgian revivalists' ideas and styles into his own writing. His translations and his own fictions, particularly those in his collection of short dramas, *Vistas*, and *The House of Usna*, a play that was encouraged by Yeats, reveal Sharp's aspiration to channel the energy of the Belgian revivalists into Scotland.

Vistas is a collection of short prose dramas, which was published by Frank Murray in Derby, and Stone and Kimball in Chicago. Stone and Kimball included the volume in their Green Tree Library, which – as we have noted – also featured *The Plays of Maurice Maeterlinck*, translated by Hovey. *Vistas* is among Sharp's best work, and perhaps the clearest example of literary symbolism produced by a Scottish writer; indeed, one critic characterised it as 'an efflorescence of the symbolistic school'.[58] Sharp himself described these dramas as 'psychic episodes', 'impressions of spiritual emotion', and 'one or two' of the dramas were even 'directly autopsychical' (he was known to write under the influence of psychic trances).[59] The dramas in *Vistas* are also highly decadent writings. In a letter to Herbert S. Stone, Sharp quotes from his friend, George Cotterell, who reportedly described Sharp's 'The Tower of Silence', which was rewritten and published in *Vistas* under the title 'A Northern Night', as 'the most remarkable and significant production of the so-called Décadent or Fin-de-Siècle school'.[60] Even if Cotterell did not say this – it is plausible that he did, considering the praise he gives to *Vistas* in his review in *The Academy*[61] – it is significant that Sharp was keen to associate his work with *fin-de-siècle* decadence.

The collection begins with a dedication to the American poet and critic, H. M. Alden, in which Sharp notes his appreciation and indebtedness to Maeterlinck and the Belgian School. However, Sharp also defends himself against claims of imitation by stating that he wrote two of the pieces ('A Northern Night' and 'The Passing of Lilith') 'anterior to the fortunate hour when I came for the first time upon "La Princesse Maleine" and "L'Intruse"'.[62] To some extent this is true, but in a diary entry from 1891 Sharp states that he finished 'A Northern Night' the day immediately after his first encounter with Maeterlinck's work, when he read *La Princesse Maleine* and *Les Aveugles* in Stuttgart in October 1891.[63] It is possible that Sharp made some late revisions, informed by his encounter with Maeterlinck's plays.

Vistas consists of eleven dramas, the first being 'Finis'. A reviewer for *The Scotsman* noted that this ironic opening was calculatedly designed to mystify the reader. This mystical quality may explain the reviewer's identification of a 'Hibernian peculiarity' in the collection.[64] Most of the eleven dramas had not been published before but some had appeared elsewhere. 'The Black Madonna', for instance, was included in Sharp's magazine, *The Pagan Review*, in 1892 under one of his earlier pseudonyms, W. S. Fanshawe. Two of the dramas, 'A Northern Night' and 'The Birth of a Soul', would appear in *The Chap-Book* later in 1894. The September issue of *The Chap-Book*, featuring 'The Birth of a Soul', was effectively devoted to Sharp and contained an essay on his verse by the Canadian poet, Bliss Carman.

Although Sharp mentions Maeterlinck and Charles Van Lerberghe in his dedication, it is arguably the work of Auguste Jenart that had the greatest impact on *Vistas*. Throughout the collection Sharp quotes from one of Jenart's texts, *The Barbarian* (1891), which Sharp translated into English. This is the only known English translation of the play and, although it is unfinished and exists only in manuscript form, it helps explain why Sharp was so interested in injecting aspects of Jenart's writing into his work. Jenart's interest in undermining 'civilisation' and performing the 'triumph of barbarism' closely complemented several of Sharp's writings.

The Barbarian can be read as a cultural nationalist play, one that draws from a foundational text of Belgian Revival literature, Charles de Coster's *Legend of Ulenspiegel* (1867). In that tale, the protagonist carries his father's ashes around his neck and they beat against his heart; in *The Barbarian*, Jenart's protagonist, Rynel de Ronçort, carries his ancestors' souls in his body and they similarly press upon his own existence. *The Barbarian* is concerned with interrogating the idea of stadialist development. In the play, the present is continually occupied and disrupted by the return of racial memories and heritage; the barbarous 'stage' is never behind them. This racial heritage is evident when the female character, Siria, contemplates how she can win Rynel from her rival, Nurh, and exposes Rynel's possible homosexual desire for the doctor:

> Siria: He alone is beautiful. Why does he prefer this Nurh? And thou also?
> The Doctor: She is a virgin.
> Siria: Virgin . . . . Six thousand years defile her.[65]

Siria here implies that no individual in the world of the play is innocent: Nurh's life is the life of her ancestors; each individual carries their own 'barbarous' past, and this notion is repeated throughout the play. This sentiment is in step with Maeterlinck's belief that the dead continue to live 'in ourselves', and the parallels between Rynel and Maeterlinck were noted[66]: one critic wrote that Rynel uses quotations from Maeterlinck and other Belgian writers throughout the dialogue.[67] These assertions of ancestral memory are important, namely because this was a period when the Belgian nationality, like the Celtic nationalities, was increasingly portrayed as marginal and 'barbaric' – wedded to a past 'stage'. As we have seen, Sharp was attentive to French framings of Belgians, including Parisians' descriptions of incoming Belgians as an 'invasion des barbares'. To the Parisian, the Belgian is 'a Barbarian, a foreigner, a Teutonic dreamer, a tiresome person whose chosen tongue happens to be French, but whose mind is Flemish, whose manner is Walloon: a mediocrity [. . .] a Belgian mediocrity'.[68] What we witness in *The Barbarian* is an attempt to undermine this stadialist reasoning, by stressing that we can never develop away from barbarity: it haunts us all. Similar to Baudelaire's ideas on the savage and Sartre's 'triumph of barbarism', characters in the play also complicate stadialist understandings by arguing that there is wisdom in supposed barbarity. Nurh's father responds to accusations of savagery by stating, 'Savage, yes. I believe terror is the original source of the emotions, and i'faith, I seek it.'[69] It is apt that Sharp described the play as 'a poetic version of *Dr. Jekyll and Mr. Hyde*'[70]: like Stevenson's novella, the play seeks to interrogate the line between supposedly civilised and barbarous peoples.

The Barbarian's resistance to stadialist understandings of historical development explains why Sharp was so enthusiastic about the play and why he quotes from it repeatedly. In speaking out against the so-called 'civilising factor' that destroyed Highland communities and in pursuing and advocating 'the old barbaric emotion', Sharp hoped to undermine these narratives of progress. Furthermore, like Jenart's protagonist, Sharp too believed that previous lives existed within him, confessing: 'we all hark back strangely at times'.[71] Sharp's belief in our ancestors' capacity to occupy our existence is reflected in his novella, *The Gypsy-Christ* (1895), which was written just eight days after he first encountered Maeterlinck's work. In that novella, the protagonist, Fanshawe (a reference to one of Sharp's pseudonyms) fails to escape his ancestors' curse.

Because *The Barbarian* spoke to many of Sharp's beliefs, he quotes from *The Barbarian* throughout *Vistas*. Almost every drama in *Vistas* is accompanied by an epigraph, and no less than three of them are quotations from *The Barbarian*. The quotation that accompanies 'The Passing of Lilith' particularly chimes with the subversion of stadialist improvement; Sharp translates Rynel's quotation as follows: 'Innumerable anterior lives are present in me: I am overcome by things of the future: I know Eternity. Am I not the Irrevocable?'[72]

But it is not just in the epigraphs that we see the influence of the Belgian Revival on Sharp's work. Like Jenart's play, several of the prose dramas in *Vistas* celebrate barbarism to rupture notions of 'civilisation' and undermine the forces of centralisation. In 'A Northern Night', for instance, set in a 'desolate district of Northern Scotland',[73] the male character, Malcolm, is to be severed from his love, Helda, who intends to marry another man. Malcolm asks, 'will he take you away? Will he take you to the South-country?' (66), invoking the threat of centralisation. They meet in a ruined keep, Iorsa Tower, but they become plagued by threatening shadows. When they frantically skate away from the shadows over a frozen loch, they discover that her fiancé is dead. In the 'death-menaced and death haunted [. . .] Scottish wilds' that Sharp describes in the dedication to *Vistas*,[74] the 'natives' surprisingly survive the threat of death and it is the centralising force that expires. The 'old barbaric emotion', while threatened, manages to resist its fragmentation.

'The Black Madonna', perhaps the best drama, which was recently published in Edinburgh University Press's anthology, *The Decadent Short Story* (2014), also features a Jenart epigraph, and it too interrogates stadialist framings of societal progress and presents barbarism as a key theme. 'The Black Madonna' concerns a pagan sacrificial custom, where youths and maidens are slain before the statue of a Black Madonna.[75] After one sacrifice, the protagonist, Bihr, tries to seduce the statue, which alludes to Wilde's poem, 'The Sphinx', where the speaker expresses his adoration for a statue. Indeed, the Black Madonna is compared to a sphinx in Sharp's drama. We learn that this Madonna is 'Ashtaroth', one of hell's angels, who is named after the Middle Eastern goddess associated with sexuality and war.[76] This Black Madonna comes to life and Bihr eventually succeeds in seducing her. But after she 'sinks as one who drowns' in his desire,[77] Ashtaroth crucifies him. The Madonna figure is exposed as 'barbaric', and the supposedly barbaric tribesman takes on the image of Christ, thus inverting the civilisation–barbarism binary. The history of the image of the Black Madonna provides a revealing context for this drama: Stephen Benko notes that the 'Black Madonna is the ancient earth-goddess converted to Christianity',[78] an image that is half-Christian, half-pagan. Many early Christians accommodated pagan tropes and symbols to help people transition to Christianity, and the Black Madonna embodies the fact that Christianity is partly underpinned by pagan 'barbarity' – an idea Sharp develops in his Fiona Macleod writings, discussed in Chapter 3. Sharp may also have known that the Black Madonna is a symbol of national resistance in Poland (the Black Madonna of Częstochowa), who is associated with their defence against Swedish invasion. By undermining 'civility' through revealing its reliance on barbarity, Sharp interrogated stadialist notions of historical progress. By continually referencing *The Barbarian* alongside his own pieces that were concerned with reclaiming and re-evaluating barbarousness, Sharp attempts to create cross-cultural solidarity between the Belgian Revival and the Scottish Revival.

This solidarity was just as marked when Sharp moved into the more concerted Celtic Revival phase of his career. Under the guise of Celtic 'Fiona', Sharp largely wrote prose, but he also wrote a few Celtic dramas, one of which was produced for the Stage Society in London. Sharp's involvement with the Stage Society is a widely ignored aspect of his life. The Stage Society was a private members' club formed in 1899, and produced innovative plays that were either banned or deemed too experimental for the commercial London stage, including works by Ibsen, Shaw and Chekhov. Sharp was a member of the first managing committee of the society and the following year he became chairman of the society. Many great dramatists were members (including Yeats, Shaw and Barrie), and the society quickly became notorious: police raided the first production, Shaw's *You Never Can Tell*, which took place on the Sabbath, in November 1899.

The fifth meeting of the Stage Society was held in April 1900 at the Globe Theatre, where one of Sharp's short Celtic plays, *The House of Usna*, was performed alongside Maeterlinck's *Interior* (translated by Archer) and *The Death of Tintagiles* (translated by Sutro). A young Harley Granville-Barker directed all three dramas. *The House of Usna* was a play encouraged by Yeats, who wanted 'Fiona Macleod' to supply work to the Irish theatrical revival.[79] Although the production was not universally well received – a reviewer for *The Outlook* stated that the evening 'began in gloom, continued in dejection and ended in despair' – the performance is an important expression of the kinship between Sharp's Celtic Revival writings and the Belgian Revival.[80] Not only did Sharp's works appear alongside Maeterlinck's but, like his *Vistas* dramas, the content and style of *Usna* were clearly informed by his interest in the Belgian Revival. In particular, *Usna* is concerned with rejecting what Symons termed the 'bondage of exteriority',[81] which is also evident in the works of several Belgian and Irish revivalists, as it helped them question the materiality of the 'advanced', utilitarian culture that they felt was undermining their cultures.

The *House of Usna* is a play that elegises the deterioration of Celtic peoples when they cannot unify. Unlike in Sharp's romantic, Ossianic writings, the Ultonian subject matter in *Usna* directly invokes Irish political and historical issues. In the play, Concobar, the High King of Ireland, wants to reconcile Ireland into 'one nation',[82] after creating many enemies in his own house and elsewhere in Ireland and Scotland. Concobar finds himself fighting against a prophecy that Ireland will die and its 'soul' will merely exist, and he hopes that his son Cormac will unite the nation and prevent it from being extinguished: 'He shall save

Eiré. The prophecies of Cathba shall be set at naught' (45). However, his son is killed by an ally, Cravetheen, for supposedly having an affair with his wife. Too many divisions have been engendered by Concobar to develop a one-nation Ireland and, consequently, we are told that 'the star of Ireland shall set in blood' (7). The play is a lament for the inability of the Celts to save themselves when they turn against each other; Ireland, we are told, can be saved only if kingliness transfers to the people, away from divisive rulers (46). While it finishes on a tragic note, unlike some of Sharp's other Celtic writings, the passing of the Celts here is not portrayed as inevitable; their end is a result of their failure 'to cohere into one compact and indispensible nation'.[83]

One of the most striking stylistic features of *The House of Usna* is the presence of disembodied voices that haunt the stage, inspired by such Maeterlinck plays as *The Seven Princesses*. Yeats also invoked supernatural or spiritual voices his work, which Joseph Lennon has commented on. These 'anti-materialistic' features were needed to counter enlightened culture that prized logical materialism; symbols and supernatural elements, Lennon argues, helped Irish revivalists celebrate 'unadulterated traditional culture'.[84] This attack on materialism and illusionism was a principal concern of Sharp's. In the Foreword to *Usna*, he distances himself from theatrical styles that are more 'congruous with the method of the mirror that gathers and reveals certain facets of the spirit, than with the spirit who as in a glass darkly looks into the mirror'. He finds such illusionistic drama too 'material', not 'symbolic'[85] – a statement that was almost certainly prompted by his discussions with Yeats.[86] The two Maeterlinck plays that follow *Usna* embody this challenge to illusionism: in both, the main events occur in enclosed spaces (one within four walls on stage, the other off stage), which the audience only ever gets glimpses of. These plays centre our attention on what happens outside the four walls by dramatising the role of the audience: like the spectators, the protagonists do not have access to the main action, and Maeterlinck evokes the tensions, miscommunications and sense of the unknown experienced between the audience and the action. *The House of Usna* is less original in its rejection of theatrical illusionism but the presence of disembodied voices that haunt the stage, common to Maeterlinck's dramas, achieves similar effects. Sharp draws on this effect of Maeterlinck's to challenge illusionistic materialism similarly in his Celtic Revival play.

Usna was the last explicit Belgian connection that Sharp built, but his work, deeply informed by the Belgian Revival, influenced other decadent and symbolist artists in Scotland. One of Scotland's most decadent artists in this period was George Dutch Davidson, who – like Beardsley – died at a very young age (just twenty-two). Davidson, who shared a studio in Dundee for a time with John Duncan, fused symbolist and Celtic lines in his highly decadent design, 'Envy' (Fig. 2.4). After he left Dundee, Davidson lived for a time in Antwerp (a further Scottish–Belgian connection), where he executed drawings based on the work of 'Fiona Macleod'. His painting, *The Hills of Dream*, was very clearly inspired by Macleod's *From the Hills of Dream*; indeed, he wrote that 'with no one do I feel so perfectly at home as with Fiona McLeod [sic]. Her "Hills of Dream" I carry next [to] my heart.'[87] For Davidson and several other key artists of the period (including Duncan and Jessie M. King), Sharp's stories and styles, inspired by the Belgian Revival, stimulated and infused their work.[88]

As *Vistas*, *The House of Usna* and various other Macleod writings, discussed in Chapter 3, reveal, Sharp's works were 'complicit in a discourse of primitivism'.[89] But, while his work does authenticate the idea that those on the margins are 'barbaric', embracing the barbaric could be a mark of cultural resistance, rather than a mere mark of resignation to accommodation, as we encountered with Fanon and Sartre. Sharp's intention in these works is to disrupt the notion of 'civilisation' and historical progress by demonstrating the superiority of the supposedly 'barbarous'.[90] These dramas pointedly attempt to destabilise some of the narratives that contributed to the marginalisation of the Celts and Celtic identity, an endeavour shared by various other cultural revivalists in Scotland. As I outline in Chapter 3, Sharp was rarely consistent in his portrayals of Celtic Scotland, and was (not infrequently) guilty of echoing the discourse of primitivism to patronise the Celt. But, in these Belgian-inspired works, we see how disruptive his work could be and how crucial cross-cultural dialogue was to his thinking. Sharp's attentiveness to the Belgian Revival was a counter-hegemonic gesture, an example of the cultural 'margins' looking to comparable nations for inspiration to embolden their movement and reveal their international awareness.

This discussion has also revealed that Sharp played a key role in translating, analysing and importing the work of the Belgian Revival into the British Isles, much like William Archer's role in importing Ibsen. And it was through Sharp's stories and dramas, which 'could hardly be rivalled outside the pages of Maeterlinck',[91] as a reviewer for *The Morning Leader* noted, that the Belgian Revival made its first distinct impression on Scottish literature. By examining Sharp's Belgian-inspired work, we witness just how international, how decadent and how symbolist Scottish writing in this period could be.

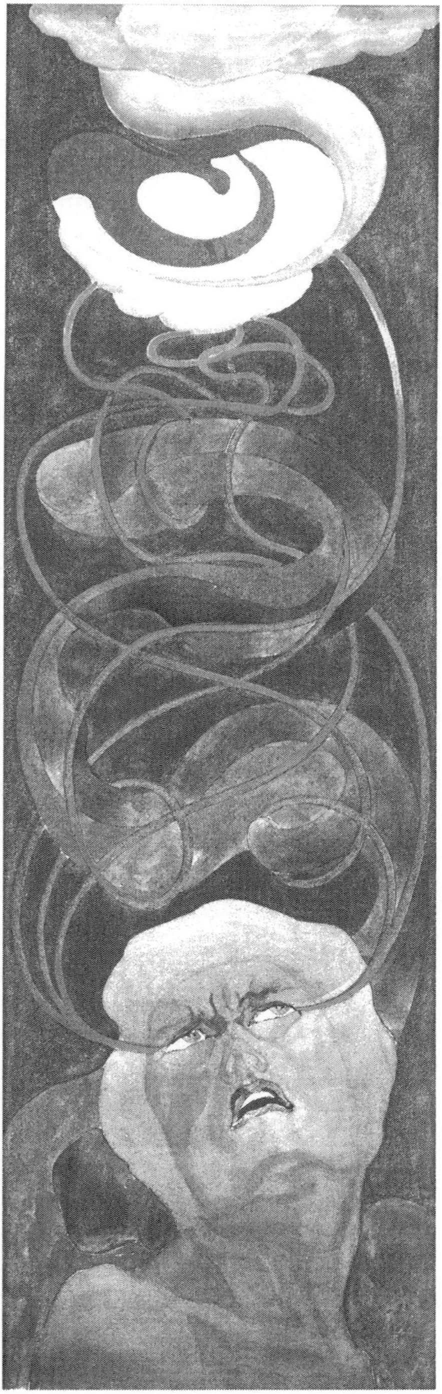

Figure 2.4 John Dutch Davidson, *Envy* (1898). © Dundee City Council (Dundee Art Galleries and Museums)

Margaret Macdonald and Maurice Maeterlinck

If Sharp was the main literary follower of Maeterlinck and the Belgian Revival in Scotland, the Glasgow School – which Geddes believed 'headed' Scotland's Celtic movement – was undoubtedly the most indebted to Belgium amongst Scotland's visual artists.[92] In the late Victorian and Edwardian periods, Glasgow's imperial wealth, coupled with its international connections and renewed focus on Scottish forms, nurtured an art culture that rivalled that of Barcelona, Vienna and Brussels, the 'capital of Art Nouveau'.[93] Unsurprisingly, there was a great deal of cultural exchange between these avant-garde cities, and Glaswegian artists were certainly looking to Belgium to help further their aims. For instance, Francis Newbery (the Director of the Glasgow School of Art between 1885 and 1917) hired Jean Delville, the noted Belgian symbolist painter and occultist, and a personal friend of Maeterlinck, to be the first Head of Painting at the Glasgow School of Art in 1900, a position he held until 1906.[94]

But the Glasgow School was looking not just to the visual arts of Belgium, but also to its literature, particularly Maeterlinck's. It is likely that these artists' interest in Maeterlinck would have been nurtured by the various performances of his work in Glasgow. For instance, in 1900, Mrs Patrick Campbell performed in *Pelléas and Mélisande* at the Theatre Royal. This was three years after the Scots composer, William Wallace, a cultural nationalist (true to his namesake), penned music inspired by the same play.[95] Later, in 1910, Maeterlinck's *The Blue Bird* was performed at the Theatre Royal, and it became his 'best known in this country'.[96] In 1911, the Scottish Repertory Theatre, discussed in the Introduction, performed *The Interior* alongside Thomas Hardy's *The Three Wayfarers* and Barrie's *Pantaloon* at the Royalty in Glasgow, which was considered an 'exceedingly interesting' triple bill.[97] The popularity of Maeterlinck's theatre and prose in the Scottish city is confirmed by the fact that he received his only honorary doctorate degree (Doctor of Laws) from the University of Glasgow in 1919.

Jessie M. King, one of the leading book artists in Scotland, who illustrated Wilde's *A House of Pomegranates* in 1915, was one Glasgow artist who took a keen interest in the works of Maeterlinck. King executed five cover designs for Maeterlinck's plays: *Alladine and Palomides* (1907), *The Interior* (1908), *The Seven Princesses* (1909), *The Death of Tintagiles* (1909) and *The Intruder* (1903), all of which were published by Gowans and Gray, in Glasgow and London. She also drew a scene from *Pelléas and Mélisande*, which was displayed in the Scottish Rooms of the Biennale, Venice, in 1899 and included in the special Winter number of *The Studio* for 1900–1 (Fig. 2.5).

Figure 2.5 Jessie M. King, *Pelléas et Mélisande*, in *The Studio: Special Winter Number* (1901): 83.

Her flattened, elongated designs, disembodied figures, use of blank spaces, limited colour range and crisp, often sinuous, lines fused symbolism with Celtic revivalism, as they did in her jewellery designs.

But Maeterlinck's impact was most pronounced on another preeminent figure of the Glasgow School, Margaret Macdonald. Maeterlinck was a favourite author of both Macdonald and her husband, Charles Rennie Mackintosh, who married in 1900. E. B. Kalas noted that their Mains Street flat in Glasgow was 'strewn with the novels of Maeterlinck',[98] and many of Macdonald's works either display marked similarities to Maeterlinck's work or (in the case of her and Mackintosh's designs for Fritz Waerndorfer's 'Maeterlinck Room') directly use Maeterlinck's plots as the subject.

Like Sharp, Macdonald 'partook of the heavy air of the Celtic Revival'.[99] 'Decorative ribbons', which characterise much Celtic imagery and metalwork, appear in several of her designs.[100] Macdonald also owned a copy of *Ossian*, featuring a bookplate by her sister Frances, and the book is prominently inscribed with Margaret Macdonald's name. Alongside these Celtic influences, Macdonald was also deeply embedded in the culture of European symbolism and decadence. Macdonald contributed two artworks to the tenth volume of *The Yellow Book*, which appeared alongside her sister's iconic peacock-inspired pastel, *The Sleeping Princess*, which Tom Hubbard describes as 'hauntingly Maeterlinckian' (Fig. 2.6).[101] As Roger Billcliffe illustrates, Macdonald's work was also deeply indebted to the figurative art of such symbolists as Jan Toorop,[102] and Margaret and Frances's *Drooko* (1896) poster design makes a very clear nod to the decadence of Beardsley too.

Figure 2.6 Frances Macdonald, *The Sleeping Princess*, in *The Yellow Book*, 10 (1896): 177.

While Macdonald's Celticism and her attentiveness to European decadence and symbolism mark similarities between her work and Sharp's, her engagement with Maeterlinck was less explicitly intended to complement or inform Scotland's cultural revival. Nevertheless, Maeterlinck did indirectly support Macdonald's and Mackintosh's interest in reviving Scottish design and forms. Mackintosh, like Sharp, was keen to reject what he termed 'wretched' utilitarianism, and his call for the recovery of traditional national forms was bound up with this project.[103] For both Macdonald and Mackintosh, as with Sharp, Maeterlinck's mysticism and symbolism helped them reject wholly utilitarian and illusionist design and embrace anti-material subjects and styles. Maeterlinck was seen as a fellow spirit, one who provided inspiration for their projects.

One of Macdonald's works that demonstrates a clear indebtedness to a Maeterlinck play was *The Mysterious Garden* (Plate 1). The painting closely resembles a scene from *The Blue Bird*, which played in Glasgow the previous year, in which two characters, Tyltyl and Mytyl, notice spirits coming out of the ground in a graveyard:

> Then, from all the gaping tombs, there rises gradually an efflorescence at first frail and timid, like steam; then white and virginal and more and more tufty, more and more tall and plentiful and marvellous. Little by little, irresistibly, invading all things, it transforms the graveyard into a sort of fairy-like and nuptial garden, over which rise the first rays of the dawn. The dew glitters, the flowers open their blooms, the wind murmurs.[104]

Macdonald's painting strikingly resembles this description. As the title indicates, the painting is also of a mysterious garden and in it a vaporous figure rises, becoming more white and virginal. The shape of the figure resembles the dewdrops referred to in the play, and the blue hue of the painting corresponds to the realm in the play where all is blue. The rigidity of the stylised figures behind the white woman is an indication that the space is somewhere between life and death. The debt to Maeterlinck is also inferred by the fact that similar rectilinear, haunting figures also appear in other Maeterlinck-inspired images by Macdonald, discussed below. In addition to *The Mysterious Garden*, Macdonald's *The Pool of Silence* (1913), which presents a near-monochrome depiction of a pool with a woman hovering on top of it, bears a striking similarity to Maeterlinck's description of a 'colourless sea of silence' in his introduction to Ruysbroeck's 'The Adornment of the Spiritual Marriage' (1891).[105] Given that Macdonald was, like

Maeterlinck, wedded to rejecting 'the old bondage of exteriority', it is unsurprising that his writings influenced her work.

Critics were quick to notice the affinities between the styles and ideas of Macdonald, Mackintosh and Maeterlinck. When attending the International Exhibition of Modern Decorative Art in Turin, 1902, Georg Fuchs admired the Scottish Section and noted that a 'neuen Sang' was being sung in Scotland.[106] His comments on 'The Rose Boudoir', one of Macdonald and Mackintosh's most acclaimed interior designs, are revealing:

> One could perform plays by Maeterlinck in these rooms; just as that poet's doomed spirits come to mind, sitting nonchalantly on these high-backed chairs like brothers of the floating figures on the rugs and utensils, at the same time one doubts that people of flesh and blood could work and relax there, eat food, and laugh, and bring up their children.[107]

Fuchs notes an important dimension of Macdonald and Mackintosh's symbolist spaces: they are designed to move the individual into a spiritual world, one that does not surrender to purely material, utilitarian considerations. Many of the features in their designs reveal this, beyond their seeming impracticality. For instance, Mackintosh's high-back chairs for Miss Cranston's Argyle Street tea rooms have oval roundels that float above the sitter's head, evocative of a halo. Mackintosh and Macdonald elevated the real world to the level of the spiritual, resembling Maeterlinck's works that resisted the material.

But the most direct and substantial influence that Maeterlinck had on the work of Macdonald (and Mackintosh) is evident in their work for Fritz Waerndorfer's music room in Vienna. Waerndorfer was a mill owner, patron and prominent collector of Gustav Klimt, an artist whose works reflect debts to the gessos that Macdonald and Mackintosh exhibited at the Vienna Secession in 1900, and also to Robert Burns's woodcut, *Natura Naturans* (1895), printed in *The Evergreen*, which clearly influenced Klimt's *Fishblood* (1898).[108] Waerndorfer was so impressed with the work of the Mackintoshes that he commissioned them to design his music room. Waerndorfer saw Macdonald and Mackintosh's work at the Eighth Secession Exhibition in Vienna and purchased 'a silver brooch by Margaret Macdonald, a drawing, and two prints' from the Scottish Section.[109] Waerndorfer also went to Glasgow to see their work. The result of the commission was a scheme called *The Seven Princesses*, based on Maeterlinck's play of the same title. In the play, seven sleeping princesses are locked in a glass room on the stage. Prince Marcellus returns by sea to visit the princesses and choose a bride but, by the time he manages to break into the room from below through the family crypt, Ursula, his chosen one, is dead. Stylistically, the play is akin to *The Interior* in presenting the audience with a glass cage, embodying the fourth wall, which no one can easily access. The haunting voices that recur throughout further subvert theatrical illusionism, replacing it with disembodied mystery. It is this plot and these styles that underpinned Macdonald's and Mackintosh's designs for the music room.

In 1903, the first pieces for the Waerndorfer commission were produced: four appliqué panels by Macdonald's sister, Frances, for the curtain separating the music room from the dining room, and two panels to decorate the piano by Macdonald, titled *Opera of the Winds* and *Opera of the Seas*. These titles refer to the ominous voices that sing 'The Atlantic' and 'We shall return no more' in the play,[110] as well as the ship on stage that eventually disappears, leaving the characters stranded. The seven princesses are represented but one has her eyes shut, referring to Ursula's death. The fusion of curvilinear and rectilinear forms also complements the tension in the play between the anxiety and supernaturalism outside the glass room and the still rigidity within. The striking use of gold against black, akin to Japanese lacquerware, gives the panels an appropriate other-worldly, spiritual atmosphere.

Large gesso panels, evoking scenes from *The Seven Princesses*, were also to feature in the room. Three completed panels by Margaret Macdonald, *The Seven Princesses* (Fig. 2.7), survive but they were discovered only in 1990 in the Vienna Museum of Applied Art. A wall had been built around the panels in the museum, which were moved there for safe storage during the war, it is believed. These efforts that were made to protect (or hide) the Macdonald panels reveal their perceived significance; Roger Billcliffe holds that they are 'undoubtedly her masterpiece'.[111] A complementary set of panels, designed by Mackintosh, was intended to face Macdonald's *Seven Princesses*. It is not known if Mackintosh's set was ever executed but his preparatory sketch survives in the Hunterian Art Gallery, Glasgow. Mackintosh depicts the return of Marcellus to choose his bride and Macdonald represents the death of Ursula, when she is carried away by her sisters; Ursula is defined by dark roses, while her sisters have white ones. The limited colour range, flattened forms and ornate, sinuous striations that bring together all of the individuals and objects are common to

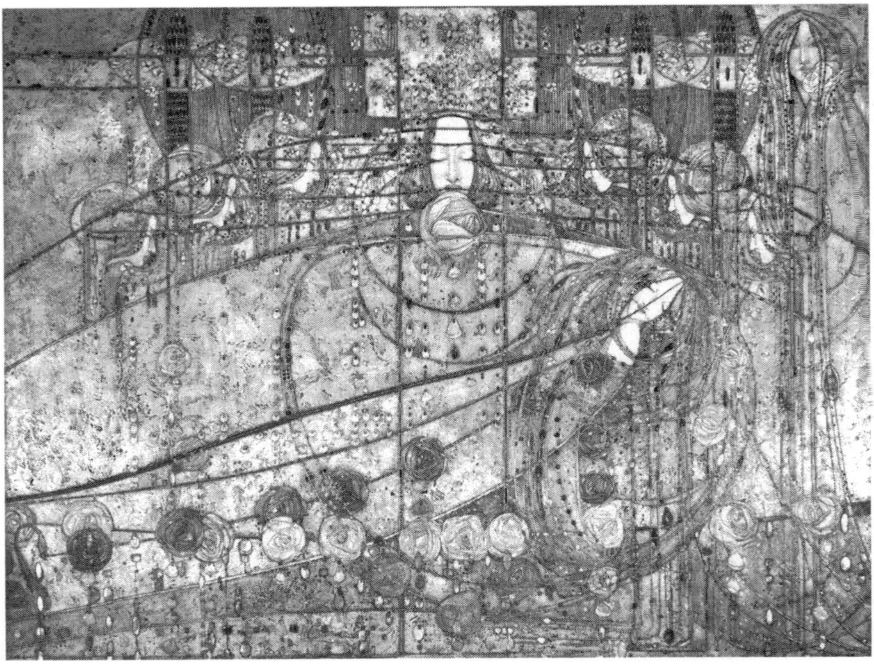

Figure 2.7 Margaret Macdonald Mackintosh, detail from *The Seven Princesses* (1906). MAK – Austrian Museum of Applied Arts / Contemporary Art. © Photograph: MAK/Georg Mayer.

Celtic Revival art. This ambitious design demonstrates how Maeterlinck's play of mortality, desire and mysticism could be sophisticatedly coupled with visual tropes associated with the Celtic Revival. Those distancing themselves from scientific and material developments were finding solidarity across borders.[112]

Previously, it has been understood that Maeterlinck's work came to the British Isles via Ireland and England. Katharine Worth argues that it 'was always a tale of three cities – Dublin, Paris and London'[113] – but such an understanding ignores the significant (if not leading) contribution that Scottish writers and artists made to kindling an interest in the works of Maeterlinck and other Belgian writers. It is important for these Scottish–Belgian connections to be rehabilitated, as they not only reveal the international awareness of Scottish cultural revivalism at the *fin de siècle* and its interest in developing counter-hegemonic relationships, but also help us unlock the continuities between the writings of the 1890s 'Scots Renascence' and the 1920s 'Scottish Renaissance' – continuities that the likes of MacDiarmid were keen to deny.

Celtic *Japonisme*

In 1895, Frank Rinder, the Scottish husband of Edith Rinder, produced a collection of Japanese tales, titled *Old World Japan: Legends of the Land of Gods* (1895), which was drawn from a variety of sources, including A. B. Mitford's and Lafcadio Hearn's writings on Japan. Audaciously, William Sharp, who was infatuated with Edith Rinder in this period, wrote a review of the collection. In the review, the author of *Vistas* and *The House of Usna* alludes to a further significant Scottish intercultural connection. He writes:

> Again and again in *Old World Japan*, which is throughout distinctively oriental and recognisably Japanese, one is reminded of our extraordinarily rich and beautiful Celtic mythology. Here are episodes, and even whole tales, which, disengaged from what is accidental, might as well have come to us through Dr. Douglas Hyde or Campbell of Islay. How many tales of Hy-Brasil, or Tir-fa-tonn, are suggested by their oriental congener, 'The Island of Eternal Youth', as beautifully retold by Mr. Rinder! Change a few names or localities, real or imaginary; for scarlet lily or lotus substitute the purple heather or the white canna [. . .] and this Japanese folk-tale might in perfect keeping be interpolated in 'The Voyage of Maelduin', or in any of the old Celtic Romances.[114]

For Sharp, Rinder's collection showcased the marked kinship between Japanese and Celtic storytelling and mythic traditions. Like Conan Doyle's *The Mystery of Cloomber*, discussed in Chapter 1, Sharp's review is an example of a Scottish revivalist attempting to 'orientalise' Scotland, building equivalences with traditional Eastern styles to distance the nation further from a purely material or utilitarian culture. As he did with Belgium, Sharp points to an international kinship that Celtic revivalists could build to mount their defence of mythology and mystery.[115]

Celtic orientalism has been examined in detail by other critics but mostly with regard to Ireland. Joseph Lennon's monograph *Irish Orientalism* traces the 'literary and intellectual links between the Oriental and the Celt', particularly between Ireland and India. These connections, Lennon argues, built on a tradition of portraying both the Celt and the Oriental as 'two antitheses of modern, enlightened Europe'.[116] But Lennon's book also demonstrates that there was 'agency' in this association (xxvi). Ireland's ancient 'inaccessible' history, for instance, could 'be accessed through a comparative study of the living Orient' (xvii) and, consequently, an 'anti-imperial and cross-colonial narrative' that supported Irish cultural nationalism emerged (xvii). Lennon makes the point that we should not see Ireland's identification with the Orient as simply 'self-deprecating and reactionary' (xix), as replaying the narrative of the Celt as divorced from modernity. As was demonstrated above, developing ties between marginalised cultures was a means of individuating nations and their contacts.

Lennon also notes how key Japan was for the Irish Revival: Yeats, for instance, used the style and tropes of the Japanese Noh to inform his nationalist drama. Claire Nally elaborates on this idea through a consideration of Yeats's fascination with masks, which were key features of Noh drama. She believes the mask stood for a 'desired alternate self', embodying Yeats's cultural nationalism.[117] Furthermore, Lennon shows that Yeats admired the simplicity of Japanese painting: it offered the 'antimaterialistic images' that he believed were needed to reclaim 'unadulterated traditional culture'.[118]

This Irish orientalism, defined by identification with, and celebration of, the Orient, contrasts with the views of the Orient held by several figures in England, who saw the Orient, and Japan specifically, as threatening (or antithetical) to English national identity. Indeed, many in England felt that the enthusiasm for Japanese styles was damaging to English art. John Ruskin, for instance, described the Japanese as a 'partially inferior race' and believed that their art was 'harmful to many of our painters'.[119] This attitude was shared by the likes of James Jackson Jarves, who claimed that 'the Oriental, the animal-human, chooses that type of human figure which thoroughly demonstrates his earthiness'.[120] Such views are also reflected in T. E. Reed's illustration *Britannia à la Beardsley*, discussed at the beginning of this chapter, which visually demonstrates how the import of Japanese styles (and decadence more widely) undermined British cultural and imperial ascendancy. For a number of figures, Japan and the Orient were imagined in a binary relationship with English 'civilisation'.

Unsurprisingly, those in England who were critical of English identity and 'civilisation' embraced Japan. As we have seen, the character Vivian in Oscar Wilde's 'The Decay of Lying' expresses enthusiasm for the art of the Orient, and Japanese art specifically, because it offers an alternative to the imitative art of the English 'degraded race' that surrounds him. English art, for Vivian, is 'the true Decadence' – a rebuttal of those who believed that a culture of utilitarian and commercial development was 'civilised'.[121] George Moore also lamented the loss of traditional Japanese culture at the hands of modernity, noting that 'even the Japanese are becoming Christian and respectable'.[122] While several figures identified Ireland with the Orient, many imagined contemporary England as the antithesis of the Orient, either to celebrate or to scold England's association with 'civilised' modernity.

While a great deal of work has been devoted to examining the presence of *japonisme* in Scotland,[123] the phenomenon has not been considered in relation to the question of national identity construction in the way that it has been with Ireland. Here, I demonstrate how important the cultural revivalist context was to Scottish *japonisme* and how it led to the development of a particular type of Celtic orientalism in Scotland. I argue that Scottish *japonisme* had a 'distinct history',[124] one that is yet to be fully explored. I begin this consideration of Scottish *japonisme* by outlining the close industrial and civic connections between Scotland and Japan at the *fin de siècle*, and the consequent enthusiasm for Japanese culture that developed in Scotland, particularly amongst Glasgow's artists. From here, I consider the ways in which various Scottish revivalists throughout the nation yoked tropes of traditional Japanese culture with Celtic and Scottish culture to orientalise and 'other' Scotland. Given that there were anxieties in both nations over how to maintain their traditional cultures and national identities whilst participating in industrialism and globalisation,[125] it is unsurprising that these equivalences and yokings developed. Building on this topic by considering Mackintosh's Glasgow School of Art building, I illustrate how Scotland's connection with Japan allowed Scots to look back to indigenous forms *and* to celebrate modernisation simultaneously, helping reconcile two dual features of the Scottish Revival.

Olive and Sydney Checkland have argued that Japan's industrial and imperial development, spurred on by the opening of its borders from 1853, owed a large debt to Glasgow: 'not surprisingly, the new Japan, in its world search for best practice, turned to Glasgow for science and engineering'.[126] In a similar vein, Olive Checkland writes elsewhere that 'Japan's railways depended on Glasgow steam engines, and Clyde-built steam ships filled her harbours'.[127] Japanese modernisers were certainly keen to establish ties with Scottish industries to develop their projects. As early as 1866, such individuals as Yamao Yōzō were sent to Glasgow shipyards to learn from the city's expertise in naval architecture. Students were also attracted to Glasgow's Chair of Naval Architecture, with one Japanese student describing the city as in the 'highest class in the world for naval architecture'. Until 1914, with the exception of London, there was a greater Japanese population in Glasgow than anywhere else in Britain.[128]

Scots also had important roles to play in Japan. Thomas Blake Glover, a merchant from Fraserburgh, went to the Far East with Jardine Matheson and Company in the middle of the nineteenth century. While in Japan, from 1859, he established naval links and contracts with Scotland, including commissions for Japanese ships that would be built in Aberdeen: *Satsuma* (1864), *Ho Sho Maru* (1868), *Jho Sho Maru* (1869) and *Wen Yu Maru* (1870). He later established Japan's first mine, 'attracting its first modern labour force',[129] and encouraged Japanese imperial expansion. Glover would also play an important role in supporting the rebel clans against the feudal militarist *bakufu*, which led to the Meiji Restoration in 1868 and played an important role in the modernising of Japan.[130]

Japan also imported other forms of Scottish engineering. As a fellow coastal nation, Scotland had an expertise in lighthouse engineering that was solicited. Consequently, Robert Louis Stevenson's family and Richard Henry Brunton, known as the father of Japanese lighthouses, built 'a complete ring of lighthouses around Japan'.[131] Henry Dyer, a further Scottish engineer, was, from 1873, the first head of the Imperial College of Engineering in Japan, at which several graduates of the University of Glasgow would become staff. There, Dyer helped set up Japan's largest engineering works, Akabane, and provided advice on Japan's first railway. James Alfred Ewing was another Scottish scientist in Japan, who has been credited with introducing many forms of physics to the nation when he was a professor there between 1878 and 1883. In this period, further ships were imported from Glasgow, including the 1874 twin-screw steamer, *Meiji Maru*. Evidently, there was a clear desire to import Scottish scientists and naval manufacturing into Japan, and this industrial connection was reflected in there being an Honorary Japanese Consul, who served in Glasgow from 1890 to 1941.

These industrial connections laid the foundations for strong cultural bonds between the two nations. Olive Checkland argues that 'no one was more excited about Japan and Japanese arts and crafts than the artistic community in Glasgow'.[132] This excitement was stimulated by a cultural exchange between the Japanese government and the City of Glasgow, which Robert Henry Smith was involved in orchestrating. As part of this exchange, in November 1878, Glasgow received thirty-one cases containing 1,150 items from Japan, and *The Glasgow Herald* reported that 'they form a collection which for variety and representative character we are safe to say is not equalled in any museum in this country'.[133] Many of these items went on display in the Glasgow Corporation Art Galleries' exhibition of oriental art (Japanese and Persian) between 1881 and 1882. This exhibition also featured a lecture from the Glasgow-born designer Christopher Dresser, who wrote *Japan: Its Architecture, Art and Manufacture*, published in 1882 after his visit to Japan.

Following the exhibition, during the 1880s, Scotland's artistic interest in Japan grew and became particularly strong at the end of that decade. The City Oriental Warehouse advertised exhibits of Japanese wares in 1888 and Alexander Reid (a friend of Vincent Van Gogh's), who had visited Japan, opened his Société des Beaux-Arts in Glasgow with an exhibition of Japanese prints (mainly Hokusai's) in 1889. Like Reid, the shipping merchant William Burrell also collected Japanese prints at this time, although he was more interested in ancient Chinese wares rather than the newly imported Japanese works. Following Reid's exhibition, J. B. Bennett & Sons held an exhibition of Chinese and Japanese ceramics in 1890, while in 1893 Paterson and Thomas exhibited Paterson's collection of over 200 Japanese prints,[134] many of which were later purchased by the British Museum and remain in their collections. Furthermore, paintings of Japanese subjects by two Glasgow Boys, E. A. Hornel and George Henry, sold remarkably well when exhibited at the Société des Beaux-Arts in April 1895. A notable demand for Japanese-inspired art clearly became established in *fin-de-siècle* Glasgow and these dealers were highly receptive to it. Similarly, Scottish carpet designers, such as Stoddard International, acquired Japanese embroideries and stencils that were used to inspire their designs. The Scottish press was attentive to this rising enthusiasm for Japanese wares too: in 1888–9, *The Scottish Art Review* – which was described as one of the *fin de siècle*'s most 'significant events' – featured articles on *kakemonos* (hanging vertical scroll pictures) and Japanese sword guards, while favourably reviewing Siegfried Bing's *Artistic Japan* magazine.[135]

Partly as a consequence of these ties, numerous comparisons between the Scottish and Japanese peoples were made. As early as 1873, similarities between the Highlander and the Japanese samurai were drawn out by David S. Miller, who had travelled from Scotland to Japan.[136] Equivalences between Scotland's and Japan's clan societies were also met with comparisons to contemporary society: in 1908, at the opening of the Japanese Section of the Scottish National Exhibition (an event discussed in Chapter 5), Sir A. R. Simpson 'commented on the similarities – in patriotism, love of education, hospitality and in other characteristics – between the people of Japan and the people of Scotland'.[137] This comparison was akin to Hornel's claim that 'in Scotland we pride ourselves on our homeliness. In Japan we see ourselves equalled in this respect.'[138] Critics too noted the similarities between the styles of Scottish and Japanese arts: in 1911, Kuno Meyer stated that, 'like the Japanese, the Celts were always quick to take an artistic hint; they avoid the obvious and the commonplace; the half-said thing to them is dearest'.[139] This racial connection was drawn out by the journal *Theosophy in Scotland*, where it was noted that 'many oriental traits still linger in the Celtic mind'.[140] There was very little hesitancy over identifying with Japan and comparing it to *fin-de-siècle* Scotland.

What is significant for this discussion about the growing industrial and imperial ties between Scotland and Japan is that cultural revivalists in Scotland did not contest these growing industrial ties with Japan. Instead, their work authenticated the bonds between the two nations and this reveals key facets of cultural nationalism in *fin–de-siècle* Scotland. The Japan connection created a site that allowed Scottish revivalists to orientalise the nation (as occurred in Ireland, primarily through its India connection), but it also allowed them to celebrate Scotland's industrial modernity too.

Several Scottish revivalists were particularly keen to yoke Japanese and Scottish culture in order to orientalise Scotland, to celebrate its traditional culture and to assert itself as 'other'. This is evident in the works of several artists and writers, one of whom was Robert Louis Stevenson. Stevenson had a greater interest in Japanese culture than tends to be recognised.[141] He wrote two articles on Japan: 'Yoshida-Torajiro' for *Cornhill Magazine* in 1880 and 'Byways of Book Illustration: Two Japanese Romances' for the *Magazine of Art* in 1883; he also intended to write an article on Hokusai for his friend, William Ernest Henley. Stevenson owned many Japanese volumes, collected Japanese prints and read Mitford's *Tales of Old Japan*, as well as Isabella Bird's *Unbeaten Tracks in Japan*. Linda Zatlin claims that Stevenson visited Japan,[142] which is unlikely, but he certainly intended to 'head for Japan' when he was travelling in the Pacific, according to a letter to his wife, Fanny Osbourne.[143] Stevenson's Davos woodcuts for his *Moral Emblems* may also have been inspired by Japanese woodcut techniques.[144]

What is significant about Stevenson's knowledge of Japan is that he often aligns Japan with Scotland and uses these discussions, as in his romance novels, to critique 'civilisation' and recover space for traditional cultures. In 'Byways of Book Illustration', Stevenson performs the 'triumph of barbarism' that is found in Sharp's Belgian-inspired texts and Baudelaire's 'Further Notes on Poe':

> There is no form of conceit more common or silly than to look down on barbarous codes of morals. Barbarous virtues, the chivalrous point of honour, the fidelity of the wild highlander or the two-sworded Japanese, are of a generous example. We may question the utility of what is done; the whole hearted sincerity of the actors shuts our mouth.[145]

Here, Stevenson not only compares the Highlander to the Japanese but vindicates their lifestyles and exposes those who would marginalise them. He applauds 'the superior duty, the duty of the clan' (9), again highlighting commonalities between the two cultures, while mocking their critics as 'silly'. He similarly discusses chieftains and castles (8): his descriptions of Japanese traditional life could easily be descriptions of Scotland. Stevenson's other Japanese essay, 'Yoshida-Torajiro' positively speaks of Yoshida's 'lively and intelligent patriotism' and of his having 'the tenacity of a Bruce'.[146] As in his South Seas writings, where Stevenson frequently assesses Polynesia through comparisons to Scotland, he evokes solidarity between Japan and Scotland here in their defence against those who would look down on the supposed barbarity of the Highlander or the Japanese samurai.

Scottish artists, particularly those associated with the Celtic Revival, were also keen to perform this 'othering' and equate Scottish and Japanese culture. It is most clearly evident in the work of John Duncan, a symbolist artist and Theosophist from Dundee, who worked closely with Patrick Geddes. Duncan, who lived for a time on Eriskay with the Celtic revivalist musician Marjory Kennedy-Fraser, was intensely involved in the Celtic Revival and created several murals and paintings that evoked Celtic figures, some of which are discussed in the following chapters. What is striking about his paintings is that his Celtic subjects often take a distinctively Japanese aesthetic.

The Glaive of Light, an oil painting by Duncan from 1897 (Plate 2), depicts two figures combating a dragon, with one wielding the sword of light. This sword of light appears in many Scottish and Irish folk tales: it is a magical, undefeatable sword that can be used to kill supernatural monsters. As such, the sword of light became a key symbol for Irish cultural and political nationalists at the *fin de siècle*; a leader of the Easter Rising, Patrick Pearse, named one of his short-lived newspapers *An Claidheamh Soluis* (The Sword of Light), for example. The black and red hair of the figures in *The Glaive of Light* point to the Celtic subject matter, as these were stereotypical features of the Celt in the late nineteenth century. The painting is a representation of Celtic defence and romance, and Duncan employed this 'sword of light' trope in several of his Celtic revivalist paintings, including one of his most recognisable, *The Riders of the Sidhe* (see Plate 12).

But while *The Glaive of Light* is a highly Celtic painting in some ways, it is very obviously not in others. The bright patterned garment of the sword-bearer, for instance, is unmistakably a kimono. The central figure even has a Japanese *obi*, or sash, tied around its waist. The monster is also based on an oriental dragon: like Chinese and Japanese dragons, it does not appear to have wings and takes a serpentine form. In this context, it is interesting to note that Duncan chose to name the subject the 'glaive of light' over the more common expression 'sword of light'. A glaive is a single-edged weapon, not like the double-edged sword represented in the painting: single-edged swords are widely associated with Japanese and Chinese warfare, such as the Japanese *naginata*. A final, very clear, allusion to Japanese arts in the painting is Duncan's signature in the bottom left-hand corner: it is a circular emblem, which he used frequently in this period, inspired by Japanese *mon* – heraldic symbols that generally draw on natural imagery. This is a painting that flaunts Celticism's otherness; it is a painting that uses Japanese details to enhance the other-worldly Celtic dimensions, while also demonstrating the internationalism of Celtic culture.

These traits are also evident in what is perhaps Duncan's greatest painting, *St Bride* (Plate 3). The medium of the painting is tempera on canvas, which Duncan was attracted to on account of tempera's strong associations with Early Renaissance art, thus helping to evoke the religiosity of his paintings. In both Irish and Scottish legend, Bride (also known as Bridget, Brighid or Brigidh) is transported from either Kildare or Iona, depending on the respective tradition, to Bethlehem to attend the nativity. Duncan was clearly fascinated with the figure of St Bride and he executed a further painting of her, *The Coming of St Bride* (1917). He was also enchanted by Iona, and was even planning to design a literary and artistic community on the island.[147] Some consider Bride to be the 'foster mother of Christ', which was certainly how Sharp described her in his short story 'Mary of the Gael', which depicts the very transportation represented in Duncan's painting (although, in Sharp's story, there are no angels). It is likely that Duncan was inspired by Sharp's story. Lindsay Errington convincingly demonstrates that other Sharp writings inform the painting: in 'The

Gaelic Heart', Sharp describes Brighid as the Celtic Demeter, who was 'born of the embrace of Poseidon', and he also describes Iona's wildlife and setting, including seals 'putting their breasts against the running tide', sea fowl, and the 'flashing white hair o' foam' on the blue body of the sea.[148] The painting, as Errington states, is a close visual embodiment of Sharp's descriptions.[149] But while this painting, like *The Glaive of Light*, has an explicitly Celtic subject matter, it also contains several oriental details. The robes, which depict the life of Christ, are again highly reminiscent of decorative kimonos – such as the one represented in Van Gogh's *The Courtesan* (1887) – while, on the inside of the kimono, near the Celtic knot trim, there are small abstract gold dots, like the abstract flower petals that appear on Japanese lacquerware. The painting is a further clear statement of Celtic orientalism by Duncan, which subverts the idea that the Celts were a lapsing, insular culture. Instead, what we see here is a vibrant internationalism, one that asserts the health of Celtic culture and one that prioritises the traditional – marking the Celts' refusal of the superiority of utilitarian modernity.

Duncan was not alone in bringing tropes of Celtic and Japanese art together in his work. David Gauld (who included many Japanese decorative features in his illustrations for the *Glasgow Weekly Citizen*) anticipates Duncan in portraying figures with 'Celtic' red and black hair wearing kimonos in his painting *Music*, while fellow Glasgow Boy, George Henry, places kimono-clad figures in an Ayrshire village in *Landscape at Barr* (1891). Agnes Middleton Raeburn signed her name vertically (typical of Japanese signatures) in her poster for the Glasgow Lecture Association (1897), which pays homage to the Celtic Revival through the Celtic knot formed by the snake's tail. These works further associate Scottish and Celtic culture with the visual vocabulary of Japan, helping to orientalise Scottish and Celtic art and tradition.

Several of the other Glasgow Boys developed an interest in Japan, none more so than E. A. Hornel, whose Japanese paintings were much admired by Duncan.[150] Alongside being a significant collector of Robert Burns editions and material culture, Hornel amassed a great number of original Japanese wares and literature on Japan: kimonos, fans and other Japanese items can be viewed in his collections at Broughton House, Kirkcudbright. In many of his artworks, Hornel brings his enthusiasm for Scottish and Japanese traditions together. This can be evidenced in his garden at Broughton House, which was one of many Japanese gardens that were created in Scotland in the period. Another was Ella Christie's in Clackmannanshire, designed by

Taki Handa in 1908, which the head of the Soami School of Imperial Garden Design, Jijo Suzuki, described as one of the most important Japanese gardens in the Western world. Although Hornel's garden is a Japanese garden, featuring a sculpture of a crane, it also contains Celtic stones, including a Dalshangan Cross. Hornel's garden successfully yokes the Celtic with the Oriental and creates an outdoor space that affirms the solidarity of the two traditions.[151] This interest in placing Celtic art alongside Japanese art is also reflected in the fact that Hornel contributed *Madame Chrysanthème* (Fig. 2.8) to the second issue of the Celtic Revival magazine, *The Evergreen*.

Hornel's Japanese collections grew when he and George Henry visited Japan in 1893, but both were aware of Japanese arts before then. The Boys would have known of *japonisme* through their enthusiasm for Whistler; his *Ten O'Clock* lecture, so celebratory of Japan, was described by Lavery as the Boys' 'gospel'.[152] It may well have been this lecture that inspired fellow Glasgow Boy, E. A. Walton, to dress as Hokusai for the Glasgow Art Club's fancy-dress ball in 1889.

Figure 2.8 E. A. Hornel, *Madame Chrysanthème*, in *The Evergreen*, 2 (1895): 101.

Walton's studio in Cambuskenneth (where Henry also worked) was decorated with Japanese prints too. The influence of Japan is also clearly evident in Hornel's and Henry's work before 1893: a contemporary critic in Belgium even noted that Hornel's decorative use of colour 'has a strong relation to Japanese art and is strongly akin to Gauguin'.[153] Hornel's focus on colour and patterning, over illusionistic detail, reflected the influence of the Japanese arts.

The painting that best demonstrates Hornel's (and Henry's) early interest in Japanese art is *The Druids – Bringing in the Mistletoe* (Plate 4), one of the most iconic artworks of the Celtic Revival. The painting, which owes a debt to Pliny's discussion on druidical processions that is quoted in J. G. Frazer's *The Golden Bough*,[154] depicts several druids who undertake a solemn procession after the chief cuts a sprig of mistletoe, which was believed to be both medicinal and miraculous, from a sacred oak tree; the mistletoe appears in the painting on the bulls' backs. It is believed that Hornel and Henry developed the subject of the painting after watching an old man in Galloway, who was interested in Celtic carvings, experience a vision about 'priests with sacred instruments and cattle'.[155] Despite the obvious Celtic nature of the piece, as with Duncan's art, there are many references to Japanese culture in the painting. William Buchanan, who organised the 1979 exhibition 'Mr Henry and Mr Hornel visit Japan', noted that the painting 'is a rich, gilded, decorative picture, and although on a Celtic theme, to many it may have had a touch of the Orient about it'.[156] A particularly Japanese feature of the painting is the presence of trees on oddly white ground, considering there is no snow on the trees. This appears to be drawn from a similar feature in Japanese prints where dark trees are printed on white ground, creating stark contrast (Plate 5). The moon in the background, against a rich blue sky, also mimics a common feature of Japanese prints. The low viewpoint of the painting may not be particularly Japanese – since Japanese prints tend to have a high viewpoint – but its effect (reducing the capacity for recession of space) is. The striking use of complementary colours, such as the ochre against the blue in the background, is also similar to Japanese prints while, more generally, the use of gilt gold details is common to oriental art. Consequently, the culture represented appears ornate and luxurious: this is no simple, rude Celticism – a feature that further complicates stadialist understandings of the Celts. The figures are also darker-skinned, which continues to orientalise the piece. The painting's various Japanese elements would not have gone unnoticed: *The Druids* was first exhibited in the Grosvenor Gallery – the 'stronghold of

Aestheticism' – whose audiences would have been sensitive to Japanese nuances.[157] As an audience, the painting invites us to recognise the sophistication (even opulence) of the Celts and the international dimensions of Celticism.

Charles Rennie Mackintosh and the Glasgow School of Art

While the artworks described above reveal the concerted attempts to 'orientalise' Scottish culture at the *fin de siècle*, it is in Charles Rennie Mackintosh's Glasgow School of Art building, described by Geddes as 'one of the most important buildings in Europe',[158] that the full complexity of the Scotland–Japan connection becomes evident. In Mackintosh's work, we again encounter the desire to orientalise Scotland, to support Mackintosh's vocal cultural revivalism, but what we also find is his proto-modernism and his interest in Glasgow's industrialism. Using Japanese and Scottish traditional styles to fuel modernism, Mackintosh undercut stadialist notions of historical progress by demonstrating that the past and modernity are not antagonists. In this way, Mackintosh's *japonisme* most successfully reconciled some of the conflicting aims of Scottish cultural revivalism: reclaiming traditional Scottish culture, while still celebrating the modernity and the 'advanced' industry of Scotland.

Mackintosh's concern with cultural revivalism is evident throughout his career. In an early lecture on architecture from 1892, he expresses reservations over adopting *japonisme* and instead favours a return to national forms:

> I think we should be a little less cosmopolitan & rather more national in our Archi[tecture], as we are with language, new words & phrases will be incorporated gradually, but the wholesale introduction of japanese senta [sic] for example would be denounced & rightly by the purist.[159]

Here, Mackintosh critiques the 'wholesale' absorption of Japan in the arts; he stresses that architecture should be fundamentally national, incorporating other cultures only by diffusion, and he attacks those who would use Japan to dilute Scottish architecture. He continues:

> the history of nations is written in stone, but it certainly would be a difficult task to read a history from the architecture of this nation at the present time. We do not build as the ancients did who in each succeeding building tried to carry to further perfection the national type. (197)

He cautions against a 'build now in Greek if we love the Classic' (197) mentality and encourages architects to focus on 'indigenous' forms, such as Scottish baronial architecture, which is 'as indigenous to our country as our wild flowers, our family names our customs or our political constitution'.[160] Indeed, the 'tradition of romantic nationalism that Mackintosh subscribes' to mimics the English medievalists, such as Pugin, who claimed that 'there is no need of visiting the distant shores of Greece and Egypt to make discoveries in art. England alone abounds in hidden and unknown antiquities of surpassing interest.'[161] To advance his cultural revivalist aims, Mackintosh extensively toured Scotland and sketched his findings,[162] which had a great impact on his architectural projects. His sketch of the observatory tower of Stirling High School very clearly influenced his Glasgow Herald Building (1893–5), for instance.

Mackintosh's stance on Japan altered, however, at least partially. By the mid-1890s he appears to acknowledge that certain uses of Japanese design did not necessarily dilute Scottish tradition; in fact, they could complement it. In this period, Mackintosh became more interested in Japanese art: contemporary photographs reveal that he and Margaret Macdonald had Japanese greetings cards (*surimono*) hung above the fireplace at 120 Mains Street, much as in E. A. Walton's studio, which appear in the Hunterian Art Gallery reconstruction. *The Studio* and Bing's *Artistic Japan* no doubt played a role in nurturing Mackintosh's interest in Japan around this time.[163]

Mackintosh's design for the Glasgow School of Art most clearly showcases his yoking of Scottish traditional forms with Japanese forms. A key architectural style underpinning Mackintosh's design for the school is Scottish baronialism. Frank Arneil Walker has noted that the south elevation of the building follows a similar design to such baronial buildings as Fyvie Castle, Aberdeenshire.[164] The eastern façade of the building also resembles Scottish buildings, particularly castles, through the rough stone, the deep-set windows that highlight the thickness of the walls, the outlook tower and the arrow-loops (Fig. 2.9). In this sense, Mackintosh's fortress of art plays into the wider late Victorian revival of Scottish architectural forms, evident in such works as Robert Rowand Anderson's Pearce Institute building in Govan. Not only does the Glasgow School of Art appear national in its architectural design but some of the decorative details are Celtic revivalist. For example, the relief above the school entrance presents figures in Celtic dress styled in a curvilinear, simple manner, typical of Celtic art and Art Nouveau alike.

However, despite the typically Scottish qualities underpinning the building, another tradition is strikingly evident. At the top of the

Figure 2.9 Charles Rennie Mackintosh, east façade, Glasgow School of Art (1896–1909). © Crown Copyright: HES.

eastern façade, so Scottish in many of its forms, Mackintosh includes an apparently redundant Japanese gable for decoration. Similarly, as Dorothy Bruce has noted, the railings on the north façade (Fig. 2.10) were inspired by Japanese *mon*.[165] According to Maggie Tatarkowski, these designs may also derive from *tsuba* (Japanese sword guards), which were discussed in Bing's *Artistic Japan*.[166] Likewise, the decorative features underneath the *mon*-inspired designs on the railings are most likely inspired by Japanese arrowheads, which would reinforce the defence theme that is also alluded to in the upper window railings, which resemble basket hilt swords. The wrought-iron grill at the top of the west staircase (Fig. 2.11) references both Japanese *shoji* designs and iron portcullises, while the Composition Room studio (Fig. 2.12) at the top of the west tower features a beam construction clearly derived from Japanese shrines. The Scottish and Japanese traditions combine harmoniously – mainly through their austerity – but they remain recognisably distinct.[167] Japan was no longer something that obscured Scottish forms but, when applied correctly, helped sharpen the 'indigenous' feel and 'otherness' of Mackintosh's architecture. Indeed, the yoking of the two sets of traditional forms creates a remarkably unique architectural and decorative scheme that helps distinguish the building from the Greek, Norman and Swiss reproductions that Mackintosh felt were diluting Scottish architecture.

Figure 2.10 Charles Rennie Mackintosh, symbol on the railings of the north façade, Glasgow School of Art (1896–1909). © Crown Copyright: HES.

Figure 2.11 Charles Rennie Mackintosh, grille at the top of the west staircase, Glasgow School of Art (1896–1909). © Crown Copyright: HES.

Figure 2.12 Charles Rennie Mackintosh, the Composition Room, Glasgow School of Art (1896–1909). © Courtesy of HES (Bedford Lemere and Company Collection).

This Scottish–Japanese fusion is found in other Mackintosh civic commissions and domestic designs too. For example, in his drawing room at 6 Florentine Terrace, which included many pieces from his 120 Mains Street flat, the influence of Japan is pronounced. Tatarkowski argues that the shape of Mackintosh's cabinets and writing bureaux are indebted to the Japanese kimono, which is certainly evident in the painted oak writing cabinet in the drawing room.[168] Furthermore, fabric room dividers, rather than doors, partition the space between the studio and drawing room, allowing for interpenetration and a fluid definition of space – a key Japanese principle of interior design. Mackintosh was evidently enthusiastic about this principle: in his baronial-style Scotland Street School,[169] classroom walls are partially made of glass and there are several other fenestrated partitions that help connect rooms to each other and to the outdoors. Like the Glasgow School of Art, the Scotland Street School is a very clear fusion of Scottish and Japanese architectural principles and detailing.

While this conflation of Scottish and Japanese art helped express Mackintosh's commitment to traditional forms, it also contributed to his commitment to modernity. In his 'Scotch Baronial Architecture' paper, Mackintosh wrote:

> From some recent buildings which have been erected it is clearly evident that this [Scottish baronial] style is coming to life again and I only hope that it will not be strangled in its infancy by indiscriminating / and unsympathetic people who copy the ancient examples without trying to make the style conform to modern requirements.[170]

Mackintosh did not use indigenous styles to reject modernity; he was responsive to it. One of the effects of his Japanese inflections is that they help Scottish baronial architecture adapt to modernity, by creating even more simplified, rectilinear forms. Mackintosh's Glasgow School of Art even celebrates the industrial, imperial culture of Scotland through the roof of the building's museum, which bears a striking resemblance to the frame of a boat's hull (Fig. 2.13) – a reference to Glasgow's shipping prowess and imperial prosperity. Mackintosh's work celebrates the 'advanced' modernity of Scotland while still observing and using traditional Scottish (and Japanese)

Figure 2.13 Charles Rennie Mackintosh, roof of the Museum, Glasgow School of Art (1896–1909). © Courtesy of HES (Bedford Lemere and Company Collection).

forms. In doing so, Mackintosh rejects a type of modernity, a utilitarian modernity, that ignores the importance of traditional culture. Mackintosh instead *relies* on traditional culture to produce his proto-modernist designs, just as many modernists would also do in the twentieth century.

It is unsurprising that Geddes admired the Glasgow School of Art building as much as he did: the building embodies his belief in harmonising the traditions of the 'Celtic world' with the new world of 'industrial and practical initiative'.[171] Indeed, Geddes praised the building for getting its 'effects with the sternest of modern conditions [. . .] never was concrete more concrete, steel more steely'.[172] As such, the Glasgow School of Art building provides one of the clearest embodiments of the duality of Scottish cultural revivalism in this period – harmonising the contemporary desire to express Scottish industrialism, while also reclaiming traditional cultures and defining Scottish nationality through art.

In 1911, at the Scottish National Exhibition in Kelvingrove Park, Glasgow, a Japanese Tea Garden was positioned beside An Clachan, the Highland Village, and across from the Irish Dairy Cottages. To visitors then, this may not have seemed so incongruous: a number of Scottish writers and artists had been consciously styling a cross-cultural solidarity with Japan for around thirty years. For these figures, the import and fusion of Japanese culture with Scotland's own traditional culture bolstered cultural revivalism in a particular way. While Belgium provided a model for the structure of Scottish revivalism, as well as a vocabulary for the 'triumph of barbarism', the Japanese link (while also supporting these ideas) expressed a different aspect of the movement: a celebration of Scottish industrialism and empire. Unlike several in Ireland who identified with India, which they felt occupied a similar colonial position to their own country, Scottish cultural revivalists did not imagine Scotland as a colony – they wanted to design a cultural friendship that highlighted the value of traditional cultures but also Scotland's modernity, industry and imperialism. The Japan connection satisfied these aims. While Scottish imperialists and industrialists played a key role in nurturing modern Japan, Japanese traditional culture, in turn, helped shape the type of modernity advocated by Scottish revivalists.

What is clear from this discussion is that Scottish culture was far from insular or parochial in this period: several Scots were explicitly developing cross-border connections to assert Scotland's international presence. I have examined only two connections in this chapter, but there are many more cultural connections waiting to be assessed in more detail, including ties with India and Egypt, which I explore in relation to occultism in Chapter 4. But what is also clear is that Scottish revivalists focused on fostering particular proximities that suited their agenda. One thing they learned from both Japan and Belgium was the importance of the traditional, the 'barbaric' or even an imagined 'original' culture to help undermine the centralising and homogenising forces of the late nineteenth century that they identified. How writers and artists in Scotland went about fashioning such imagined origins for the nation is the central concern of the next chapter.

Notes

1. For more on decadence and the anxiety of imperial decline, see Arata, *Fictions of Loss*.
2. Elliot, p. 271.
3. Letter from Patrick Geddes to R. E. Muirhead [Centre for Research Collections, University of Edinburgh: E2208.54] (4 December 1928).
4. Branford and Geddes, 'Prefatory Note': 8.
5. Geddes's Franco-Scottish endeavours are discussed in detail in Fowle and Thomson's *Patrick Geddes* and Reynolds's *Paris–Edinburgh*.
6. Talbott: 405.
7. Letter from Geddes to Muirhead [CRC E2208.54].
8. Gibbons: 272.
9. Ibid.: 274.
10. Nordau, pp. 9–10, 227.
11. This motto appears on the front cover of Wanliss's book, *The Bars to British Unity: A Plea for National Sentiment*.
12. Leela Ghandi theorises the notion of international solidarities at the *fin de siècle* in her book, *Affective Communities* (2006).
13. (Cited in) Meier-Graefe, p. 62.
14. Nordau, p. 560.
15. For more on the *fin-de-siècle* relapse into barbarism, see Brantlinger, pp. 229–30.
16. Gagnier, 'The Victorian *Fin de Siècle* and Decadence', pp. 33, 336.
17. Baudelaire, *The Painter of Modern Life and Other Essays*, p. 93.
18. For more on Schopenhauer's ideas on progress, see Nisbit, pp. 319–20.
19. Rousseau, pp. 153–4.
20. Carruthers, *Scottish Literature*, p. 9.
21. Symons, 'In Praise of Gypsies': 298.
22. Sartre, p. 18.
23. Fanon, pp. 169, 178.

24. Wilde, *Plays, Prose Writings and Poems*, p. 80.
25. Carpenter, *The Healing of the Nations*, p. 219.
26. William Morris, p. 107.
27. Gagnier, *Insatiability*, p. 152.
28. Bru, 'The Prism of Propaganda': 43–62; McCulloch, *Scottish Modernism and its Contexts*, p. 16.
29. (Cited in) McCulloch, *Scottish Modernism*, p. 16.
30. (Cited in) McCulloch, *Modernism and Nationalism*, p. 52.
31. (Cited in) Ibid., p. 52.
32. Carruthers, Goldie and Renfrew, p. 16.
33. For a detailed examination of the various ways in which writers attempted to appease the anxiety of influence, see Bloom.
34. Varty, p. 140.
35. For more on the Theatre of the Absurd, see Esslin.
36. Bru, 'The Low Countries', p. 290; Mus and Vandevoorde, p. 341.
37. 'La Jeune Belgique': 1.
38. Worth, *Oscar Wilde*, p. 54.
39. The Yeats–Sharp friendship is thoroughly examined in William F. Halloran's two articles titled 'W. B. Yeats, William Sharp, Fiona Macleod: A Celtic Drama' for *Yeats Annual*.
40. Patrick Geddes, Rough notes relating to *The Evergreen* [Archives and Special Collections, University of Strathclyde: T-GED 8/1/3].
41. 'Miscellaneous Books', p. 4.
42. Letter from William Sharp to Catharine Janvier, *The William Sharp "Fiona Macleod" Archive*, available at <http://www.ies.sas.ac.uk/research/current-projects/william-sharp-fiona-macleod-archive/william-sharp-fiona-macleod-archive> (last accessed 15 December 2018) (12 August 1893).
43. William Sharp, '*The Princess Maleine*': 270–2.
44. William Sharp, 'A Note on the Belgian Renascence': 153.
45. Pittock, *Celtic Identity*, p. 71.
46. William Sharp, *The Washer*, p. 4; William Sharp, *The Winged Destiny*, pp. 164, 273; William Sharp, *The Sin-Eater*, p. 13.
47. (Cited in) Maley: 170.
48. William Sharp, 'The Irish Muse': 697.
49. Grilli: 21.
50. William Sharp, 'A Note on the Belgian Renascence': 152.
51. Baudelaire, *Œuvres posthumes*, III, p. 20.
52. William Sharp, 'A Note on the Belgian Renascence': 150.
53. William Sharp, 'La Jeune Belgique': 416, 418.
54. William Sharp, 'A Note on the Belgian Renascence': 156.
55. Ibid.: 150.
56. Ibid.: 151.
57. Several of the historical Scottish–Belgian connections are outlined in Grant, pp. 142–72.
58. Clarke: 159.

59. Letter from William Sharp to Herbert S. Stone, *The William Sharp 'Fiona Macleod' Archive*, available at <http://www.ies.sas.ac.uk/research/current-projects/william-sharp-fiona-macleod-archive/william-sharp-fiona-macleod-archive> (last accessed 15 December 2018) (22 December 1894); for more on Sharp's autopsychical writing, see Benham, pp. 38–41.
60. Letter from William Sharp to Herbert S. Stone (22 December 1894).
61. Cotterell: 182–3.
62. William Sharp, *Vistas*, p. 3.
63. Elizabeth A. Sharp, *William Sharp*, p. 190.
64. 'New Books', p. 2.
65. William Sharp, Manuscripts and typescripts of dramas [National Library of Scotland: MS 8776].
66. Maeterlinck, *The Treasure*, pp. 142–3.
67. 'Les Livres': 227.
68. William Sharp, 'La Jeune Belgique': 416.
69. William Sharp, Manuscripts and typescripts of dramas [National Library of Scotland: MS 8776].
70. William Sharp, 'La Jeune Belgique': 433.
71. (Cited in) Elizabeth A. Sharp, *William Sharp*, p. 188.
72. William Sharp, Manuscripts and typescripts of dramas [National Library of Scotland: MS 8776].
73. William Sharp, *The Pagan Review*: 61.
74. William Sharp, *Vistas*, p. 3.
75. This sacrifice to a goddess may have been inspired by the opening of J. G. Frazer's *The Golden Bough*, set on the banks of Lake Nemi.
76. Ashtaroth would later feature in John Buchan's 'The Grove of Ashtaroth' (1912). In Buchan's story, a man of Scottish descent, Lawson, is seduced by a non-Christian religion that threatens rationality.
77. William Sharp, *The Pagan Review*: 109.
78. Benko, p. 215.
79. Ellmann, p. 132.
80. 'Music and Maeterlinck': 434.
81. Symons, *The Symbolist Movement*, p. 8.
82. William Sharp, *The House of Usna*, p. 3.
83. William Sharp, 'Introduction', p. xxxiii.
84. Lennon, pp. 281–3.
85. William Sharp, *The House of Usna*, pp. xxvi–xxvii.
86. Ellmann, p. 132.
87. (Cited in) Jarron, p. 69.
88. For more on George Dutch Davidson and his links to William Sharp, see Hardie, pp. 123–6.
89. Castle, p. 10.
90. Sharp's concern with the 'triumph of barbarism' is reflected in the title of one of his short story collections written as Fiona Macleod, *Barbaric Tales* (1897).

91. (Cited in) Elizabeth A. Sharp, *Lyra Celtica*, p. 432.
92. Patrick Geddes, Notes for a lecture to the Celtic Society [Archives and Special Collections, University of Strathclyde: T-GED 5/2/9].
93. Mus and Vandevoorde, p. 336.
94. Newbery also hired Frederick Cayley Robinson as Professor of Figure Composition between 1914 and 1924. Robinson was an important illustrator of Maeterlinck's work, who designed sets for *The Blue Bird* that were approved by Maeterlinck.
95. William Wallace composed various pieces of orchestral music inspired by Scottish history, including a symphonic poem, *Sir William Wallace* (1905), and an overture, *In Praise of Scottish Poesie* (1894).
96. 'Recognition of War Services', p. 7.
97. 'Glasgow', p. 8.
98. Pamela Robertson, p. 61.
99. Helland, pp. 71–2.
100. Billcliffe, *Charles Rennie Mackintosh*, p. 34.
101. Hubbard, p. 273.
102. Billcliffe, *Charles Rennie Mackintosh*, p. 36.
103. Mackintosh, 'Untitled Paper on Architecture (c. 1892)', p. 196.
104. Maeterlinck, *The Blue Bird*, p. 213.
105. Maeterlinck, *Ruysbroeck and the Mystics*, pp. 26–7.
106. Pamela Robertson, p. 51.
107. (Cited in) Pamela Robertson, p. 51.
108. Billcliffe, *Charles Rennie Mackintosh*, p. 134.
109. Vergo, p. 28.
110. Maeterlinck, *The Plays of Maurice Maeterlinck*, p. 344.
111. Billcliffe, *Charles Rennie Mackintosh*, p. 167.
112. For Maurice Maeterlinck's interest in the Pre-Raphaelites, see William Sharp, '*The Princess Maleine*': 271.
113. Worth, *The Irish Drama*, p. 10.
114. William Sharp, 'Old World Japan': 516.
115. Sharp's attraction to Japanese culture was reciprocated: his 'Fiona Macleod' writings became popular in Japan in the 1920s and are still in print today; see Shimokusu.
116. Lennon, pp. xv–xvii.
117. Nally, pp. 149, 168.
118. Lennon, pp. 281, 283.
119. Zatlin, p. 26.
120. Watanabe, p. 161.
121. Wilde, *Plays, Prose Writings and Poems*, pp. 80–1.
122. Moore, p. 142.
123. Several critical pieces have treated Scottish *japonisme* but not in the context of cultural revivalism; these include Ono; Holt; Checkland, *Japan and Britain*, pp. 142–50; MacMillan; Suzuki; and Bruce.
124. Lennon, p. xviii.

125. Gardiner, *At the Edge of Empire*, p. 124.
126. Checkland and Checkland, p. 149.
127. Checkland, *Japan and Britain*, p. 22.
128. Checkland, *Britain's Encounter*, pp. 134, 141.
129. Checkland and Checkland, p. 160.
130. Gardiner, *At the Edge of Empire*, pp. 45–66, 153–4.
131. Checkland and Checkland, p. 23.
132. Checkland, *Japan and Britain*, p. 116.
133. Lovelace, p. 12.
134. Fowle, p. 66.
135. Murdoch, *The Renaissance*, p. 15.
136. 'Lecture on Japan', p. 4.
137. 'The Exhibition', p. 7.
138. Hornel, p. 11.
139. (Cited in) Sims-Williams, p. 102.
140. Atisha: 61.
141. For more on Stevenson and Japan, see Gardiner, 'Robert Louis Stevenson and the Meiji Enlightenment'.
142. Zatlin, p. 23.
143. (Cited in) Tanabe, p. 48.
144. For more on Stevenson's Davos illustrations, see Hill.
145. Robert Louis Stevenson, 'Byways': 9.
146. Robert Louis Stevenson, 'Yoshida-Torajiro': 329.
147. John Duncan, Notebook: Italy and France (c.1911) [National Library of Scotland: MS 6866/4], pp. 64–73.
148. William Sharp, *The Winged Destiny*, p. 196; William Sharp, *The Divine Adventure*, pp. 242–3.
149. Errington, pp. 52–3.
150. Duncan particularly admired the way Hornel painted kimonos; see Checkland, *Japan and Britain*, p. 150.
151. For a detailed consideration of Hornel's Japanese garden, see Holt.
152. Buchanan, 'Japanese Influences', p. 292.
153. Buchanan, *Mr Henry and Mr Hornel*, p. 9.
154. Frazer, pp. 597–8.
155. Billcliffe, *The Glasgow Boys*, p. 218.
156. Buchanan, 'Japanese Influences', p. 294.
157. Helland, p. 70.
158. Patrick Geddes, 'Aesthetics – on the utilitarian contempt, indifference and distrust of aesthetics', (n.d.) [Archives and Special Collections, University of Strathclyde: T-GED 5/3/70].
159. Mackintosh, 'Untitled Paper on Architecture', p. 196.
160. Mackintosh, 'Scotch Baronial Architecture', p. 51.
161. Frank Arneil Walker, pp. 36–7.
162. Mackintosh's Scottish notebook is reproduced in Grogan, pp. 9–46.
163. Buchanan, 'Japanese Influences', p. 298.

164. Frank Arneil Walker, p. 36.
165. Bruce, p. 28.
166. Tatarkowski, pp. 212–20.
167. Jones, p. 9.
168. Tatarkowski, p. 216.
169. The turrets for the Scotland Street School were most likely inspired by Mackintosh's sketch of Falkland Palace c.1901 [Hunterian Art Gallery: GLAHA 41423].
170. Mackintosh, 'Scotch Baronial Architecture', p. 63.
171. Patrick Geddes, Notes for a lecture to the Celtic Society (1897) [Strathclyde: T-GED 5/2/9].
172. Patrick Geddes, 'Aesthetics – on the utilitarian contempt, indifference and distrust of aesthetics' [Archives and Special Collections, University of Strathclyde: T-GED 5/3/70].

Chapter 3

Neo-Pagan Scotland: Fashioning Origins

While *fin-de-siècle* Scottish nation-building often relied on interrogating Scotland's deep-rooted cultural and racial divides, building international cultural bonds and defending the value of traditional cultures in the face of the 'uniformity' of modernity, Scottish writers and artists also actively participated in the process of myth-making, to define the nation's 'indigenous origins'.[1] The importance of myth-making to the construction of national identity has been foregrounded in recent decades by Anthony D. Smith's work on nationalism. Challenging 'dominant modernist orthodoxy' on nationalism,[2] Smith argues that national consciousness formation and sustenance are at least as reliant on symbolic resources, 'myths, memories, traditions, and symbols of ethnic heritage', as the institutions of modernity, industrialism and capitalism.[3] For Smith, these various facets of what he terms 'ethno-symbolism' create a shared cultural memory, which is central to the existence of the nation. Together, these symbolic resources forge an '*ethnie*' – an imagined community connected by shared memories and ancestry, a common understanding of their origin, and an association with a homeland (12–13). Smith is keen to highlight that these constructed memories and ideas of ancestry are not fixed: national communities evolve by rediscovering and reappropriating pasts and myths of descent. This reappropriation, he contends, is dictated by the socio-political imperatives of the time, where intellectuals 'furnish the community with "maps," both cognitive and territorial, and "moralities," both individual and collective, for its new destiny'.[4] Thus, in Smith's framing, myths of origin do not simply form nationalities but allow them to endure and adapt. Smith also argues that a key feature of a nation's 'ethno-symbolism' is a designated 'golden age' of heroism, one that binds people and helps 'regenerate' the community, although these golden ages too are adaptable and reflect the contemporary context.[5] Across the various facets of ethno-symbolism that Smith outlines, the importance of collectively associating with a past and a common origin to build and sustain the nation is stressed.

Smith's understandings of nation-building are provocative when considered in relation to Victorian Scotland. Colin Kidd has argued that Scotland's marked Celt–Saxon racial divide during the nineteenth century, discussed in Chapter 1, 'diluted the ethnocentric element which was such an important feature of nineteenth-century nationalisms'.[6] For Kidd, the inability to reconcile Scotland's racial divisions c.1780–1880 partly explains why Scottish nationalism was, in his view, 'inhibited' during this period – Scotland's *ethnie* was compromised. But, as we move towards the *fin de siècle*, when cultural revivalists were actively challenging the Celt–Saxon divide and hoping to promote more national cohesiveness, there was increased concern with the 'ethnocentric element' of nation-building in Scotland. This chapter considers how cultural revivalists hoping to defend Scottish identity and revive aspects of Scottish culture attempted to develop a national '*ethnie*' and embraced the rise of neo-paganism in the late nineteenth century to do so. The increasing enthusiasm for pagan mythologies and rituals was drawn from not only to help form a collection of symbols for Scotland, but to design imagined origins, rooted in heroes, that reflected cultural revivalists' desire to defend Scottish identity.

Across murals, paintings, prose writings and poetry in *fin-de-siècle* Scotland, we find cultural revivalists turning to Scotland's Celtic pagan inheritance. But, as the material treated in this chapter frequently demonstrates, they seldom turned to Scotland alone. As with cultural revivalist enthusiasm for *japonisme* and Belgian literature, discussed in the previous chapter, writers and artists who appropriated pagan origins and myths engaged in international colloquies to develop their national myths and symbolic resources – the recurrent fusing of Celtic and Hellenic motifs, highlighted throughout this chapter, attests to the internationalism of cultural revivalist attempts to define Scotland's national origins. Scottish cultural revivalism was seldom purely autochthonous. Indeed, cultural revivalists also commonly subverted autochthonism by highlighting Scotland's shared Celtic mythologies with Ireland, despite the fact that Celtic myths were often employed in tellingly different manners across the North Channel. In line with Smith's belief that myths and pasts are appropriated to suit each community's needs at a particular time, I argue here that the contrasting uses of Celtic pagan mythology in Scotland and Ireland reflect the differing accents of the two nations' constitutional and cultural concerns at the *fin de siècle*.

Along with demonstrating the ways in which neo-pagan myths and ideas supported Scottish cultural revivalism in the works of Patrick Geddes, John Duncan, Mona Caird, Robert Louis Stevenson and 'Fiona Macleod', this chapter also considers the resistance to neo-paganism in the work of the poet John Davidson, who was vigorously opposed the Scottish cultural revival (as well as the Scottish and Irish Home Rule campaigns) too. Davidson's desire to resist the cultural revival is further confirmation of its presence and imprint at the *fin de siècle*, but his work also reveals the ways in which cultural revivalism and neo-paganism became associated in the eyes of those who wanted to style both concepts as anti-modern returns to the past.

Neo-Paganism and National Identity in the British Isles

The neo-paganism that developed in the late nineteenth century across Europe was symptomatic of several socio-political issues associated with modernity. Christopher Wood argues that various peoples looked to antiquity in the hope of finding alternative life-styles and social models to counter 'the ugliness, materialism and industrialism of their own age'.[7] Wood here portrays the return to antiquity as a subversive or escapist act, which it often was, but Victorians were also returning to Ancient Rome and Greece for 'paradigms and reference points' for imperialism, industry and politics.[8] The pre-Christian world was used by some to support, and by others to combat, the Victorian bourgeoisie's narratives of progress, civilisation and cultural decline.

Nevertheless, neo-paganism was often framed as a disruptive return to the past at the *fin de siècle*. For instance, William Barry, who identified differing engagements with antiquity in his 1891 essay 'Neo-Paganism', labelled the subversive appreciation of the pre-Christian past 'neo-pagan'. In contrast to those who looked to antiquity to help advance science, order and the progress of civilisation, Barry believed that there was a group of dissidents who turned to antiquity to appreciate the 'sensual curiosity', passion, intoxication and revelry of the Greeks and the Romans, and he labelled this group 'neo-pagans'.[9] Barry believed that this 'sect of modern heathens' (294) were 'opposed to the intellect no less than the moral development which Christian civilization has pursued' (292–3). In his framing, neo-paganism was not simply an interest in the pagan past, but a *subversive* interest in it – a desire to displace, replace or complicate civilised, modern, Christian society. Barry's neo-pagans are concerned not only with attacking modernity, but also with the teleological understanding of the progress of history: rather than believing society progressively improves through a civilising process, neo-pagans hold that 'all varieties of civilization since the Greek are steps on a decline' (285). As such, Barry firmly associates neo-paganism with another *fin-de-siècle* phenomenon that questioned historical progress: decadence. He wrote that the 'disciples of the school known as Decadent, though by no means classic in a noble sense, are unquestionably Pagan' (293). Barry primarily associates these decadent neo-pagans with France, and attempts to distinguish England and the German 'Teuton' from neo-paganism, making only brief reference to Swinburne, Symonds and Pater in the context of neo-paganism (297).

Barry's association of neo-paganism with dissidence is confirmed by the number of *fin-de-siècle* figures that were dissatisfied with, or alienated by, their contemporary culture and who turned to the pagan world. Not only did classical antiquity provide alternatives to Christian belief but it also supported other forms of socio-political dissidence. Jennifer Hallett has argued that neo-paganism informed Edward Carpenter's socialism, for instance,[10] and it provided ideological structures to legitimise same-sex love, as in the case of Symonds, Carpenter, Crowley, Levy, R. Murray Gilchrist and Forster.[11] As this chapter will demonstrate, new women were also turning to the pagan past to further their critiques of hegemonic Victorian gender hierarchies. In both literature and lifestyle, several figures used the pagan past to authenticate, or provide a historical basis for, their unorthodox ideas, styles and customs that subverted Victorian middle-class ideals.

One use of neo-paganism, to legitimise and authenticate potentially disruptive ideas, was its role in the development of cultural revivals and nationalist political campaigns. The importance of returning to pre-Christian culture to define and defend national identities has been identified across European cultures (as in Owen Davies's consideration of Lithuania and Mary Helen Thuente's exploration of Celtic pagan folklore as a key resource for Irish nationalists, including Lady Wilde and Douglas Hyde),[12] and this was similarly the case in Scotland. Like cultural revivalists in Wales and Ireland, Scottish cultural revivalists looked to the Celtic paganism to authenticate myths of origin. This was not a difficult endeavour at the *fin de siècle*, when several anthropologists were casting Scotland as a site of 'residual culture', to use Raymond Williams's term, where aspects of pagan lifestyle were believed to remain active. Numerous studies and articles were published on Scotland's continuing, active paganism at the *fin de siècle*, with titles including 'Survivals of Paganism in Foula', 'Still Pagan Scotland', 'A Remnant of Pagan Scotland' and 'Some Survivals of Paganism in Scotland'. Although J. G. Frazer's *The Golden Bough: A Study in Comparative Religion* (1890) states that 'the curtain must soon descend on savagery forever' – a stadialist view – he nevertheless identified the presence of various continuing pagan customs and beliefs across Scotland too.[13] These studies made it easier for cultural revivalists to explore the nation's pagan past and to help build connections between Scotland's pagan mythology and its contemporary national community.

This understanding of the Celtic nations as sites of 'residual culture' was endorsed not only by anthropologists, but also by authors. In several *fin-de-siècle* writings, we find England portrayed as a nation lacking a native paganism, where English characters can experience paganism only through it being imported from, or through their travelling to, Celtic nations. The association of England with pagan absence is found in several writings by aesthetes or proto-aesthetes, which tend to portray England as too industrialised to sustain a pagan energy. In *Culture and Anarchy*, Matthew Arnold argued that English culture (especially after the Reformation) was defined by Christian Hebraism, which foregrounded discipline and self-sacrifice over the that pagan Hellenism that celebrated the 'spontaneity of consciousness'.[14] Pater also found England removed from, and inferior to, antiquity: Sparta was an 'idealised' England for him. In his framing, Greece represented what England could be, were it not 'weakened by the industrial revolution', as Richard Jenkyns argues.[15] Wilde similarly dramatises the differences and distance between England and the pagan gods, as in his poem 'Panthea'. When commenting on the dwelling of the pagan gods, the speaker of the poem states, 'There never does that dreary north-wind blow / Which leaves our English forests bleak and bare' (ll. 61–2).[16] In his poem 'Before a Crucifix' (1871), Swinburne, who frequently used his poetry to escape from England to a Mediterranean pagan past, perhaps goes furthest in portraying the 'rottenness and rust' of an oppressive industrialism, from which Christianity offered little reprieve.[17] For several cultural figures in England, there was a longing for the pagan past, a longing that acknowledged the fact that England had become too industrial and commercial to connect to it. For many *fin-de-siècle* writers, England was the land where 'the Gods are dead'.[18]

Related to this association of England with pagan absence was the belief that the pagan past could be experienced by the English only if it was imported (often from the 'Celtic nations') or if they travelled from England. In Arthur Machen's *The Great God Pan*, initially published by *The Whirlwind* in 1890 and subsequently by the Bodley Head in 1894, Pan is portrayed as living in a remote wood, which, although not stated, is almost certainly in Wales. Not only do the initial descriptions of the country surrounding Dr Raymond's house and the village Mary lives in correspond to Machen's descriptions of Wales in the introduction – which he tells us provided the 'fountains of [his] story'[19] – but the final fragments reveal that Helen (the daughter of Mary and Pan) lived in Caermaen. A threatening paganism is imported into England through Mary's encounter with Pan in Wales. Machen's 'The Novel of the Black Seal' (1895) confirms the association of Wales with paganism. In this story, the protagonist, Professor Gregg, takes a house near Caermaen, a land 'more unknown to the Englishmen than the very heart of Africa',[20] to investigate a black stone. There, Gregg discovers the existence of the 'little people' of Celtic legend, who are associated with 'ancient Babylon'.[21] In Machen's work, Wales is represented as a site of ethnic preservation and continuing paganism, which is juxtaposed with England.

This idea was replayed in the Edwardian period, when it was even more firmly believed (as Christopher Wood notes) that 'the old gods were dead'.[22] Forster's short stories dramatise the inability of paganism and English identity to co-habit in the same space, unlike in Italy and Ireland. In 'The Story of a Panic' (1904), set in Italy, a particularly priggish Englishman, the narrator Mr Tytler, cannot understand or believe that the young boy, Eustace, has been occupied by a pagan spirit, which enters him amongst the woods. The boy's experiences are simply dismissed as symptomatic of the 'Southern mind'.[23] The man of English nationality refuses to understand, or is unable to identify with, paganism in this story. These ideas are revisited in Forster's 'Other Kingdom' (1909), where the English male (Mr Worters) seeks to 'civilise' the copse he has acquired, Other Kingdom, for his fiancée, Miss Beaumont, with paths and bridges. However, Miss Beaumont, who has been brought back from Ireland and defends learning the Classics, rejects this. Miss Beaumont not only is more closely connected to the environment than the other characters but she can physically fuse with the trees: she disappears, spiritually and materially immersed within them, by the end of the story. Forster's short stories most clearly exhibit the proximity of Catholic and Celtic peoples to paganism and render England's divorce from it. Much like D. H. Lawrence's 'Pan in America' (1936), which argues that old Pan is 'still alive' in the Rocky Mountains of New Mexico, paganism is associated with locales beyond England in these Forster stories.[24]

The association of Celtic territories with survivals of pagan lifestyle and mythology 'othered' these nations, highlighting their (at least partial) dissonance from industrial, commercialised modernity. The notion that Celtic locales were preserves of a supposedly past 'stage' of historical development was often used to marginalise them, but it also helped assert Scotland, Wales and Ireland's difference from England. As Barry Cunliffe notes, the '"Celtic spirit" stood in defiance of the centralising imperatives of London and Paris'.[25] In turning to their pagan inheritance, Celtic revivalists not only developed their own particular myths of origin and collective symbolism to unify and define their nations, but also asserted their difference from their larger neighbour, which, as we have seen, was not infrequently encoded as disconnected from paganism at the *fin de siècle*.

The Ramsay Garden Common Room Murals

One of the most striking examples of Scottish cultural revivalism intersecting with the dissident neo-paganism that Barry identifies is the Ramsay Garden common room mural sequence in Edinburgh, executed by the painter John Duncan. While Duncan painted these murals, the sequence was largely designed and overseen by Patrick Geddes; Geddes had founded University Hall in 1887 (Edinburgh's first student halls of residence) with the aim of encouraging 'the Art of living sociably, of how to behave as a social unit', as one artist who had lived at University Hall for two winters, James Cadenhead, put it.[26] Ramsay Garden was the latest of University Hall's residential projects, which was built around, and incorporated, Allan Ramsay's house, Ramsay Lodge, by Edinburgh Castle's esplanade. Like *The Evergreen* magazine, which was inspired by Ramsay's 1724 cultural revivalist poetry anthology of the same name, Ramsay Garden and its decorations bore the mark of Scottish cultural revivalism. Although the project incorporated a feature associated with English university life – residential student living – the Ramsay Garden buildings themselves were designed by Stewart Henbest Capper and Sydney Mitchell 'in revival of the old Scottish Domestic architecture so characteristic of Old Edinburgh', with staired towers, crow-stepped gabling, harled stone and 'red freestone dressings'.[27] As a Scottish domestic fortress standing alongside Edinburgh Castle, the complex shocked 'the devotees of drab'.[28] Cultural revivalism is also clearly at work in one of the central rooms of Ramsay Garden, which Geddes intended to be elaborately designed with Duncan's murals, which would feature key figures of Scottish history and education (from the warrior of Celtic mythology, Cuchullin, to Charles Darwin), interspersed with Celtic decorations by Helen Hay, Helen Baxter and Marion Mason, who had each contributed decorations to *The Evergreen*.[29] Taken together, the range of figures presented in the mural told an unorthodox narrative of Scottish history, featuring a unique collection of heroes and symbols for the nation, which reflected the particularities of Geddes's cultural revivalism.

The Ramsay Garden mural scheme is deeply complex: it attempts to furnish Scotland with mythological origins and a collection of heroes, as well as posing a challenge to hegemonic Victorian narratives of progress, but it also expresses enthusiasm for science and industry. To understand the logic of this mural scheme and the form of cultural revivalism that it promotes, we first need to grasp Geddes's relationship to Victorian modernity. In his writings and talks, Geddes continually stressed that commercial, industrial, urban society was not superior to subsistence lifestyles and highlighted the continuing dependence of present-day industries on the ancient past. In one talk, he critiques those who style Neolithic miners as 'barbarians', and instead highlights the fact that they were the 'essential founders of most of the main elements of our present civilization'.[30] He repeatedly reclaims the significance of non-commercial aspects of society: the hunter is no 'rude survivor of primitive society, but a type of permanent and increasing significance in history' (66). Geddes even makes a direct attack on stadialist thinkers who break society and history up into distinct phases, mocking their 'bookish habit to speak of [. . .] successive "stages" [. . .]. And these too simply as "phases" before the present predominance of the industrial and commercial urban order' (68). He strongly rebukes this stadialist vantage by reminding us that 'all these fundamental occupations we have always with us' (68). For Geddes, 'the peaceful agricultural world outlives all', and this fact symbolises 'the victory of the peasant' (69) – a sentiment that would resurface during the later Scottish Renaissance in Lewis Grassic Gibbon's *Sunset Song* (1932). Geddes's celebration of the peasantry resonates with Smith's belief that the peasant is 'sacred' for ethno-symbolists, as the peasantry embodies the continuity of a nation's ethnicity, its 'myth of descent'.[31] It is no surprise that Geddes and Branford commended the early twentieth-century Scout movement for reviving the 'primitive hunting life' and that Geddes wanted his children to learn from 'the stones of the common people' over public schooling.[32] Commenting on Scotland's megalithic peoples and their culture, he similarly stated his desire for today's children to grow up 'to express these traditions [. . .] within this modern civilization which absorbs us all'.[33] For Geddes, it was important that modernity was not imagined as superior, or in opposition, to the past or rural life; for him, they were all mutually dependent and synthetic, which prompted him to look to the past and activate its presence in modernity. Throughout his work, we find what Smith terms 'retrogressions' to counter 'unilinear evolutionism'.[34]

Thus, Geddes – the botanist, biologist, sociologist and town planner – was not opposed to modernity itself, but to a type of modern thinking that failed to appreciate the value of tradition and cultural legacy, one that simply privileged the 'commercial urban order'. For Geddes, art – crucially, public art – could play a key role in overcoming modernity's reliance on commerce and self-interest, and help usher in an alternative social model rooted in 'mutual co-operation [. . .] wealth as weal'.[35] In his essay, 'Political Economy and Fine Art', which opened the second volume of *The Scottish Art Review* in 1889, Geddes attacks the private ownership of art, panels that 'flap idly upon rich men's walls',[36] which he believed nourished 'high living and plain thinking'.[37] Inspired by John Ruskin's writings,[38] he proposes an alternative principle: 'private simplicity and public magnificence' (3). These pithy statements distil Geddes's belief that society (especially the wealthy in society) should focus on investing in elaborate, civic artworks that would enrich the public realm and better the civic economy; he expressed his hope that Lawrence Alma-Tadema, Frederic Leighton and George Frederic Watts might soon be put to task executing civic murals.[39] In 'Political Economy and Fine Art', Geddes commends eighteenth-century France for understanding art's 'special importance to the national wealth' (3). Art provided permanent, storable, valuable products that bolstered national and municipal economies: 'thus, and thus only, grew rich the great old cities of the world' (3). In a direct refutation of Adam Smith's *The Wealth of Nations*, which he considered 'dismal science' (3), Geddes wrote that 'the wealth of nations must commence once more with the permanent treasure of the public, not be everlastingly measured in private winnings and public debt' (4). This promotion of public art could be best facilitated, in Geddes's view, by turning to Celtic design, which he believed was a 'democratic' and 'costless' art; indeed, in one of his unpublished essays, he imagines how the Celtic cross might displace 'the tombstone of commerce'.[40] His association of Celtic culture with democratic art may help explain why the price of *The Evergreen* was kept relatively low for such a high-quality production, which inevitably made the magazine financially unsustainable.[41] For Geddes, looking to traditional artforms like Celtic decoration to develop valuable public art was a means of challenging the facets of modernity that he abhorred, principally the ignorance of the past and the privileging of self-interest.

Geddes's resistance to what he termed 'paleotechnic finance' (modern economics that prioritised competition)[42] led him to develop an interest in *fin-de-siècle* decadence. As I have demonstrated elsewhere, Geddes's relationship with decadence was deeply ambivalent.[43] While he critiques the 'all-pervading "Decadence"' in 'The Scots Renascence',[44] his other contributions to *The Evergreen* reveal a more complex engagement with decadence. In a draft plan for the second volume of *The Evergreen* ('Autumn'), which was circulated to prospective contributors, Geddes suggests potential essay topics:

> In Section III Autumn in the World may probably be a historic paper dealing with Fruition in history, with the evolution of Cities or the like – while the modern and cosmopolitan note may be represented in an essay dealing with the Decadence treated critically yet appreciatively, as not only expressing the decay of old things but containing also the seed of the new.[45]

Geddes appears to have ended up contributing this essay himself, giving it the title 'The Sociology of Autumn'; in it, he expresses his admiration for decadent artists' ability to detach themselves from mercantile 'modern life'. Although he critiques the 'inaction' associated with decadence and *ennui*, he nevertheless believes that the decadents' distance from 'Philistine' modernity is something that should be harnessed to help critique the current state of society and 'imagine it as it might be'.[46] Decadence is portrayed not as an end in itself, but as a phase that may lead to cultural revival. As Geddes and Branford put it in the 'Prefatory Note' for *The Evergreen*'s 'Autumn' volume, we must 'pass, through Decadence, towards Renascence'.[47] Appropriately, Geddes concludes 'The Sociology of Autumn' by stating, 'Thanks then, and even honour, to the art and science of the Decadence' (38). Geddes's critical but appreciative attitude towards decadence explains why some critics believed *The Evergreen* was a Scottish equivalent of *The Yellow Book*, and others thought it was a Scottish rebuttal of it: *The Evergreen* was both at once.

Geddes's resistance to aspects of industrial modernity, his belief in the potential of civic art to overcome self-interested Victorian liberalism, and his Scottish cultural revivalism all underpin the design for the Ramsay Garden common room murals. The room presents a sequence of Scottish and Celtic figures, chronologically arranged, that encircles the room's four walls. The sequence begins with the Celtic pagan warriors, Cuchullin and Fionn, followed by 'The Taking of Excalibur', a painting featuring King Arthur, Merlin and Queen Morgan Le Fay (figures Geddes was keen to claim as Scottish, as discussed in Chapter 5). St Mungo, Johannes Scotus Erigena, Michael Scot and the Admirable Crichton are then represented, and the final five panels focus on modern figures: John Napier, James Watt, Walter Scott, Charles Darwin (whose attendance at Edinburgh University justifies his place in this collection of Scottish and Celtic heroes) and Lord Lister. As a collection of notable male figures through time, the scheme is not dissimilar to William Hole's phallocentric mural procession of Scottish historical figures in the Scottish National Portrait Gallery, but the figures Geddes selects and the Celtic decorations throughout the room make it very distinctive. Ever modest, Geddes believed the scheme formed 'the vastest and most elaborate Celtic illumination in the modern world',[48] and it was highly consistent with his belief in creating elaborate civic art to overcome private property. As Geddes stated, 'if there is literal gilding within a building, it will free its occupants from the lust for further gold'.[49]

Two of the dissident notes in this mural scheme are its critiques of historical progress and centralisation. These critiques are both implied in the inscription over the door that students would have entered the room from: 'As it hath been / So it shall be.' As Murdo Macdonald notes, this is an adaptation of a quotation from a poem attributed to St Columba, 'But ere the world come to an end / Iona shall be as it was,'[50] which was reproduced in Patrick Geddes and Colleagues' volume, *Songs and Tales of St Columba and His Age*, and also in Geddes's essay, 'The Scots Renascence'. Iona – known as the origin of Celtic crosses and for the production of the Book of Kells in the ninth century – was championed by Geddes as a remote, small island that had nevertheless made a major contribution to world culture. Iona embodied the notion that culture did not have to rely on a metropolis or centralisation, which Geddes neatly summed up in a remark that he recurrently uttered: 'it is not for London to educate Iona; it is for Iona to educate London'.[51] Alongside subtly imbuing the room with Geddes's resistance to centralisation, the quotation is also a challenge to teleological, unilinear understandings of progress. The quotation implies that the past can return and highlights the circularity of history. Bearing the Iona reference in mind, there is also a suggestion that the Celtic past (and Celtic cultural importance) specifically can return. By placing this quotation alongside the first painting in the sequence – of the Celtic warrior, Cuchullin – Geddes encourages us to consider the reanimation of Celtic culture.

The Awakening of Cuchullin (Plate 6) itself strikes a dissident neo-pagan note. The painting depicts the pagan warrior, Cuchullin, who stirs after being urged to sleep by his father, Lugh. Resembling a Pre-Raphaelite 'stunner', with a thick neck and long, flowing red hair, Cuchullin is both aestheticised and sexualised here. But while this aestheticised, languid moment dilutes Cuchullin's military potency, Celtic resistance is nevertheless inferred through the invocation of the 'sleeping hero' tradition.[52] In their study of Scottish folklore, Jennifer Westwood and Sophia Kingshill's note that 'such "sleeping heroes" are usually said to wait in enchanted slumber until the day they are needed to save their land from some enemy'.[53] Several Scottish Celtic revivalists were invested in this concept of the sleeping hero who may return to defend their people: Geddes references it with regards to King Arthur in 'The Scots Renascence' (137), as does William Sharp in *Green Fire*, where it is noted that 'Arthur the Celtic hero would come again out of Flath-innis, and redeem his lost, receding peoples.'[54] By invoking this context of the 'sleeping hero' that arouses to defend its threatened people, this painting (in a cultural revivalist room) subtly suggests that a Scottish defence is awakening. Indeed, Smith argues that the image of 'reawakening' is common to *ethnie*-building projects.[55] And the fire and light motifs that run throughout the murals, which Clare Willsdon has identified, are representative of this revitalisation too.[56] The painting is by no means equivalent to the images of Cuchullin that were propagated by some Irish Celtic revivalists, such as Patrick Pearse, who used the Cuchullin myth to arouse Irish militancy (discussed in Chapter 5). The fact that Duncan's image of Cuchullin arousing from sleep is foregrounded, rather than the mid-battle scenes in the background, makes the image less threatening and emphasises Duncan's and Geddes's stress on the defensive, rather than the combative. Indeed, diffusing combativeness is also evident in the next painting in the sequence, *The Combat of Fionn*, as the two competitors represented, Fionn and Swaran, would dine together as friends post combat. But *The Awakening of Cuchullin* nevertheless embodies a desire to defend the nation. Although Scottish cultural revivalists like Geddes shunned 'militant nationality',[57] pagan myth was not used here to represent 'a fading civilization', as Murray Pittock argues.[58] There is clear discontent over the position of Scottish and Celtic culture, and Geddes and Duncan draw on a Celtic pagan figure to help visually distil their resistance to the marginalisation of the Celt.

While this mural sequence presents a collection of Scottish historical figures and heroes in a bid to highlight Scottish strength and achievement throughout history – and to articulate Scotland's Celtic, pagan origins – the scheme does not draw on paganism to endorse an autochthonous image of the Scottish race. As John Morrison notes, in drawing from Celtic pagan myths that were shared with Ireland, Duncan and Geddes did not 'simplistically parade Scotland's supposed Celtic heritage as a mark of difference and therefore singularity'.[59] Typical of Geddes's projects, he was keen to style Scotland as a European and international nation and to highlight commonalities with other traditions. Aligning Scotland with Ireland also helped to endorse a Celtic counter-hegemony to England's dominance, much like the counter-hegemonies that Sharp was keen to nurture through his Belgian-inspired work, discussed in Chapter 2. And the fact that an Englishman, Charles Darwin, also appears in one of the later panels is further evidence of the open notion of Scottish nationality that this scheme promotes: there is a concerted effort to resist autochthonous paganism in this scheme.

The interest in Celtic pagan mythology in Geddes's circle was by no means limited to this mural scheme. It was complemented by *Lyra Celtica: An Anthology of Representative Celtic Poetry* (1896), edited by Elizabeth Sharp and published by Patrick Geddes and Colleagues, which includes ancient poems featuring pagan figures, including Fionn, Cuchullin, Maev, Deirdre and Ossian. Elizabeth Sharp chose to include these ancient poems under the one category, 'Ancient Irish and Scottish', which again demonstrates the desire to evoke shared mythical origins with Ireland. The company's publication of Macpherson's *Ossian* (edited by William Sharp and also published in 1896) is a further example of Geddes's wider interest in distributing literature about the lives of such figures as Fionn and Ossian.

But Celtic paganism was not the only form of paganism that Geddes's circle was concerned with. In the Ramsay Garden common room we find references to Mediterranean paganisms, further diminishing any autochthonous element of the mural scheme. Here, in the 'Athens of the North', Hellenic and Celtic pagan figures confront each other. Towards the end of the mural sequence, there are two panels devoted to James Watt (Plate 7) and Charles Darwin (Plate 8), which were completed by Duncan only in 1927 when a donor was found to support finishing the scheme.[60] Both of these scientists are placed alongside a pagan figure: Watt is pictured in front of Prometheus, who 'is seen bringing light from heaven for the service of man', and Darwin sits, listening to Pan play his pipes.[61] Unlike many who turned to paganism as an alternative to Victorian modernity, this sequence does not pit paganism against industry and science. For Geddes, the past and modernity could complement each other, a sentiment that is reflected in these murals. For instance, Geddes was particularly keen to celebrate the rise of electricity, which he portrayed as a fairy godmother in his essay 'Cinderella', for helping to liberate women from hard labour.[62] In the James Watt panel, modern energy and paganism meet. Throughout his writings, Geddes heralds Watt as 'a second Prometheus', capable of creating energy and teaching 'its applications to a thousand other purposes'.[63] In 'The Valley Section', he also claimed that Watt was akin to the 'primal' woodsman and was 'the perfect linking of the old industrial order with the new' (66). As in this mural panel, Geddes links pagan origins and industrial modernity in order to subvert teleological notions of 'progress' and instead highlight constancy and continuity throughout history. Duncan's style further complements this return of the primal as it was influenced by the French muralist, Pierre Puvis de Chavannes, who often represented figures in a simplistic, vitalist manner with sharp lines, a restrained colour palette and little illusionistic detail – a primitivist style that was admired by decadent figures, such as Joséphin Péladan, and vehemently resisted by anti-decadents, like Max Nordau.[64] Duncan's mural also embodies John Stuart Blackie's desire to fuse Greek mythology with the 'modern gentleman'.[65] As such, these murals challenge the view that modernity necessitates a break with the past and instead highlight the importance of traditional cultures and primalism to modernity – a recurrent feature of Scottish revivalist art.

This subversion of teleology also underpins the appearance of Charles Darwin and Pan on the penultimate panel of the mural scheme. Geddes was a correspondent with Darwin, and Darwin even wrote two letters of recommendation on Geddes's behalf when he applied to science chairs in Scotland,[66] but Geddes was nevertheless a critic of the concept of 'survival of the fittest', which he believed promoted competition and self-interest.[67] Challenging the association of Darwin with competitive evolutionism and disenchantment, Duncan and Geddes style Darwin, like Pan, as an embodiment of 'the All'.[68] Darwin is cast here as a theorist of inheritance and relatedness, of the inability to separate the past from the present. As Duncan wrote when describing the mural, Pan symbolised the 'unified whole [. . .] half brute, half man', and Darwin is portrayed as reactivating this 'unified whole'.[69] By highlighting how paganism can inform contemporary science, Geddes and Duncan's return to antiquity resembles the 'noble' engagement with the pagan past that Barry identifies: using antiquity to help improve modernity. But these murals also subvert the notion of historical progress and civilisation, which Barry associates with the ignoble neo-paganism. Historical circularity, rather than progress, is endorsed in these murals; pagan figures do not just inspire modernity, they are capable of returning to and confronting the commercial, competitive order.[70]

Together, these images form a cultural revivalist cycle of Scottish and Celtic heroes, both mythic and educational. But the scheme does not simply highlight great historical figures and Scotland's contribution to the development of education. By beginning the scheme with pagan origins; recounting the lasting, continuing imprint of paganism in contemporary culture and modernity; and suggesting an awakening defensiveness of Celtic culture, Geddes creates a scheme that asserts a tone of resistance. While the scheme bears similarities to Yeats's desire to build a 'common symbolism' for Ireland, as well as his interest in 'return[ing] to an originary, pre-Colonial Irishness', the form of resistance presented in the Ramsay Garden murals is not anti-colonial or anti-Union.[71] Indeed, some of the other wall decorations at Ramsay Garden include the heraldry of three kingdoms that comprise the United Kingdom. But, equally, there are other decorations at Ramsay Garden where England's heraldry and symbolism are omitted: on several occasions, Scotland's thistle, for instance, is linked with heraldic emblems associated with France (the fleur-de-lis) and Ireland (the shamrock), and England's rose is neglected. Such gestures 'severed the union of the flowers' – an idea that created anxieties for some unionists in the period – and asserted Scotland's own engagements and interactions with Europe.[72] In his interrogation of centralisation to London, Geddes resisted the notion that Scotland had to speak to the world via London, and this scheme embodies both the assertion of Scottish nationality and its own European connections. Thus, while in no way attempting to undermine the existence of the United Kingdom, we should be careful about interpreting the murals as 'inclusively British' or as 'not mark[ing] a change in Scottish attitudes to nationhood', as John Morrison claims.[73] They certainly look beyond Scotland but they nevertheless reflect growing anxieties in *fin-de-siècle* Scotland, relying on pagan figures and motifs to reassert Scottish and Celtic culture.

Fiona Macleod and *The Pagan Review*

Perhaps the most popular phenomenon of the Scottish Celtic Revival was the literature penned by an elusive figure, 'Fiona Macleod', which proved to be a commercial hit. 'Fiona Macleod' was a pseudonym developed by Geddes's colleague, William Sharp, and many of 'her' writings were published by Patrick Geddes and Colleagues in high-quality volumes, featuring stunning gilt decorations. But Macleod was much more than a pseudonym: Sharp created an entire identity and history for Macleod. Macleod was often styled as Sharp's cousin, who lived in remote parts of the Highlands and Islands, and he cast himself as her literary representative, even arranging her press conferences (which, of course, had to be cancelled at the last minute). As he confessed in a letter to his wife, he felt Fiona Macleod was a person in her own right: 'W.S. and F.M. are becoming two persons – often married in mind and one nature, but often absolutely distinct.'[74] Maintaining his secret dual life, which few were privy to until his death in 1905, proved exhausting for Sharp.

Criticism on the formation of the Fiona Macleod identity has noted various influences, including Sharp's participation in esoteric societies and his indebtedness to his muse, Edith Wingate Rinder,[75] to whom his first Macleod novel, *Pharais* (1894), was dedicated.[76] But some of the most provocative criticism has argued that the development of the Macleod identity was a result of Sharp's own 'sexual tensions'.[77] There is certainly evidence to support the fact that Sharp did not see himself as singularly male. For instance, he acknowledged that 'in some things I am more a woman than a man',[78] a statement that resembles one by another Celtic revivalist who wrote under a pseudonym that some interpreted as female, George Russell ('Æ'), who stated in a letter to Yeats: 'perhaps [. . .] I am half a woman inside'.[79] Observers of Sharp similarly noted his gender fluidity: his secretary, Lilian Rea, implicitly compared him to Hermaphroditus when she noted that 'in him seemed to live again the child of Hermes and Aphrodite'.[80] Some have even claimed that Sharp dressed as a woman to write the Macleod texts.[81] The fluidity and duality of Sharp's gender are reflected in his recounting of a dream to Yeats's friends, in which he featured as a woman who made love to a male incarnation of Fiona Macleod.[82] He would also occasionally write as a fusion of the two identities, under the hybrid name 'Wilfion'. Sharp's various expressions of gender fluidity have prompted Terry L. Meyers to examine whether they were indicative of a repressed sexuality crisis.[83] Meyers is right to note that the formation of the Fiona identity is (at least partly) a reflection of Sharp's interest in gender fluidity and an unsettling of the binary between masculinity and femininity. But rather than using Sharp's expressions of gender fluidity as a springboard to speculate on his sexuality, I propose here that it is more fruitful to consider Sharp's concern with gender in relation to cultural and political debates at the *fin de siècle*. Sharp's transgression of gender divides informs not only his proto-feminism and neo-paganism, but also his role in the Scottish Celtic Revival.

The Fiona Macleod writings are set almost exclusively in the Highlands and Islands of Scotland and they announce themselves as not only Celtic revivalist but also neo-pagan. In *The Washer of the Ford* (1896), published by Geddes, Macleod utters her desire to reclaim the 'pagan sentiment', 'the old barbaric emotion', to overcome the uniformity of modernity and 'bastard utilitarianism'.[84] In writing the vast majority of his Celtic revivalist works through his female heteronym, critics have read the Macleod identity as a facet of Sharp's Arnoldian Celticism, a Celticism that some Celtic revivalists found patronising for endorsing the idea that the Celt was feminine, intuitive, emotional and relatively illogical in comparison to the Saxon,[85] as discussed in Chapter 1. Sharp himself encourages us to read his work in the context of Arnoldian Celticism: in his introduction to *Lyra Celtica*, he frequently draws on Arnold to highlight the ways in which Celtic culture can contribute, and has contributed, to Saxon culture, a project that Daniel Williams labels Celtic contributionism.[86] Sharp's 'contributionism' in *Lyra Celtica* is rooted in his defeatist attitude. Quoting Macleod, he argues that the only hope for the preservation of Celtic culture is in its influence on Saxon culture: 'the Celt falls, but his spirit rises in the heart and brain of the Anglo-Celtic peoples'.[87] This defeatism chimes with the introduction to *The Sin-Eater*, where Macleod styles the Celt as having 'reached his horizon' with 'no shore beyond',[88] and in *Pharais* (1894), which proleptically elegises Celtic identity, symbolised by the splitting of a boat named Fionnaghal. Sharp's 'cultural necrophilia', as Murdo Macdonald terms it,[89] along with his belief that the only future for Celticism lies in its potential to enrich English or Saxon culture, incensed some of Sharp's fellow Celtic revivalists, especially those across the North Channel. George Russell, who told Yeats that he had 'declared war on Fiona Macleod', wrote that 'she glories in the name Britisher and wants us to incarnate in England'.[90] One can only imagine Russell's response, had he read Sharp's unpublished poem, 'West Britain: An

Appeal', in which Sharp not only attacks Irish nationalists, but condemns their attempts to 'degrade the might of England':[91]

> Shall this foul shame be yours, shall this foul wrong
> Be done by you, West Britons, kith and kin?
> Shall the red flames of civil war wave long
> Athwart your isle? Think well ere ye begin. (ll. 23–6)

This poem never acknowledges the 'West Britons' as Irish: it is an assimilationist representation that styles the Irish as British. The 'English' nationality is encoded throughout as noble, strong and masculine (defending female England) while the Irish are violent pillagers, who would 'seize [England's] greatness with rebellious rape' (l. 8). This performance of both British and English nationalism was not limited to Sharp's unpublished notes either: anticipating T. S. Eliot's dismissal of Scottish literature as a field, Sharp noted that 'there is, for us all, only one English literature. All else is provincial or dialectic.' This statement from the Macleod essay, 'Celtic', which also professed his pride in being British and his opposition to 'pseudo-nationalism', was especially abhorred by Russell.[92]

Based on the above quotations, it is easy to see why several critics have labelled the Macleod writings as 'instinctive[ly]' anti-nationalist (even if Sharp's British/English nationalism in 'West Britain' complicates this).[93] But to represent the Macleod writings solely through this lens would leave us with a partial understanding of them. As was demonstrated in Chapter 2, Sharp's views were seldom consistent: he did distance himself from national defence and revival efforts when writing under his own name, but he also made innovative contributions to those efforts (both Scottish and Irish) and expressed his opposition to the processes of centralisation and cultural homogenisation. This inconsistency was no different in the case of Fiona Macleod. While the Celticism of the Fiona Macleod writings often embodied twilight rather than revivalism, and even promoted Saxon and English culture at the expense of Highland and Scottish culture, some of the Macleod writings were also deeply critical of the treatment of Scottish Highlanders and aimed to defend and preserve Celtic mythology; Mark Williams has demonstrated that the Macleod writings were invested in expanding and enriching Scotland's Celtic myths and deities too.[94] In *The Winged Destiny*, Macleod adopts a far more revivalist and defensive stance when criticising the 'depopulation' of the Highlands and resisting 'what in bitter unconscious irony is called the civilising factor [. . . the] crushing curse of a growing materialism in Scotland; the

Plate 1 Margaret Macdonald Mackintosh, *The Mysterious Garden* (1911). National Galleries of Scotland. Purchased with help from The Art Fund 2011.

Plate 2 John Duncan, *The Glaive of Light* (1897). University of Dundee Museum Services.

Plate 3 John Duncan, *St Bride* (1913). National Galleries of Scotland. Purchased 1946.

Plate 4 E. A. Hornel and George Henry, *The Druids – Bringing in the Mistletoe* (1890). © CSG CIC Glasgow Museums and Libraries Collection.

Plate 5 Utagawa Hiroshige, *Maple Trees at Tsuten Bridge* (c.1834). © The Trustees of the British Museum.

Plate 6 John Duncan, *The Awakening of Cuchullin* (c.1895). Historic Environment Scotland.

Plate 7 John Duncan, *James Watt* (c.1927). Historic Environment Scotland.

Plate 8 John Duncan, *Charles Darwin* (c.1927). Historic Environment Scotland.

Plate 9 Phoebe Anna Traquair, *Pan* (1912). National Galleries of Scotland. Bequest of the artist 1936.

Plate 10 Phoebe Anna Traquair, *The Progress of a Soul: The Victory* (c.1902). National Galleries of Scotland. Bequest of the artist 1936.

Plate 11 Charles Rennie Mackintosh, detail of a design for a stencilled mural decoration, Miss Cranston's Tea Rooms, Buchanan Street, Glasgow (1896). © The Hunterian, University of Glasgow.

Plate 12 John Duncan, *The Riders of the Sidhe* (1911). © Dundee City Council (Dundee Art Galleries and Museums)

Plate 13 John Duncan, *The Taking of Excalibur* (c.1895). Historic Environment Scotland.

paralysing selfishness of both native and alien landowners' – making a rare intervention in the Land War debate.[95] Sharp's celebration of the 'superb efflorescence'[96] of 'national idiosyncrasies' at the *fin de siècle* and his calls for individual anthologies of Scottish, English, Welsh and Irish poetry are also testament to his interest in cultural revivalism.[97] And while some Irish nationalists came to wage war on Macleod, Russell was initially moved by her writings, much like Yeats, who 'succumbed to the spell' of Macleod and hoped her work could be staged at the Irish Literary Theatre, which became the Abbey Theatre in 1904.[98] Criticism has rightly identified the defeatist and 'contributionist' aspects of the Macleod writings, but I argue here that there are other threads in the Sharp weave: some of the Macleod writings reflect and embody cultural revival efforts in both Scotland and Ireland. The readings I present here, when placed alongside those that have focused on the defeatist aspects of the Macleod writings, reveal just how inconsistent and conflicted Sharp could be.

Sharp's engagement with neo-paganism was perhaps the most pronounced of *fin-de-siècle* Scots, and in his Macleod work we witness how various facets of *fin-de-siècle* neo-paganism supported Scottish cultural revivalism. The Macleod neo-pagan writings that I examine here are not solely concerned with Scottish cultural revivalism: they focus on questioning the subjugation of various different groups. In these writings, the dominance of men over women, man over nature, and Christianity over paganism is questioned in the name of nurturing more mutual respect. But, as part of Sharp's project of resisting the process of subjugation in these writings, he also invokes the relationship between the Saxon and the Celt, between the English and the Scots, and it is here that the cultural revivalism of the Macleod writings emerges.

Sharp's interest in interrogating subjugation in the Fiona Macleod writings, and his belief that neo-paganism could help facilitate this, built on a work he had written before the first Macleod volume: his little magazine, *The Pagan Review* (1892). *The Pagan Review* featured short stories, poetry and prose dramas, including 'The Black Madonna', which we encountered in Chapter 2, that were all seemingly written by different contributors. But each of the authors' names presented throughout the magazine was, in fact, a pseudonym, disguising the fact that the magazine was authored solely by Sharp himself. The vocal dissidence of the magazine may partly explain why Sharp was keen to distance his name from the title. As Koenraad Claes notes, *The Pagan Review* was described by Remy de Gourmont as an 'imitation or parody of French Symbolist magazines', and

The Pagan Review announced its dissidence on the cover page via its motto 'Sic Transit Gloria Grundi', a playful proclamation that the reign of Mrs Grundy (the embodiment of Victorian propriety) was now over.[99] Readers hoping to relieve themselves of societal prudishness would not be disappointed: the 'Foreword' alone advocated the view that 'literature dominated by the various forces of the sexual emotion should prevail'.[100] Such irreverence towards prudishness was reflected more broadly in *fin-de-siècle* Scotland: the following year, for instance, James Herbert MacNair would paint *The Lovers* (1893), a watercolour that leaves little to the imagination.

The Pagan Review was especially aimed at a 'younger generation', those who believe that 'the religion of our forefathers has not only ceased for us personally, but is no longer in any vital and general sense a sovereign power in the realm' (2). The 'Foreword' makes little reference to the pre-Christian era itself but instead embraces 'paganism' as a term to unite those who champion youth, 'sexual union' and women's rights. Indeed, overcoming the subjugation of women was placed at the centre of Sharp's neo-pagan ideology:

> A new epoch is about to be inaugurated [. . .] a new epoch in civil law, in international comity, in what, vast and complex though the issues be, may be called Human Economy. The long half-acknowledged, half-denied duel between Man and Woman is to cease, neither through the victory of hereditary overlordship nor the triumph of the far more deft and subtle if less potent weapons of the weaker, but through a frank recognition of copartnery. This new comradeship will be not less romantic, less inspiring, less worthy of the chivalrous extremes of life and death, than the old system of overlord and bondager [. . .]. Far from wishing to disintegrate, degrade, abolish marriage, the 'new paganism' would fain see that sexual union become the flower of human life. But, first, the rubbish must be cleared away; the anomalies must be replaced by just inter-relations; the sacredness of the individual must be recognised; and women no longer have to look upon men as usurpers, men no longer to regard women as spiritual foreigners. (2)

Sharp, who was friends with Mona Caird and was married to another new woman, Elizabeth Sharp, plays the 'new man' in this quotation. Olive Schreiner believed that the new man was a figure who stood 'side by side with the New Woman [. . .] anxious to possess her only on the terms she offers', and Sharp embodies this idea here through his recognition of women's independence and his desire to replace inter-gender dominance with 'just inter-relations'.[101] In response to anti-new woman propagandists, many of whom argued that the rise of the new woman would diminish marriage,[102] Sharp posits that the rise of 'co-partnery' and the end of 'overlordship' would not undermine marriage but enrich that 'sexual union'. The association of neo-paganism with women's emancipation here is akin to Edward Carpenter's essay, 'Civilization: Its Cause and Cure', where Carpenter calls for a return to 'the naive insouciance of the pagan and primitive world' to reject 'forms of dominance' that turn 'the woman into the property of the man'.[103]

Significantly, Sharp's resistance to the dominance of men over women often invokes the language of nationhood and national division: women are currently 'usurped', making men and women 'foreign' to each other, and this problem can be solved only by just inter-relations and a new era of 'international comity'. Nations' attempts to dominate others are correlated to male overlordship over women, and this intersection between gender politics and national identity politics is developed by Sharp in one of the stories in *The Pagan Review*, 'The Pagans'. This story, written under a pseudonym that draws from the lexis of early modern Scots, 'Willand Dreeme', features a Scottish narrator, Wilfrid Traquair, who speaks of the 'deep comradeship' between him and his French lover, Claire (24). Against the wishes of Claire's brother Victor, who rejects her pairing with a 'beggarly Scot' (28) – also described as an 'offensive Scot' (26) – these two 'outcast pagans' leave Victor and 'go forth into the green world' together (28). Victor's name symbolises his belief in hierarchy, and his desire to denigrate the Scot reflects this: Victor is the 'overlord' figure that Sharp discusses in the 'Foreword', who has little respect for 'comradeship'. But Victor's assertion of his dominance – in terms of both nationality and gender – is subverted in the story, when it is revealed that Victor and Claire have Scottish ancestry. By articulating this, Sharp complicates attempts to dissociate and degrade others, and instead reveals connection. The story reveals Sharp's intermittent interest in resisting attempts 'to crush, to subdue, to usurp, to retaliate' in any form, between nationalities or genders.[104] Like the mythical weaver of the Celtic underworld, Orchil, who appears in various Fiona Macleod writings,[105] several of Sharp's works strive for synthesis over dominance. *The Pagan Review* reveals how Sharp's interest in resisting subjugation could support Scottish cultural revivalism, and this intersection is developed more fully in certain Fiona Macleod writings.

The Washer of the Ford, published by Patrick Geddes and Colleagues as part of their Celtic Library, is one of the Macleod texts that announces its desire to highlight Scotland's 'surviving antique paganism' (6). Its title alone is a reference to Celtic paganism as Cuchullin came across a washer (typically a supernatural, prophetic figure in Celtic mythology) at a ford.[106] Dedicated to the American artist, Catherine Ann Janvier, the short stories presented in this book focus on 'the strange complexity of paganism and christianity' in the Highlands and Islands of Scotland, and highlight the fact that the 'militant Christian saints' of early Scottish Christianity – Columba, St Patrick and Kentigern – 'were merely transformed pagans' (6). These thoughts illustrate Sharp's debt to several contemporary anthropological surveys, which argued that 'Christianity is but a thin veneer upon the solid timber of Paganism'.[107] The collection is partly a mythical retelling of the origins of Christianity in Scotland, and also an attempt to challenge the notion that 'barbaric' paganism is inferior 'civilised' Christianity. As James Ashcroft Noble noted, Sharp's neo-pagan writings have a 'barbaric element' that 'breaks up even the thick crust of an elaborated civilization' and instead searches for 'stirrings of a conscious kinship'.[108] Typical of Sharp's other writings, discussed in Chapter 2, *The Washer of the Ford* demonstrates that he is keen to reclaim the barbaric and to challenge Christianity's supposed domination and overlordship over paganism.

Various stories in *The Washer of the Ford* are concerned with the relationship between paganism and Christianity. On several occasions, Sharp questions Christian dominance over paganism not only by portraying the pagans as wise but also by representing the 'barbaric' tendencies of the Christians. This is evident in two conjoined stories: 'The Dark Nameless One' and 'The Three Marvels of Hy'. The first story relates Colum's (or St Columba's)[109] encounter with Angus MacOdrum (or Black Angus), who is 'one of the race of Odrum the Pagan' (139), thus foregrounding a Christian–pagan dialogue. 'Odrum' is a reference to the North Uist legend of Clan MacCodrum of the Seals, seals that were 'held to be the children of a Scandinavian king under spells'.[110] The story implies that Angus is a selkie, capable of changing from seal to human form, and Colum believes that he is 'no friend of Christ' and is instead 'of the evil pagan faith' (138): it is locally understood that Angus took a servant of Christ, Kirsteen McVurich, out to sea and there she became the sea-witch of Erraid, the small tidal island near Iona that David Balfour is marooned on in *Kidnapped*.[111] Consequently, Colum is told that the soul of Angus 'is Judas' (142), prompting Colum to crucify Angus. A clear conflict between Christianity and paganism is staged in the initial story.

However, in the successor story, 'The Three Marvels of Hy', Colum is informed by Angus's daughter, the Moon-Child, that Angus was 'a man under spells' (167). Colum regrets his action, realising he has left the child alone in the world, and he then asks the Moon-Child, of the pagan race, '"Teach me the way to God, O little child"' (171). The pagan becomes the leader of the Christian and, in turn, the Christian's denigration of the pagan is defused. Significantly, the Moon-Child then transforms gender and becomes Christ:

> there were no seaweeds in her hair and no shell in the little wee hands of her. For now, it was a male Child that was there, shining with a light from within: and in his fair sunny hair was a shadowy crown of thorns, and in his hand was a pearl of great price. (171)

Sharp subtly transforms the pagan sea imagery into Christian images: the seaweeds become a crown of thorns and the shell becomes the pearl of great price. The suggestion here is that the way to Christianity is through paganism, not against it. Like Hornel and Henry's sister paintings, *The Druids: Bringing in the Mistletoe* and *The Star in the East*, which 'equalize Pagan and Christian values' – as well as the decorations in *The Evergreen* that integrate Christian and pagan forms – the Christian–pagan hierarchy is questioned here.[112] Christian and pagan are levelled, male and female become interchangeable, and forms of dominance are consequently diminished.

Another form of dominance that is implicitly resisted in these stories is the marginalisation of the Celt. The setting of these two stories near Iona is significant in this context, as Sharp was keen to reactivate Iona's mythology and reclaim its importance. In a manner akin to Geddes, who believed it was time for Iona 'to educate London', Sharp told Dr John Goodchild that 'out of Iona is again to come a Divine Word [. . .] that Iona, the little northern isle, will be as it were the tongue in the mouth of the South'. In another letter to Goodchild, he stated that a new 'redeeming' figure would come to Iona, 'a woman who will express the old Celtic Bride or Brigit'.[113] Like Duncan, who painted St Bride on several occasions and was enchanted by Iona, Sharp was captivated by the image of Bride, and he represents her journey from the Western Isles to Bethlehem through a portal of arched trees in a story included in *The Washer of the Ford*, 'Muime Chriosd' (or 'Foster-Mother of Christ') (48). Sharp's interest in Bride, or Brighid, is unsurprising, as she features in both pagan and Christian mythology, thus helping to reconcile the two traditions, but she is also portrayed as a female, Celtic redeemer.[114] Removed from his defeatist writings, these Macleod mythologies suggest the potential for a Celtic redemption and revival. In his retellings and reanimations of 'the Celtic past',[115] principally focusing on Bride and St Columba, several of the Macleod writings hoped to demarginalise the 'Celtic fringe'.

A further feature of Macleod's neo-paganism, which also had ties to Scottish cultural revivalism, was overcoming the divisions between humans and nature, a feature of Sharp's writing that was partly inspired by his enthusiasm for Walt Whitman. One of the most striking images of synthesis and symbiosis between man and nature is evident in the story 'The Annir-Choille' (The Wood-nymph), in *The Washer of the Ford*. In this tale, the protagonist (Cathal) renounces women and paganism in favour of Christianity. However, when he encounters his future lover, Ardanna, he rejects Christianity and returns to paganism. He also gives up his Christianity-infused surname (Gille-Mhoire – servant of Mary) and returns to being Cathal mac Art 'of the race of Alpein' (183), a name that alludes to the man who is often considered to be the first king of Scotland, Alpin. In doing so, Sharp ties Cathal's pagan affirmation to his rediscovery of Scottish identity. This reading is substantiated by the fact that, when Cathal is caught, he is left in the hollow of an oak tree, most likely a reference to Charles II, who hid in an oak tree to evade the Roundheads at the Battle of Worcester, which led to the oak tree becoming a key Jacobite symbol. The name Cathal can also be anglicised as Charles, supporting this association of Cathal with Jacobitism. Furthermore, when Cathal looks out from the oak tree, he can see in the stars the sword of Fionn and the harp of Brigidh, significant figures in Scottish neo-paganism of the period.

Through the oak tree, Cathal experiences the 'green life', where spirits can live in, and pass through, trees. This idea may have developed from J. G. Frazer's *The Golden Bough*,[116] which describes at length the 'savage' belief that 'the world in general is animate, and trees are no exception to the rule', or it may have derived from Pater – much admired by Sharp for his interrogation of the divide between Christianity and paganism in *Marius the Epicurean* – who asserted his belief that even in modernity humans have 'a life in the green world' and can recognise the souls of flowers and leaves.[117] As we have seen, Forster would draw on this idea in 'Other Kingdom', where trees house individuals and are invested with pagan energies. In 'The Annir-Choille', humans and trees draw life from one another. Referring to the trees, Deòin, the 'Druid of the trees' (213), states, '"the tree is my body [. . .] they are as I am"' (212). This green life was even practised by Sharp himself: Lady Gregory related a time when Sharp embraced a tree and felt his soul flowing through the sap.[118] For Sharp himself, and in this Macleod story, nature and man are one and the same. In these respects, Sharp's writings have close connections with the German youth movement that formed 'a pantheism that integrated man, nature and the nation, directing attention away from the physical and toward national mythology'.[119] It is also easy to see the eco-political vein of neo-paganism, which Dennis Denisoff has identified, in Sharp's representations.[120] It is in this state, literally absorbed in nature, that Scotland's pagan gods return to Cathal.

Pan in Scotland

One of the gods who made frequent returns to *fin-de-siècle* Scotland was Pan. Pan, the god of the wild and rustic music, was a key figure across *fin-de-siècle* Europe, inspiring the German decadent magazine, *Pan* (1895–1900), and the Norwegian novelist Knut Hamsun's 1894 novel, *Pan*. While some lamented that 'the Gods are dead' or that they had emigrated to America, several writers represented the re-emergence of Pan in Europe. As we have witnessed, Machen evoked the threatening return of Pan in *The Great God Pan*, and Machen's interest in Pan was not limited to that novella; as Alex Murray shows, Machen drew upon Pan's Roman equivalent – Faunus – in *The Hill of Dreams* (1907) too.[121] Through Machen's writings and their increasing popularity, Pan has primarily come to be associated with Wales in the British Isles at the *fin de siècle*. But Pan also featured in various Scottish artworks and writings, several of which have been either forgotten or under-examined.[122] Indeed, Scottish cultural revivalists were keen not only to portray Pan but also to associate him with Scotland and the Celtic territories more widely. As a figure that united man and nature, Pan was widely embraced as a deity that symbolised connection: this half-man, half-animal helped undermine the 'teleology of civility' that idealised societies and individuals that had shed off any barbaric or animalistic impulses.[123]

Pan makes a distinctive imprint on the writings of Fiona Macleod, where he or his relatives are portrayed as living in the Highlands. In 'The Annir-Choille', an obscure figure is referenced when Deòin tells Cathal the name of his god: Keithoir. Keithoir is a Celtic deity fashioned by Sharp who appears in several Macleod writings, but his identity is best clarified in the dedication of *Pharais* to Edith Rinder:

> In the mythology of the Gael are three forgotten deities, children of the Delbaith-Dana. These are Seithoir, Teithoir and Keithoir [. . .]. Keithoir is the god of the earth; dark-eyed, shadowy brother of Pan; and his fane is among the lonely glens and mountains and lonelier isles of "Alba cona lingantaibh" [Scotland with its lochs]. It is because you and I are of the children of Keithoir that I wished to grace my book with your name.[124]

Sharp here builds a Scottish 'neo-myth', to use Mark Williams's term,[125] that draws from Celtic and Hellenic sources, which he believed were complementary (a view shared by T. W. Rolleston).[126] For Sharp, Keithoir is a Celtic version of Pan, the 'god of the earth', who he situates in Scotland. In creating a Celtic Pan, resident in Scotland, and by suggesting that he and Rinder are the descendants of Keithoir, Sharp attempts to activate and associate the energy of Pan with Scotland, ancient and present. As a symbol of synthesis, it is unsurprising that Pan appealed to Sharp: Pan was a deity that helped embody the Macleodian vision of a reconnected 'green world', resistant to cultural and social subjugation.

We have encountered this association of Pan with synthesis in the Ramsay Garden common room mural scheme, where Pan meets Charles Darwin (Plate 8). That mural panel was just one example of Pan's presence in Ramsay Garden. Geddes believed that Pan's spirit had been best 'preserved here in the north', and the numerous mural embodiments of Pan at Ramsay Garden reflect this belief.[127] Geddes's flat in Ramsay Garden was decorated with another mural scheme by Duncan, titled *The Evolution of Pipe Music*, and Pan and his descendants make several appearances. Although this mural scheme no longer exists and few photographs are known to have survived, Duncan outlined the scheme in a letter to William Craigie and he included woodcut versions of the early subjects in the first two issues of *The Evergreen* (Figs 3.1 and 3.2), a magazine that was itself described as 'purified-Pagan'.[128] In this mural scheme, as Duncan tells us, one of the opening subjects is Pan teaching Apollo to 'play upon pan-pipes', followed by a Bacchanalian Procession, 'Bacchus and Silenus', which bears compositional similarities to John Duncan Fergusson's modernist painting, *Les Eus* (c.1910). In light of growing campaigns for temperance and prohibition at the *fin de siècle*, 'Bacchus and Silenus' was particularly subversive in depicting a joyous bacchanal that foregrounds the love of revelry and indulgence. Indeed, the image features a god of drunkenness, Silenus, who was often portrayed in

Figure 3.1 John Duncan, *Apollo's Schooldays*, in *The Evergreen*, 1 (1895): 39.

Figure 3.2 John Duncan, *Bacchus and Silenus*, in *The Evergreen*, 2 (1895): 90–1.

Greek myth as the son of Pan, riding on a donkey. Alongside Silenus, we see satyrs playing on bagpipes, and these references prefigure the later sections of *The Evolution of Pipe Music*. Duncan tells us that the mural moved from Arcady through to the Pied Piper of Hamlin and ended with a sombre note, where a leading Jacobite who was slain at the Battle of Killiecrankie, John Graham of Claverhouse, is 'carried from the field with the pipes of the Highland Clans'.[129] And here, the spirit of the pipes 'dies away among the Highland hills'.[130] Through this mural, Scotland is portrayed as the resting place of Pan's pipe music. Although this scheme appears to suggest death, there is also a revivalist dimension to it. Besides the portrayal of Pan returning to meet Darwin, Geddes associated Pan with Scotland in *The Masque of Ancient Learning*, discussed in Chapter 5, where he notes that Pan is reviving in Scotland, having been preserved there 'by kindly folk-lore, and by the protection of the poets, Burns above all', correlating Burns's 'deil' to Pan.[131] The fact that this re-emerging Pan was partly associated by Geddes and Duncan with Jacobite Scotland (symbolic of national resistance) suggests a further note of dissidence lurking beneath the presence of Pan in these murals.

Another figure connected to Geddes's projects that took an interest in Pan, and pagan themes more widely, was Phoebe Anna Traquair. Traquair was an Irish-born Arts and Crafts artist who was deeply influenced by Early Renaissance painting and the Pre-Raphaelites. On behalf of the Edinburgh Social Union, which Geddes established, Traquair executed a commission to decorate the mortuary chapel of the Royal Hospital for Sick Children, which demonstrated a debt to William Morris. The Union also offered a commission to decorate the new Scottish National Portrait Gallery, which she declined in favour of decorating the Catholic Apostolic Church in Mansfield Place, where she sets several biblical tales against Scottish landscapes, as Sharp did in his story, 'The Last Supper'. Aside from creating mural decorations, Traquair was an oil painter, furniture decorator and embroiderer, and several of her artworks featured pagan subjects. Pan appears across all of these mediums, such as in her painting *Pan* (1912), which features Pan playing pipes, with a baby faun (holding a wine carafe) on his shoulder (Plate 9). The luminous colours of this painting, as well as Pan's leopard skin, are clear reprisals of an earlier Traquair artwork, *The Progress of a Soul* (1895–1902), a set of four large embroideries that loosely draw from 'Denys L'Auxerrois', a story by Walter Pater, who Traquair was reading at this time.[132] In Pater's Dionysian tale, the narrator comes upon stained-glass windows and a series of tapestries that feature a figure 'muffled in skins', 'a suffering, tortured figure [. . .] a pagan god', whose demise is charted throughout.[133] As in Pater's story, Traquair presents a figure 'muffled in skins' and chronicles his fall through the four embroideries: 'The Entrance', 'The Stress', 'Despair' and, finally, 'The Victory' (Plate 10), in which the figure is redeemed by an angel. It is almost as if Traquair attempted to recreate the tapestries and the stained glass that the narrator encounters through these embroideries, which feature luminous colours, mimicking stained glass. In portraying the angel in 'The Victory', which we do not see in Pater's story, *The Progress of a Soul* redeems this 'pagan god' and presents us with a more circular 'rise and fall' (or, 'fall and rise') narrative than a linear decline. The final note is one of revival and Christian–pagan fusion, which we are denied in 'Denys'.

Beyond Geddes's circle in Edinburgh, other cultural revival figures in Scotland incorporated Pan into their writings. Referring to himself as a 'kind old pagan' in *The Silverado Squatters*, Robert Louis Stevenson comments on the spread of phylloxera in French vineyards and laments that 'it is not Pan only; Bacchus, too is dead'.[134] Stevenson's ironic reference to Pan's death here contrasts with the presentation of Pan in his essay, 'Pan's Pipes' (1878). Here, Stevenson provides a cheerier appraisal of Pan's health, asserting that 'for youth and all ductile and congenial minds, Pan is not dead'.[135] In much the same manner as Geddes and Sharp, Stevenson presents Pan as symbolising the fusion between man and natural impulse: part-animal Pan is valorised as a figure that subverts stadial 'evolution' and those 'highly respectable citizens who flee life's pleasures' (12–13). As we witnessed in Chapter 1, subversions of linear progress were key to Stevenson's cultural revivalism, and Pan is held up as a deity of such subversions here. Like Stevenson, his friend J. M. Barrie also drew upon Pan's associations with youthfulness when rendering the eponymous character of *Peter Pan* (1904), the boy who would not grow up. And Stevenson's association of Pan with nature, and with remedying unbridled modernity, is reflected in a masque performed at the Glasgow School of Art in 1909, titled 'The Birth and Growth of Art', to celebrate the opening of Mackintosh's building. In that masque, Pan features as the narrator and expressly critiques 'huddled civilization'.[136] Aside from these uses of Pan by cultural revivalists, others were clearly enthused by the figure: George Henry addressed E. A. Hornel as 'Pan' in a letter,[137] and Robert Crawford notes the presence of Pan on the cover of John Buchan's *Scholar Gypsies* (1896).[138] While the uses of Pan by each writer briefly considered here differed, several cultural revival figures in Scotland were celebrating Pan as a symbol that highlighted man's connections to nature and animality, challenging the stadialist progress that was felt to undermine both Scotland and traditional culture. If Pan represented a threatening virility in the works of Machen and Crowley, in these writers' and artists' works he was almost exclusively representative of a healthy synthesis and interconnection.

Mona Caird's Neo-Pagan New Women

A close friend of William and Elizabeth Sharp was the English-born author, suffragist, anti-vivisectionist and Theosophist, Mona Caird.[139] Although she was born in England, Caird's father was the inventor John Alison of Midlothian and she married a Scottish land-owner, James Alexander Henryson-Caird, making her the daughter-in-law of the Stirling Burghs MP and agriculturalist, Sir James Caird; consequently, she spent much of her time in Scotland, and her fiction reveals an acute concern with Scottish identity. Caird is best known as one of the most prominent and controversial new women of the *fin de siècle*; Elizabeth Sharp described her as the most 'loyal and devoted advocate of the cause of women' in the dedication to her anthology *Women Poets of the Victorian Era* (1890).[140] Caird gained particular notoriety on the publication of her article 'Marriage' (1888), published in the *Westminster Review*, which defined marriage as a failed institution, prompting thousands of disconsolate readers to submit contributions to a quickly established *Daily Telegraph* series, 'Is Marriage a Failure?'. Although Caird occupied a precarious place in William Sharp's love triangle (she was not only friends with Sharp's wife, but also a cousin by marriage to his muse, Edith Rinder, who he most likely had an affair with),[141] Sharp was keen to advocate her work. He proposed that Patrick Geddes and Colleagues should publish Caird – a proposal that Geddes agreed to, although a volume never emerged.[142]

There are several instances where the *fin-de-siècle* new woman movement and the Scottish cultural revival came into contact, besides in *The Pagan Review*. Elizabeth Sharp was devoted to giving women a stronger voice in publishing: she edited not only *Women Poets of the Victorian Era* but also an anthology titled *Women's Voices*, for which Phoebe Anna Traquair designed an elaborate cover. On the west coast, the female artists of the Glasgow School were characterised by the press as new women artists: Roger Billcliffe has recently disinterred a six-stanza poem on Margaret and Frances Macdonald's work from *The Glasgow Evening News* that associates them with 'the Woman New' (l. 11)[143] and portrays the figures in their paintings as subversive:

> For if Caliban was mated
> With a feminine gorilla
> Who her youth had dissipated
> O'er the book yclept the Yellow
> The daughters of the wedding
> Would be something such as these –
> Sadly scant of fleshly padding
> And ground-spavined at the knees. (9–16)

Bearing the 'Beardsley leering glance' (l. 28), the Macdonalds' figures are explicitly equated with decadence, gender-bending and *The Yellow Book*, to which both sisters contributed artworks. *The Yellow Book* and decadence were often associated with the new woman, in part because John Lane published the Keynotes series, featuring decorations by Beardsley, which included some seminal new women writers, including George Egerton. Fiona Macleod, a 'manly' woman in a different way, placed herself within this new woman *milieu* by contributing *The Mountain Lovers* (1895) to the series. Sharp's proto-feminism was even recognised in *Votes for Women*, the suffragette newspaper, which ran an article that described him as allied to the cause.[144] Geddes had a more complicated relationship with the woman question: his belief in 'differential nature' based on 'female passivity and male energy'[145] divorced him from the views of many new women, but his belief in women's 'business capacity' brought him closer.[146] *The New Evergreen* was less ambivalent: it announced that 'When the New Woman has cast forth the Old Adam, the Utopia may be found out.'[147] Across these various examples, we find Scottish cultural revivalists either actively attaching themselves to the new woman movement or finding themselves associated with it, usually by figures keen to malign their dissidence.

But Caird is undoubtedly the most prominent new woman figure who had interests in Scottish cultural revivalism. Paganism and antiquity are key themes in several of Caird's novels, including *The Pathway to the Gods* (1898) and *The Stones of Sacrifice* (1915), the latter of which features several Scottish characters. But the text that most explicitly (although complicatedly) depicts Anglo-Scottish tensions and Scottish cultural defence, and contains pagan elements, is *The Daughters of Danaus* (1894). The novel's title is a reference to a

Greek myth referenced in Ovid's *Metamorphoses*, where the daughters of Danaus 'murder their cousin husbands' on their wedding night and are forced to spend eternity carrying water in sieves as punishment.[148] This myth was selected by Caird to embody the repetitive futility of women's lifestyles at the *fin de siècle*. As the protagonist, Hadria, tells her sister, Algitha, 'Women will go on patiently drawing water in sieves, and pretend they are usefully employed because it tires them.'[149] The novel concerns Hadria's efforts to emancipate herself from a life of feminine futility, but the novel ultimately demonstrates the near-impossibility of Hadria's efforts as various social and familial forces conspire against her.

The Daughters of Danaus begins in Scotland, before moving to England and France, and, as Alexandra Gray demonstrates, Anglo-Scottish relations feature prominently. Gray writes that

> Caird's choice of name for her central heroine immediately establishes her as a Scottish rebel figure. [. . .] Since Caird's text concerns an unhappy marriage between a controlling Englishman and a wild and spirited Scot, her heroine's name can be read as symbolising the metaphorical walls she both demolishes and constructs.

Beyond Hadria's name and her 'Celtic blood',[150] there is further evidence of an Anglo-Scottish tension in the text. For instance, Hadria is keen to undermine her future husband's Anglocentricism:

> 'Don't you ever come to town?' he asked.
> 'We go to Edinburgh occasionally', she replied with malice, knowing that he meant London. (88)

Hadria's desire to reclaim Scotland from English marginalisation here is also evident in her appreciation of landscapes. Rather than seeing the 'wild', uncontrollable Scottish landscapes as uncivilised, she finds them liberating. Instead, it is the English landscape that offends her when she travels south: 'Hadria suffered from a gnawing home-sickness; a longing for the rougher, bleaker scenery of the North. [. . .] The calm, sweet English landscape affected her at times with a sort of disgust.' The garden landscapes of southern England are explicitly correlated to patriarchal subjugation here: the English landscape has been 'torn, and wounded, and furrowed'; it is an example of 'Mother earth submissive to the dictatorship of man' (173). The association of Scotland with uncontrollable liberation and England with patriarchal subjugation is further evident in Hadria's musical abilities:

we are told that there is a 'strong Celtic element' in her music – 'wild and strange, yet essentially sane' (266) – and through it she seems capable of communing with pagan Scotland: 'it fills me with bewildering memories [. . .] it seems almost as if I had lived before, among some ancient Celtic people' (137). Later in the novel, she also imagines joyfully dancing in pagan Greece (289–90). But Hadria's love of music, deeply enmeshed in Scotland and paganism, gradually deteriorates as she loses opportunities to play in her marriage. As Gray notes, 'Hadria is eventually conquered and made to give up her music, a talent connected directly to her sense of Celtic identity and the landscape that encodes her (initially) untameable nature' (59). From these pieces of evidence, the Scottish landscape is showcased as the ideal setting for the growth of the new woman, who feels compromised when she leaves Scotland.

Although the novel largely associates Scotland with the defiant, free new woman and England with an order keen to dominate, the novel does at times complicate this reading. For example, the 'national' music and reels that Hadria is absorbed in at the New Year's dance prove partly responsible for intoxicating her into a state where she accepts Temperley's marriage proposal (137–9). And, as Wendy Parkins illustrates, although Hadria passionately adores the Scottish landscape, she also associates its mountains with the 'boundary of her horizon'.[151] Furthermore, her sister, Algitha, who moves to London, ultimately achieves greater liberation as a new woman. In the association of Scotland with the new woman, there are several notes of discord, which, Parkins argues, help to evoke Hadria's liminality,[152] but we are nevertheless invited to equate Scotland with the new woman that other characters, male and female, 'lay siege' to (210). As Lady Engleton tells Hadria, 'really, Mrs Temperley, you are not born for an English village' (290). As in the Fiona Macleod writings, the questioning of both national identity hierarchies and gender hierarchies intersect in Caird's novel.

John Davidson: Resisting Revivals

As we have witnessed, several figures who were keen to defend Scottish cultural identity and define the nation's mythological origins, as well as its heroes, embraced the *fin-de-siècle* enthusiasm for neo-paganism. Neo-paganism also helped critique the stadialist belief in linear progress, a critique that was so key to Scottish cultural revivalism. But not all late Victorian Scots were supportive of neo-paganism. Unsurprisingly, certain stadialist thinkers in Scotland were harsh critics of the return to antiquity, and of cultural (and political) revival efforts more widely. The poet, playwright and novelist John Davidson embodies this resistance to neo-paganism and cultural revivalism to the extreme. Born in Barrhead in 1857, Davidson taught in schools throughout Scotland in the late 1870s and 1880s before moving to London. In London, he joined the Rhymers' Club, where he came into contact with several Irish revivalists and decadent writers, who he had contested relationships with. Davidson's relationship to decadence is particularly complicated: he satirised decadence (especially one of its key writers, Oscar Wilde) in his novels *Earl Lavender* (1895) and *Baptist Lake*,[153] but, like several decadents, he developed a pseudo-aristocratic sensibility defined by a loathing of democracy and uniformity. The most iconic decadent illustrator, Aubrey Beardsley, would provide an illustration for an anthology of Davidson's plays, written in Scotland and published by John Lane, and there are also several Nietzschean elements to his work: nihilistic materialism and his enthusiasm for social Darwinism can be traced in several works.[154] This daring, independent vision made Davidson particularly attractive to several modernists, including T. S. Eliot and Hugh MacDiarmid, and John Sloan has gone so far as to label him the 'first of the moderns'.

While Davidson had a complicated association with decadence, his relationship with cultural revivalism was less complex. Although he was anthologised in Elizabeth Sharp's *Lyra Celtica* (1896) and his work reveals a debt to some Scottish writers,[155] Davidson's writing regularly resists Scottish cultural revivalism by demeaning Scotland and actively attempting to assimilate Scottish nationality into English nationality. In Davidson's work, with its commitment to stadial progress and cultural assimilation in Britain, we find extreme examples of what Scottish cultural revivalists found themselves up against.

Davidson regularly expressed his opposition to neo-paganism and returns to antiquity, especially in the name of building myths. Although he wrote plays that featured pagan characters, including *Scaramouch in Naxos* (1888), first performed in Crieff, his writings frequently reveal his antagonism towards those enthused by the pagan past. Sloan tells us that he took little interest in his Classics classes with the cultural revivalist and Home Ruler, John Stuart Blackie, at Edinburgh University (1876–7), believing that 'dead languages remain dead'.[156] This dismissiveness towards classical antiquity is reflected in Davidson's *The Testament of an Empire-Builder*, where it is stated that 'dwellers in legend, burrowers in myth' are the 'Materials of Hell'.[157] Riffing on Nietzsche, Davidson describes such individuals (who presumably include Scotland's myth-making cultural revivalists) as 'deniers of the will to live' (76). When his work does invoke classical paganism, it is often as a means to attack both it and Christianity. The best example of such attacks is in *The Testament of John Davidson*, where the poet destroys various figures associated with Mediterranean and Germanic paganisms, including Thor, Aidoneus and Apollo. As Douglas Bush notes, the poetic subject here banishes 'the fear of hell, the worship of God and chastity, and all the other bogies which have hindered man from realising his unfettered supremacy'.[158] Davidson also associates these gods with particular races: the implication is that it is only when ethnicities are eradicated that the gods will die.[159] In his resistance to classical paganism and Christianity, Davidson's resistance to nationhood, and especially nation-building projects rooted in mythology, is expressed.

It is therefore unsurprising that Davidson launched sustained and strident attacks on both Irish and Scottish nationalism in this period. Several of Davidson's writings, political and literary, explicitly reject the Home Rule movements, denigrate Scottish and Irish nationality, and encode the 'Celtic nations' as English. These facets of his writing are clearly evident in his political writings. Douglas Gifford has commented on Davidson's letter to the House of Lords in 1908, which makes the 'radical suggestion Ireland, Wales and Scotland should all yield to the evolutionary inevitability – and honour – of being supporting players to a superior race in a Westminster-and-English dominated Britain'.[160] This letter formed the dedication of *The Testament of John Davidson* (1908), which attacks the campaigns for Irish Home Rule, women's enfranchisement and socialism (13). Addressing Irish Home Rulers, Davidson concedes that Ireland, Scotland and Wales can be 'national' in their own nations, but he demands that they reconcile themselves not only to an international Englishness but also to the superiority of England:

> In your relations to the other British kingdoms, to the Empire, and to the world, England requires you to be English, as the Welsh are English, as the Scots are English. The Welsh and the Scots, having accepted England and the meaning of England, remain magnanimous. The Irish, having refused England and the great meaning of England, are less fortunate [. . .]. We recommend you heartily to cease thinking of demands on England, and of what England should do for Ireland. Set yourselves, rather, to study and understand what England requires of you, and what you should do for England. (15–16)

Ask not what your country can do for you, ask what you can do for your country. Davidson's passage here is not dissimilar in its tone to Sharp's unpublished poem, 'West Britain: an appeal': both attempt to enforce English nationality on the Irish and urge them to recognise the superiority of the English nationality, just as the Scots and the Welsh have done. As we have seen, Davidson's depiction of Scotland's supposed acquiescence to English identity was far from true; just a few years before this essay was penned, 104,647 Scots signed a petition to Queen Victoria, objecting to the use of the word 'England' to refer to 'Britain', for instance.[161] But Davidson was keen to style the Scots as English and to undermine the Scottish nationality. In this essay alone, he ironically proposes granting Home Rule to 'the Highlands of Scotland, and to the Lowlands',[162] a proposal brazenly designed to undercut Scottish nation-building by rebooting the division between the Highlands and Lowlands that had compromised Scottish unity in the nineteenth century, as discussed in Chapter 1. What Davidson exhibits in this passage is not anti-nationalism but a forceful, imperialist English nationalism, one that seeks to discredit, disintegrate and absorb the 'Celtic fringe'.

Davidson's attempt to denigrate and mock Scottish nationality, and to highlight the superiority of English nationality, is not limited to this letter; it is found in several of his literary works too. In his play *Bruce* (1886), for instance, Davidson diminishes Scottish culture and history, seeking 'to cut himself off from his national heritage'.[163] The play charts the events leading up to the Battle of Bannockburn, where Edward II seeks an England that 'shall stretch from Orkney to Land's End'.[164] With sharp wit, Davidson mocks Scottish nationhood by portraying Bruce, an emblem of Scottish nationality, not only as an irresolute king (138) but as a king who almost agrees with Edward II's position. This is evident in the fourth act, when Bruce discusses Britain with his soldiers:

> 2nd Soldier: But might it not have been a benefit
> If Rome had conquered Scotland too, and made
> Between the Orkneys and the Channel Isles
> One nation?
> Bruce: A subtle question, soldier;
> But profitless, requiring fate unwound.
> It might be well were all the world at peace,
> One commonwealth, or governed by one king;
> It might be paradise; but on the earth
> You will not find a race so provident
> As to be slaves to benefit their heirs. (183)

Bruce here contemplates the benefit of Scotland being absorbed into one assimilated nation, and Davidson's use of meter, having Bruce finish the pentameter of the second soldier's final line, emphasises the interchange's concern with integration. The few rousing nationalist speeches made in the play are punctured with such considerations of assimilation. Scotland's other national hero, William Wallace, is also portrayed as favouring assimilation: 'Who doubts our lands are destined to be one? / Who does not pray for that accomplishment' (168–9). Scottish nationality is also patronised: its national heroes are associated with backwardness, as opposed to English civility. While Wallace is described as having 'gothic hands' (164), Edward is associated with 'order' (164). As several Scottish revivalists and Home Rulers tried to rekindle a feeling for national heroes (particularly evident in the pageants discussed in Chapter 5), Davidson maligns them in order to promote a pan-Britain English nationality. The play even infantilises the Battle of Bannockburn, a battle often associated with Scottish liberation and preservation, through it being described as 'child's play' (212). In various ways, the play mocks Scotland's claim to nationhood and portrays that nationhood as inferior to England's.

Davidson's attempt not only to portray Scottish identity as inferior to English identity, but to recast the Scots as English (imaginatively completing his fantasy of assimilation) is evident in other literary writings, particularly his poem 'St George's Day' (1895). This poem, published by John Lane, features various characters who attempt to bring a sceptic, Menzies, round to their belief in the continued greatness of England. Here, Davidson portrays the Scots as reconciled to England's superiority, happily identifying themselves as English. Sandy, a name commonly used to personify Scotland, claims that Wallace and Bruce were Englishmen:

> Sandy: The Bruce and Wallace wight I ken,
> Who saved old Scotland from its friends,
> Were mighty northern Englishmen.[165]

Davidson's attempt to recast Scottish characters as English is not limited to 'St George's Day'. The surname of the Scottish character in his novel *Baptist Lake* (1894), John Inglis, reveals Davidson's broader concern with associating the Scots with Englishness; indeed, Inglis's son also declares that 'the Scotch are just northern English'.[166] In 'St George's Day', the various characters around Menzies eventually succeed in persuading him to accept their belief in the supremacy of

England, and the poem finishes on a chorus of English nationalism and assimilationism:

> All: By bogland, highland, down, and fen,
> All Englishmen, all Englishmen![167]

With Scots merrily declaring themselves Englishmen, it is easy to understand why Caroline McCracken-Flesher has read this poem as 'joking'.[168] But when it is placed alongside the various other declarations of the supremacy of England in Davidson's work, it is clear that there is little irony here; as John Sloan highlights, Davidson himself believed in these pro-England sentiments expressed in 'St George's Day'.[169] Despite his materialist individualism and his supposed denouncing of nationalism,[170] Davidson's work often reveals a propagandistic imperialist English nationalism.

Given these contexts, the fact that a prominent Scottish nationalist, Hugh MacDiarmid, became one of Davidson's strongest champions in the twentieth century seems strange. But MacDiarmid appears to have been well aware of this anti-Scottish strain in Davidson's writings and mocked him for it: his excessive references to the Scottishness of Davidson and his poetry in his essay on Davidson are most likely ironic bids to counteract Davidson's diminishment of Scotland.[171] This diminishment of the nation that we find in Davidson's writings reveals just how strident British or English assimilationism could be at the *fin de siècle*. Davidson's works help explain why cultural revivalists felt the need to define their origins, challenge the Highland–Lowland divide and interrogate the supposed backwardness of Scottish culture: prominent figures like Davidson were trying to undermine and divide the nation further.

This chapter has presented just a few examples of cultural revivalism and neo-paganism intersecting in *fin-de-siècle* Scottish literature and art. But what these intersections reveal are the ways in which cultural revivalists used neo-paganism as a tool to develop and define Scottish nationhood, and the complexities of such projects. Neo-myths were created to help expand Scotland's mythologies, pagan deities were celebrated to define a Scottish collection of heroes, and survivals and revivals of paganism were endorsed in order to undermine the stadialist notions of societal progress that were felt to malign traditional cultures and Scottish nationality. But, as we have seen, these uses of neo-paganism (which were common across Europe in this period) differed from those of other nations in that they asserted and defended Scottish identity but did not intend to challenge the existence of an Anglo-Scottish union. Rather than using neo-paganism to foster militarist resistance, the neo-paganism of Scottish cultural revivalists prioritised the recovery of those that were marginalised and promoted greater equality between races and cultures within Britain. As John Davidson's writings demonstrate, there were concerted efforts to demean and assimilate Scottish nationality in this period. Embracing the neo-paganism that Davidson abhorred, Scottish cultural revivalists looked to Celtic and Hellenic myths to help defend the nation from its *fin-de-siècle* threats.

Notes

1. Gibbons: 273.
2. Smith, *Myths and Memories*, p. 13.
3. Ibid., p. 9.
4. Smith, *Ethno-Symbolism*, p. 56.
5. Ibid., p. 65.
6. Kidd, 'Teutonist Ethnology': 46.
7. Wood, p. 17.
8. Vance, p. 5.
9. Barry: 293.
10. Hallett, pp. 199–200.
11. Meyers, pp. 49–52; Owen, p. 216.
12. Davies, p. 115; Thuente, pp. 63–73.
13. Frazer, pp. 24, 182, 482, 476, 694.
14. Arnold, *Culture and Anarchy*, pp. 162–3, 173.
15. Vance, p. 223.
16. Wilde, *Complete Poetry*, p. 94.
17. Swinburne, pp. 195–201 (l. 140).
18. Wilde, *Complete Poetry*, p. 29 (l. 1).
19. Machen, *The Great God Pan*, p. 4.
20. Machen, *The White People*, p. 40.
21. Ibid., p. 60.
22. Wood, p. 257.
23. Forster, p. 21.
24. D. H. Lawrence, p. 82; for more on Pan in America, see Fontelieu.
25. Cunliffe, p. 123.
26. James Cadenhead, [untitled paper] (c.1912) [Archives and Special Collections, University of Strathclyde: T-GED 12/1/167].
27. 'University Hall Extension': 140.
28. Armour: 103.
29. For more on the decorations in *The Evergreen*, see Kooistra.
30. Geddes, 'The Valley Section': 66.
31. Smith, *Myths and Memories*, p. 85.

32. Branford and Geddes, *The Coming Polity*, p. 106; Patrick Geddes, 'Keltic Art' (26 July 1899), p. 6 [Archives and Special Collections, University of Strathclyde: T-GED 5/2/7].
33. Geddes, 'The Megalithic Builders': 144.
34. Smith, *Myths and Memories*, p. 67.
35. Geddes, *Cities in Evolution*, p. 386.
36. Geddes, *Everyman His Own Art Critic*, p. 27.
37. Geddes, 'Political Economy and Fine Art': 2.
38. For more on Ruskin's influence on Geddes's views of art, see Shaw, 'Aestheticism and Decadence in Patrick Geddes's Socio-Economics', pp. 167–9.
39. Geddes, *Every Man His Own Art Critic*, p. 28.
40. Patrick Geddes, [untitled paper on the Celtic Cross], pp. 1, 8–9 [Archives and Special Collections, University of Strathclyde: T-GED 5/2/13].
41. Grilli: 29–31.
42. Geddes, *Cities in Evolution*, pp. 386–7.
43. See Shaw, 'Aestheticism and Decadence'.
44. Geddes, 'The Scots Renascence': 136.
45. Papers and correspondence relating to The Evergreen and Messrs. Patrick Geddes and Colleagues [Archives and Special Collections, University of Strathclyde: T-GED 8/1/2].
46. Geddes, 'The Sociology of Autumn': 27–38.
47. Branford and Geddes, 'Prefatory Note': 8.
48. *The Interpreter of Seven Pictures of Black and White* (Edinburgh, 1896), p. 14 [Archives and Special Collections, University of Strathclyde: T-GED/5/3/33].
49. (Cited in) Jarron, p. 53.
50. Murdo Macdonald, 'Visual Culture Japan – Scotland', available at <www.thenorthernmirror.com/pdf/Macdonald_Visual.pdf> (last accessed 28 August 2018).
51. Geddes, 'Keltic Art', p. 8 [University of Strathclyde: T-GED 5/2/7].
52. Geddes, 'The Scots Renascence': 137.
53. Westwood and Kingshill, p. 450.
54. Sharp, *Green Fire*, p. 32.
55. Smith, *Myths and Memories*, p. 68.
56. Willsdon, p. 276.
57. 'The Scots Renascence': 138.
58. Pittock, *Celtic Identity*, p. 90.
59. Morrison, *Painting the Nation*, p. 187.
60. Letter from Patrick Geddes to John Duncan, 2 February 1926 [National Library of Scotland: MS 10517].
61. *Interpretation of the Pictures in the Common Room of Ramsay Lodge*, p. 13.
62. Geddes, 'Cinderella': 327–31.
63. *Interpretation of the Pictures*, p. 13; Geddes, *Cities in Evolution*, p. 60.
64. Di Pasquale: 56; Nordau, p. 11.

65. Wallace, pp. 193–4.
66. Sutherland: 352.
67. Geddes, *Cities in Evolution*, p. 275.
68. Boardman, p. 99.
69. *Interpretation of the Pictures*, p. 15.
70. In light of the subjects in these murals, it is unsurprising that Geddes and Sharp planned lectures on 'The Return of the Gods' for the Edinburgh Summer School; see William Sharp, Miscellaneous Prose, iv. 99 [National Library of Scotland: MS 8777].
71. Howe, pp. 52, 70.
72. 'The Court', p. 4.
73. Morrison, 'Nationalism and Nationhood', pp. 187, 201.
74. (Cited in) Elizabeth A. Sharp, *William Sharp*, p. 285.
75. Richardson, pp. 201–2, 219–20; Alaya, pp. 124–6.
76. Halloran, 'W. B. Yeats, William Sharp and Fiona Macleod: A Celtic Drama, 1897': 160.
77. For more on discussions on Sharp's 'sexual tensions', see Meyers.
78. (Cited in) Crichton-Miller: 39.
79. Russell, p. 10.
80. (Cited in) Alaya, p. 112.
81. Fletcher, p. 163.
82. Yeats, p. 129.
83. See Meyers.
84. William Sharp, *The Washer*, p. 4; William Sharp, *The Sin-Eater*, p. 13.
85. Pittock, *Celtic Identity*, pp. 64–6.
86. Daniel G. Williams, p. 73. For more on Arnoldian readings of Sharp, see Stroh, pp. 218–36.
87. William Sharp, 'Introduction', p. li.
88. William Sharp, *The Sin-Eater*, p. 8.
89. (Cited in) Mark Williams, p. 379.
90. Russell, pp. 22–3.
91. William Sharp, Manuscripts of Poems [National Library of Scotland: MS 8775].
92. William Sharp, *The Winged Destiny*, pp. 181–2; for more on Sharp's anti-nationalism, see Tania Scott, pp. 127–41.
93. Alaya, p. 15; Blamires, p. 36; Mark Williams, p. 77.
94. Mark Williams, p. 384.
95. William Sharp, *The Winged Destiny*, p. 273.
96. William Sharp, 'Introduction', p. l.
97. William Sharp, 'The Irish Muse – I': 689; as editor of the Canterbury Poets series, Sharp was responsible for publishing numerous volumes of verse by Scottish writers, including *Contemporary Scottish Verse* (1893), edited by George Douglas.
98. Halloran, 'W. B. Yeats, William Sharp and Fiona Macleod: A Celtic Drama, 1897': 159.
99. Claes, pp. 84–6.

100. William Sharp, *The Pagan Review*: 3.
101. Schreiner, p. 272.
102. Ledger, pp. 11–12.
103. Carpenter, *Civilization*, pp. 3–5.
104. Sharp, *Green Fire*, p. 280.
105. Mark Williams illustrates that Orchil was invented by Standish O'Grady, before being appropriated by other Celtic revivalists, pp. 383–4.
106. Rolleston, p. 231.
107. Sands, p. 8.
108. *Recently Published and Forthcoming Books Issued by Patrick Geddes and Colleagues*, p. 9.
109. For more on the broader enthusiasm for Columba in this period, see Bradley, *Celtic Christianity*, pp. 136–7.
110. George Henderson, p. 261.
111. In Jason Marc Harris's reading of the story, McVurich is equated with the 'legendary figure of Jewish Folklore, Lilith'; see Harris, p. 184.
112. Cumming, 'Celtic Influenced Art', p. 110; Kooistra, p. 108.
113. (Cited in) Blamires, pp. 204–5.
114. For more on Sharp's interest in Bride, see Mark Williams, p. 375.
115. (Cited in) Elizabeth A. Sharp, *William Sharp*, p. 159.
116. It is most likely that Sharp used *The Golden Bough* as a source for several of the pagan customs he represents, such as sin-eating. Sharp's creation of Fiona Macleod may also have been indebted to *The Golden Bough*: he told Ernest Rhys that she was born to him 'on the banks of Lake Nemi', the location of the golden bough. For more on Fiona Macleod and Lake Nemi, see Rhys, *Everyman Remembers*, pp. 79–80, and Blamires, pp. 71–5.
117. Frazer, p. 51; William Sharp, 'Marius the Epicurean': 341–54; Pater, *Greek Studies*, p. 11.
118. Halloran, 'W. B. Yeats, William Sharp and Fiona Macleod: A Celtic Drama, 1897': 185.
119. Mosse: 83.
120. Denisoff: 433.
121. Murray, *Landscapes of Decadence*, p. 150.
122. The similarities between Macleod's work and Machen's may not be entirely coincidental: the title of Machen's *The Hill of Dreams* (1907) bears a striking resemblance to Macleod's *From the Hills of Dream* (1896).
123. Pittock, *Scottish and Irish Romanticism*, pp. 17, 60–1.
124. William Sharp, *Pharais*, p. viii.
125. Mark Williams, p. 380.
126. William Sharp, Manuscripts and typescripts of dramas [National Library of Scotland: MS 8776]. Rolleston, p. 22; unlike Sharp, Rolleston defines Celtic culture in opposition to 'barbarous' culture.
127. Geddes, *Dramatisations of History*, p. 52.

128. 'The Evergreen', *Glasgow Herald*, p. 11.
129. Letter from John Duncan to Sir William Craigie, 25 April 1893 [National Library of Scotland: MS 9987].
130. Armour: 103.
131. Geddes, *The Masque of Ancient Learning*, p. 46.
132. Cumming, 'Phoebe Anna Traquair HRSA', pp. 226, 297.
133. Pater, *Imaginary Portraits*, p. 60.
134. Robert Louis Stevenson, *The Silverado Squatters*, p. 47.
135. Robert Louis Stevenson, *Pan's Pipes*, p. 5.
136. Newbery, p. 3.
137. Letter from George Henry to E. A. Hornel (3 December 1895) [Broughton House: 2668].
138. Crawford, *Scotland's Books*, pp. 526–7.
139. Caird joined the Theosophical Society in 1904, around the same time that William Sharp was contributing to the *Theosophical Review*.
140. Elizabeth A. Sharp, ed., *Women Poets of the Victorian Era*, p. v.
141. Mark Williams, p. 388.
142. See William F. Halloran, ed., *The Letters of William Sharp 'Fiona Macleod'* (January–June 1895), available at <http://sas-space.sas.ac.uk/342/14/1895.Jan-June.pdf> (last accessed 15 September 2018), p. 36.
143. (Cited in) Billcliffe, *Charles Rennie Mackintosh*, p. 55.
144. Emmeline Pethink Lawrence, p. 226.
145. McCulloch, *Scottish Modernism*, p. 81.
146. Geddes and Thomson, p. 238.
147. Branford, 'A Series of Remarks': 33. Beyond the circles of decadence and Celticism, Glenda Norquay illustrates that the best-selling writer and suffragist, Annie S. Swan, who would go on to become a founding member of the Scottish National Party, offers a 'sentimental celebration of motherland' in her *fin-de-siècle* writing; see Norquay, 'Geographies of Self', pp. 154–5.
148. Ovid, p. 154.
149. Caird, p. 472.
150. Gray, pp. 17, 58–9.
151. Parkins, p. 82.
152. Ibid., p. 81.
153. Kingston, pp. 130–5.
154. For more on the ties between Davidson and Nietzsche, see Ritchie Robertson.
155. Hynd: 87–96.
156. Sloan, pp. 15–17.
157. Davidson, *The Testament of an Empire-Builder*, p. 76.
158. Bush, p. 467.
159. Davidson, *The Testament of John Davidson*, p. 107.
160. Gifford, 'From Celtic Revival to Scottish Renaissance?', p. 221.

161. Morton, 'Scotland is Britain': 128.
162. Davidson, *The Testament of John Davidson*, p. 14.
163. Townsend, p. 67.
164. Davidson, *Plays*, p. 208.
165. Davidson, *Selected Poems*, p. 155.
166. Davidson, *Baptist Lake*, p. 66.
167. Davidson, *Selected Poems*, p. 160.
168. McCracken-Flesher, 'Fin-de-Siècle Scotland', p. 188.
169. Sloan, p. 146.
170. For a detailed discussion of Davidson's individualism, see Gagnier, *Individualism, Decadence and Globalization*, pp. 97–110.
171. MacDiarmid, *Selected Essays*, pp. 197–204.

Chapter 4

The Occult Revival

> There is this small island entirely covered by what was still a habitable but empty castle. The last man who lived there had been Dr [Douglas] Hyde's father who, when a young man, lived there for a few weeks. All round were the wooded and hilly shores, a place of great beauty. I believed that the castle could be hired for little money and had long been dreaming of making it an Irish Eleusis or Samothrace. An obsession more constant than anything but my love itself was the need of mystical rites – a ritual system of evocation and meditation – to reunite the perception of the spirit, of the divine, with natural beauty. [. . .] Various trees corresponded to cardinal points, and the old gods and heroes too, their places gradually in a symbolic fabric that had for its centre the four talismans of the Tuatha de Danaan, the sword, the stone, the spear and the cauldron, which related themselves in my mind with the suits of the Tarot.[1]

Taken from his *Memoirs*, this quotation concerns W. B. Yeats's envisaged Order of Celtic Mysteries, a project he developed intermittently between 1895 and 1903, centred on the empty fortress on Castle Rock in Lough Key, Country Roscommon. Yeats dreamed of creating an occult order, not dissimilar to the recently established Hermetic Order of the Golden Dawn, of which he was an initiate. But in contrast to the pan-British Golden Dawn, Yeats hoped to develop an order that was distinctively Irish, one that would draw on Celtic mysteries and symbolism to develop new rites and rituals. Like the Eleusinian Mysteries that were rooted in the Grecian mythical figures Demeter and Persephone, these Irish rites would be inspired by figures of Irish mythology, especially the Tuatha Dé Danaan – the otherworldly pantheon that included Lugh and Brigid. In part, the order was designed to encourage spiritual awakening amongst its initiates, but it was also intended as a space to nurture an ancestral, druidic Irish identity,[2] one where 'those setting forth on some great task for Ireland might through lonely meditation on Ireland harmonise their individual effort with national endeavour', as Maud Gonne noted.[3] Gonne, who was closely involved in developing this 'Castle of the Heroes' with Yeats, highlights its aim to foster unity of purpose amongst Irish nationalists through common rituals and establishing a secret, secluded space to develop their ideas.[4] Although Yeats's order never came to fruition, the plan presents a clear instance of cultural revivalism intersecting with the rising interest in occultism at the *fin de siècle*.

The *fin de siècle* witnessed the proliferation of occult societies, as well as academic and popular interest in occultism, throughout Europe and beyond. As Nicholas Goodrick-Clarke notes, occultism entered 'public discourse on a scale not seen since the sixteenth century' at the *fin de siècle*.[5] Amongst the notable occult societies formed in this period were the Theosophical Society, founded in 1875 in New York by several figures, including Helena Petrovna Blavatsky and Henry Steel Olcott, which quickly developed an international following, and the Hermetic Order of the Golden Dawn, which spread across the United Kingdom after its founding in 1887. As will be demonstrated below, these two groupings took very different forms, but, at their most rudimentary, they were both devoted to the study of the hidden, driven by the conviction that there are realms beyond those of common material perception that can be penetrated or understood. The increasing turn towards esoteric, Rosicrucian, mystical and hermetic ideas at the *fin de siècle* is often characterised as a 'desire for unorthodox numinous experience in a post-Darwinian age'.[6] It is certainly true that occult societies provided creative alternatives to (or ways of engaging with) established religions that were under scrutiny, but the occult also captivated its broadly middle-class audience for other reasons beyond reconciling scientific discoveries with established religion. As Alex Owen demonstrates, diverse groups or professions were drawn to the occult for particular reasons: occultism's alternative hierarchies, she argues, provided women's rights activists (such as Annie Besant and Florence Farr) with a space to exert female leadership and authority, for instance.[7] Amongst the diverse groups who became enthusiasts of *fin-de-siècle* occultism were cultural revivalists and Home Rulers, most notably in Ireland and in India.[8]

While the growing enthusiasm for occult orders lent itself well to Yeats's Celtic mysticism, and Theosophy became closely intertwined with the Indian Home Rule movement,[9] *fin-de-siècle* occultism was no straightforward ally of national revival or defence projects. The complex relationship between national revivalism and occultism becomes particularly apparent when occultism's relationship to imperialism is considered. Patrick Brantlinger compellingly argues that imperialism and occultism were closely related at the *fin de siècle*: the late Victorian enthusiasm for the occult – for exploring hidden, numinous realms – was partly impelled by the late imperial desire to control and dominate other nations and their cultures. For Brantlinger, the occult sphere was especially important at the *fin de siècle*, as it provided new spiritual geographies and realms to conquer in an age marked by 'the waning of opportunities for heroic adventure'.[10] In this framing, *fin-de-siècle* occultism was complicit in cultural domination, helping to satisfy and sustain the desire for imperial expansion. Nevertheless, as Frantz Fanon reminds us, the 'occult sphere' was also a key defensive weapon for nations threatened by empire. In *The Wretched of the Earth* (published in French in 1961), Fanon presents a theory of colonial resistance by focusing on the Algerian War. Here, he identifies the presence of a 'magical superstructure which permeates the native society',[11] and he considers the effect of living in such a society, underpinned by magic and myth:

> The atmosphere of myth and magic frightens me and so takes on an undoubted reality. By terrifying me, it integrates me in the traditions and history of my district or of my tribe, and at the same time it reassures me, it gives me a status, as it were an identification paper. [. . .] By entangling myself in this inextricable network where actions are repeated with crystalline inevitability, I find the everlasting world which belongs to me, and the perenniality which is thereby affirmed of the world belonging to us. (43)

The occult sphere, in Fanon's framing, 'is a sphere belonging to the community' that provides and supports native identity: it offers a limited space, distinct from the settler, where native culture can be expressed and preserved. It also instils fear, which, Fanon believes, helps unify that culture. For Fanon, the occult sphere is a forceful weapon in colonial resistance: in that realm, 'the settler's powers are infinitely shrunken' (43). Although Fanon's focus is on an 'underdeveloped' colony in the twentieth century (43), *The Wretched of the Earth*, like Yeats's order, signals the ways in which occultism could foster myths, delimit spaces and help defend national cultures that were felt to be under threat or marginalised, despite occultism's connections to *fin-de-siècle* imperialism.

When we turn to Scotland, we witness the clear intersection of occultism with cultural defence efforts, which closely reflected Irish developments. Over the course of the *fin de siècle*, Scottish cultural revivalists became invested in occultism in various ways. Not only was occultism embraced to help engage with and promote the Celtic mysteries, but Scottish cultural revivalists also joined occult societies and even planned an occult Celtic order, which bears striking affinities with Yeats's Order of Celtic Mysteries. As this chapter illustrates, a key reason that occultism was embraced by cultural revivalists was that it endorsed the notion of unseen, hidden phenomena that could be contacted, experienced or reanimated. This notion appealed to several cultural revivalists, who were keen to style ancestral, apparently healthier, Scottish and Irish cultures as, not dead, but hidden. Responding to Ascendancy historians who had branded an ancestral Irish self as dying or dead,[12] Daniel Corkery's *The Hidden Ireland* (1924), for example, aimed to counteract this idea by showing that an ancestral self was merely hidden, alive in the Gaelic verse of Munster, and Corkery hoped to re-engage with and recover it. Similar rhetoric is found in Scotland's interwar period: Edwin Muir's poem, 'Scotland's Winter' (1935), for instance, depicts Scots as living a 'frozen life',[13] walking over (and oblivious to) the icy graves of their national heroes. These heroes in Muir's poem are simultaneously portrayed as dead and animate, capable of hearing people walking over their 'winter casket[s]' (l. 3). The implication of the poem is that a stronger national self, which Scots are not aware of, lies frozen in the ice, capable of being thawed and uncovered. I argue here that the sentiment of Muir's poem was not without precedent: in *fin-de-siècle* Scottish writing, we find depictions of healthier, frozen forms of Scottish nationality, and the occult is portrayed a means to contact, recover or sustain such hidden ancestral selves. As such, via occultism, we find further lines of continuity between *fin-de-siècle* cultural revivalism and the later Scottish Renaissance.

This chapter hopes to complement recent gains in scholarship that have identified and analysed the roles of other aspects of practical supernaturalism in Scotland's Celtic Revival. Elsa Richardson and Michelle Foot have explored the ways in which spiritualism, second sight, psychical research and cultural revivalism conversed in *fin-de-siècle* Scotland. Richardson examines several figures we have already encountered – including Andrew Lang,[14] William Sharp and John Crichton-Stuart, the third Marquess of Bute – and reveals their roles in representing, or supporting research on, Scottish second sight.[15] Richardson contends that several of these figures were keen to endorse the notion of second sight as a national attribute (18), helping to distinguish the Scottish self. She also demonstrates the complementary agendas of certain revivalists and psychical researchers, who were both seeking to 'represent the lives and beliefs of marginal people to a cosmopolitan public' (202). Similarly, through her considerations of Daniel Dunglas Home, Helen Duncan and Alexander Duguid, Foot demonstrates the ways in which the Celtic races in general, and Scots in particular, were styled as especially sensitive to the supernatural in this period.[16] Indeed, Foot reveals that spiritualists came to defend Scottish Celticism, worrying that the encroachment of 'stolid' Anglo-Saxon features into Scotland would undermine the nation's spiritualist gifts (207). Beyond the external spiritualist enthusiasm for Scotland, Foot also notes that the Home Ruler, John Stuart Blackie, attended séances (221–2), and she provides a detailed account of the spiritualist dimensions of John Duncan's work. While Richardson's and Foot's researches have uncovered the ways that spiritualism, second sight and psychical research interacted with the Scottish Celtic Revival, the present chapter focuses on esoteric occult societies and orders – such as Theosophy and the Golden Dawn, and their Hermetic and Rosicrucian influences – to reveal the marked influence that they also had on the Scottish cultural revival. As we shall see, the lines between the various forms of practical supernaturalism at work in *fin-de-siècle* Scotland were often porous, and a common element of each was their participation in cultural revivalism.

Egyptomania in Scotland

The revival of interest in the occult at the *fin de siècle* was, in no small part, informed by the late Victorian enthusiasm for Ancient Egypt. As Caroline Tully argues, occult orders like the Hermetic Order of the Golden Dawn looked to and 'augmented the Hermetic Egyptosophical tradition [imaginary notions of Egypt] with the latest findings from academic Egyptology'.[17] The Golden Dawn's interest in Egypt was so acute that every temple of the order was given an Egyptian name, including the Edinburgh temple, Amen-Ra.[18] The Theosophical Society equally borrowed from Egyptology, and an alternative name for the society, the Egyptological Society, was even debated.[19] Like these occult orders, Scottish cultural revivalists (several of whom would go on to participate in occult orders) looked to Egypt and incorporated the symbolism of Egyptian Hermeticism into their works, partly to reanimate the myth of the Scots' Egyptian descent.

In this period, there was widespread fascination with Egyptian culture and Hermeticism on an international scale. Interest in Egypt was evident throughout the nineteenth century, but it was stimulated further at the *fin de siècle* by new archaeological discoveries, pioneered by the likes of Flinders Petrie, who held the first Chair in Egyptology in the United Kingdom. British interest in Egypt also arose as a result of the Anglo-Egyptian War (1882) and the Convention of Constantinople (1888), which brought the Suez Canal under the protection of the United Kingdom. Concurrently, influential publications on Egypt were released, including E. A. Wallis Budge's facsimile editions of the Papyrus of Ani, published in 1890 and 1894, which prompted debates on whether Egyptian religion derived from Africa (Budge's view)[20] or from Caucasian invasion (the theory advanced by Petrie). *Fin-de-siècle* literature reflects this sensitivity to Egypt: Oscar Wilde's poem, 'The Sphinx', Bram Stoker's *The Jewel of the Seven Stars* (1903) and Arthur Conan Doyle's *The Ring of Thoth* (1890) are all testament to the *fin-de-siècle* lure of Egypt.

As *The Ring of Thoth* indicates, Scotland was by no means removed from Egyptomania, where it developed a particular accent. Indeed, one observer noted that 'the sons and daughters of Scotland [. . .] appear to be most strongly influenced by Egypt',[21] an influence that is particularly evident in the artworks of *fin-de-siècle* Glasgow and Edinburgh. Visual references to Ancient Egypt were especially marked in Glaswegian artworks, as the Victorian art critic Joseph Gleeson White noted when commenting on the influence of Egypt on 'Young Glasgow'.[22] Glasgow artists benefited from a wealth of Egyptian resources on their doorstep. The city's substantial museum collections of Egyptian culture – including the mummies in Glasgow's Corporation Galleries and the Hunterian Museum, which drew the attention of the Egyptologist Peter le Page Renouf – provided first-hand engagements with Egyptian iconography.[23] Egyptian culture had also become imprinted on Glasgow's urban geography as a result of Alexander 'Greek' Thomson's recently erected buildings that showcased clear influences from Egypt, such as his Egyptian Halls (c.1872).

The Glasgow School's interest in Ancient Egyptian iconography and myth was also nourished by W. R. Lethaby's *Architecture, Mysticism and Myth* (1892), which Charles Rennie Mackintosh is known to have read.[24] Besides outlining Kabbalistic concepts, this book discusses iconography found in Ancient Egyptian art, as well as Ancient Egyptian myths, including an incident where a king encounters his father, Ra, in an obelisk sun temple.[25] The presence of the figures and symbols that Lethaby discusses can be found in various works by the Glasgow Four,[26] such as Mackintosh's wall decorations for Miss Cranston's Buchanan Street Tea Rooms (Plate 11), which were designed in 1896 as part of a commission secured by the architect and designer George Walton. Sacred, symbolic trees are discussed throughout Lethaby's book and, in this mural, we find spiritual, symbolic trees intersecting with Egyptian motifs. As part of the scheme, which also featured some large aesthetic peacocks, Mackintosh presents several elongated female figures that emerge from roots in the ground and take on the form of trees. These women face a stylised tree that, in turn, takes on abstract human features, including eyes that resemble those in Egyptian temple paintings. The form of this tree also bears similarities to a sketch by a fellow enthusiast of Egyptian culture, and co-founder of the Golden Dawn, S. L. MacGregor Mathers.[27] Mathers depicted an emblematic tree of the Garden of Eden in one of his notebooks – a representation of the Kabbalistic tree of life that fuses a tree with human bodies, and presents the roots beneath the tree, with a crown on top – that is highly akin to Mackintosh's design. Serpents also feature on Mackintosh's mural, which are 'symbols of the royal house in Ancient Egypt'.[28] Like various other Glasgow artists who were fascinated by symbolic trees (especially trees of life and trees of knowledge),[29] Mackintosh adds an Egyptian finesse to this mural design, which also resembles occultist portrayals of emblematic trees.

Aside from this mural scheme, various other works by the Glasgow School include Egyptian features. For instance, Dai Vaughan identifies the scarab beetle form at the centre of Mackintosh's *The Wassail* gesso panel.[30] Given its associations with 'renewal and regeneration', it is unsurprising that the scarab beetle also features in *The Evergreen* (see Fig. 4.7). Margaret and Frances Macdonald's candle sconce (Fig. 4.1) similarly showcases a debt to Egypt, by including several eyes that resemble the eye of Horus. Fusing Egyptian tropes with those of aestheticism, these eyes surround the edges of a peacock in the Macdonalds' design.

The various Egyptian and esoteric references in the Glasgow School's works have prompted critics to consider the extent to which their works were 'neo-occult'.[31] Timothy Neat argues that, while there is little evidence to confirm Mackintosh and Macdonald's engagement with occult orders and societies, their works suggest their creators' familiarity with the occult.[32] John Berger similarly believes that art critics have yet to grasp the thinking behind several of their esoteric works, stating that 'no doubt in Glasgow there is a Rosetta Stone, which makes clear the tangled reading of these designs',[33] but

Figure 4.1 Margaret Macdonald Mackintosh and Frances Macdonald, candle sconce (c.1896). © Victoria and Albert Museum, London.

it has not yet been found. While the extent of the Glasgow School's participation in occultism cannot be precisely defined, their work undoubtedly reveals borrowings from the iconography of Ancient Egypt that were consistent with those of *fin-de-siècle* occultists.

Cultural revivalists in Edinburgh, especially those associated with *The Evergreen*, also embraced Egyptomania and incorporated the iconography and designs of Ancient Egypt into their work, at times placing it alongside Celtic culture. *The Evergreen* itself is suffused with Egyptian visual references. Sphinxes appear on several occasions: for instance, in Pittendrigh Macgillivray's *Der Zeitgeist* and John Duncan's *The Sphinx* (Figs 4.2 and 4.3). In the former, Macgillivray portrays pyramids and a sphinx alongside Christ and an angel that symbolises time – an expression of how Ancient Egypt, the return of the past, and the spiritual defined the 1890s zeitgeist. Duncan's illustration presents a despairing figure crouched over the base of a sphinx. Placed alongside a quotation from the Book of Job, the image evokes the resilience of art and culture against the mortality of man. Besides these two illustrations, several of the occult-inspired images in *The Evergreen*

Figure 4.2 Pittendrigh Macgillivray, *Der Zeitgeist*, in *The Evergreen*, 2 (1895): 149.

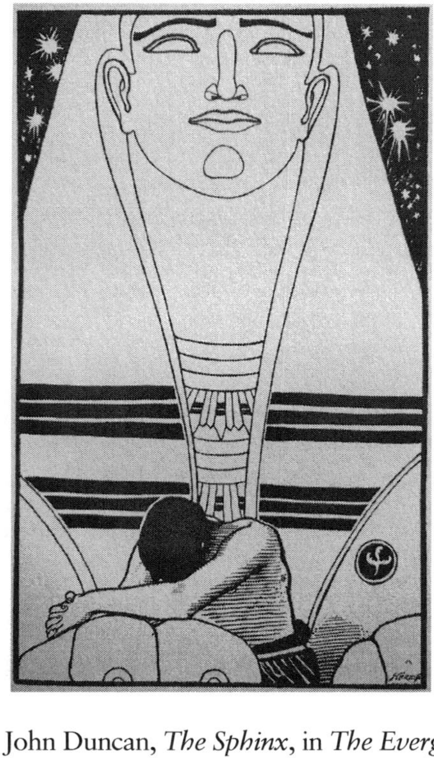

Figure 4.3 John Duncan, *The Sphinx*, in *The Evergreen*, 4 (1896): 65.

(see Figs 4.6 and 4.7) also feature Egyptian references, including sphinxes. The fact that these Egyptian-inspired images appear in a Celtic magazine may seem odd but it is less surprising when its publisher's writings are considered. Patrick Geddes was keen to equate Celtic and Egyptian traditions: in an unpublished essay, he styled the Celtic cairn and the Egyptian pyramid as equivalent memorials, describing the cairn as a 'primeval pyramid – the essential origin of the Egyptian temple'.[34] Geddes's upbringing in Ballater, where a large pyramidal cairn to Prince Albert was erected in 1862, most likely inspired this conflation. Geddes also admired the Ancient Egyptian focus on regeneration and renewal: 'the regularity of the seasons [. . .] with the assured hope of returning life'.[35] As such, the recurrent appearance of Ancient Egypt, which Geddes equated with Celtic culture and renewal, is less surprising in this Celtic revivalist seasonal.

A further explanation for the coupling of Celticism and Egyptomania lies in the revival of a further Scottish myth of descent at the *fin de siècle,* besides those we encountered in Chapter 3. This myth styled the Scots as descendants of Egyptians and it was referenced by at least two revivalists. At the *Scottish National Pageant* at Saughton Park (1908), which Duncan and various other cultural revivalists contributed to (discussed in Chapter 5), several mythological origin figures for Scotland were paraded before thousands of spectators. Among them, in the 'Celtic' section organised by Duncan, was Scota Pharaoh. Scota Pharaoh makes an appearance in Geoffrey Keating's history of Ireland (c.1630), a text that responded to Galfridian claims that Britain had first been settled by Brutus. Keating argued that Niul – husband of Scota, an Egyptian Pharaoh's daughter who bore the child Gadelas – was sent abroad to conquer foreign territories and 'ordered his people, who he designed to settle as a Colony in some convenient Country, not to forget that they were Natives of Scythia, that they should distinguish themselves by the name of Scuit or Scots'.[36] According to the myth, these settlers landed in both Ireland and Scotland, making the Scots the descendants of Egyptians (as well as Scythians). As I discuss below, Mathers also reanimated this myth by explicitly casting himself as a descendant of Scota to bolster the legitimacy of his Scottish ancestry, as well as his Rites of Isis.[37] The Egyptian foundation myth appears throughout Scottish history: it is referenced in the Declaration of Arbroath (1320), Scotland's declaration of independence, which describes the Scots as descendants of 'Greater Scythia', and Allan Ramsay was interested in the myth as he looked to the 'Doric' tongue of Theocritus, the Egyptian court poet, to help inspire the revival of Scottish vernacular literature.[38] At the *fin de siècle*, cultural revivalists reanimated this myth, as it complemented various aims of the Revival: it not only helped distinguish Scotland and suggest its alternative origins to England, but also linked Scottish identity more closely to its Celtic heritage and to Ireland. The resurrection of this myth at the *fin de siècle* may help explain why so many Egyptian references appear in Scottish art. Given Duncan's role in resurrecting the Scota Pharaoh myth at the Scottish National Pageant, it is certainly possible that the proliferation of Egyptian-inspired decorations in *The Evergreen* (several by Duncan) owe a debt to Scota.

The Theosophical Society and the Golden Dawn

Besides drawing from similar iconographical resources as occultists, a number of Scottish cultural revivalists were active members of occult orders and societies, or participated in their events and publications. These occult groups appealed to cultural revivalists for two main reasons: not only did they help authenticate particular notions of Scottish identity (especially its association with Jacobitism and Catholicism) but they also offered spaces for revivalists to express their dissidence. One of the most widespread occult societies of this period, which hoped to make 'the mysteries of ancient Egypt [and . . .] the great Oriental philosophies thinkable to the average European',[39] was the Theosophical Society. Established in New York City in 1875, the Theosophical Society soon became an international phenomenon. Bearing the motto, 'there is no religion higher than truth', the society was primarily concerned with finding the hidden, unifying force that the world's religions had emerged from. Through lectures, demonstrations and discussion, the society advocated a comparative study of religion and occult texts, and by fusing Christianity, Kabbalah, astral projection, and Buddhist and Hindu belief, the society hoped the foster its central ideal – universal brotherhood. Unlike other *fin-de-siècle* occult groups, Theosophy (on the whole) was not a closed-off society but one that encouraged participation, which helped it spread as widely as it did. By 1910, there were seventeen different national sections of the society, including the Scottish section.

While the distinctive Scottish section was formed in 1910, theosophical lodges had been active in Scotland since 1884, with the founding of the 'Scottish lodge' in Edinburgh. This lodge appealed 'especially to men of science and intellect', and its third president was the lawyer, John William Brodie-Innes, who penned several texts on magic and would go on to play a leading role in Edinburgh's Golden

Dawn temple.[40] The transactions of the 'Scottish lodge' were edited by Brodie-Innes and were regularly published under the title *Occult, Scientific, and Literary Papers, Read at the Scottish Lodge*. This elite 'Scottish lodge', with its 'drawing-room character',[41] was soon accompanied by an 'Edinburgh branch' in 1891, which aimed to make the society more accessible; this branch followed the first Glasgow lodge, which was established in 1888. By the 1910s, theosophical lodges or branches could be found in towns and cities across Scotland; even relatively small towns of 10,000 inhabitants (such as Bo'ness) possessed a Theosophical Society branch. This national interest was nourished by a new periodical, *Theosophy in Scotland*, edited by the Fabian and future Labour MP David Graham Pole, which reported on affairs from across Scotland. Theosophy's appeal was not limited to men either: amongst the various female members was the astrologist and translator of Ibsen, Isabelle M. Pagan, who was an active member of the Edinburgh lodge, and Mona Caird, a member of the Blavatsky Lodge in London between 1904 and 1909.

As I have illustrated elsewhere, Theosophy had close ties to Scottish cultural revivalism, as well as the Scottish Home Rule movement.[42] For instance, in a speech to the SHRA in 1919, one of the United Kingdom's leading Theosophists and socialists, Annie Besant, declared her support for the cause. Besant, who had critiqued the suppression of native religions and government in India by missionaries and imperialists, used her speech in Glasgow to assert the importance of national autonomy, stressing that a nation must be 'free to develop the possibilities within itself'. She also drew on spiritual language to bolster her argument, affirming that 'God has written a sentence' 'over the cradle of every nation', a statement that reworks another she made in 1910, which characterised every nation as 'a spark from the divine fire'.[43] Theosophy was not simply connected to Scotland's political activism, though; by authenticating the notion of Scotland as Celtic, and commending the abiding significance of spiritual traditions in Scotland, Theosophy also supported the cultural revival. In one article published in *Theosophy in Scotland*, 'The Future Work of Scotland', a Theosophist, 'Brother Atisha', notes that 'in many respects Scotland is a chosen land [. . .] some of the sacred spots seem still to be *alive* with the spirit of the old gods and initiates'.[44] Scotland here is styled as one of the principal sacred enclosures, a land where mysticism and occultism have survived modernity. The article also portrays the Celts more broadly as a race 'capable of penetrating into the deep mysteries of the East; for many Oriental traits still linger in the Celtic mind'.[45]

Given Theosophists' celebration of national autonomy and their authentication of Scotland's Celticism, it is unsurprising that several revivalists were drawn to it. As I illustrate in 'Theosophy in Scotland', Geddes, who was friends with Annie Besant and had formerly tutored her, attended Theosophical Society lectures, while William Sharp took 'deep interest in genuine theosophical work', and contributed a short story and poetry to *The Theosophical Review* between 1904 and 1905.[46] While Geddes and Sharp demonstrated a concerted interest in Theosophy, their *Evergreen* colleague, John Duncan, was an active member of the Theosophical Society in Edinburgh. In 1909, Duncan joined the Edinburgh lodge, before transferring his membership to Edinburgh's Orpheus lodge, which focused on art and drama, with his wife, Christine Allen.[47] Duncan not only donated artworks to the Theosophical Society in Scotland, but also undertook a commission for Ananda College in Sri Lanka, established by the Buddhist Theosophical Society, for which he painted a cycle of the life of the Buddha.[48] Theosophy's authentication of hidden phenomena would have appealed to Duncan, who claimed to experience visions of Celtic mythological figures. Several of these visions were recorded in his paintings, artworks that Duncan believed helped people 'mediate with the unseen'.[49] *The Riders of the Sidhe* (Plate 12),[50] for example, depicts the Celtic faery people, who are believed to emerge from their underground mounds on May Night (30 April), on horseback. According to Duncan's acquaintance Charles Richard Cammell, Duncan had seen these faery people:

> He told me that he himself had seen the people of the *Sidh* (pronounced *Shee*) with his own eyes. He told me and my wife that he could teach us how to see these faery-folk; that you never see them in front of you, but sidelong through the corners of your eyes, that is, with the *oblique* glance, to which one finds allusions in these old legends. Duncan had painted the *Sidh* from memory; so vividly had they impressed themselves on his mind.[51]

Duncan uses his art to allow audiences to behold the occult, casting himself as a medium who can bring hidden, mythological figures to wider audiences. Like his Irish equivalent, George Russell (Æ), who countered the fey, childlike representations of Celtic mythological figures (especially faeries) at the *fin de siècle*, Duncan presents potent, regal faeries in this painting. They each carry symbols, three of which are magical jewels of the Tuatha Dé Danaan – the stone of destiny, the cauldron of the Dagda (or the Grail cup) and the sword of light.

As we have seen, Yeats, a fellow member of the Theosophical Society whose poem, 'The Hosting of the Sidhe' (1899), may have inspired Duncan's painting, was similarly enchanted by these jewels and hoped that they would adorn his Castle of the Heroes in Lough Key.[52] The fourth faery in Duncan's painting carries a wand and a tree of life, which were commonly referenced symbols at the *fin de siècle* in occult orders, including the Golden Dawn. Through his art, Duncan not only demonstrates the strength and nobility of these Celtic occult figures, but highlights art's capacity to serve as an intercessor between physical and occult words at the *fin de siècle*.

While the Theosophical Society helped authenticate Celtic mysticism and the image of Scotland as a Celtic territory, the Hermetic Order of the Golden Dawn supported Scottish cultural revivalism in other ways, principally by allowing individuals to recover and express dissident identities that valorised aspects of Scottish culture associated with its pre-Union history (such as Jacobitism). Featuring a range of prominent cultural figures amongst its initiates, such as Florence Farr, W. B. Yeats, Arthur Machen and William Sharp, the Hermetic Order of the Golden Dawn was founded in 1888 by three Freemasons – Samuel Liddell MacGregor Mathers, William Wynn Westcott and William Robert Woodman. In the mid-1880s, Mathers, Westcott and Woodman endeavoured to create a magical order that would embody the teachings of the Cipher Manuscripts.[53] As a result, the Golden Dawn was rooted in a curriculum that included both theoretical and practical magic, covering Kabbalah, astrology, geomancy and tarot divination. By passing examinations, initiates of the Golden Dawn could ascend the various grades of the order, from the introductory Neophyte grade to the most advanced, Ipsissimus. The first temple, Isis-Urania, was established in London in 1888, before spreading throughout the United Kingdom and to Paris. In 1893, Edinburgh's temple, Amen-Ra, was founded, following the Horus temple in Bradford and the Osiris temple in Weston-super-Mare (1888). Due to frustrations with Mathers's management of the Golden Dawn towards the turn of the century, there were a series of schisms amongst the initiates, leading to the formation of four new orders, including the Stella Matutina (based in London, which Yeats became a member of) and the Alpha et Omega (based in Paris, which Edinburgh's Amen-Ra temple affiliated with). While the Golden Dawn's hierarchical system and process of examination distinguished it from the Theosophical Society, it nevertheless attracted several Theosophists. The President of the Theosophical Society's 'Scottish lodge', Brodie-Innes, became the Imperator, or chief, of Amen-Ra, and styled himself as the Head of the Order in Scotland.

Similarly, the Theosophical medical missionary Robert Felkin joined the Golden Dawn upon the founding of Amen-Ra in Edinburgh.

Amen-Ra, the 'Scottish Temple',[54] was established in 1893 and largely followed the teachings of the wider order, as Emily Drummond's 'Book of Rituals' reveals.[55] While the location of the temple in Edinburgh remains unknown, we know that it contained a movable altar that was decorated with the symbol of the temple (a holy cross positioned above a triangle that framed a sunrise).[56] The Golden Dawn's address book lists fifty-six initiates at Amen-Ra, who were required to pay an annual subscription of twelve shillings and sixpence, and it is believed that the temple was active until 1912, when it officially became 'Alpha and Omega 2'.[57] As with the other Golden Dawn temples, each member had a magical motto or secret name; for example, Brodie-Innes's motto was H. Frater Sub Spe (meaning 'brother under hope'). Given the temple's association with the Egyptian sun god, Ra, the temple also included biannual Equinox ceremonials that every initiate was expected to attend.[58]

As with Theosophists, Scotland proved attractive to Golden Dawn initiates, who wanted to associate themselves with a land where faith in magic and hidden realms had survived modernity. Among these figures were MacGregor Mathers and Aleister Crowley, the latter one of the most notorious initiates of the Golden Dawn. Both of them not only associated themselves with Scotland but cast themselves as Scottish nationals. Foot notes that Mathers 'embellished himself with an invented Scottish lineage to strengthen the perception of his magus powers',[59] and he was not alone in claiming a Scottish lineage or wearing traditional Scottish dress. Crowley also attempted to align himself with Scottish nationality and even moved to Boleskine House, near Loch Ness, to develop his Thelemic system. But Mathers and Crowley did not style themselves as Scottish simply to link themselves to a locale that was felt to be especially mystical at the *fin de siècle*; they also did so to advance their neo-Jacobitism.

The Jacobite Revival and Neo-Catholicism

Amongst the various dissident revivals that took hold in the 1890s was the Jacobite Revival. As Ian Fletcher and Murray Pittock have demonstrated, identification with Jacobitism and support for restoring the House of Stuart was expressed in this period 'on a scale unwitnessed since the eighteenth century'.[60] Pittock argues that *fin-de-siècle* opposition to materialist, bourgeois society 'led many artists of the Symbolist period to espouse the politics of an aristocratic pre-bourgeois past in both their art and society beyond it'.[61] Across the United Kingdom, those looking for a golden, pre-Puritan age in which art, culture and aristocracy were cherished championed the Stuart era. As a consequence, Jacobite periodicals emerged, most notably *The Royalist* (1890–1903), and Jacobite societies were founded, including the Order of the White Rose (1886) and the more political Legitimist League (1891). The former order included James Abbott McNeill Whistler (who wrote of his descent from the McNeills of Barra)[62] among its members, as well as Andrew Lang.[63] The latter league published work by the Home Ruler, Theodore Napier, who dedicated his plea for Stuart restoration, *The Royal House of Stuart* (1898), to the Queen – Maria Theresa of Austria-Este, Jacobite claimant to the British crown. In Napier's work, Scottish nationalism and neo-Jacobitism became mutually supportive – a trend that has also been identified in the work of the Gaelic revivalist, Stuart Erskine,[64] who edited the Jacobite, epicurean newspaper, *The Whirlwind* (1890), to which Whistler and Walter Sickert contributed.[65] Besides the Stuart age's association with art, pre-Union Scotland and aristocracy, certain figures were also attracted to Jacobitism because of the enthusiasm for 'Rosicrucianism, astrology, natural magic, and inner light' during the Stuart era, as Earl Miner identifies.[66] As a culture that had once been 'condemned to secrecy',[67] and had devised secret societies and a language of hidden symbols to sustain itself during the years of sedition,[68] Jacobitism would have had an additional lure for *fin-de-siècle* occultists.

The Golden Dawn most clearly embodies the late Victorian occultist turn towards the Stuart age and, in aligning themselves with Jacobitism, several initiates participated in critiquing the constitutional formation of the United Kingdom. As has been well documented, both Mathers and his rival Crowley were neo-Jacobites who tried to adopt Scottish nationality. As John Symonds notes:

> Crowley, at a later date, dubbed himself the Laird of Boleskine and Abertarff for no greater reason than that he had a one-storeyed house of that name on the shore of Loch Ness. Later, Mathers transposed his adopted and real names to become Mathers MacGregor; then, after he had gone to live in Paris, to the Chevalier MacGregor. Nightly he changed into Highland dress and danced the sword dance with a knife (*skean-dhu*) in his stocking, a remarkable performance for the son of a merchant's clerk, an Englishman who never set foot in Scotland until the spring of 1897, when he inspected the Golden Dawn's Amen-Ra Temple in Edinburgh and caught a cold.[69]

There are several parallels between Crowley's and Mathers's performances of Scottish nationality. Like the Laird of Boleskine, Mathers and his wife Moina (sister of Henri Bergson) styled themselves as the Count and Countess of Glenstrae in an attempt to claim Scottish nobility.[70] And, like Mathers, Crowley was known to don traditional Scottish garb,[71] not least the MacGregor tartan,[72] to further the image of himself as a Scottish nobleman. Crowley also adopted the name of MacGregor, signing letters Aleister MacGregor,[73] and, not unlike Moina Mathers who changed the spelling of her name (from Mina) to sound more Celtic, Crowley changed one of his forenames (Alexander) to its near-equivalent in Gaelic, Aleister.[74] He even identified himself as a 'High Tory and Jacobite' in a bid to live out his childhood fantasy of having ancient, aristocratic Druidic roots.[75]

Mathers's neo-Jacobitism was particularly strong, to the extent that it started to compromise the Golden Dawn. Mathers's motto in the Golden Dawn was 'S Rioghal Mo Dhream'[76] ('my race is royal' – the MacGregor clan motto), and he also cast himself as both James IV reincarnated and '"the last descendent of a Scottish king"'.[77] At a time when Mathers was increasingly distracted by Jacobite politics, Annie Horniman was expelled from the Golden Dawn for refusing to give Mathers money because he was using it for political over magical purposes.[78] Horniman's frustration was further fuelled by Brodie-Innes,[79] who had boasted that 'he was in continual correspondence on political matters with Mr Mathers *not* on Order business'.[80] There is speculation that Brodie-Innes was member of a neo-Jacobite White Rose Society, while his father was a member of the New Spalding Club, which published historical papers on the Jacobite period in 1895. Mathers's Jacobite distractions and his despotic rule of the Golden Dawn proved to be key factors in the order's fragmentation.

In his turn to Scottish Jacobitism, Mathers participated in Scottish cultural revivalism and uttered statements that suggested he was supportive of Home Rule for Scotland. Mathers styled himself as a defender of Scottish cultural and political identity: Yeats stated that Mathers 'imagined a Napoleonic role for himself, a Europe transformed to his fancy, Scotland a principality, Egypt restored'.[81] It is not exactly clear what a Scottish principality means here, but it implies some form of royal or political autonomy. Mathers also sought to re-establish the Celtic pantheon (like Yeats), which was partly the purpose behind his planned magazine *Isis*, an allusion to the Egyptian goddess.[82] Mathers's conflation of Celtic and Egyptian culture reflected his conviction that he was a descendant of Scota

Pharaoh; he even described himself as 'the last ring' of Scota's 'sacred chain'.[83] In his calls for Scottish political or monarchical distinction and his authenticating Scottish myths of descent, Mathers's ideas reflected some of the more eccentric ones found amongst Scottish cultural revivalists. Relatively conventional, Brodie-Innes's writings were also consistent with revivalist thinking, especially in their concern with defending Celtic identity from Saxon incorporation. In 1917, he wrote:

> Altogether the foot of the Saxon has been very heavy on the west, and the old occultism and the old fairy lore have retreated out of sight, and largely I fear out of mind [. . .]. I have tried to string together a few rambling memories [. . .]. I can only vouch for their truth as personal experiences of a time when the occultism of the Celtic west was not only a very real thing, but was looked on as utterly natural.[84]

Brodie-Innes here associates Celticism with occultism and voices his desire to preserve both Celtic lore and its occult features, in the face of them being wiped out. Brodie-Innes also worked to maintain the independence of the Scottish lodge of the Theosophical Society, according to R. A. Gilbert – an expression of his institutional nationalism.[85] These high-profile initiates of the Golden Dawn, in their turn to Jacobitism, found themselves countering Saxonism and articulating myths of descent that brought them into rhetorical proximity with other revivalists, many of whom were also turning their attention to the Stuart age.

As we witnessed in Chapter 1, Robert Louis Stevenson, Violet Jacob and Andrew Lang revived and reimagined the Jacobite romance genre at the *fin de siècle*, and their work spoke to a broader literary interest in Jacobitism in Scotland: *The Song of the Stewarts* (1909), by *The Yellow Book* contributor and acquaintance of Oscar Wilde, Douglas Ainslie, and W. G. Blaikie Murdoch's writings on Jacobitism and aestheticism further reflect the renewed Scottish enthusiasm for the Jacobites.[86] Among the various cultural revivalists who were inspired by the Stuart age were the contributors to *The Evergreen*, several of whom associated that period with a healthier state of Scottish nationality. *The Evergreen*'s title alone makes a covert allusion to Jacobitism in that it harks back to *The Ever Green* (1724), a poetry anthology edited by a well-known Jacobite sympathiser, Allan Ramsay. *The Evergreen*'s contents also include several references to the Jacobite past. In 'The Scots Renascence', for instance, Geddes writes:

> One day noble traditions long forgot will rouse a mightier literature, nobler localities still unvisited bring forth more enduring labours for their crown. Though Charlie may no come back again, though the too knightly king, so long expected back from Flodden, lie for ever 'mid the Flowers o' the Forest, though Mary's fair face still rouse dispute as of old, the Wizard's magic book still waits unmouldering in his tomb. The prophetic Rhymer listens from Elfland, Arthur sits in the Eildon Hills, Merlin but sleeps in his thorn. (137)

Geddes's interest in the occult is evident in this quotation: he imagines hidden localities that are yet to be uncovered, and reveals his enthusiasm for wizardry, magic and foresight (through referencing the prophet Thomas the Rhymer and Merlin). Geddes alludes to three Stuart figures here – Charles Edward Stuart, James IV and Mary Stuart – and, while he portrays this Stuart era as over, he nevertheless imagines their times as nobler, and believes that the traditions of past eras can be aroused and revived to create a 'mightier literature'. The Stuart era is styled as a time of stronger Scottish culture, whose spirit may be uncovered, contacted and revived. As Merlin and Arthur lie waiting to rise (an idea I explore in greater detail in Chapter 5), the Stuarts might still come to inspire Scottish culture. Geddes's naming of his 'Scots College' in Montpellier is a further example of his neo-Jacobitism, as Scots Colleges (Roman Catholic seminaries in Europe) had served as refuges for Jacobite exiles in the eighteenth century.

Alongside Geddes's implication that the Stuart era still had the potential to ennoble Scottish culture, despite being over, John Duncan's *Anima Celtica*, printed in *The Evergreen*, similarly suggests that Jacobitism can revive Scottish art. The illustration (Fig. 4.4) is accompanied by an epigraph by Duncan, which states that, although 'the past has been and shall not be again', the 'disarmed, deposed' soul of the Celts can yet open 'a wide new kingdom in the minds of men'. While Duncan participates in associating Celtic identity with a past, defeated 'stage' here, consistent with some of William Sharp's imaginings of Celtic identity that we encountered in Chapter 3, the image (which Sharp critiqued)[87] nevertheless associates Jacobitism with this Celtic soul that can inspire culture. The soul of the Celt is surrounded by Celtic mythical figures, including Fingal, Cuchullin, Ossian and Malvina, but on the table in front of this female embodiment of the Celt is 'a dirk and bonnet typical of the weapons and dress of the 1745 Jacobite uprising'.[88] By foregrounding these militarist symbols, Duncan highlights how the spirit of Jacobite resistance, fused with Celtic mythology, can animate Scottish culture.

Figure 4.4 John Duncan, *Anima Celtica*, in *The Evergreen*, 1 (1895): 107.

A further reference to the Stuarts in *The Evergreen* is the illustration that immediately follows Geddes's 'The Scots Renascence' essay, *Maria Regina Scotorum* (Fig. 4.5) by Pittendrigh Macgillivray, who addressed the '45 Club in 1911 and also published neo-Jacobite poems in his collection, *Pro Patria* (1915).[89] Through the Latin title and her crucifix necklace, Macgillivray highlights Mary Stuart's Catholicism.[90]

Mary Stuart's association with the ritualism and spiritualism of Catholicism, as well as her tragic end, led to her becoming an iconic figure for Catholics, occultists and dissidents at the *fin de siècle*. For instance, Marie Sinclair (Lady Caithness), who was President of the Société Théosophique d'Orient et d'Occident in Paris, asserted her 'devotion' to Mary Stuart and claimed to channel her spirit. In *A Midnight Visit to Holyrood* (1887), Sinclair relates Mary Stuart's appearance to her, with Stuart telling Sinclair that men are incapable of listening 'to the voice of the Deific forces'.[91] As occultists associated Mary Stuart with the divine feminine, aesthetic writers were drawn to the romance of her life and times: Algernon Charles Swinburne wrote a trilogy of plays about Mary Stuart,[92] while Pater noted that her story was characterised by 'heroic and vehement hatreds and love' when demonstrating the influence of the Stuarts on Dante Gabriel Rossetti.[93] *The Tragic Mary*, by Michael Field (the pseudonym of Katherine Bradley and Edith Cooper), presented Stuart as a '*femme fatale*', a 'decadent artist and aesthete'.[94] With these contemporary associations, the inclusion of Mary Stuart in *The Evergreen* is consistent with the various forms of *fin-de-siècle* dissidence that the magazine spoke to: decadence, occultism and neo-Jacobitism.

Figure 4.5 Pittendrigh Macgillivray, *Maria Regina Scotorum*, in *The Evergreen*, 1 (1895): 141.

Due to the inclusion of such illustrations as *Maria Regina Scotorum* and the magazine's wider neo-Jacobitism, contributions to *The Evergreen* were slighted by *The Glasgow Herald* as 'neo-Catholic' and 'too vague and gushing for our coarsened Presbyterian tastes'.[95] Among those contributions specified by *The Herald* as 'neo-Catholic' was Victor Branford's 'Awakenings in History', which portrays the medieval Catholic church as an 'ideal society', responsible for ushering in 'the most wide-spread awakening of all'.[96] This neo-Catholicism was by no means limited to the pages of *The Evergreen*. Decadent writers and artists across Europe found themselves turning to Catholicism for spiritual and artistic awakening: J. K. Huysmans, Aubrey Beardsley, Paul Verlaine, Ernest Dowson, 'Michael Field', John Gray, Oscar Wilde and Lionel Johnson all converted to Catholicism.[97] As Miriam Elizabeth Burstein cautions, this did not necessarily make each convert a devout Catholic[98]: several decadents turned to Catholicism to express a religious dilettantism or, much like neo-Jacobites, because they were attracted to the aesthetic dimension of Catholic ritualism, which had been promoted by John Henry Newman and the Tractarians in the mid-nineteenth century. Because of this ritualism, several occultists also turned to Catholicism, most notably Joséphin Péladan, whose Ordre de la Roise + Croix fused Rosicrucian occultism with Catholicism.[99] Nevertheless, these decadent converts did share the view that modernity 'was defined by moral, political and cultural decay' and embraced neo-Catholicism in symbolic defiance of industrialism, democracy or empiricism.[100]

Although Scotland is often neglected in considerations of *fin-de-siècle* neo-Catholicism, several occult-inclined revivalists participated in it, often through denouncing the Protestant Reformation and its disenchanting influence on Scottish culture. Despite being brought up in the Free Church of Scotland and associating it with Celticism – describing the Free Church as 'our Celtic religious movement' – Geddes could be virulent in his attack on the Reformation and its aftermath.[101] A committed Europhile, Geddes believed the Reformation fragmented European educational cohesiveness, declaring, 'I wish to undo that evil result of the Reformation, the breaking of the intellectual unity of Europe.'[102] When writing with Branford, Geddes also identified the 'moral narrowness of Calvinism',[103] and elsewhere described the Free Church's principle of endurance as diffusing 'sordid ugliness' and 'bacterial dirt' that were the 'shame of puritan Edinburgh'.[104] The naming of his Scots College in Montpellier was a further suggestion of his neo-Catholicism. Sharp, writing as Fiona Macleod, also believed that Calvinism had caused the health of Scotland to deteriorate, describing it as 'a curse to our despoiled land'.[105] Sharp imagined Macleod and her writings as a remedy to this curse: not only did she prophesy the redemption of Celtic Scotland in her writings, as we encountered in Chapter 3, and critique Calvinism in her stories, but Sharp explicitly identified Macleod as Catholic.[106] This respiritualising redemption from Calvinism was connected to Sharp's occultism. As several critics have thoroughly demonstrated, Sharp's membership of the Golden Dawn brought him closer to the mysticism of Yeats,[107] while his Catholic alias was also closely tied to the occult. At times, Sharp styled his Macleod texts as automatic writings: he told fellow writer Ernest Rhys that, following his discovery of Fiona on the banks of Lake Nemi, near Rome, his 'pen wrote as if dipped in fire, and when I sat down to write prose, a spirit hand would seize the pen and guide it into inspired verse'.[108] Sharp also used his anti-Calvin pseudonym to participate in psychic experimentations (via correspondence) with Yeats and MacGregor Mathers in Paris.[109]

Geddes's and Sharp's strident attacks on Calvinism and the Reformation at the *fin de siècle* prefigure similar critiques by writers of the Scottish Renaissance in the interwar period. Scholars of Scottish modernism have argued that writers of the later Renaissance project (from the 1920s onwards) appealed to 'pre-Reformation cultural forms'.[110] These appeals are particularly evident in Edwin Muir's and Hugh MacDiarmid's work: MacDiarmid saw the Reformation as 'a blight on Scottish arts and affairs', and Muir associates John Knox and Andrew Melville with the 'desolation' of the nation in 'Scotland 1941'.[111] Further into the twentieth century, George Mackay Brown's 'The Storm' described Scotland as a 'Knox-ruined nation'.[112] Pre-Reformation and pre-Union Scotland are associated with stronger national health in these texts; as Linden Bicket notes of MacDiarmid, he 'allied the greatness of Scotland's medieval art with its former status as an independent polity'.[113] While *fin-de-siècle* cultural revivalists were not attacking the Reformation from an anti-Union vantage, those twentieth-century Renaissance writers' association of cultural revivalism with a resistance to Calvinism can be very clearly traced back to the 1890s.

Patrick Geddes's Evergreen Club

Neo-Catholicism and occultism most clearly met in Joséphin Péladan's Order of the Rose + Croix at the *fin de siècle*. Péladan was a French Catholic novelist who founded an occult order, the Kabbalistic Order of the Rose-Cross, with Stanislas de Guaíta in 1888.

Due to tensions within the group, Péladan broke from the order and established his own, the Order of the Rose + Croix, in Paris in 1890, which included many symbolist painters among its members. Captivated by the medieval Rosicrucian Brotherhood, Péladan's order hoped to fuse 'Catholic devotion' with Rosicrucianism, and it has been described as a cultural renewal project 'symptomatic of late nineteenth-century reactions against Positivism, which had disavowed the inner life in favour of reason and the hard sciences'.[114] More specifically, it was an order that expressed nostalgia for the *ancien régime*.[115] This order underpinned the Salon de la Rose + Croix, a series of six art salons hosted by Péladan in Paris, which took place between 1892 and 1897, displaying mystical artworks by a range of prominent European symbolists. These symbolists included Puvis de Chavannes, whose mural paintings influenced John Duncan; Carlos Schwabe and Jan Toorop, whose work left an imprint on the Glasgow School, according to Jessie Newbery;[116] and Jean Delville, a future lecturer at the Glasgow School of Art who painted Péladan posing in robes as the 'Grand Master of the Rosicrucians' in 1895. The subjects of the paintings at the salons were also akin to those of Scottish revival art: sphinxes, holy grails, pagan deities, angels and figures of Catholic devotion appeared in many. As with *The Evergreen*, woodcuts were a favoured form of medium for the salons' artists too.

A further parallel between the artworks of Péladan's Salon de la Rose + Croix and *The Evergreen* magazine can be found lurking amongst Patrick Geddes's manuscript archives at the University of Strathclyde. These archives hold six notecards on which Geddes devised his own occult order, titled 'The Evergreen Club'. Along with various other tropes of *fin-de-siècle* occultism that appear in these notes, including references to Celtic symbols, secret names and initiation rituals, 'Rose Croise' is explicitly referenced on the cards. Geddes's planned club reveals how deeply engaged he was with *fin-de-siècle* occultism, and how similar Scottish developments were to Yeats's planned Order of Celtic Mysteries and European Rosicrucian orders.

Before exploring these notes in detail, it is necessary to understand how pervasive Geddes's interest in occultism was. Geddes has been characterised as a scientist suffering from 'excessive empiricism',[117] but throughout his work we find a concern with the noumenal, which is tied to his cultural revivalism and the thinking behind his Evergreen Club. In 'The Scots Renascence', the significance of the noumenal and spiritual are clearly evident. Here, Geddes describes Edinburgh as an 'ice-pack of frozen culture',[118] in a manner that anticipates Muir's 'Scotland's Winter', while resembling his own description of Celtic culture as 'frozen' in his essay 'Celtic Cross'.[119] Like Muir's poem, the essay also references the tombs of national heroes. Geddes stands over the tomb of John de Graham, an ally of William Wallace, and considers how a seemingly lost spirit can be revived to nourish a cultural revival:

> Yet here the teacher will some day bring his scholars and read them Blind Harry's verse. And so in some young soul here and there the spirit of the hero and the poet may awaken, and press him onward into a life which can face defeat in turn. Such is our Scottish, our Celtic Renascence – sadly set betwixt the Keening, the watching over our fathers dead, and the second-sight of shroud rising about each other. Yet this is the Resurrection and the Life, when to faithful love and memory their dead arise.[120]

Couched in the language of spiritualism, Geddes defines the Scots Renascence: a movement that requires lamenting, but also reawakening, the memory of the dead. There is a melancholy to these lines, but they also express Geddes's belief in the 'indestructible sovereignty of the ever-returning past', and his concerted effort to present 'a tradition of continuity' between the Scots and their heroes, which Anthony Smith sees as crucial to nation-building efforts.[121] In making these points, spiritualist contact with the dead and second sight are adopted as metaphors for the cultural revival – Scottish society must commune with, remember and reanimate the past. Geddes's points resemble William Sharp's depiction of the soul of the Celt as living in a 'spell-bound trance' – a dormant culture, belonging to the occult sphere, waiting for a 'blast' to be roused.[122] But Geddes's references to the noumenal here were not simply rhetorical: across his writings and projects, his conviction about practical supernaturalism and its potential to nourish contemporary culture recurrently appears, and underpinned his desire to establish the Evergreen Club.

Beyond his interest in Indian spiritualism and Theosophy, noted above, which led Philip Boardman to describe him aptly as 'a sceptical Western scientist *and* an Indian mystic',[123] Geddes was enthusiastic about witchcraft, Western esotericism and the Bahá'í faith. Geddes's concern with Scottish witchcraft and magic is evident throughout his writings and he associated his Celticism with it, sometimes referring to Scottish witchcraft as 'Celtic witchery'.[124] He was so taken by the history of Scottish witchcraft that the emblem of the Outlook Tower, which decorated the building and featured in Patrick Geddes and Colleagues publications, includes three witches flying over Edinburgh. This emblem related to the Outlook Tower's history – witches were burned at the stake on the site of Ramsay Garden, a fact that was commemorated with a fountain beside Ramsay Garden, designed by John Duncan, known as the Witches' Well. The executed occultist Major Thomas Weir had also lived in this area in the seventeenth century. The Ramsay Garden common room mural sequence, discussed in Chapter 3, is testament to Geddes's (and Duncan's) interest in the history of Scottish magic, as several subjects were chosen because of their connections to the occult. The guide to the murals tells us that the scheme features 'pictures of the imagination, of magic and romance': ideas that are not 'dead, but modern and increasing'.[125] We are told that Michael Scot dealt 'mainly with astrology, alchemy, and the occult sciences'; St Mungo practised 'gentle magic'; and John Napier of Merchiston 'dabbled in the occult'.[126] Geddes and Duncan clearly selected Scottish figures who they believed had links to practical magic. In doing so, they attempted to authenticate the notion of Scotland as a nation where magic and the supernatural flourish, much like the collector of magical literature, John Ferguson, who wrote that 'a belief in magic in Scotland is older than any literature which has come before me'.[127] But it also reflected Geddes's and Duncan's own participation in *fin-de-siècle* occultism and their belief in hidden phenomena.

Geddes was certainly stimulated by the Bahá'í faith, which was closely allied to Theosophy in its desire to find commonality between the world's religions. Geddes even gave Abdu'l-Bahá a tour of the Outlook Tower when he visited Edinburgh, after paying a visit John Duncan's house, and Geddes conducted town plans in Haifa, Palestine, that were authorised by Bahá.[128] Geddes appears to have taken an interest in the Golden Dawn too, although his connections are obscure. As yet, no textual evidence has been found to suggest that he was a member of the Golden Dawn; however, Alexander Farquharson, who was Secretary of Le Play House, a hub of Geddes and Branford's social betterment movement, claimed that 'Geddes was connected with the GD [Golden Dawn].'[129] It is possible that Geddes could have been a member, as the order's address books, which contain lists of the initiates, are far from authoritative. However, even if Geddes was not an initiate of the Golden Dawn, it is undeniable that he was aware of it and its ideas. For example, he made notes from Arthur Edward Waite's *The Mysteries of Magic: A Digest of the Writings of Eliphas Levi*. Waite was a prominent member of the Golden Dawn and his book elucidates various occult beliefs and concepts that the Golden Dawn adopted, including Kabbalistic doctrines, conjuration, the astral body and tarot. Geddes's notes make specific reference to the second part of Waite's book, 'Doctrines of Occult Force'.[130] Among his other occult readings, Geddes is known to have read Edouard Schuré's history of esoteric religions, *The Great Initiates* (1889), and Maeterlinck's *The Great Secret* (1921).[131]

Geddes was keen not only to study the literature of *fin-de-siècle* magic and occultism but to put it into practice, which is evident in his descriptions of the Outlook Tower and his unpublished essay, 'What is the Mystic Life'. Geddes's Outlook Tower, adjacent to Ramsay Garden, may have been a museum and sociological centre, featuring a camera obscura, but Geddes referred to it in alternative terms. He named the Outlook Tower a 'Temple of Vision', with an aim 'to produce trained seers', and referred to the camera obscura as a 'wizard's mirror'.[132] Like several public buildings in the late nineteenth century, including Alois Bastl's planned scheme for a 'Palace for Scientific Occult Societies' (1902) in Paris, the Outlook Tower reflects the growth of quasi-religious, spiritual spaces in an age when the church no longer 'possessed the monopoly of reflection', as Nietzsche wrote;[133] temple designs also featured in Péladan's Parisian salons. Geddes wanted his Edinburgh temple and its seers to reveal the 'hiddenness of the obvious', an idea that he expands on in his paper, 'What is the Mystic Life'.[134] In this essay, Geddes outlines his desire to encourage a mystic life that can 'calm the ordinary life and subdue it' in order to awaken alternative states of consciousness, where 'new activities may develop, and upon a higher plane than customary ones'.[135] To do this, the essay proposes 'withdraw[ing] from all of the ordinary external activities and even, as far as may be, from all external receptivities, e.g., food', as well as performing raja yoga and entering a 'Yogi trance' (1–2). This 'suppression of environment and ordinary responses' would, Geddes wrote, lead to 'light visions', as well as the 'touch of loving hands and sexual ecstasies generally' (2). The association of sexual ecstasy with a 'higher plane' here is not dissimilar to Crowley's interest in sex 'magick' – using 'sexual energy' to ascend 'to the level where magick may be worked'.[136] These alternative, heightened states of mind, Geddes writes, would prompt a 'transvaluation', a 'renewal' that would move the participant 'through vision and to action' (3–4). Consistent with his commitment to social and cultural revival, Geddes defines the ways in which the mystic life can move individuals to a 'higher plane' that subdues the ordinary and familiar, and promotes 'renewal'. In making these points, Geddes defines not only the benefits of practising occultism, but also his interest in encouraging the practice of it and producing 'trained seers'.

One observer of, and participant in, Geddes's circle further confirms his concern with *fin-de-siècle* occultism. Riccardo Stephens was a Cornish writer, physician and occultist, who settled in Edinburgh and was one of the 'workers, thinkers, and dreamers who congregated in the settlement founded by Professor Patrick Geddes on the site of Allan Ramsay's residence – "New Edinburgh", as University Hall [was] sometimes called'. Filled with 'Celtic fire', Stephens contributed poetry to *The Evergreen* and Elizabeth Sharp's anthology, *Lyra Celtica* (1896), and published poems on the history of Edinburgh Castle.[137] He was also the secretary of Geddes's Edinburgh Summer School in 1895. In the mid-1890s, Stephens lived at 8 Coltbridge Terrace, Edinburgh, with William and Christine Peck, prominent adepts of the Amen-Ra temple, and Stephens himself became a member on 27 July 1896, bearing the motto 'sic itur ad astra' [thus one journeys to the stars]. Forming the clearest tie between Geddes's circle and the Golden Dawn, Stephens was especially sensitive to the occult happenings around Ramsay Garden, which inspired his novel *The Cruciform Mark* (1896). This novel, narrated by the 'Celtic' Richard Tregenna, focuses on life in University Hall, and recounts the various strange deaths of students and staff after beholding a ghostly female face. The novel very clearly references Geddes and his efforts. The Ramsay Garden common room and its murals – painted by a man who is 'a bit decadent' – appear, while Professor Grosvenor, the 'volatile scientist', is at least partly inspired by Geddes. Grosvenor's interest in the 'Philosopher's Stone', 'ascending spirals', 'the tree of Knowledge' and 'the past and the future' over the present (as well as the mention of the 'snake of Æsculapius' when Tregenna converses with him) align Grosvenor very closely to several of the occult concepts and symbols that Geddes was interested in, outlined below.[138] The novel also depicts the recurring appearance of a sphinx and references magic and secret societies. Stephens's representations confirm Geddes's enthusiasm for the occult while also furthering the association of Scotland with a disruptive magic. His novel is akin to Conan Doyle's 'John Barrington Cowles' (1886), set in Edinburgh, which also contains a dangerous female mesmerist and helps render the capital as a gothic space.

While he was deeply invested in occultism around the 1890s, Geddes nevertheless felt that ritualism was lacking from his projects based around the Outlook Tower. When writing to Branford in 1902 on esotericism and encouraging him to read Schuré's *The Great Initiates*, Geddes told his colleague, 'we have a temple, but what of the Mysteries? What of the initiation?'[139] Geddes's archival manuscripts reveal that he was actively attempting to remedy this problem, by brainstorming a plan to create an occult order that would be defined by ritualism and involve a process of initiation. Amongst the University of Strathclyde's Geddes archive are six small cards that Geddes penned, entitled 'The Evergreen Club'. It seems as though the club would consist of the contributors to *The Evergreen*, as, elsewhere in papers on the periodical, he refers to an 'Authors' Society (+ Club)'.[140] In some ways, the fact that Geddes was planning an occult order for *The Evergreen*'s contributors is unsurprising, considering that the magazine itself was described as symptomatic of 'cette invasion de tous les ésotérismes'.[141] Like occult orders, 'The Evergreen Club' was intended to be more than simply a social club: it would include a 'ritual of initiation' involving a 'Book of Chivalry', and the initiates would have secret names. The society would also have rules and a motto, the 'central idea of extirpating Boredom', and it was intended to support 'spiritual art – abjure cynical + decadent' and to stimulate a 'movement for directing moral upheaval'. Besides being a positive remedy to what Geddes saw as a debilitating decadence – in opposition to the potentially productive decadence discussed in Chapter 3 – the club not only was similar in structure to *fin-de-siècle* occult orders but also was closely bound up with the ideas and practices of the Golden Dawn and Péladan's order. Some of the words Geddes uses in his cards reveal this when they are considered together; they include 'Arbor Vitae', 'Rose Croise', 'Thelema', 'Chapel – PG', 'robes' and 'wreaths'. Beyond these terms, we also find references to Celtic symbolism that invite comparisons with Yeats's planned order. Each of these features will be considered here to demonstrate the striking ties between Geddes's planned club and *fin-de-siècle* occult orders, and the ways in which Geddes's cultural revivalism intersected with the occult.

The 'Arbor Vitae', or tree of life, was a central symbol of the Golden Dawn, drawn from Kabbalah, which represents ten sephirot (spiritual principles) and the twenty-two paths between the bottom one, Malkuth (earth), and the top, Kether (invisible sublimity). Geddes's knowledge of the tree of life is reflected in the final contribution to the Spring edition of *The Evergreen*, which presents a tree of life, the *Arbor Saeculorum* (Fig. 4.6). Bearing his initials, 'PG', Geddes's tree (guarded by sphinxes) does not present a symbolic representation of an individual's spiritual development, as in Kabbalah, but instead the development of society, stemming from roots in the animal world and flourishing with a bud at the top, which is highly reminiscent of the ascension and crown at the top of many Kabbalistic trees. Geddes

Figure 4.6 *Arbor Saeculorum*, in *The Evergreen*, 1 (1895): 143.

wrote of this tree that it is 'perpetually renewed' from its roots and that 'the spirals of smoke which curl among its branches' are representative of the blindness of 'thinkers and workers of each successive age to the thought and work of their precursors'.[142] As such, Geddes's *Arbor Saeculorum* embodies his attack on stadialist thinking and his conviction in the 'ever-returning past'. The serpent-like smoke that links all of the various ages of man together in Geddes's design also echoes several representations of the tree of life in Kabbalistic iconography[143] and what Mathers refers to as the 'serpent of wisdom'[144]: a 'centripetal force, ever seeking to penetrate into Paradise'.[145] Yeats similarly described this force as 'the Kabbalistic serpent-winding nature'.[146] Such ascending, helical spirals are also found in Mackintosh's tea room murals for Miss Cranston, which feature a serpent. Geddes's order and his designs, like Mackintosh's, suggest a marked debt to Kabbalistic thinking.

The 'Rose Croise', or Rosy Cross, is a very clear reference to the symbol of the Rosicrucian Order, believed to have been established by the legendary alchemist Christian Rosenkreuz around the fifteenth century, consisting of a cross with a rose in the centre. Rosicrucianism, which fused Eastern philosophy with traditional Christian beliefs and claimed to harbour 'esoteric secrets',[147] was reviving across Europe in this period, most notably with Péladan's Ordre de la Rose + Croix. For Max Nordau, Rosicrucianism was one of the features that marked the androgynous Péladan, who he discusses in detail, as a 'delirious' degenerate.[148] There had been a strong tradition of Rosicrucianism in Scotland: David Stevenson demonstrates that modern Freemasonry, and lodges with ritual functions, originated in Scotland in the seventeenth century from town craft guilds, and that these lodges were implicated in the development of Rosicrucianism from 1598.[149] The 'Rosicrucian quest' for hidden knowledge led many curious Scots to Masonic lodges, which claimed 'possession of arcane secrets'. Stevenson also shows that there was detailed knowledge of Rosicrucianism throughout Scotland.[150] Geddes's notes reflect the continuance of Rosicrucian ideas in Scotland but also his attentiveness to broader *fin-de-siècle* occultism, and his desire to develop a counter-cultural club that was concerned with the hidden.[151]

Geddes's reference to Thelema is striking and complex, especially considering that it is not precisely clear when these cards were written. It is logical to assume that they were penned at the time Geddes was working on *The Evergreen*, thus 1895–6. However, Thelema became an idea particularly associated with occult orders only in 1901, through Crowley, who established a magical system entitled Thelema, and named Boleskine House, which he bought from Mary Rose Hill Burton (a friend of Geddes's who contributed decorative panels to Ramsay Garden), his Abbey of Thelema.[152] This system's philosophy was 'do what thou wilt – then do nothing else'.[153] Crowley, like Geddes, was clearly drawing upon Rabelais, who wrote of an

Abbey of Thélème in *Gargantua and Pantagruel*, where 'do what thou wilt' and the pursuit of pleasure defined the abbey's philosophy. Strikingly, Boardman notes that Geddes established his own 'Abbey de Thélème' in the Mediterranean, to be used for excursions from Scots College in Montpellier, to improve university life and further his 'Agenda Synthetica' – his belief in amalgamating schools of religious thought, much like the syncretism that had fuelled Péladan's order.[154] Although Geddes is not generally associated with the hedonistic pursuit of pleasure, we can see hints of this attitude in his thinking, such as when he stated to his daughter Norah, 'I am still out for adventure, for all risks; and [do] not need Nietzsche to teach me to live dangerously.'[155] In this case, it is possible that Geddes's conflation of Thelema with Rosicrucianism and Kabbalah predates Crowley's and could be further proof that Geddes had greater ties and influence on the Golden Dawn than previously believed.

It is likely that the reference to the egotistical 'Chapel – PG' is also related to Geddes's Agenda Synthetica and a proto-occult mysticism. When commenting on religion, Geddes wrote:

> Of course I believe in the Bible [. . .] and in the Koran, and in all the bibles of all people, whether savages or Buddhists, Celts or Christians. To those vast storehouses of past wisdom, one makes one's contribution. I make mine by seeing that Life is bigger and more wonderful than has been thought; and that all the gospels put together cannot encompass it. The ecstasy of the highest Mystics is one with the elemental life-emotion of the Biosphere.[156]

These comments, which have ties to mysticism, Theosophy and the Bahá'í faith's belief in the unity of religions, reveal that Geddes was interested in fusing and augmenting established religious ideas, and it seems likely that such principles would be the basis of his chapel. The reference to 'wreaths' and 'robes' in Geddes's notes is also a key reflection of *fin-de-siècle* occultism, as initiates of the Golden Dawn and Péladan's Rose-Croix used robes and headdresses in ceremonies and performances. Taken together, these small cards demonstrate numerous concordances between Geddes's proposed Evergreen Club and prominent *fin-de-siècle* occult orders, revealing Geddes's desire to create his own occult order in Edinburgh.

What would distinguish this occult order from the Golden Dawn's Amen-Ra temple in Edinburgh was that its symbolism was infused with Celticism, reflecting the Celtic revivalism of *The Evergreen*'s contributors. Geddes proposed that the symbolism of the club should incorporate a Celtic 'Druid Oak Tree' (and initially 'oak leaves'), a tree that he says is for 'the healing of the nations'. This biblical phrase, which refers to the tree of life and its remedial leaves, is ambiguous: it can be interpreted as referring to nations overcoming their divisions, which is consistent with Geddes's interest in promoting a common identification with Celticism across Scotland, or as signifying the need for greater internationalism, a key facet of Geddes's thinking and his vision for Scottish culture. Both interpretations cohere with Geddes's cultural revivalism. Furthermore, Geddes's notes for the Evergreen Club mention a 'Round Table'. These two symbols – the round table and the druid oak tree – would reappear at Scots College in Montpellier: an oak tree and 'King Arthur's table' were placed in the garden precinct.[157] As is discussed at length in Chapter 5, Geddes styled Arthur as a Scottish and Celtic hero; thus these two symbols were united in their Celticism. The fact that he wanted to include these Celtic symbols in his occultist Evergreen Club parallels Yeats's Order of Celtic Mysteries; indeed, Geddes's reference to the Druids in his plans resembles Yeats's concern with 'reviving Druidic mysteries', as George Russell stated to Fiona Macleod.[158] The Evergreen Club may even have provided a space, like the Golden Dawn, to express *The Evergreen*'s neo-Jacobitism as 'oak leaves', which Geddes references in his plans, were strongly associated with the Stuarts, on account of Charles II famously hiding in an oak tree in 1651. Oak leaves appear in other neo-Jacobite projects in this period: in Mount Stuart House, designed by Robert Rowand Anderson for the Catholic Home Ruler and neo-Jacobite, John Crichton-Stuart, oak leaves are abundant in the interior decoration. The symbolism referred to in Geddes's notes strongly appears to suggest that he was developing a Celtic occult order in Scotland, which would help support the Scottish Revival and bear several similarities to Yeats's plans for an Irish Celtic order.

The revivalist dimension of the Evergreen Club is confirmed by the final decoration for the final issue of *The Evergreen*, *Lapis Philosophorum* (Fig. 4.7), which also featured in the interior decor of the Outlook Tower. The image, similar in design to the *Arbor Saeculorum* and also bearing the initials 'PG', concerns the philosopher's stone and its associated idea of transmutation, which was an important symbol in Golden Dawn magic. The philosopher's stone was key for Geddes too[159]: he believed it was 'scattered through the world',[160] and he conflated it with the Elixir Vitae, the potion that grants eternal life.[161] When writing on this image, and scorning the 'official scientist' who is 'so contemptuous of occultisms', Geddes

Figure 4.7 *Lapis Philosophorum*, in *The Evergreen*, 4 (1896): 157.

notes that the symbols are 'essentially hieroglyphic [. . .] by the initiated for the initiated', reflecting Geddes's concern with occultism and Egypt.[162] While the sphinxes, obelisk, bursts of sunrays and scarab beetle provide obvious connections to Egypt, the Masonic square and compass (albeit upside down) and the alchemical symbol of the Rod of Asclepius nod to esoterica.[163] In the University of Strathclyde's Geddes archive, there is a key to these hieroglyphs, which reveals that the symbols are arranged to represent how a more primitive existence (the bottom group of symbols on the obelisk) can generate community (the middle group) and lead society to 'Eutopia' (the upper group). The arrows pointing both upwards and downwards suggest, like *Arbor Saeculorum*, that these states are all interdependent. Importantly, Geddes includes a thistle on the obelisk in *The Evergreen*, representative of Scottish nationality, alongside other symbols that he states represent 'comradeship' and 'communion'.[164] This is indicative of the importance of collectivism, nationhood and internationalism for Geddes, serving as the foundation of his Utopian vision of society. In this image, as in his plans for the Evergreen Club, we witness the interdependence of nationhood and occultism in Geddes's idealism.

A final visual clue as to the importance of occultism to the Scottish Revival is present in the decorative designs for the book covers of the Celtic Library, published by Patrick Geddes and Colleagues. The gilt designs for the front and back covers of Fiona Macleod's *The Washer of the Ford*, for instance, borrow from several occult forms and also feature symbols of Scottish nationality. Most notably, the image on the front cover, which consists of two thistles (Fig. 4.8),

Figure 4.8 Front [left] and back [right] cover designs, *The Washer of the Ford* (1896).

stresses upward ascension, and the interlinking nature of the forms in the middle column is not unlike those of the Kabbalistic tree. These forms also resemble interlinking compasses, symbols common to Freemasonic orders. The image on the back cover – featuring concentric circles, triangles, hidden thistles and a bursting sun – also includes symbols that were common to the Golden Dawn's iconography: the bursting sun presents a literal golden dawn. Again, the designs here suggest a strong affinity between the assertion of Scottish nationality and the occult sphere in Geddes's thinking.

Conclusions relating to occultism and secret societies are particularly difficult to form. As Murray Pittock has argued of Jacobite secret societies and languages, 'they resist comprehensive analysis for the same reasons that made them successful in the first place': they were designed to be secretive.[165] Despite this, some broad trends are apparent. Writers and artists of the Scottish Revival, based in various locales, were clearly taken by (or actively participating in) *fin-de-siècle* occultism, and they were often doing so to further the Revival. Egyptian esoterica, for instance, offered revivalists the opportunity to outline a further Scottish myth of descent, to help unify and distinguish the national community. *Fin-de-siècle* occult societies and orders also offered spaces to help express and preserve ancestral, potentially disruptive Scottish selves, and helped authenticate the notion that supposedly past, healthier ages of the nation's history could be contacted and recovered. For others, the ritualism and symbolism of the occult sphere would help bind the revivalist community. In these respects, occult orders and esoteric ideas supported Scottish cultural revivalism, even if such orders and ideas were experienced only by the initiated few. To popularise the cultural revival beyond the initiated, alternative artforms would have to be developed, including those that define the following chapter: masques and pageants.

Notes

1. Yeats, pp. 123–5.
2. Nally, pp. 22–30.
3. Gonne, p. 24.
4. For more on the intersection of occultism and nationalism in the Order of Celtic Mysteries, see Nally, pp. 1–30.
5. Goodrick-Clarke, p. 13.
6. Owen, p. 7.

7. Ibid., pp. 91–2; Joy Dixon issues a caution on the issue of women's spiritual empowerment via occultism, arguing that *fin-de-siècle* occultism was often patriarchal in nature (see Dixon, p. 85).
8. Owen, pp. 30–1.
9. Chandra, p. 35.
10. Brantlinger, pp. 238–40.
11. Fanon, p. 43.
12. Corkery, p. 24.
13. Muir, 'Scotland's Winter', l. 28.
14. For more on Lang and psychical research, see Luckhurst.
15. Richardson, p. 198.
16. Foot, p. 200.
17. Tully, p. 131.
18. Ibid., p. 142.
19. Santucci, p. 233.
20. Budge, ed., p. 269.
21. White: 88.
22. Ibid.
23. 'Glasgow and its Mummy Cases', p. 4.
24. Brett, p. 142.
25. Lethaby, pp. 12, 39, 108.
26. The Glasgow Four were four *fin-de-siècle* Glaswegian artists: Mackintosh, Margaret Macdonald, Frances Macdonald and Herbert MacNair.
27. The Mathers sketch is reproduced in Raine, p. 188.
28. Neat, p. 117.
29. See Hardie, p. 116, and Billcliffe, *Charles Rennie Mackintosh*, pp. 34–7; a tree of life also appears in the Mortuary Chapel in Compton, Surrey, designed by the Scottish Celtic revivalist, Mary Watts.
30. Vaughan: 4.
31. Brett, p. 61.
32. Neat, p. 23.
33. (Cited in) Ibid., p. 181.
34. Patrick Geddes, untitled paper on the Celtic Cross, pp. 1–3 [Archives and Special Collections, University of Strathclyde: T-GED 5/2/13].
35. Geddes, *The Masque of Ancient Learning*, pp. 15–16.
36. Geoffrey Keating, p. 97.
37. These Ancient Egyptian rites were first performed by Mathers and his wife, Moina Mathers, at the Théâtre Bodinière, Paris in 1899.
38. Pittock, *Material Culture and Sedition*, p. 65.
39. 'Introductory': 2.
40. 'Scotland': 520.
41. Dick, 'Scotland': 520.
42. Shaw, 'Theosophy in Scotland'.
43. *Self Determination for Scotland*, pp. 7–8.
44. Atisha: 61.

45. Ibid.
46. 'Life after Death as Viewed in the Religion of Humanity' [Archives and Special Collections, University of Strathclyde: T-GED 11/3/94]; Scott and Bromley, pp. 48–51, 78.
47. For more on Christine Allen's occult interests, see Benham, p. 39.
48. Shaw, 'Theosophy in Scotland', p. 35.
49. John Duncan, Notebook, 1913 [National Library of Scotland: AC6866–6].
50. Gonne, pp. 23–4; Foot provides extensive analysis of the various symbols of this painting, and questions whether the four prominent figures are all *sidhe* (pp. 231–44).
51. Cammell, p. 229.
52. Gonne, pp. 22–3.
53. The Cipher Manuscripts form a collection of magical theories, structured as a syllabus; the origin of the manuscripts remains disputed.
54. Regardie, *What You Should Know*, p. 33; Letter from John William Brodie-Innes to Robert Felkin [The Library and Museum of Freemasonry: GBR 1991 GD 4/3/2/5/a].
55. Emily Drummond, 'The Book of Rituals' [The Library and Museum of Freemasonry: GBR 1991 GD 2/1/7]. Drummond was second in command, Praemonstratrix, of the temple.
56. Summons of Amen-Ra Temple [The Library and Museum of Freemasonry: GBR 1991 GD 2/3/4/3].
57. Owen, p. 83.
58. Bye-Laws of the Amen-Ra Temple [The Library and Museum of Freemasonry: GBR 1991 GD 2/3/4/2]
59. Foot, pp. 202–3.
60. Fletcher, pp. 83–123; Pittock, *Spectrum*, p. 98.
61. Pittock, *Spectrum*, pp. 96–7.
62. Letter from James Whistler to unidentified correspondent, August 1892 [GUL Whistler X26].
63. Fletcher, pp. 83–123; Pittock, *Spectrum*, p. 101.
64. For more on Napier's and Erskine's neo-Jacobitism, see Pittock, *The Invention of Scotland*, pp. 127–33.
65. For more on Erskine and *The Whirlwind*, see Murray, 'Decadent Conservatism': 197.
66. (Cited in) Pittock, *Spectrum*, p. 99.
67. Fanon, p. 191.
68. For more on Jacobite secret societies, see Pittock, *Material Culture and Sedition*, pp. 64–72.
69. Symonds, p. 22.
70. Colquhoun, p. 69.
71. Ibid., p. 32.
72. Ibid., p. 58.
73. Churton, p. 57.

74. Ibid., p. 5.
75. Ibid., pp. 42, 20.
76. Owen, p. 57.
77. Colquhoun, pp. 80, 85; Churton, p. 40.
78. Letter from Annie Horniman to William Peck (25 December 1896) [The Library and Museum of Freemasonry: GBR 1991 GD 2/4/1/12].
79. Ibid.
80. Letter from Horniman to Peck (25 December 1896) [The Library and Museum of Freemasonry: GBR 1991 GD 2/4/1/12].
81. (Cited in) Colquhoun, p. 93.
82. Ibid., p. 88.
83. Gaucher: 449.
84. Brodie-Innes, pp. 101–2.
85. Gilbert, p. 10.
86. Murdoch, *The Royal Stuarts*; Murdoch, *The Renaissance*.
87. Murdo Macdonald, '*Anima Celtica*', p. 35.
88. Ibid., p. 32.
89. Pittock, *The Invention of Scotland*, p. 127.
90. John Duncan would also paint Mary Stuart in his c.1929 work, *Mary, Queen of Scots (1542–1587), at Fotheringhay*.
91. Sinclair, p. 38.
92. For discussions of Swinburne's neo-Jacobitism, see Dahl.
93. Pater, *Appreciations*, p. 225.
94. Vadillo, p. 133.
95. 'The Evergreen', *Glasgow Herald*, p. 11.
96. Branford, 'Awakenings in History': 88, 90.
97. Burstein, p. 106.
98. For a discussion of late Victorian Scottish Catholic writers, see McCluskey and Bicket: 59–81.
99. Di Pasquale: 56.
100. Ibid.
101. Notes by Patrick Geddes for a lecture to the Celtic Society, 1897 [Archives and Special Collections, University of Strathclyde: T-GED 5/2/9].
102. (Cited in) Stewart Alan Robertson, p. 9.
103. Branford and Geddes, *Our Social Inheritance*, p. 16.
104. Patrick Geddes, 'A Northern College: An Experimental Study in Higher Education', p. 4 [Archives and Special Collections, University of Strathclyde: T-GED 12/1/61].
105. William Sharp, *The Sin-Eater*, p. 13.
106. For more on Sharp's neo-Catholicism, see Alaya, pp. 166–8.
107. See Halloran, 'W. B. Yeats, William Sharp and Fiona Macleod: A Celtic Drama, 1897': 159–66; Jeffares, pp. 107–9; Blamires, pp. 125, 154–8, 183–4; Hodd: 39; Benham, pp. 38–41.
108. Rhys, *Everyman Remembers*, pp. 79–80.

109. Richardson, pp. 218–20.
110. Lyall, '"That Ancient Self"': 83.
111. (Cited in) Ibid.: 81; Muir, 'Scotland 1941', l. 12.
112. (Cited in) Bicket, p. 4.
113. Bicket, p. 9.
114. Greene, p. 15.
115. Rapetti, pp. 88–9.
116. Billcliffe, *Charles Rennie Mackintosh*, p. 36.
117. Leonard, p. 79.
118. Geddes, 'The Scots Renascence': 135.
119. Geddes, 'Celtic Cross' [T-GED 5/2/13].
120. Geddes, 'The Scots Renascence': 139.
121. Ibid.: 138; Smith, *Myths and Memories*, p. 150.
122. William Sharp, 'Introduction', p. xliii.
123. Boardman, p. 452.
124. Card notes on Witchcraft, 1905 [Archives and Special Collections, University of Strathclyde: T-GED 11/1/22].
125. *Interpretation of the Pictures in the Common Room of Ramsay Lodge*, p. 1.
126. Ibid., pp. 6, 9, 12.
127. John Ferguson, p. 4.
128. I discuss Geddes's links to the Bahá'í faith in more detail in 'Theosophy in Scotland'. Bahá's visit to Edinburgh is also covered in Khursheed.
129. Colquhoun, p. 89.
130. Notes by Patrick Geddes on the theory of magic as religious awakening, c.1897 [Archives and Special Collections, University of Strathclyde: T-GED 11/1/13].
131. Boardman, pp. 194, 450–1.
132. Kelman, pp. 5–6.
133. (Cited in) Whyte, pp. 16–17.
134. Kelman, p. 15.
135. Patrick Geddes, 'What is the Mystic Life', p. 2 [Archives and Special Collections, University of Strathclyde: T-GED 11/1/93].
136. Churton, p. 138.
137. Elizabeth A. Sharp, *Lyra Celtica*, p. 444.
138. Stephens, pp. 28, 48, 51–2, 193, 206, 219.
139. (Cited in) Boardman, p. 194.
140. Rough notes by Patrick Geddes relating to *The Evergreen*, c.1895–6 [Archives and Special Collections, University of Strathclyde: T-GED 8/1/3].
141. 'Some Illustrated Books', p. 13.
142. Patrick Geddes, 'Arbor Saeculorum' [Archives and Special Collections, University of Strathclyde: T-GED 12/1/397].
143. For an example of this serpent, see Regardie, *The Golden Dawn*, p. 62.
144. Mathers, 'Concerning the Symbolism', p. 131.

145. Mathers, *The Kabbalah Unveiled*, p. 42.
146. (Cited in) Jeffares, p. 107.
147. Di Pasquale: 56.
148. Nordau, pp. 219–24.
149. David Stevenson, p. 96.
150. Ibid., pp. 101, 104.
151. Neat argues that the Glasgow School were also influenced by Rosicrucianism; see Neat, pp. 120–32.
152. Churton, p. 253; Geddes also visited Boleskine in 1895 to write on Celtic crosses.
153. Crowley: 26.
154. Boardman, p. 451.
155. (Cited in) Stephen, p. 37.
156. (Cited in) Boardman, p. 451.
157. Schimmerling, p. 52.
158. (Cited in) Ellmann, p. 123.
159. Westcott, pp. 179–91.
160. Notes by Patrick Geddes on the association of ideas, alchemy, psychology, society and education [Archives and Special Collections, University of Strathclyde: T-GED 3/4/13].
161. Notes by Patrick Geddes on the Philosopher's stone and the Elixir Vitae [Archives and Special Collections, University of Strathclyde: T-GED 11/1/67].
162. Geddes, *Dramatisations*, pp. 76–7.
163. *A First Visit to the Outlook Tower* (1906) proposes a reading of these various symbols, pp. 23–6.
164. Notes by Patrick Geddes on University Halls, etc. [Archives and Special Collections, University of Strathclyde: T-GED 12/1/28].
165. Pittock, *Material Culture and Sedition*, p. 94.

Chapter 5

The Pageant Revival: Popularising Renascence

At the beginning of the twentieth century, a cultural epidemic dubbed 'pageantitis' broke out in the United Kingdom.[1] Historical pageantry became a hugely popular international phenomenon in this era, often attracting thousands of participants and, at times, tens of thousands of spectators. Although formats varied from pageant to pageant, they tended to take place in outdoor settings, with the audience seated on specially constructed grandstands. Participants, dressed up as historical, mythological or allegorical figures, would then relate a town or nation's history by enacting successive historical episodes, generally with minimal dialogue, or by processing in front of the huge crowds of spectators.[2] Special effects, mechanically operated dragons and animal costumes were also commonly employed to entertain the crowds. As such, pageants hoped to appeal to large audiences of all ages; indeed, they are sometimes considered participatory, historical variants of motion pictures, which were also becoming increasingly popular at the beginning of the twentieth century.[3]

Much of the literature on Edwardian pageantry has focused on pageants in England, which tended to take place in small towns. These pageants presented versions of a specific town's history that would help educate those involved and strengthen the local participants' and audience's sense of their identity.[4] These identities were often, at least partly, encoded as Saxon in English pageantry through their focus on local and national histories prior to the Norman Conquest; as Angela Bartie et al. illustrate, Edwardian English pageantry built on the 'Victorian cult of the Anglo-Saxons'.[5] Pageantry's success in England was also underpinned by growing concerns over urbanisation, resulting in a desire to defend localities from the processes of modernity.[6] Louis Napoleon Parker, one of England's leading pageant-masters, for example, wrote that the 'modernising spirit' is 'precisely the kind of spirit which a properly organised and properly conducted pageant is designed to kill'.[7] Historians have recently questioned whether Edwardian English pageants were as conservative and nostalgic as Parker suggests here, or if they were strategies to 'cope with and accommodate change', as Paul Readman argues.[8] Either way, these pageants reveal the increasing importance of narrating, displaying and performing particular versions of history to mass audiences in order to bind communities in the face of modernity.

Scotland was by no means immune to the spread of pageantitis; indeed, there is evidence to suggest that historical pageants were being performed in Scotland in 1900, before Parker's *Sherborne Pageant* (1905), which is often cited as beginning the twentieth-century pageant tradition in the United Kingdom.[9] Among those who embraced this growing artform were Scotland's cultural revivalists, including many of the writers and artists we have encountered in the preceding chapters. Patrick Geddes, Phoebe Anna Traquair, John Duncan, Margaret Macdonald, Jessie M. King, William Hole and Theodore Napier all performed in, or contributed to, historical pageants. Scottish revivalists were attracted to pageantry, in part, because of its potential to disseminate to wider audiences the histories and myths of origin that they had painted or written. Pageants helped promote what Anthony D. Smith terms a 'sense of continuity' more widely through chronicling a national line (or lines) of descent.[10] As such, pageants produced by Scottish revivalists were less concerned with the small town than Parker's – indeed, many were staged in large cities, including Glasgow and Edinburgh – and they placed far greater emphasis on building a national sense of community through performing national histories and mythologies. To complement these aims, as we shall see, the cult of the Celts was continued in Edwardian Scottish pageantry, and some Scottish pageant-masters actively resisted the Saxonism that often underpinned contemporary pageants in England. Alongside pageantry's capacity to reanimate the past to educate audiences about a community's history and mythology, revivalists would also have been attracted to the ritualism of pageantry, as well as its reliance on symbols. Pageantry's connections to Pre-Raphaelitism, identified by Deborah Sugg Ryan,[11] would have appealed to several revivalists too – including Geddes, Duncan and Traquair – who admired Pre-Raphaelite art.

Moreover, Scottish cultural revivalists' enthusiasm for pageantry reflected a broader desire to create elaborate public art that was educational. As we encountered in Chapter 3, Geddes was keen to promote mural paintings to help educate and enrich civic society, and the Ramsay Garden common room murals, painted by Duncan, bear resemblances to pageantry in illustrating various episodes and historical figures in Scottish mythology and history through time. As Clare Willsdon notes, 'the visualisation of history in murals' was 'a first cousin of theatre, and several mural artists were also stage and costume designers for plays and pageants'.[12] Because of their similarities, various Scottish Revival muralists were drawn to pageantry. For instance, William Hole, who designed the pageant-like mural procession of Scottish historical figures that features in the Scottish National Portrait Gallery in Edinburgh, not only performed in pageants but designed a large number of costumes for the historical section of one of the largest Scottish pageants, the *Scottish National Pageant of Allegory, History and Myth* in Edinburgh (1908). Duncan, who executed various murals and would go on to paint a series of processionals, such as his *Masque of Love* (1921), designed costumes for the same pageant, as did Phoebe Anna Traquair, known for her Pre-Raphaelite-inspired mural decorations in the Catholic Apostolic Church and the mortuary chapel of the Royal Hospital for Sick Children in Edinburgh. Beyond the capital, the Dundee painter and associate of Duncan's, Stewart Carmichael, designed a banner to represent Dundee for the *Scottish National Pageant*. Carmichael would go on to paint Celtic revivalist work, including his *Anima Celtica* (1932), and he had already executed murals of Scottish historical figures, such as the *Leaders of Scottish Liberty* mural (1901) for the Dundee Liberal Club. Featuring various Scottish heroes and intellectuals through time, including the most famous opponent of the 1707 Union, Fletcher of Saltoun, Carmichael's mural reflects the Liberals' increasing discontent with Scotland's constitutional arrangements at the *fin de siècle*. These various mural projects by prospective pageanteers demonstrate Scottish revivalists' desire to bring narratives of Scottish history and liberty to civic spaces; pageantry helped extend that aim further by presenting such myths and histories to large crowds.

Aside from Juliet Kinchin's, Jude Burkhauser's and Elizabeth Cumming's foundational introductions,[13] Edwardian Scottish pageantry remains broadly absent in narratives of Scottish theatre, history and design. In turn, Scotland is often conspicuously absent from assessments of Edwardian British pageantry.[14] In response to such neglect, this chapter hopes not only to historicise these pageants and demonstrate their importance to cultural revivalism in *fin-de-siècle* Scotland, but also to help rectify some of the more Anglocentric understandings of British pageantry that have taken hold, including the notion that the only major pageants held in British cities before 1914 were in London and Liverpool.[15] By turning our attention to Scotland, alternative understandings are revealed and a more complex picture of British pageantry emerges.

Cultural Memory and Pageantry

Fin-de-siècle pageants were part of a broader culture of creating and disseminating shared memories through public spectacle, which had grown throughout the nineteenth century. The nineteenth century witnessed the rise of public festivals, ceremonies and monuments that were principally concerned with looking to the past and commemorating it. Roland Quinault has noted that 'in modern Europe centenary commemorations were rare before 1800 and uncommon before the mid-nineteenth century. Thereafter, however, the number and scope of centenary commemorations grew rapidly and by the late nineteenth century, a "cult of the centenary" had become established.'[16] In the United Kingdom, this cult was advanced by the Handel and Burns centenaries held in the Crystal Palace in 1859; Ballantine's chronicle 'records a mind-boggling total of 876 celebratory events' for Burns that year.[17] Quinault argues that 'the contemporary emergence of History as a distinct academic discipline and the growth of learned historical societies and journals' stimulated the growth of centenaries,[18] along with 'local patriotism and commercial interest'.[19] Or, as Aleida Assmann puts it, centenaries were part of the appropriation of 'common traditions in order to create an identity for the new political subject "the people"'.[20]

Public commemoration was a widespread phenomenon in Victorian Scotland, expressed through a variety of forms.[21] Cultural figures were commemorated as part of local festivals, including Burns at the Ayr Festival of 1844[22]; cairns were erected to commemorate historical events, such as the Culloden memorial cairn (1881); and landmark monuments to Walter Scott and William Wallace were erected to dominate the skylines of Edinburgh and Stirling, respectively. There was also a proliferation of statues in civic spaces, and annual demonstrations were organised to commemorate specific events, such as the Bannockburn Day demonstration, which began in 1901 and featured pageant-participant Theodore Napier in his 'customary pre-Revolution Highland dress'.[23] As such, Victorian Scotland witnessed the transformation of public spaces and landscapes into sites of historical commemoration.

In recent years, cultural memory studies has explored the role that such historical commemorations played, and continue to play, in shaping and defining communities. For Ann Rigney, memory 'refers in the first instance to the ways in which individuals recall their own experience, and as such it cannot be automatically or easily transferred to the social domain'.[24] However, she goes on to map out an alternative form of memory, cultural memory, 'in which images of the past are communicated and shared among members of a community through public acts of remembrance through publicly accessible media'.[25] Thus, cultural memory 'is always "external"'[26] rather than personal – it is sustained through memorials, ceremonies and monuments. Rigney argues that these cultural memories are not fixed; they are always vicarious as they 'evolve in the course of time'[27] and are 'mediated by texts and images'.[28] Rigney also highlights the fact that 'authenticity may not always be relevant to memorial dynamics, and certain things may be recalled because they are meaningful to those doing the recalling rather than because [. . .] they are actually true'.[29] Thus, cultural memories often tell us more about the community recalling: for Rigney, 'this recovery project is itself linked in complex ways to contemporary identity politics and to the desire of particular groups to profile their common identity by claiming distinct roots in a particular historical experience'.[30] As such, cultural memory is a 'working memory'[31] that communities sustain, elaborate and alter over time. What Rigney's work foregrounds is the role of publicly accessible commemorative monuments in defining a collective memory, a sense of a shared past, which is intended to promote collective cohesiveness. Cultural memories can be viewed as an extension of Anthony Smith's *ethnie*, discussed in Chapter 3: these memorials took fashioned notions of the past into public realms, to help nurture a wider collective identification with a shared past that would help bind a group or nation.

Anticipating Rigney and Smith, late nineteenth-century figures themselves spoke on the need to choose a past selectively to define the nation. In his essay, 'The Use and Abuse of History' (1874), Friedrich Nietzsche identifies a problem with nineteenth-century life that he is keen to remedy – the fact that 'historical knowledge streams on [modern man] from sources that are inexhaustible'.[32] Nietzsche stresses that the rising pool of historical knowledge was starting to suffocate individuals and nations (16). He writes that the proliferation of historical detail undermines the coherence of the self: 'there is a degree of sleeplessness, of rumination, of "historical sense", that injures and finally destroys the living thing, be it a man or a people or a system of culture' (9). To remedy this situation, he proposes that a limited, focused engagement with the past is needed:

> cheerfulness, a good conscience, belief in the future, the joyful deed, all depend, in the individual as well as the nation, on there being a line that divides the visible and the clear from the vague and the shadowy: we must know the right time to forget as well as the right time to remember. (10)

Nietzsche's thoughts here resemble Geddes's point that 'tradition is truer than history'[33]: a selected, partial notion of the past was needed to sustain coherent histories that were believed to form the bases of cultures and nationalities. Cultural memory played a key role in defining and distributing those selective histories to broader audiences.

It is in this context, when cultural memories were being defined and there was greater stress on choosing a selective historical memory, that pageants became dominant. *Fin-de-siècle* pageantry was not without its antecedents: there was a long tradition of pageantry dating back to the Middle Ages, which tended to involve a religious procession and the performance of religious plays,[34] and there had been historical re-enactments in the nineteenth century, such as Ayrshire's Eglinton Tournament (1839). But *fin-de-siècle* pageants broadly differed from these antecedents in their focus on chronicling the history of a locality or nation. As one contemporary commentator put it, Edwardian pageants were 'more consciously historical' than previous forms of pageantry.[35] Like other forms of *fin-de-siècle* public commemoration, pageants were often held to mark centenaries or anniversaries, and they were concerned with nurturing collective identification with specific historical figures or versions of the past. But we can also distinguish pageantry from other forms of *fin-de-siècle* cultural memory, such as monuments, in that they were deeply participatory.[36] Local participants not only performed in pageants but designed costumes and staging for them. Parker was insistent on this, hoping that pageantry would reveal that 'talent and technical skill is lying dormant in the English provincial towns'.[37] And in comparison to the fixed and portable historical monuments that Rigney discusses,[38] pageants were ephemeral: the vast majority of pageants were staged only a few times, although they were widely photographed and some, including the *Scottish National Pageant*, were even filmed. But this ephemerality did not deter Scotland's revivalists: pageantry's ability to promote public engagement with a community's origins and its fashioned lines of historical descent enchanted a number of them.

The Scottish National Pageant of Allegory, History and Myth (1908)

Several revivalists were attracted to other forms of cultural memory, besides pageantry. For instance, Geddes applauded the Wallace Monument for reactivating 'our long Celtic memory' – a statement that characterises the national hero as Celtic, complementing Geddes's various attempts to unify Scotland around Celtic culture.[39] Geddes was also keen to include statues in his projects, such as his proposed sculpture of Ossian (designed by Duncan but never executed) for the Bee Alley Gardens, Dunfermline.[40] But it was pageantry that especially captivated Geddes; he noted that pageants were 'the most ambitious and comprehensive' activities that he and the Outlook Tower circle were engaged in.[41] Geddes believed masques and pageants (terms that he used interchangeably)[42] were central to the development of the cultural revival, a view he expressed in his unpublished essay 'Significance and Purpose of the Masques'. There, he writes that the 'railways age and its centralising influences' had 'pushed back the whole romantic movement until even Scottish folk songs or the German art-songs to which they gave impulse' were little more than 'culture-reminiscences'.[43] For Geddes, masques and pageants could counter this centralisation and 're-establish a common culture, civic, national and general' (6) by reanimating histories and traditions: 'traditions must be recovered, new minstrels must again arise, in sympathy with their own people' (4). To help 're-Muse' Scottish culture,[44] Geddes called for a pageant of Scottish history. In 1904, he wrote that W. G. Burn Murdoch's processional mural design, 'A Procession of Scottish History', covering 700 years from the eleventh century, as well as John Duncan's Ramsay Garden murals and William Hole's Scottish National Portrait Gallery murals, were 'awaiting fitting realization in sculpture, in colour, and in actual periodic pageant'.[45] Four years later, an equivalent pageant to that which Geddes proposed, the *Scottish National Pageant*, was staged in Edinburgh, and various other Edwardian pageants, including his own, reflected his concern with 're-Musing' Scotland and heralding the 'Mythopoetic age'.[46]

Scottish pageants undoubtedly 'contributed to a modern British tradition',[47] but they also formed a distinctive tradition. While the pageants produced by Parker and others in England in this period tended to focus on a small town, the emphasis of Scottish pageants was broadly on the nation. The local emphasis of English Edwardian pageantry is embodied by the titles of some of the pageants performed there: the *Sherborne Pageant* (1905), the *Warwick Pageant* (1906), the *Oxford Historical*

Pageant (1907), the *Bury, St Edmunds Pageant* (1907), the *St. Albans Pageant* (1907), the *Liverpool Pageant* (1907), the *Chelsea Pageant* (1908), the *Winchester Pageant* (1908), the *Dover Pageant* (1908), the *Colchester Pageant* (1909), the *Bath Pageant* (1909), the *Chester Pageant* (1910) and *The Pageant of London – A Masque of Empire* (1911). These local pageants did not ignore the context of national history – Paul Readman argues that provincial English pageants often articulated 'the local roots of national identity'[48] – but, like William Chauncy Langdon's pageants in America, the locality was nevertheless 'the hero'.[49] This emphasis on the town and its history in Edwardian English pageants is in stark contrast to the pageants of Edwardian Scotland. A sampling of titles alone reveals a particularly national emphasis in Scottish pageantry. They include the *Mary Queen of Scots Pageant* (1906), the *Scottish National Pageant* (1908), the *Grand Historical Pageant* of Scottish women, organised by the Women's Social and Political Union (1909),[50] *The Pageant of The Bruce* (1911),[51] the *Robert Burns Pageant* (1911), a proposed *Jacobite Pageant* to be penned by Neil Munro (1911),[52] and the *Bannockburn Pageant* (1914), which sought the talents of the Outlook Tower Masquers.[53] In the 1920s, the *Masque of Scottish Women* (1926) and the *Scottish Historical Pageant* (1927) would be staged. Even some of the pageants that did not include a reference to the Scottish nation in the title were heavily centred on Scottish history, such as the *Glasgow University Pageant* (1908), which partially reprised the *Scottish National Pageant*. These pageants were strongly centred on the Scottish nation or on key national figures, such as Mary Stuart, Bruce and Burns: heroes that were used to embody and celebrate the national identity.[54] The differing emphases of Scottish and English pageants were so marked that they were noted by one of the first historians of Edwardian pageantry, Robert Withington, in 1920: he wrote that England had not had an equivalent to the 'Scotch and Welsh national pageants' because 'the small place' was prized in England and the alternatives were felt to be too 'politicized'.[55] In Scotland, the 'small place' alone was rarely the hero; instead, the nation was.

In this respect, the Scottish pageant tradition was closer to those in Ireland and Wales, where several had a national emphasis, such as the *National Pageant of Wales* (1909).[56] Patrick Pearse's pageants in Ireland – discussed below – were also more nationally focused, even encouraging a militarised nationalism to defend Ireland. A number of Scottish, Welsh and Irish revivalists collaborated too by staging a pageant together during the Celtic Congress of Caernarfon in 1904, where the members donned historical dress to perform as various

Celtic figures for an audience on the closing day.[57] Like several small-town English pageants, which hoped to resist the town's 'complete submergence' in 'the great tide of London',[58] Scottish, Irish and Welsh pageants also resisted the process of centralisation to reassert cultural traditions and identities in the face of modernity. But the resistance to centralisation in these nations was often coupled with national revival efforts, which gave many pageants in Ireland, Scotland and Wales a distinctively national emphasis.

The Scottish pageant that had the greatest national emphasis and attracted a wide variety of revivalist participants was the *Scottish National Pageant of Allegory, History and Myth*. This took place in Saughton Park, Edinburgh, during the Scottish National Exhibition in 1908. Events like the Scottish National Exhibition and Glasgow's Scottish Exhibition of National History, Art and Industry (held in Kelvingrove Park in 1911) were important facets of the cultural revival themselves. Alongside rollercoaster rides and palaces of art and industry, often designed in Scots baronial style, they celebrated imperialism and Scottish culture. The 1908 exhibition featured a 'Scottish National Day' on 24 June, commemorating the anniversary of the Battle of Bannockburn. The day included a pipe band contest, Highland dancing, a concert, and an eye-catching procession of cyclists dressed as Walter Scott's characters.[59] Members of the organisation committee for 'Scotland's Day' were drawn from a range of patriotic groupings, including the Scottish Rights Association, Scottish Patriotic Association and the Gaelic Society.[60] These national exhibitions also attempted to present unified images of Scotland by featuring Highland villages, and it was deemed pivotal that all of the employees in An Clachan, the village in the 1911 exhibition, spoke Gaelic to avoid 'a caricature of the Highlands being given to the public'. The expertise of the Co-Operative Council of Highland Home Industries was also solicited to create the village.[61] The 1911 exhibition was cultural revivalist not only in form but also in motivation: it was designed to fund a Chair of Scottish History and Literature at Glasgow University, thus promoting Scottish history and literature as distinct academic disciplines. These exhibitions were hugely popular: nineteen days after opening, the Scottish Exhibition of National History, Art and Industry (1911) in Glasgow had attracted 1.1 million visitors.[62] Because of their high footfall and capability of hosting large audiences, such exhibitions became popular sites for staging pageants. Like the 1908 exhibition, which staged the *Scottish National Pageant*, pageants were also performed at Glasgow's 1911 exhibition, which focused on the lives of Robert the Bruce and Robert Burns.

The *Scottish National Pageant* was designed to raise funds for the Children's League of Pity. It was several years in the making, which resulted in a spectacular display that chronicled Scottish history from its mythological origins to the eighteenth century. The pageant's executive committee was led by the artist Cecile Walton and its members included fellow artists, such as John Duncan, James Paterson and Phoebe Anna Traquair. The pageant was staged twice on 13 June 1908, involving nearly 1,800 players, and was described as 'simply enormous'.[63] While rehearsals took place in fine weather on the sports ground, the first staging of the pageant had to be moved into the concert hall, on account of a downpour. Reporters lamented that the new setting compromised the spectacle: certain features, including banners, could not be displayed and the figures were huddled too closely together.[64] Nevertheless, at four o'clock, when the clouds broke, a second procession took place outside, 'with a fair amount of éclat'.[65] Some short pieces of footage documenting the pageant are publicly available via Scottish Screen Archive,[66] and various other primary sources survive, including a wealth of photographs in *The Scots Pictorial*, costume design sketches by William Hole,[67] and a pageant handbook. After the Edinburgh performances, sections of the pageant were reprised at Aberdour Castle in Fife and at the University of Glasgow.

The *Scottish National Pageant* bears a striking resemblance to other forms of *fin-de-siècle* cultural revivalism, featuring very similar mythic heroes and narratives of Scottish history to those we have encountered in previous chapters. Preceding the 'historical section' (the episodes for which were partially decided by the public, through a competition in *The Scottish Review* that was won by C. A. Malcolm)[68] were three sections that bore the mark of revivalism: Celtic, Arthurian and Early Church. Each of these sections was organised and designed by a key cultural revival artist: John Duncan, Jessie M. King and Phoebe Anna Traquair, respectively. Duncan's Celtic scheme included the heroes that featured in his Ramsay Garden common room murals, Cuchullin (Fig. 5.1), played by the sculptor H. S. Gamley, and Fionn, played by James Cadenhead, as well as other subjects that feature in both his art and Fiona Macleod's Celtic fiction – the *sidhe*, Scathach, Bride and Ossian (Fig. 5.2). A further Scottish mythological origin figure, Scota Pharaoh, whose role in Scottish cultural revivalism was discussed in Chapter 4, also featured in Duncan's Celtic section. Duncan himself played in the pageant as Cormac, alongside another Edinburgh painter, Henry Taylor Wyse (Faolan), and Geddes's children (Norah as a daughter of Maeve, Alastair as

Figure 5.1 H. S. Gamley as Cuchullin, *Scottish National Exhibition Pageant* (1908). Private Collection. With thanks to the Digital Imaging Unit, Edinburgh University Library.

Figure 5.2 Archibald Menzies as Ossian, *Scottish National Exhibition Pageant* (1908), in *The Scots Pictorial*, 4 (1908): 241.

one of the Riders of the *sidhe* and Arthur as Fionn's Fairy Harper). Although Geddes appears to have had minimal input in the pageant (if any),[69] his wife, Anna Geddes, was involved in organising costumes for the Celtic kings.[70] Like Duncan, King also performed in her Arthurian section, discussed below, as the Angel of the Holy Graal. Traquair's Early Church section focused on the age of Columba, a period that greatly inspired the work of Fiona Macleod and Duncan. This section presented various styles of cross (Fig. 5.3), perhaps in a bid to provide a more unified image of Scottish religion than that which existed in a period defined by rising sectarian tensions.

Taking these summaries together, the pageant was a scheme that gave space to express and define the mythologies and histories that Scottish revivalists were preoccupied with, and to disseminate these to wider audiences. Consequently, individuals connected to Scottish cultural revivalism applauded the pageant's ambition. Theodore Napier, who performed in the Jacobite group of the 'historical' section alongside J. W. Brodie-Innes and Alexander Carmichael, noted in *The Fiery Cross* that 'we regard this Scottish Historical Pageant [. . .] as a good

Figure 5.3 The Early Church section, *Scottish National Exhibition Pageant* (1908). Courtesy of the University of St Andrews Library. RMA-S-574-Y.

sign of the reviving Scottish national spirit and sentiment'.[71] *The Fiery Cross* would also publish a poem on the pageant in its 1908 October issue. As we shall see below, one of the central revivalists, Geddes, lauded the pageant's Arthurian section.

Besides its focus on national histories and mythological figures, the *Scottish National Pageant* reflected the wider revival in another sense: it was a national endeavour, drawing collaborators from across Scotland. While the Parkerian pageant tended to be produced by, and involve the participation of, the local community, the *Scottish National Pageant* looked beyond Edinburgh and solicited talents from across Scotland. The Arthurian section, for instance, was also known as the Glasgow section because its contributors – including Margaret Macdonald (Morgan le Fay), the pioneering photographer James Craig Annan (King Arthur) and E. A. Taylor (Sir Galahad) – were associated with the Glasgow School and the Glasgow Art Club. As previously mentioned, one of Dundee's most notable artists, Stewart Carmichael, also contributed to the pageant. These participants, all acclaimed visual artists, reveal that the pageant was not simply an endeavour of national collaboration, but a celebration of the nation's art culture too. The central designers alone – Duncan, King and Traquair – were amongst Scotland's most renowned, and they helped generate lavish, detailed costumes. Unlike Parker's pageants and several in America, which tended to feature basic costumes,[72] the designs for the *Scottish National Pageant* were defined by their visual splendour. As such, the pageant embodied the art of 'public magnificence' that Geddes had heralded, which he juxtaposed with the 'capitalistic' private magnificence that he felt was preferred amongst the artists of South Kensington.[73] For Geddes, it was pageantry that could most effectively meet the aims of the Arts and Crafts movement: he wrote that, in them, 'neither head, hand nor heart may be lacking',[74] an allusion to the Arts and Crafts conviction that practicality, labour and beauty must be intertwined.

Although the *Scottish National Pageant* helped disseminate myths and heroes that were privileged by several revivalists to large audiences, and celebrated the nation's art cultures, one feature of pageantry that threatened to undermine its revivalism was the kinship between pageants and stadialist narratives of history. Such processionals often presented society moving through various historical stages on a teleological trajectory. In his study, *American Historical Pageantry*, David Glassberg demonstrates that American pageants of the 1910s often represented an orderly narrative from primitivism towards civilisation, as evidenced in the design for the pageant programme of the *Boston Pageant*, entitled *Cave Life to City Life*, which presents a primitive man looking out to modern industrial society (including aeroplanes) on the horizon. Glassberg argues that such representations of 'successive stages of community development' helped authenticate the idea of 'orderly, stable progress' in America.[75] He also highlights how the idea of 'community destiny' was developed to such a degree in American pageants that some represented the '"historical inevitability" of white conquest'.[76]

Despite the appropriateness of the pageantry form for representing stadialist narratives of history, Scottish pageants tended not to present history as a teleological development. The *Scottish National Pageant*, for example, indulges in mythological narratives and elides industrial modernity, concluding with the fall of the Jacobites. Produced just one year after the bicentenary of the Acts of Union 1707, the pageant also skims over this landmark event in Scottish history that is often associated with the nation's transition to modernity. The elision was not isolated. As Ewen Cameron has demonstrated, there were very few attempts to celebrate the Union in 1907, which prompts Cameron to question whether this era truly was the high-water mark of unionism.[77] He cites an article in the *Dundee Courier*, which highlights the fact that Scottish constitutional discontent was partly responsible for the neglect:

> The bicentenary of the Union is occurring at a time when the disadvantages accruing to Scotland from it are decidedly more conspicuous than the advantages [. . .] the Scottish people, therefore, can hardly be expected to be in a mood for rejoicing over an event which at the moment seems to have had no other effect than to deprive them of their legitimate rights.[78]

In line with Rigney's characterisation of cultural memory, this quotation reminds us that historical commemoration often tells us more about the community recalling than it does about the past, and that, as Ernest Renan put it, what is forgotten is just as important to national identity construction as what is remembered.[79] The elision or suppression of the Union in historical commemoration reveals that a number of *fin-de-siècle* Scots felt the Union to be increasingly compromising the nation, or antithetical to the expression of Scottish nationality – a marked shift from the unionist–nationalist dimensions of Noel Paton's memorial to the Wars of Independence in the mid-Victorian period, discussed in the Introduction. By commemorating over a hundred Jacobite leaders instead, the *Scottish National Pageant* embraces a culture associated with cultural defence to define the national self.

Other pageants produced in this period also questioned modernity and the notion of historical progress. For instance, in *The Birth and Growth of Art* masque, performed to celebrate the opening of Mackintosh's Glasgow School of Art building, the narrator, Pan, heralds the fact that 'primeval senses wake from hidden depths',[80] and expresses his opposition to the 'huddled civilisation' of modernity.[81] Similarly, Geddes's book, *Dramatisations of History*, written to accompany his pageant on education, *The Masque of Learning*, which I discuss in greater detail below, characteristically critiques stadialist notions of historical development. He writes that 'history is no mere retrospect of the past, nor excavation in it: what it reveals to us, above all, is the past working on within our apparent present'.[82] He also mentions the 'undying past' and,[83] when discussing the primitive in an unpublished paper on the *Masque*, states that 'our pageant thus recapitulates this past more and more fully, age by age; in each phase, as far as may be, with some suggestion of its return to Nature, and for its fresh impulse of development'.[84] In their critiques of modernity and their focus on reanimating pre-industrial histories and mythologies, pageants by Scottish revivalists carefully avoided, and even subverted, the presentation of stadialist narratives that the pageantry form could so easily support.

Although a number of pageants in Scotland focused on the nation, it would be wrong to deny that they were also concerned with localities and civic cultures. Geddes described pageants as the 'sociological and civic stage',[85] a concept that Victor Branford explains in more detail when commenting on town planning:

> No city-plan is adequate to future requirements which fails to find a place for the Civic Theatre, and for one designed on large and generous proportions – a spacious portico for pageant, masque and processional.[86]

In tune with Parker's thoughts, Branford styles pageantry as a means of binding a locality, rather than a nation. Several Scottish pageants exhibit a concern with locality, including the *Scottish National Pageant*, which began with 'An Allegory of the City of Edinburgh', featuring various symbols of the city, including the River Forth and Edinburgh Castle. Nevertheless, Edinburgh's status as the nation's capital cannot be ignored: even in this civic allegory, Edinburgh is styled as the 'Queen City of the Realm of Scotland', supported by 'All the Burghs of Scotland'.[87] There were some civic elements to the *Scottish National Pageant* but even these reveal its deeply national emphasis and its aim to nurture a national sentiment in the audience. Judging by the commentaries on the event, it appears to have succeeded: one reviewer walked away from the pageant thinking 'I am one of no mean nation.'[88]

Arthurian Scotland

> *No Scottish historic Arthur! – the dry-as-dust historian of mere records tells us.*[89]

So exclaimed one advocate of including the Arthurian cycle in pageants of Scottish history – Patrick Geddes – in his book *City Development* (1904). Critiquing historians who prioritise textual evidence, Geddes here asserts his view that the truth of Scottish history is instead 'written deep in geography first, place, name, memory and legend next' (144), all of which, he believes, suggest that King Arthur was Scottish. Geddes's statements here build on research undertaken by his acquaintance, J. S. Stuart Glennie,[90] whose study of Arthurian topography, *Arthurian Localities* (1869), stresses that Cymric, pre-medieval southern Scotland (including what is currently the north of England) offered the true origins of Arthur.[91] Glennie identifies various references to Arthur in southern and eastern Scottish topography, such as Arthur's Seat, Camelon and Arthur's O'on, and examines several aspects of Scottish folk tradition that allude to the Arthurian cycle, including the beliefs that Arthur's Round Table is situated below Stirling Castle (the King's Knot) and that Merlin, Guinevere and Arthur are buried in Scotland, to make his argument.[92] These elements of folklore are in tune with Geoffrey of Monmouth's narrative poem, *Vita Merlini* (c.1150), which details Merlin's life in the Forest of Calidon in Scotland.[93] Glennie also contrasts the various references to Arthur in southern and eastern Scottish topography with references to the Fingalian tradition in the west and north, including the various Dun Fions.[94] He concludes that early medieval Scotland was composed of two main cultures: Pictish Celts and Cymric Celts, traditions that were similar enough to develop a united Scottish nationality.[95]

Glennie's endorsement of a Lowland Celtic mythology, which complemented a Highland Celtic mythology, drew Geddes to Glennie's research. Geddes not only mentions Glennie in *City Development*, but planned to republish Glennie's *Arthurian Localities* as part of the Celtic Library.[96] Geddes also corresponded with Glennie, who was due to give two lectures at the Outlook Tower – the first on 'The Localities of the Arthurian Tradition', the second on 'The Characters of Arthurian Romance'.[97] What Glennie's work offered Geddes and other Scottish revivalists was evidence of a Lowland Celtic mythology, which allowed them to style Scotland, as a whole, as Celtic. Although such a Lowland mythology authenticated differences between the Highlands and the Lowlands, it nevertheless helped to develop the image of a pan-Scottish Celticism, with complementary mythological cycles, that might dilute the identification of Lowland and eastern Scotland with Saxon heritage. Consequently, Scottish revivalists, especially Geddes, went to great lengths to define and represent a Scottish Arthurian mythology, and pageantry proved to be a key means of promoting identification with the Arthurian cycle.

Scholars have previously argued that the Arthurian elements of *fin-de-siècle* Scottish art, in drawing from an 'English source', were marks of an 'inclusively British' unionism.[98] While I argue here that the Arthurian presence in Scottish revivalist literature, art and pageantry demonstrates that Scots were happy to share a mythic vocabulary with England and Wales, there were nevertheless more defensive dimensions to *fin-de-siècle* Scottish Arthurianism too. Several figures I examine here wanted to reclaim Arthur as a Scottish source, not endorse the notion that Arthur was English or Welsh, and they were keen to do so to develop greater national unity and overcome the Lowland Saxonism that was felt to be dividing the nation, as discussed in Chapter 1. At a time when Arthur's association with Celtic identity was being increasingly 'ignored' in England, as Stephanie Barczewski demonstrates, Scottish revivalists, like those in Wales, were keen to reinscribe Arthur's Celtic legacy.[99]

Geddes's interest in Arthurian Scotland is reflected throughout his work, but most explicitly in the Ramsay Garden common room, discussed in Chapter 3, which features *The Taking of Excalibur*, a panel that depicts Merlin rowing Arthur to meet Queen Morgan Le Fay, who arises out of a loch wielding his sword Excalibur (Plate 13). Placed directly beside *The Combat of Fionn*, the panel immediately speaks to the complementary Arthurian and Fingalian Celtic cycles that Glennie outlined. The panel's connections to Glennie's ideas are further enhanced by the description of it in the guidebook, published by Patrick Geddes & Colleagues, with commentaries offered by Duncan and Geddes's colleague, Arthur Thomson. In Thomson's description of this panel, it becomes clear that the scene is set in Edinburgh:

> Upon the slopes of a hill now called Arthur's Seat the king would build a mighty fortress; but all the efforts of the builders were in vain [. . .]. Merlin instructed the king to dig deep under the foundations, saying that in a subterranean cave two great serpents lay imprisoned, sleeping by day, but in the night time waking to battle with each other. The king caused the hillside to be opened, and two huge dragons – one white like a cloud and the other red as the sun at evening – soared into the air biting and tearing at each other. The red dragon at length subdued his adversary, and the two sank to the place from which they had issued. Merlin, calling to those who had come to see this wonder, said that on the morrow the red dragon would rise from the loch (now below Duddingston) in the form of a sword, and to him who had the hardihood to grasp it, the sword would be yielded.[100]

This description appropriates a tale that is related in one of the foundational texts of Arthurian lore, Geoffrey of Monmouth's *The Prophecies of Merlin* (c.1150). In that text, Merlin and King Vortigern witness a battle between a red and a white dragon. In response, Merlin prophesies, 'Alas for the red dragon, its end is near. Its caves will be taken by the white dragon, which symbolises the Saxons whom you have summoned. The red represents the people of

Britain, whom the white will oppress.'[101] Thomson's description of Duncan's mural panel not only situates this battle in Scotland, thus claiming Arthur and Merlin as Scottish Celtic mythological figures while authenticating the Arthurian inheritance of Arthur's Seat, but it also inverts the inevitable defeat of the Celts that is prophesied in Geoffrey's text. There, the white (Saxon) dragon subdues the red (Celtic) dragon, but in Thomson's revision, it is the red, Celtic dragon that is the victor. The potent sword Excalibur, a manifestation of that victorious Celtic dragon, is then given to Arthur to wield, while Merlin wears a bright red cloak, a further reference to the victory of the Celts. The panel, therefore, both advances a Lowland Scottish Arthurian cycle, and embodies the resistance and empowerment of the Celt – a sentiment that was deeply in tune with other panels in the common room, such as *The Awakening of Cuchullin*, discussed in Chapter 3.

While the Ramsay Garden mural sequence forms the clearest embodiment of Geddes and his circle's desire to reclaim a Celtic Arthur for Scotland, it is not isolated. Throughout *The Evergreen*, Geddes makes references to Arthur and Merlin. In 'The Scots Renascence', Geddes repeats Glennie's idea that 'Arthur and all his court are said to lie in enchanted sleep' underneath the Eildon Hills in the Borders,[102] a myth that also features in Riccardo Stephens's *The Cruciform Mark*, which includes many references to Geddes's interests.[103] Furthermore, 'The Scots Renascence' and *City Development* both argue that the spirit of Arthur was taken up by the Jacobites and William Wallace, who Geddes describes as a 'veritable Arthur'.[104] Geddes is keen to conflate the image of Arthur with that of Scottish national defence. In 'The Sociology of Autumn', he also refers to aesthetes and decadents as 'our new Merlins', who 'brighten our winter with their gardens of dream'.[105] It comes as no surprise that Geddes named his youngest son Arthur (b.1895): around this time, Geddes was deeply committed to activating Scotland's Celtic Arthurian inheritances, writing that the 'Celtic art stream', which had been dormant since the time of King Arthur, was now reviving.[106]

Other figures besides Geddes shared an interest in Arthurian Scotland. Duncan's paintings featured Arthurian subjects, including *Merlin and the Fairy Queen* and *Tristan and Isolde* (1912); Edith Rinder contributed 'Sant Efflamm and King Arthur' to the Winter issue of *The Evergreen*; and, as was noted in Chapter 3, Sharp described Arthur as the defender of the Celts. Sharp was also interested in the quest for the grail, in both his life and his work. His novella, *The Gipsy Christ* (1895), traces the line of Kundry, a character who features in Richard Wagner's Arthurian-inspired opera on the quest for the holy grail, *Parsifal* (1882).[107] Merlin is also the subject of Fiona Macleod's poem, 'The Last Fay', and Sharp's manuscript notes reveal that he was planning two other Arthurian texts, 'Merlin: A Romance' and 'The Saga of Merlin'. The plan for the latter follows several of Glennie's and Geddes's ideas: Sharp intended to portray the Arthurian cycle emerging from the end of the Fenian cycle, and to cover Arthur and Guinevere (or Guenevêre) in Scotland, as well as Merlin's relationship with Oisin – highlighting the relationship between the Fingalian and Arthurian traditions.[108] Beyond *The Evergreen*'s contributors, Robert Louis Stevenson places Merlin in the Caledonian Forest in his unfinished novel *Heathercat* (1897),[109] while John Veitch's *Merlin and Other Poems* (1889) depicts Merlin's wanderings in the Borders. Furthermore, Margaret and Frances Macdonald created striking illustrations for William Morris's *The Defence of Guenevere* in 1897, and the Glasgow School of Art held an evening of *tableaux vivants* titled 'Idylls of the King', rooted in Arthurian lore, in 1909. Phoebe Traquair's Arthurian triptych *The Passing of Arthur* (1905) was clearly influenced by Edward Burne-Jones's *The Last Sleep of Arthur in Avalon* (1881). Geddes was obviously not the only revivalist who was drawn to Arthur and Merlin – two figures who were renowned for challenging the Saxons – and for attempting to situate them in Scotland.

This interest in the Arthurian cycle amongst those associated with the Scottish Revival is clearly reflected in the pageants of the period, particularly the most national ones. The *Scottish National Pageant* included a large Arthurian section, which was designed by figures associated with the Glasgow School: namely, Jessie M. King, following her illustrations for *The High History of the Holy Graal* in 1903. Geddes especially admired this section, writing that it 'was probably the masterpiece of pageantry as yet produced either side of the Tweed'.[110] King's designs were also applauded by reviewers for their symbolism: one described the section as being less an 'embodiment of history' and more 'the symbolic representation of the spirit of Romance'.[111] This Arthurian section then reappeared at the *Glasgow University Pageant* (Fig. 5.4), which also included the Arthurian myth in its chronicling of Scottish history. Not only did the Arthurian section feature 'the spirit of the water' that wields Excalibur, depicted in Duncan's mural, but Arthur's association with Scottish Celticism was also indicated by having a 'seanachie' (a bearer of lore in Scottish and Irish Gaelic culture) proclaim the approach of King Arthur, as well as the inclusion of the Queen of the Outer Isles.[112] Furthermore,

Figure 5.4 Queen Guinevere, *Glasgow University Pageant* (1908). University of Glasgow, Archives & Special Collections.

Arthur and Merlin appeared in the Celtic section of Geddes's *The Masque of Ancient Learning*, discussed below, with Geddes performing as Merlin.[113] In the book that accompanies the masque, Geddes asks us to think back to Duncan's Ramsay Lodge murals:[114] again, he stresses the importance of understanding the Arthurian tradition alongside Scotland's Fingalian figures, who Arthur sits alongside in that scheme. These various examples show that there was a clear attempt in the period to integrate the Arthurian myth into narratives of Scottish history and myths of descent, and that pageantry became a key tool for weaving the Arthurian myth into the Celtic Revival and distributing it to a wider populace.

Despite the fact that Arthurianism helped advance Scottish cultural nationalism in various ways, by advocating a myth that also had a legacy in England and Wales, revivalists opted to share myths of origin with other parts of Britain, marking their lack of hostility towards a loose cultural Britishness. The fact that a *Masque of St George and the Dragon*, featuring Walter Crane as the patron saint of England, concluded the *Scottish National Pageant* further confirms this British dimension, even in the most national of Scottish pageants. Unlike Patrick Pearse's pageants in Ireland, which imagined the Cuchullin cycle as the Irish alternative to the Arthurian cycle,[115] in Scotland Arthur and Cuchullin co-habited. The British dimension of Scottish Arthurianism is exemplified in the poem 'The Arthurian Legends' in the programme for the *Glasgow University Pageant*, which includes the line 'Oer Brittaine Arthur Kynge did rayne' (l. 5).[116] Arthur could support not only a Scottish myth of descent, but also a pre-Saxon Britishness more widely. As such, the Arthurian myth perfectly fitted the needs of many *fin-de-siècle* Scottish revivalists: it helped define Scotland in opposition to Saxon ethnicity, promoting greater unity within Scotland through identification with Celticism, while not defying cultural unionism outright.

Geddes's Pageants and Scottish Education

In 'promoting local interest in history and heritage', pageantry had a clear 'educational function', which was harnessed by revivalists hoping to disseminate their understandings of Scottish myth and history further.[117] But pageantry also attracted certain Scottish revivalists because, as a form, it was felt to nourish Scotland's distinctive educational traditions. Geddes, whose pioneering role in the development of historical pageantry was quickly 'forgotten',[118] was one of the pageant-masters most concerned with the ways in which pageantry and education intersected: not only would he stage a pageant on that theme, *The Masque of Learning: A Pageant of Education* (1912; Fig. 5.5), which was performed in Edinburgh and London, but also he wrote books and essays on pageantry and education. Besides pageantry's ability to reanimate the past, Geddes was drawn to masques and pageants because he believed they helped collapse the divide between town and gown, promoting greater 'synthesis' in education – a trait that underpinned his understanding of Scottish education.[119] For Geddes, civic pageants helped nurture 'student-citizens' with 'City and University ever renewing their own life and vigour as they enrich and widen, deepen and brighten that of youth'.[120] In his eyes, pageantry helped promote and defend the laudable features of Scotland's educational culture.

Throughout his life, Geddes was a committed polymath, who, as Murdo Macdonald demonstrates, embodied the Scottish generalist education tradition that George Davie outlines in his book, *The Democratic Intellect* (1961).[121] In contrast to what he saw as England's

Figure 5.5 Patrick Geddes, *The Masque of Learning* (1912). Archives and Special Collections, University of Strathclyde Library: T-GED 12/4/8.

specialist education tradition, Geddes admired Scotland's generalist, 'synthetic' tradition, helping learners understand the connections and interaction between various disciplines and subjects. Rejecting 'the manifold specialisms of modern universities', Geddes described the great Scottish thinkers as 'seekers for synthesis', and noted that this tradition resembled Celtic culture in its rootedness in 'synthesis'. Beyond disciplinary connections, he also felt that the Scottish education tradition promoted dialogue between nations: he wrote that 'Oxford will retain its manifold advantages and charms; but our renewal of contacts with the continent generally [. . .] remains none the less the paramount desideratum of our Scottish Universities.'[122] Although several of Geddes's educational efforts were inspired by English developments,[123] he was keen to valorise these aspects of the Scottish tradition, and he was not alone. Several *fin-de-siècle* cultural revivalists similarly cast Scottish education as superior: as we have seen, Stevenson compared the 'thoughtful, Bible-quoting ploughman' of Scotland with the 'neglected peasant' of England[124]; the narrator of Conan Doyle's *The Firm of Girdlestone* notes that the best Scottish students are 'men of the world while their *confrères* in England are still magnified schoolboys'[125]; and Buchan compared the 'kindergarten' of Oxford to the 'strenuous life of Glasgow'.[126] These revivalists shared a desire to define the differences between the Scottish and English education traditions and they often encoded the Scottish features as strengths.

While Geddes valorised certain features of Scottish education, he also expressed the need for reform. The health of Scottish education was, he felt, under threat from growing trends in educational practice, including the rise of specialism and examination, and the dominance of university management. He even called for a revolt against university management and its philosophy of 'Futilitarianism' – the futile focus on education's utility. Instead, he wanted university life to be refocused on teachers and students, writing 're-enter Guru and disciples, master and scholars: exeunt Chancellors, University Courts and Boards'.[127] He also launched attacks on contemporary pedagogical practice, believing that 'our docile memorising and general "good order" are far too much mere submission and stupor; symptoms of our decline, even of nearness to death'.[128] To combat examination, memorisation and university management, Geddes endeavoured to 'replace the stereotyped methods of education' with alternative 'synthetic' practices,[129] leading him to develop an enthusiasm for both Summer schools and pageantry.[130]

Pageantry became a key means of furthering the 'synthetic' education tradition that Geddes sought to revive. As has been noted, he believed that masques and pageantry were the Outlook Tower's 'most ambitious and comprehensive' project to remedy conventional education, and he wrote and produced several himself. Undoubtedly, his most ambitious pageant was *The Masque of Learning*, later performed as two separate pieces, *The Masque of Ancient Learning and The Masque of Medieval and Modern Learning*. Produced at the same time that Geddes was planning and designing the Edinburgh Zoological Garden (now Edinburgh Zoo),[131] *The Masque of Learning* was first performed in Edinburgh at the Synod Hall, featuring 650 players, in 1912 and then in London in 1913. The pageant presents the development of education from the Babylonian and Assyrian age through to Ancient Egyptian, Hebrew, Chinese, Indian, Hellenic and Celtic times, and then on to the medieval and modern periods, including episodes on James IV and Erasmus, Queen Mary and John Knox, Edinburgh University (an episode that featured George Buchanan and the Admirable Crichton), and a 'gathering of Edinburgh notables', including Burns, Scott, Robert Adam and James Watt.[132] In Marshall Wane's photographs of the actors, the Admirable Crichton, played by the author of the homoerotic story 'Evensong and Morwe Song' (1908) and future translator of Marcel Proust's *À la recherche du temps perdu*, Charles Kenneth Scott Moncrieff, strikes a pose that is identical to Crichton's stance in the Ramsay Garden murals, reflecting Geddes's view that pageants should be inspired by civic murals.[133]

From the outset of the pageant, *The Masque of Learning* announces its resistance to conventional methods of education. It begins with a prologue, set outside Edinburgh University, where a schoolboy encounters a 'friendly professor' who inspects his 'crowded' schoolbag. The professor states, 'this overgrown arithmetic book is the very spirit of the commercial and financial age: this old examination paper bears the stamp of its bureaucracy: and this cram-book to prepare for it is the encyclopædia in miniature'. Geddes writes that these books and methods 'depress, even repel, the student'.[134] The professor asks the boy to succumb to the true 'spell' of education and 're-enter' the past, and from here the pageant begins. After beholding the 'Pageant of Life and Learning', the performance concludes by refocusing on the boy, who is now celebrated as a citizen-student: 'although University and City came in separately upon our stage, they go out together; and with our whilom schoolboy, now a citizen-student, as torch-bearer, leading the way'.[135] Not only does the boy gain a more 'synthetic' understanding, through the pageant's reanimation of scientific and artistic figures, but also town and gown are portrayed as uniting through pageantry. As Geddes wrote, 'to link up [. . .] resources more fully, to diffuse them more generally to direct them more definitely towards the life of citizenship on one hand, of, inward culture upon the other' was the aim of pageantry.[136] As part of this synthetic relationship between town and gown, Geddes hoped that pageantry would change the way in which universities conducted their research. For example, he encouraged anthropologists and archaeologists to present their findings in the form of a masque, rather than in an academic journal, anticipating academia's current interest in public engagement. He wrote, 'why should research societies always hunt for subscriptions in one quarter, and then publish their learned work mainly in another, when they might so readily, as Masquers, widely popularise their science'?[137] Consequently, in *The Masque of Learning*, historical artefacts were used, including a spear that was 'borne in the Battle of Flodden', thus bringing history closer to civic society.[138] In various ways, *The Masque of Learning* embodied Geddes's determination to advance educational synthesis.

The Masque of Learning was also concerned with synthesis in another sense: nurturing unity between Scotland's sects of Christianity. At the end of *The Masque of Ancient Learning*, it is proposed that a statue of St Columba should be erected in Edinburgh's Lawnmarket, where Columba 'may most probably have preached'. It is highly unlikely that Columba ever preached in Edinburgh but such mythologising is telling: it reflects Geddes's desire to connect Scotland's Lowland capital with Hebridean, Celtic culture. Columba's 'synthetic' role is highlighted when we are told that he is the 'one single figure who all sections, divisions, classes, faiths of this much divided land have accepted as representative'.[139] Although this statue was never realised, it was sketched by Percy Portsmouth and appears on the cover of Branford's *St Columba* (1912). Besides helping to unify Scottish religion and society, as well as Columba's association with Iona, Geddes's enthusiasm for Columba may have reflected his own tacit support for Scottish Home Rule too: Geddes kept a cutting of an article in *The Scotsman* that described Columba as Scotland's first Home Ruler, liberating the Scots from foreign (Irish) control.[140]

The Masque of Learning was not alone in promoting synthesis and generalism. For instance, the front cover of the handbook for the *Scottish National Pageant* shows Lugh 'hurling the sun against the Powers of darkness'. Lugh was commonly understood by *fin-de-siècle* Celticists as the great Celtic generalist, 'the presiding deity of all human knowledge and of all artistic and medicinal skill',[141] and the pageant handbook even acknowledges this, describing him as 'inventor of all the arts'.[142] By placing Lugh on the front cover, the handbook raises the profile of this pagan generalist.

Pageantry was thus a means of promoting educational 'synthesis' between disciplines and between town and gown, helping to advance Scotland's 'synthetic' educational tradition, while also fostering greater national unity. But Geddes was also attracted to the form because he wanted Scots to develop a greater appreciation for the theatrical. He believed that Scots found theatre 'scarcely serious as compared with Church and State' and wrote that pageants could remedy this.[143] The visuality of pageants was also important, as Geddes felt that 'we do not clearly think, much less clearly idealise, until we visualise, and energise: that is, until we dramatise'.[144] Indeed, the pageants he designed were almost entirely communicated through visuals: they were 'silent or almost wordless performance[s]'.[145] Connected to his interest in visualising and dramatising, Geddes hoped that his pageants might become successful motion pictures. He wrote:

> just as the Picture House freshens the public mind by showing things far from our everyday street, so we might at any rate be pardoned even were we but rehearsing – so as to be worthy some day of appearing in a new film – one too which with all its faults might surely hold its own with many others on the market.[146]

This statement reveals Geddes's conviction about educational entertainment and his interrogation of conventional teaching mechanisms; he is quoted as saying, 'if you divide education and entertainment you will fail with both'.[147] Pageants were the ideal form for embodying Geddes's desire to raise the profile of visuals, dramatisation and entertainment in Scottish education.

On a variety of levels, pageantry supported Geddes's project of cultural revivalism, but his pageants were very distinct from those educational pageants performed by revivalists in Ireland. The impetus to educate and promote revivalism through pageants was evident in Ireland in this period too, but it took a very different form in the events performed at Patrick Pearse's St Enda's School, Dublin. Several pageants were performed at St Enda's (a school for boys) between 1909 and 1915, which were mainly arranged and organised by Pearse's brother, William.[148] Like Geddes's *Masque*, these pageants focused on the figure of the schoolboy, but they were often used as a means to educate the boys towards militant nationalist ends, as is particularly evident in *The Boy Deeds of Cúchulainn*. Here, the Celtic hero, Cuchullin, was chosen as a role model to ignite a nationalist drive in the children who performed. Pearse stated, 'the noble personality of a Cúchulainn forms a true type of Gaelic nationality, full as it is of a youthful life and vigour and hope',[149] and said that the school was 'anxious to send our boys home with the knightly image of Cúchulainn in their hearts and his knightly words ringing in their ears'.[150] In doing so, a militant 'nationalist masculinity' would be nurtured in the boys.[151] Pearse's agenda reached its peak in the school's 1911 Passion Play at the Abbey Theatre, which was, as Mary Trotter notes, 'a violent metaphor: a call for the Irish nationalist to accept his/her own cross and be prepared to die for Ireland'.[152] It was believed that the Acts of Union 1800 were emasculating Ireland and that one way of counteracting this was to instil the image of the masculine Gael, as opposed to the fey Celt, in the children from an early age.[153] Pearse's pageants used mythology not simply to form a cultural identity, but to stimulate political change through potential militancy.

The pageants at St Enda's School provide a useful comparison for considering the intersection between education and nationalism in Scotland. Although there were some representations of national military combat in work by those in Geddes's circle (such as John Duncan's submission to the Glasgow Corporation Bannockburn Centenary competition in 1914 – portraying Bruce slaying de Bohun – which tellingly lost out to John Hassall's portrayal of the pre-battle prayer), there was very little interest in consciously encouraging militancy in Scotland. Geddes's enthusiasm for 'the university militant' idea, outlined by Charles Ferguson in 1912, was concerned with improving the culture of education in universities rather than political militancy.[154] As we have previously encountered, Geddes was content to see 'militant nationality' ebb, and hoped that the Scottish Revival could be advanced by 'gentler voices'.[155] Alongside Pearse's, Geddes's pageants highlight the characteristics and limits of Scottish revivalism, encouraging a sense of Scottish nationality and enriching Scotland's educational traditions while in no way challenging unionism.

This consideration of historical pageantry in Edwardian Scotland reveals not only that it was alluring to *fin-de-siècle* Scottish cultural revivalists but that it supported the distinctive nature of the Scottish Revival in various different ways. As forms of cultural memory, pageants helped define and circulate Scottish Celtic mythologies and histories, its myths of descent, that were constructed to help foster the nation's sense of its own identity. But pageants did not simply provide a national 'sense of continuity'; they celebrated the greatest artists and designers of the Celtic Revival, and Scotland more widely, provided platforms for national collaboration, and became a means of advancing Scotland's educational traditions (or, at least, Geddes's perception of what these traditions were). As such, Scottish Edwardian pageantry also reveals the complexity of British pageantry in this period: as in Wales and Ireland, Scottish revivalists developed particular forms of pageantry and particular narratives, many of which are starkly different from those found in Parker's pageants in small-town England. Scottish Edwardian pageantry reminds us of our need to be careful over generalising about British historical pageantry: most pageant-masters may have been defying the processes of centralisation, but revivalists in the 'Celtic nations' were resisting the centre in very distinctive manners.

Notes

1. For more on contemporary references to 'pageantitis', see Sugg Ryan.
2. Freeman: 424.
3. For more on how some pageant-masters in America were inspired by (and resisted) the commercialism of motion pictures, see Glassberg, p. 118.
4. Freeman: 426.
5. Bartie et al.: 874–80.
6. Hulme: 270.
7. Parker: 143.
8. Readman: 191.
9. Robert Withington wrote to Geddes, asking for information about a pageant Geddes staged on Arthur's Seat in Edinburgh in 1900. See Letter to Patrick Geddes from Robert Withington [Archives and Special Collections, University of Strathclyde: T-GED 9/1194]. There is also evidence of historical pageants being held as early as the 1880s, such as the *Grand Pageant at Ripon Yorkshire* (1886).
10. Smith, *Myths and Memories*, p. 151.
11. Sugg Ryan: 68.
12. Willsdon, p. 20.
13. See Kinchin; Burkhauser, pp. 67–9; and Cumming, *Hand, Heart and Soul*, p. 180.
14. For instance, see Simpson.
15. Hulme: 271.
16. Quinault: 303.
17. Rigney, 'Embodied Communities': 71.
18. Quinault: 321.
19. Ibid.: 322.

20. Assmann, p. 129.
21. For more on Victorian Scottish commemorations, see Coleman.
22. For more on this festival, see Pittock and Whatley.
23. Pittock, *The Invention of Scotland*, p. 130.
24. Rigney, 'Portable Monuments': 365.
25. Ibid.: p. 366.
26. Rigney, 'Plenitude': 25.
27. Rigney, 'Portable Monuments': 377.
28. Ibid.
29. Ibid.: 381.
30. Rigney, 'Plenitude': 13.
31. Ibid.: 17.
32. Nietzsche, II, p. 31.
33. Patrick Geddes, 'The Celtic Races', 1896 [Archives and Special Collections, University of Strathclyde: T-GED 5/2/8].
34. For more discussion of an example of earlier pageantry, see Johnston and Dorrell.
35. 'The Warwick Pageant': 12.
36. Withington, 'Louis Napoleon Parker': 512.
37. (Cited in) 'Mr. Louis N. Parker on Pageantry': 598.
38. Rigney, 'Portable Monuments': 383.
39. Patrick Geddes, 'The Celtic Renascence – Columbian and Contemporary', p. 6 [Archives and Special Collections, University of Strathclyde: T-GED 5/2/6].
40. Geddes, *City Development*, p. 147.
41. Patrick Geddes, 'Significance and Purpose of the Masques', pp. 7–8 [Archives and Special Collections, University of Strathclyde: T-GED 12/1/395].
42. Masques were generally considered to be more allegorical versions of pageants; see Glassberg, p. 120.
43. Patrick Geddes, 'Significance and Purpose of the Masques', p. 6 [Archives and Special Collections, University of Strathclyde: T-GED 12/1/395].
44. Geddes, 'Significance and Purpose of the Masques', p. 4. [T-GED 12/1/395].
45. Geddes, *City Development*, pp. 144–5.
46. Geddes, *Dramatisations*, p. 91.
47. Cumming, *Hand, Heart and Soul*, p. 180.
48. Readman: 178–9.
49. (Cited in) Glassberg, p. 78.
50. The suffragette pageant presented various key figures from Scottish history, including Queen Margaret, Jenny Geddes and Mary Stuart. It was partly organised by a Glaswegian suffragette, Frances McPhun, who would go on to be imprisoned in 1912 for smashing windows in central London.
51. *The Pageant of the Bruce*, which was performed at the national exhibition in Kelvingrove Park, Glasgow, in 1911, was written by George Douglas.

52. Kinchin and Kinchin, p. 104.
53. Postcard invitation to participate in a Bannockburn Pageant at Falkirk, June 1914 [Archives and Special Collections, University of Strathclyde: T-GED 7/8/78].
54. For more information on heroism in *fin-de-siècle* Scottish art, see Murdo Macdonald, *Scottish Art*, p. 129.
55. Withington, *English Pageantry*, II, pp. 202–3.
56. For more on this pageant, see Edwards.
57. For more on this congress and its pageant, see Löffler.
58. 'The Revival of Pageantry', p. 6.
59. 'Scottish National Exhibition', *The Scots Pictorial*: 235.
60. 'National Exhibition: Scotland's Day': 290.
61. Printed correspondence relating to Scottish Exhibition of National History, Art and Industry, Glasgow [Archives and Special Collections, University of Strathclyde: T-GED 4/2/11].
62. 'The Scottish Exhibition', p. 6.
63. 'The Pageant and Masque', p. 7.
64. 'The Grand Scottish Historical Pageant': 240.
65. 'The Scottish National Pageant', p. 3.
66. 'Scottish National Exhibition', Scottish Screen Archive, available at <http://ssa.nls.uk/film/1699> (last accessed 12 June 2014).
67. William Hole, Costumes designed for the Scottish Historical Pageant held in Edinburgh on 13th June 1908 (design sketches, 1908) [National Library of Scotland: NF.1481.a.21].
68. Geddes possessed this issue; see 'Journal: *The Scottish Review*. Vol. V. No. 112' [Archives and Special Collections, University of Strathclyde: T-GED 12/2/192].
69. Geddes wrote to the Exhibition's Provisional Committee between 1905 and 1906, mentioning pageantry in one letter to Bailie Fraser Dobie; see Archives and Special Collections, University of Strathclyde: T-GED 7/1/14/1–2 and 7/1/13.
70. Letter from Daisy to Mrs Geddes, 30 May 1908 [Archives and Special Collections, University of Strathclyde: T-GED 9/840].
71. 'The Scottish Historical Pageant', p. 7.
72. Baltz: 211–12.
73. Patrick Geddes, untitled essay on the Celtic Cross, pp. 6–9 [Archives and Special Collections, University of Strathclyde: T-GED 5/2/13].
74. 'Significance and Purpose of the Masques', p. 8 [University of Strathclyde: T-GED 5/2/13].
75. Glassberg, p. 139.
76. Ibid., p. 143; it should be acknowledged that American pageants were not always stadialist: American pageants in this period could also look to the past to provide 'a guide to proper behaviour in the present' (Glassberg, p. 124).
77. See Cameron.

78. 'Celebrating the Union', p. 4.
79. Renan, p. 251.
80. Newbery, p. 5.
81. Ibid., pp. 4, 11.
82. Geddes, *Dramatisations*, p. iv.
83. Ibid., p. xii.
84. Papers by Patrick Geddes regarding Masques of Learning [Archives and Special Collections, University of Strathclyde: T-GED 12/1/397].
85. Geddes, *Dramatisations*, p. iv.
86. (Cited in) 'The Civic Theatre': 445.
87. *Scottish Children's League of Pity Pageant Handbook*, pp. 3–4.
88. 'The Scottish National Pageant', p. 3.
89. Geddes, *City Development*, p. 144.
90. Glennie had written a play on Arthur, *King Arthur* (1870), and he became a supporter of Home Rule All Round; see Glennie, *The Liberal Party*, p. 36.
91. Glennie, *Arthurian Localities*, p. 17.
92. Ibid., pp. 125–7. For more on the burial sites of Arthurian figures in Scotland, see Westwood and Kingshill, p. 216.
93. *Vita Merlini* was referenced in W. F. Skene's *The Four Ancient Books of Wales*, which Glennie read (see Glennie, *Arthurian Localities*, p. i). For more on this poem, see Clarkson, pp. 5–12.
94. Glennie, *Arthurian Localities*, pp. 101–2.
95. Ibid., pp. 109–10.
96. Rhys, *The Fiddler of Carne*, p. 358.
97. Letter from J. S. S. Glennie to Patrick Geddes, 24 May 1901 [Archives and Special Collections, University of Strathclyde: T-GED 9/343].
98. Morrison, 'Nationalism and Nationhood', pp. 201–4.
99. Barczewski, pp. 153, 236.
100. *Interpretation of the Pictures in the Common Room of Ramsay Lodge*, p. 5.
101. Geoffrey of Monmouth, p. 144.
102. Geddes, 'The Scots Renascence': 137; Glennie, *Arthurian Localities*, p. 66.
103. Stephens, *The Cruciform Mark*, p. 308.
104. Geddes, *City Development*, p. 144.
105. Geddes, 'The Sociology of Autumn': 36.
106. Diagram by Patrick Geddes illustrating the Celtic art stream from the Classic art stream [Archives and Special Collections, University of Strathclyde: T-GED 5/2/5].
107. For more on Sharp's interest in the grail, see Benham.
108. William Sharp, manuscripts and typescripts [National Library of Scotland: MS 8777].
109. Robert Louis Stevenson, *Romances*, p. 91.
110. Geddes, *Dramatisations*, p. 54.

111. 'The Pageant and Masque', p. 7.
112. *Scottish Children's League of Pity Pageant Handbook*, p. 9.
113. Geddes, *Dramatisations*, p. 51.
114. Ibid., p. 54.
115. Augusteijn, p. 170.
116. Programme of the Pageant held at the University of Glasgow, 10 October 1908 [Special Collections, Glasgow University Library: Sp Coll Mu21-d.56].
117. Freeman: 425; Bartie et al.: 870.
118. Defries, p. 47.
119. Geddes was instrumental in establishing the Town and Gown Association in Edinburgh in 1896.
120. Geddes, *Dramatisations*, p. 180.
121. For more on Geddes's generalism, see Murdo Macdonald, 'Patrick Geddes's Generalism'.
122. Geddes, *Dramatisations*, pp. 187, 120; Patrick Geddes, 'The Celtic Cross', p. 2 [Archives and Special Collections, University of Strathclyde: T-GED 5/2/13].
123. See Sutherland: 357.
124. Stevenson, *The Lantern-Bearers*, p. 167.
125. Doyle, *The Firm of Girdlestone*, p. 33.
126. (Cited in) Paul H. Scott, p. 186.
127. Geddes, *Dramatisations*, pp. 87–8
128. Ibid., p. 116.
129. Elizabeth A. Sharp, *William Sharp*, p. 249
130. For an introduction to Geddes's Summer schools in Edinburgh, see Meller, pp. 66–70.
131. For more on Geddes's role in the establishment of the Edinburgh Zoological Garden, see Thompson.
132. Geddes, *Dramatisations*, p. 154.
133. 'The Masque of Ancient Learning', p. 613.
134. Geddes, *Dramatisations*, pp. 1–2, 190.
135. Ibid., p. 180.
136. Ibid., p. 101.
137. Ibid., pp. 69–70.
138. Hay, p. 11.
139. Geddes, *Dramatisations*, pp. 58–9.
140. 'The First Home Rule Act for Scotland', p. 8; this cutting can be found in the Archives and Special Collections, University of Strathclyde: T-GED 4/2/13.
141. Rolleston, p. 112.
142. *Scottish Children's League of Pity Pageant Handbook*, p. 6.
143. Papers and Notes relating to Masques of Learning, c.1912–1914 [Archives and Special Collections, University of Strathclyde: T-GED 12/1/174].

144. Geddes, *Dramatisations*, p. v.
145. Ibid., p. 194.
146. Patrick Geddes, 'Use of the Masque', p. 7 [Archives and Special Collections, University of Strathclyde: T-GED 12/1/158].
147. Defries, p. 282.
148. Trotter, p. 148.
149. (Cited in) Sisson, p. 79.
150. (Cited in) Trotter, p. 152.
151. Sisson, p. 113.
152. Trotter, p. 138.
153. Sisson, p. 85.
154. For more on Geddes's interest in 'the university militant' see Scott and Bromley, pp. 157–60.
155. Geddes, 'The Scots Renascence': 138.

Envoy

In 1925, Richard Le Gallienne, an English poet and contributor to *The Yellow Book*, noted that 'all our present-day developments amount to little more than pale or exaggerated copying of the '90s'.[1] This statement, casting modernist literary innovations as unoriginal, is an exaggerated attempt to highlight the significance of the 1890s. But, beneath the exaggeration, the quotation reveals that certain figures in the 1920s were attentive to the debts that modernist developments owed to the late Victorian period. Scholars of modernism and decadence are increasingly acknowledging the debts that Le Gallienne alludes to. Laura Marcus et al.'s collection, *Late Victorian into Modern* (2016), and Kate Hext and Alex Murray's *Decadence in the Age of Modernism* (2019) are just two recent examples of scholarly attempts to interrogate the supposed divisions between modernism and the late Victorian period. Rather than a radical break, these studies highlight the continuities between the nineteenth and twentieth centuries.

It is hoped that this book, in uncovering the nature of cultural nationalism in *fin-de-siècle* Scotland, as well as its reliance on decadence and international colloquy, provides a platform to scrutinise more fully the ties between the late Victorian and the modern in Scotland – ties that Hugh MacDiarmid was especially keen to obscure. As we encountered in Chapter 2, MacDiarmid made various bold statements, denying the health, sophistication and internationalism of Scottish culture in the 1890s in order to advance his 'impulse for Renaissance'; he even went so far as to describe the Victorian and Edwardian years as perhaps 'the most jejune and uninspired period in Scottish literature'.[2] But, even in MacDiarmid's writings, we find several inheritances from the *fin de siècle* (besides the Scottish–Belgian connection), which help us grasp Scottish modernist debts to (and divergences from) the *fin de siècle*.

For instance, in his collection of autobiographical essays, *The Company I've Kept*, MacDiarmid devotes a section to Patrick Geddes, where he outlines his intense admiration for Geddes's work:

> Prophets are proverbially without honour in their own country, but even so the neglect or ignorance of Sir Patrick Geddes in Scotland goes to an uncommon degree and throws a very disconcerting light on our whole national condition, since he was one of the outstanding thinkers of his generation, not merely in Britain but in the world, and not only one of the greatest Scotsmen of the past century but in our entire history.[3]

MacDiarmid's respect for Geddes is reflected in his keenness to seek out his company, through correspondence and his intention to visit Geddes in Montpellier.[4] Elsewhere, MacDiarmid praised *The Evergreen*, which 'touched an international note, and kept up the spirit of the best ideals in literature and art',[5] and he also described Geddes's Outlook Tower as enabling 'the fullest understanding of the place by its people'.[6] Geddes's generalism, his internationalism and his focus on locality clearly impressed and inspired MacDiarmid.

And Geddes was not the only *fin-de-siècle* figure who earned MacDiarmid's respect. Despite his dismissive attacks on the 'mongrel work' of Fiona Macleod, other MacDiarmid writings reveal that such charges were largely rhetorical bravado; for instance, he commended 'Macleod's amazing powers of word-painting and of spiritual insight', and also described her as one of the six best short-story writers Scotland had ever produced.[7] MacDiarmid himself mapped out continuities between Fiona Macleod's writings and Scottish modernism, identifying Neil Gunn's dialogue with Macleod's work in Gunn's story, 'Half Light', where the schoolmaster, Iain Mackay, discusses Macleod.[8]

Beyond Macleod and Geddes, MacDiarmid cited Cunninghame Graham as one of his major sources of inspiration: indeed, he wrote that his decision to 'make the Scottish cause, cultural and political, my life-work' dated from the moment he met Cunninghame Graham,[9] noting that 'there is no finer figure in all the millenary pageant of Scotland's writers'.[10] The Dundee artist, Stewart Carmichael, who began his career in the 1890s and painted into the modernist period, was a further *fin-de-siècle* figure who MacDiarmid revered.[11]

As these few, brief examples demonstrate, there was substantial appreciation for *fin-de-siècle* Scottish writings in the 1920s, which lie behind MacDiarmid's rhetorical attempts to write the Victorian and Edwardian periods off. By recovering Scotland's *fin de siècle*, we not only grasp the complexities of constitutional and cultural tensions in the United Kingdom around the 1890s, and uncover Scottish contributions to several European literary and artistic developments, but also advance our understanding of Scottish modernism.

Besides raising questions on the influence of *fin-de-siècle* Scottish literature and art, it is hoped that this study prompts various other queries. Far from offering the final word on the Scottish Revival, there are several topics, only fleetingly touched on here, that deserve their own book-length studies. What were the class politics of the Scottish Revival, and to what extent did cultural revivalism diffuse beyond the groups of largely middle-class writers and artists examined here? What role did the Scots language play in the Scottish Revival? To what extent were features of the Revival reflected in the Gaelic literature of the period? Was the Celtic revivalist enthusiasm for La Jeune Belgique reciprocated in Belgium? These, and many other questions, await fuller exploration.

Notes

1. Le Gallienne, p. 137.
2. MacDiarmid, *Contemporary Scottish Studies*, p. 358.
3. MacDiarmid, *The Company I've Kept*, p. 79.
4. Letter from C. M. Grieve to Patrick Geddes, 6 October 1930 [Archives and Special Collections, University of Strathclyde: T-GED 9/1717].
5. (Cited in) Hanna: 2.
6. (Cited in) Lyall, *Hugh MacDiarmid's Poetry*, p. 45.
7. MacDiarmid, *Contemporary Scottish Studies*, pp. 20, 22, 318.
8. Ibid., pp. 310–12.
9. MacDiarmid, *Albyn*, p. 132.
10. MacDiarmid, *Cunninghame Graham*, p. 40.
11. See Jarron, p. 90.

Bibliography

Archival Sources

Archives and Special Collections, University of Strathclyde
T-GED 3/4/13, T-GED 4/2/11, T-GED 4/2/13, T-GED 5/2/5, T-GED 5/2/6, T-GED 5/2/7, T-GED 5/2/8, T-GED 5/2/9, T-GED 5/2/13, T-GED 5/3/33, T-GED 5/3/70, T-GED 7/1/13, T-GED 7/1/14/1–2, T-GED 7/8/44, T-GED 7/8/78, T-GED 8/1/1, T-GED 8/1/2, T-GED 8/1/3, T-GED 9/343, T-GED 9/1194, T-GED 9/840, T-GED 9/1194, T-GED 9/1717, T-GED 11/1/3, T-GED 11/1/22, T-GED 11/1/67, T-GED 11/1/93, T-GED 11/3/94, T-GED 12/1/28, T-GED 12/1/61, T-GED 12/1/158, T-GED 12/1/167, T-GED 12/1/174, T-GED 12/1/395, T-GED 12/1/397, T-GED 12/2/192, T-GED 22/1/British Isles/Scotland/539/1

The Arthur Conan Doyle Encyclopedia
<www.arthur-conan-doyle.com>

Beinecke Library of Rare Books and Manuscripts, Yale University
GEN MSS 664/11/288, GEN MSS 664/12/304

Broughton House, Kirkcudbright
2668

Centre for Research Collections, University of Edinburgh
E2208.54

Hunterian Art Gallery
GLAHA 41423

The Library and Museum of Freemasonry, London
GBR 1991 GD 2/1/7, GBR 1991 GD 2/3/4/2, GBR 1991 GD 2/3/4/3, GBR 1991 GD 2/4/1/12, GBR 1991 GD 4/3/2/5/a

National Library of Scotland, Edinburgh

Acc. 9058/5/1, AC6866–6, MS 6866/4, MS 8775, MS 8776, MS 8777, MS 9987, MS 10508A, MS 10517, MS 27416/4, NF.1481.a.21

Special Collections, Glasgow University Library
Whistler X26, Mu21-d.56

The William Sharp 'Fiona Macleod' Archive
<https://www.ies.sas.ac.uk/research-projects-archives/william-sharp-fiona-macleod-archive>

Printed Sources

Ad Rem, 'Bathgate Sons Aye to the Fore', *West Lothian Courier*, 1 November 1884.

Alaya, Flavia, *William Sharp – 'Fiona Macleod'* (Cambridge, MA: Harvard University Press, 1970).

Arata, Stephen, *Fictions of Loss in the Victorian Fin de Siècle: Identity and Empire* (Cambridge: Cambridge University Press, 1996).

— 'Stevenson, Morris, and the Value of Idleness', in *Robert Louis Stevenson: Writer of Boundaries*, ed. David Ambrosini and Richard Dury (Madison: University of Wisconsin Press, 2006).

Armour, Margaret, 'Mural Decoration in Scotland. Part I', *The International Studio*, 1 (1897): 100–6.

Arnold, Matthew, *Culture and Anarchy: An Essay in Political and Social Criticism* (London: Smith, Elder, 1869).

— *On the Study of Celtic Literature* (London: Smith, Elder, 1867).

Assmann, Aleida, *Cultural Memory and Western Civilization* (Cambridge: Cambridge University Press, 2011).

Atisha, Brother, 'The Future Works of Scotland', *Theosophy in Scotland*, 4 (1910): 61.

Augusteijn, Joost, *Patrick Pearse: The Making of a Revolutionary* (Houndmills: Palgrave Macmillan, 2010).

Baltz, Trudy, 'Pageantry and Mural Painting: Community Rituals in Allegorical Form', *Winterhur Portfolio*, 15.3 (1980): 211–28.

Barczewski, Stephanie, *Myth and National Identity in Nineteenth-Century Britain: The Legends of King Arthur and Robin Hood* (Oxford: Oxford University Press, 2000).

Barrie, J. M., *Farewell Miss Julie Logan: A Barrie Omnibus* (Edinburgh: Canongate, 2000).

— 'Mr. Plagiary Lang', *The Scots Observer*, 4 (1890): 97–8.

— *Peter Pan and Other Plays*, ed. Peter Hollindale (Oxford: Oxford University Press, 1995).

Barry, William, 'Neo-Paganism', *The Quarterly Review*, 172 (1891): 273–4.

Bartie, Angela, Linda Fleming, Mark Freeman, Tom Hulme, Alexander Hutton and Paul Readman, 'Historical Pageants and the Medieval Past in Twentieth-Century England', *English Historical Review*, 133 (2018): 866–902.

Baudelaire, Charles *Œuvres posthumes*, 3 vols (Paris: Louis Conard, 1952).

— *The Painter of Modern Life and Other Essays*, trans. and ed. Jonathan Mayne (London: Phaidon, 1995).

Benham, Patrick, *The Avalonians* (Glastonbury: Gothic Image, 1993).

Benko, Stephen, *The Virgin Goddess: Studies in the Pagan and Christian Roots of Mariology* (Leiden: E. J. Brill, 2004).

Bicket, Linden, *George Mackay Brown and the Scottish Catholic Imagination* (Edinburgh: Edinburgh University Press, 2017).

Billcliffe, Roger, *Charles Rennie Mackintosh and the Art of the Four* (London: Frances Lincoln, 2018).

— *The Glasgow Boys* (London: Frances Lincoln, 2008).

Blackie, John Stuart, *Essays on Subjects of Moral and Social Interest* (Edinburgh: David Douglas, 1890).

— 'The Highland Crofters', *The Nineteenth Century: A Monthly Review*, 13 (1883): 604–16.

— *The Scottish Highlanders and the Land Laws: Historico-Economical Enquiry* (London: Chapman and Hall, 1885).

— *A Song of Heroes* (Edinburgh: William Blackwood and Sons, 1890).

— *The Union of 1707 and its Results: A Plea for Scottish Home Rule* (Glasgow: Morison Brothers, 1892).

Blair, Kirstie, '"Whose cry is Liberty, and Fatherland": Kossuth, Garibaldi and European Nationalism in Scottish Political Poetry', *Scottish Literary Review*, 10.2 (2018): 71–94.

Blamires, Steve, *The Little Book of the Great Enchantment* (Arcata: R. J. Stewart, 2008).

Blathwayt, Raymond, 'A Talk with Dr. Conan Doyle', *The Bookman*, 8 (1892): 50–1.

Bloom, Harold, *The Anxiety of Influence: A Theory of Poetry* (Oxford: Oxford University Press, 1997).

Boardman, Phillip, *The Worlds of Patrick Geddes: Biologist, Town Planner, Re-Educator, Peace-Warrior* (London: Routledge & Kegan Paul, 1978).

Bold, Valentina, and Andrew Nash (eds), *Gateway to the Modern: Resituating J. M. Barrie* (Glasgow: Scottish Literature International, 2014).

Boyce, D. G., '"The Marginal Britons": The Irish', in *Englishness: Politics and Culture 1880–1920*, ed. Robert Colls and Philip Dodd (London: Croom Helm, 1986).

Bradley, Ian, *Celtic Christianity: Making Myths and Chasing Dreams* (Edinburgh: Edinburgh University Press, 1999).

Branford, Victor, 'Awakenings in History', *The Evergreen*, 1 (1895): 85–90.

— 'Old Edinburgh and the *Evergreen*', *The Bookman*, 9 (1895): 88–90.

— 'A Series of Remarks', *The New Evergreen: The Christmas Book of University Hall* (1894): 33.

Branford, Victor, and Patrick Geddes, *The Coming Polity: A Study in Reconstruction* (London: Williams & Norgate, 1917).

— *Our Social Inheritance* (London: Williams & Norgate, 1919).

— 'Prefatory Note', *The Evergreen*, 2 (1895): 8.

Brantlinger, Patrick, *Rule of Darkness: British Literature and Imperialism, 1830–1914* (Ithaca, NY: Cornell University Press, 1988).

Brett, David, *C. R. Mackintosh: The Poetics of Workmanship* (London: Reaktion, 2000).

Brodie-Innes, J. W., 'Some Celtic Memories', in *The Sorcerer and his Apprentice: Unknown Hermetic Writings of S. L. MacGregor Mathers and J. W. Brodie-Innes*, ed. R. A. Gilbert (Wellingborough: Aquarian Press, 1983), pp. 101–14.

Brown, Ian, *History as Theatrical Metaphor: History, Myth and National Identities in Modern Scottish Drama* (London: Palgrave Macmillan, 2016).

— *Scottish Theatre: Diversity, Language, Continuity* (Amsterdam: Rodopi, 2013).

Bru, Sasha, 'The Low Countries: Introduction', in *The Oxford Critical and Cultural History of Modernist Magazines*, ed. Peter Brooker, Sascha Bru, Andrew Thacker and Christian Weikop, III (Oxford: Oxford University Press, 2013), pp. 290–2.

— 'The Prism of Propaganda: Hugh MacDiarmid's Modernism and the Belgian Literary Revival', *Scottish Literary Review*, 3.1 (2011): 43–62.

Bruce, Dorothy, *Alexander Reid and the Japanese Influence: Art, Ships and Plants* (Blairmore: Cowalfest, 2009).

Buchan, John, *Grey Weather: Moorland Tales of My Own People* (London: John Lane, 1899).

— *John MacNab* (Edinburgh: Polygon, 2007).

— *Prester John* (New York: John H. Doran, 1910).

Buchanan, William, 'Japanese Influences on the Glasgow Boys and Charles Rennie Mackintosh', in *Japonisme in Art: An International Symposium* (Tokyo: Kodansha International, 2001), pp. 291–301.

— *Mr Henry and Mr Hornel Visit Japan* (Glasgow: Scottish Arts Council, 1979).

Budge, E. A. Wallis, ed., *The Book of the Dead* (New York: Gramercy, 1999)

Burkhauser, Jude, 'The Visible Woman Vanishes!', in *Glasgow Girls: Women in Art and Design 1880–1920*, ed. Jude Burkhauser (Edinburgh: Canongate, 2005), pp. 63–70.

Burstein, Miriam Elizabeth, 'Catholicism and the Fin de Siècle', in *The Edinburgh Companion to Fin-de-Siècle Literature, Culture and the Arts*, ed. Josephine M. Guy (Edinburgh: Edinburgh University Press, 2018), pp. 106–23.

Burton, Richard, *The Context of Baudelaire's 'Le Cygne'* (Durham: University of Durham, 1980).

Bush, Douglas, *Mythology and the Romantic Tradition in English Poetry* (Cambridge, MA: Harvard University Press, 1937).

Caird, Mona, *The Daughters of Danaus* (New York: Feminist Press, 1993).

Calder, Jenni, 'Figures in a Landscape: Scott, Stevenson, and Routes to the Past', in *Robert Louis Stevenson: Writer of Boundaries*, ed. David Ambrosini and Richard Dury (Madison: University of Wisconsin Press, 2006), pp. 121–32.

Cameron, Ewen, '"Offensive to national sentiment"? The Bicentenary of the Union of 1707', in *The Age of Anniversaries: The Cult of Commemoration, 1895–1925*, ed. T. G. Otte (London: Routledge, 2018), pp. 82–100.

Cammell, Charles Richard, *Heart of Scotland* (London: Robert Hale, 1956).

Campbell, Ian, *Kailyard* (Edinburgh: Ramsay Head Press, 1981).

Carlyle, Thomas, *Chartism* (London: James Fraser, 1840).

Carpenter, Edward, *Civilization: Its Cause and Cure and Other Essays* (London: Swan Sonnenschein, 1891).

— *The Healing of the Nations and the Hidden Sources of Their Strife* (London: George Allen & Unwin, 1915).

Carruthers, Gerard, 'The Invention of Scottish Literature During the Long Eighteenth Century', PhD thesis, University of Glasgow, 2001.

— *Scottish Literature* (Edinburgh: Edinburgh University Press, 2009).

Carruthers, Gerard, David Goldie and Alastair Renfrew, 'Introduction', in *Scotland and the 19th-Century World*, ed. Gerard Carruthers, David Goldie and Alastair Renfrew (Amsterdam: Rodopi, 2012), pp. 15–20.

Castle, Gregory, *Modernism and the Celtic Revival* (Cambridge: Cambridge University Press, 2001).

'Celebrating the Union', *Dundee Courier*, 31 January 1907, p. 4.

Chandra, Jyoti, *Annie Besant: From Theosophy to Nationalism* (Dehli: K. K. Publications, 2001).

Checkland, Olive, *Britain's Encounter with Meiji Japan, 1868–1912* (Houndmills: Macmillan, 1989).

— *Japan and Britain after 1859: Creating Cultural Bridges* (London: RoutledgeCurzon, 2002).

Checkland, Olive, and Sydney Checkland, *Industry and Ethos: Scotland 1832–1914* (Edinburgh: Edinburgh University Press, 1989).

Churton, Tobias, *Aleister Crowley: The Biography* (London: Watkins, 2011).

'The Civic Theatre', *Review of Reviews*, 48 (1913): 445.

Claes, Koenraad, *The Late-Victorian Little Magazine* (Edinburgh: Edinburgh University Press, 2018).

Clarke, Helen A., 'Maeterlinck and Sharp', *Poet-Lore*, 7 (1895): 157–61.

Clarkson, Tim, *Scotland's Merlin: A Medieval Legend and its Dark Age Origins* (Edinburgh: John Donald, 2016).

Coleman, James J., *Remembering the Past in Nineteenth-Century Scotland: Commemoration, Nationality and Memory* (Edinburgh: Edinburgh University Press, 2014).

Colls, Robert, 'Englishness and the Political Culture', in *Englishness: Politics and Culture 1880–1920*, ed. Robert Colls and Philip Dodd (London: Croom Helm, 1986), pp. 29–61.

Colquhoun, Ithell, *Sword of Wisdom: MacGregor Mathers and the Golden Dawn* (New York: G. P. Putnam's Sons, 1975).

'Conan Doyle and Home Rule', *Belfast Evening Telegraph*, 22 September 1911, p. 5.

Corkery, Daniel, *The Hidden Ireland: A Study of Gaelic Munster in the Eighteenth Century* (Dublin: Gill and Macmillan, 1986).

Corr, Helen, 'Crawfurd, Helen (1877–1954)', *Oxford Dictionary of National Biography*, <doi:10.1093/ref:odnb/40301> (last accessed 29 October 2018).

Cotterell, George, 'Vistas', *The Academy*, 1139 (1984): 182–3.

Coupland, Sir Reginald, *Welsh and Scottish Nationalism: A Study* (London: Collins, 1954).

'The Court', *The Scotsman*, 18 July 1889, p. 4.

Craig, Cairns, 'Arcades – The Turning of the Nineteenth Century', in *The Edinburgh Companion to Twentieth-Century Scottish Literature*, ed. Ian Brown and Alan Riach (Edinburgh: Edinburgh University Press, 2009), pp. 15–24.

— 'The Case for Culture', *The Scottish Review of Books*, 10.3 (2014): 19–20.

— *Out of History: Narrative Paradigms in Scottish and English Culture* (Edinburgh: Polygon, 1996).

— *The Wealth of the Nation: Scotland, Culture and Independence* (Edinburgh: Edinburgh University Press, 2018).

Crawford, Robert, 'Dedefining Scotland', in *Studying British Cultures: An Introduction*, ed. Susan Bassnett (London: Routledge, 2003), pp. 88–103.

— *Scotland's Books: The Penguin History of Scottish Literature* (London: Penguin, 2007).

— 'Scottish Literature and English Studies', in *The Scottish Invention of English Literature*, ed. Robert Crawford (Cambridge: Cambridge University Press, 1998), pp. 225–46.

Crichton-Miller, H., 'William Sharp and *The Immortal Hour*', *British Journal of Medical Psychology*, 5.1 (1925): 35–44.

Crichton-Stuart, John Patrick, *Parliament in Scotland* (Glasgow: Scottish Home Rule Association, 1889).

Crowley, Aleister, 'The Message of the Master Therion', *The International*, 12 (1918): 26.

Cumming, Elizabeth, 'Celtic Influenced Art', in *Celtic Culture: An Historical Encyclopedia*, ed. John Thomas Koch (Santa Barbara: ABC-CLIO, 2006), pp. 110–12.

— *Hand, Heart and Soul: The Arts and Crafts Movement in Scotland* (Edinburgh: Birlinn, 2006).

— 'Phoebe Anna Traquair HRSA (1852–1936) and Her Contribution to Arts and Crafts in Edinburgh', PhD thesis, University of Edinburgh, 1986.

Cunliffe, Barry, *Druids: A Very Short Introduction* (Oxford: Oxford University Press, 2010).
Cunninghame Graham, R. B., *Progress: And Other Sketches* (London: Duckworth, 1911).
Dahl, Curtis, 'Swinburne's Loyalty to the House of Stuart', *Studies in Philology*, 46.3 (1949): 453–69.
Daly, Nicholas, *Modernism, Romance and the Fin-de-Siècle* (Cambridge: Cambridge University Press, 1999).
Davidson, John, *Baptist Lake* (London: Ward and Downey, 1894).
— *Plays* (London: Elkin Mathews and John Lane, 1894).
— *Selected Poems* (London: John Lane, 1905).
— *The Testament of an Empire-Builder* (London: Grant Richards, 1902).
— *The Testament of John Davidson* (London: Grant Richards, 1908).
Davies, Owen, *Paganism: A Very Short Introduction* (Oxford: Oxford University Press, 2011).
Defries, Amelia, *The Interpreter Geddes: The Man and His Gospel* (New York: Boni & Liveright, 1928).
Demoor, Marysa (ed.), *Dear Stevenson: Letters from Andrew Lang to Robert Louis Stevenson* (Leuven: Peeters, 1991).
Denisoff, Dennis, 'Dissipating Nature of Decadent Paganism from Pater to Yeats', *Modernism/Modernity*, 15.3 (2008): 431–46.
Devine, T. M., *The Great Highland Famine: Hunger, Emigration, and the Scottish Highlands in the Nineteenth Century* (Edinburgh: John Donald, 1988).
Dewey, Clive, 'Celtic Agrarian Legislation and the Celtic Revival: Historicist Implications of Gladstone's Irish and Scottish Land Acts 1870–1886', *Past and Present*, 64 (1974): 30–70.
Di Pasquale, Maria E., 'Joséphin Péladan: Occultism, Catholicism, and Science in the *Fin de Siècle*', RACAR, 34 (2009): 53–61.
Dick, Fred J., 'Scotland', *Lucifer*, 9 (1891): 520.
Dixon, Joy, *Divine Feminine: Theosophy and Feminism in England* (Baltimore: Johns Hopkins University Press, 2011).
Doyle, Arthur Conan, *The Edinburgh Stories*, ed. Owen Dudley Edwards (Edinburgh: E.U.S.P.B, 1981).
— *The Firm of Girdlestone* (London: Chatto & Windus, 1890).
— *His Last Bow: A Reminiscence of Sherlock Holmes* (New York: George H. Doran, 1917).
— 'Home Rule', *Daily Mail*, 4 April 1912.
— *The Lost World* (New York: A. L. Burt, 1912).
— *Memories and Adventures* (Oxford: Oxford University Press, 1989).
— *The Mystery of Cloomber* (London: Hesperus Press, 1889).
— *The Poison Belt* (Toronto: Hodder and Stoughton, 1913).
— *The Sign of Four* (London: Spencer Blackett, 1890).
Dusinberre, Juliet, *Alice to the Lighthouse: Children's Books and Radical Experiments in Art* (Houndmills: Palgrave Macmillan, 1999).

Edwards, Hywel Teifi, *The National Pageant of Wales* (Llandysul: Gwasg Gomer, 2009).

Elliot, Bridget Jane, 'Aubrey Beardsley's Images of New Women in the Yellow Book', PhD thesis, University College London, 1985.

Ellmann, Richard, *Yeats: The Man and the Masks* (London: Penguin, 1988).

Errington, Lindsay, 'Celtic Elements in Scottish Art at the Turn of the Century', in *The Last Romantics: The Romantic Tradition in British Art*, ed. John Christian (London: Lund Humphries, 1989), pp. 47–54.

Erskine, Stuart, 'The Independency of Scotland', *The Albemarle*, 1 (1892): 100–3.

Esslin, Martin, *The Theatre of the Absurd* (New York: Vintage, 2004).

'The Evergreen', *Glasgow Herald*, 27 May 1895, p. 11.

'The Evergreen: A Northern Seasonal', *The Scotsman*, 29 May 1895, p. 6.

'The Exhibition', *The Scotsman*, 11 July 1908, p. 7.

Facos, Michelle, *Nationalism and the Nordic Imagination: Swedish Art of the 1890s* (Berkeley: University of California Press, 1998).

Fanon, Frantz, *The Wretched of the Earth*, trans. Constance Farrington (London: Penguin, 1967).

Farrell, Joseph, *Robert Louis Stevenson in Samoa* (London: MacLehose, 2017).

Fenyô, Krisztina, '"Contempt, Sympathy and Romance": Lowland Perceptions of the Highlands and the Clearances during the Famine Years, 1845–1855', PhD thesis, University of Glasgow, 1996.

Ferguson, John, *Bibliographical Notes on the Witchcraft Literature of Scotland* (Edinburgh: Edinburgh Bibliographical Society, 1897).

Ferguson, Megan C., 'Patrick Geddes and the Celtic Renascence of the 1890s', PhD thesis, University of Dundee, 2011.

Fielding, Penny, *Writing and Orality: Nationality, Culture, and Nineteenth-Century Scottish Fiction* (Oxford: Oxford University Press, 1996).

Finlay, Richard J., *A Partnership for Good?: Scottish Politics and the Union Since 1880* (Edinburgh: John Donald, 1997).

'The First Home Rule Act for Scotland: Our Political Debt to St Columba', *The Scotsman*, 18 September 1897, p. 8.

A First Visit to the Outlook Tower (Edinburgh: Patrick Geddes and Colleagues, 1906).

Fletcher, Ian, *W. B. Yeats and His Contemporaries* (Brighton: Harvester Press, 1987).

Fontelieu, Sukey, *The Archetypal Pan in America: Hypermasculinity and Terror* (Abingdon: Routledge, 2018).

Foot, Michelle, 'Modern Spiritualism and Scottish Art between 1860 and 1940', PhD thesis, University of Aberdeen, 2016.

Forster, E. M., *Selected Stories*, ed. David Leavitt and Mark Mitchell (London: Penguin, 2001).

Fowle, Frances, *Van Gogh's Twin: The Scottish Art Dealer Alexander Reid* (Edinburgh: National Galleries of Scotland, 2011).

Fowle, Frances, and Belinda Thomson (eds), *Patrick Geddes: The French Connection* (Oxford: White Cockade, 2009).

Fraser, Robert, *Victorian Quest Romance: Stevenson, Haggard, Kipling and Conan Doyle* (Plymouth: Northcote House, 1998).

Frazer, J. G., *The Golden Bough: A Study in Comparative Religion* (Edinburgh: Canongate, 2004).

Freeman, Mark, '"Splendid Display; Pompous Spectacle": Historical Pageants in Twentieth-Century Britain', *Social History*, 38 (2013): 423–55.

Gagnier, Regenia, *Individualism, Decadence and Globalization: On the Relationship of Part to Whole, 1859–1920* (Houndmills: Palgrave Macmillan, 2010).

— *The Insatiability of Human Wants: Economics and Aesthetics in Market Society* (Chicago: University of Chicago Press, 2000).

— 'The Victorian *Fin de Siècle* and Decadence', in *The Cambridge History of Twentieth-Century English Literature*, ed. Laura Marcus and Peter Nicholls (Cambridge: Cambridge University Press, (2005), pp. 30–49.

Gardiner, Michael, *At the Edge of Empire: The Life of Thomas B. Glover* (Edinburgh: Birlinn, 2008).

— 'Robert Louis Stevenson and the Meiji Enlightenment', *The Yearbook of English Studies*, 41.2 (2011): 58–72.

Gaucher, André, 'Isis à Montmartre', *L'Écho du merveilleux*, 1 (1890): 446–53.

Geddes, Patrick, 'Cinderella', *The Blue Blanket*, 1 (1912): 327–31.

— *Cities in Evolution: An Introduction to the Town Planning Movement and to the Study of Civics* (London: Williams and Norgate, 1915).

— *City Development: A Study of Parks, Gardens and Culture-Institutes* (Edinburgh: Geddes and Company, 1904).

— *Dramatisations of History* (Edinburgh: Patrick Geddes and Colleagues, 1923).

— *Everyman His Own Art Critic* (London: John Heywood, 1887).

— *The Masque of Ancient Learning* (Edinburgh: Patrick Geddes and Colleagues, 1913).

— 'The Megalithic Builders', *The Evergreen*, 4 (1896): 142–51.

— 'Political Economy and Fine Art', *Scottish Art Review*, 2 (1889): 2–4.

— 'The Scots Renascence', *The Evergreen*, 1 (1895): 131–9.

— 'The Sociology of Autumn', *The Evergreen*, 2 (1895): 27–38.

— 'The Valley Section', *Architect's Yearbook*, 12 (1968), 65–71.

Geddes, Patrick, and J. Arthur Thomson, *Sex* (London: Williams and Norgate, 1914).

Geoffrey of Monmouth, *The History of the Kings of Britain*, trans. Neil Wright (Woodbridge: Boydell Press, 2007).

Gibbons, Luke, 'Peripheral Modernities: National and Global in a Post-Colonial Frame', *Nineteenth Century Contexts: An Interdisciplinary Journal*, 29 (2007): 271–81.

Gifford, Douglas, 'From Celtic Revival to Scottish Renaissance?', in *Gael and Lowlander in Scottish Literature*, ed. Christopher MacLachlan and Ronald W. Renton (Glasgow: Scottish Literature International, 2015), pp. 216–35.

Gilbert, R. A., 'Introduction', in *The Sorcerer and His Apprentice: Unknown Hermetic Writings of S. L. MacGregor Mathers and J. W. Brodie-Innes*, ed. R. A. Gilbert (Wellingborough: Aquarian Press, 1983), pp. 7–12.

'Glasgow', *The Scotsman*, 3 October 1911, p. 8.

'Glasgow and its Mummy Cases', *Glasgow Herald*, 1 December 1891, p. 4.

Glassberg, David, *American Historical Pageantry: The Uses of Tradition in the Early Twentieth-Century* (Chapel Hill and London: University of North Carolina Press, 1990).

Glennie, John S. Stuart, *Arthurian Localities; Their Historical Origin, Chief Country, and Fingalian Relations; with a Map of Arthurian Scotland* (Edinburgh: Hertford, 1869).

— *The Liberal Party: Its True Character: Betrayals of the Workers: and Deserved Extinguishment*, Pamphlet (1895).

Gonne, Maud, 'Yeats and Ireland', in *William Butler Yeats: Essays in Tribute*, ed. Stephen Gwynn (Port Washington: Kennikat Press, 1965), pp. 15–34.

Goodrick-Clarke, Nicholas, *The Western Esoteric Traditions: A Historical Introduction* (Oxford: Oxford University Press, 2008).

Goudsward, David, *The Westford Knight and Henry Sinclair: Evidence of a 14th Century Scottish Voyage to North America* (Jefferson: McFarland, 2010).

'The Grand Scottish Historical Pageant', *The Scots Pictorial*, 4 (1908): 240–5.

Grant, James, *The Scottish Soldiers of Fortune* (London: George Routledge and Sons, 1889).

Gray, Alexandra, *Self-Harm in New Woman Writing* (Edinburgh: Edinburgh University Press, 2017).

Greene, Vivien, 'Introduction', in *Mystical Symbolism: The Salon de la Rose+Croix in Paris, 1892–1897* (New York: Guggenheim Museum, 2017).

Grilli, Elisa, 'Funding, Publishing, and the Making of Culture: The Case of the *Evergreen* (1895–97)', *Journal of European Periodical Studies*, 1.2 (2016): 19–43.

Grogan, Elaine, *Beginnings: Charles Rennie Mackintosh's Early Sketches* (Oxford: Architectural Press, 2002).

Haggard, H. Rider, 'About Fiction', *The Contemporary Review*, 51 (1887): 172–80.

— *King Solomon's Mines* (Oxford: Oxford University Press, 2006).

Halkett, George R., 'Sir Joseph Noel Paton, RSA', *Magazine of Art*, 3 (1880): 1–6.

Hallett, Jennifer, 'Wandering Dreams and Social Marches: Varieties of Paganism in Late Victorian and Edwardian England', in *Paganism: Critical Concepts in Religious Studies*, ed. Barbara Jane Davy, 3 vols (London: Routledge, 2009), I, pp. 119–220.

Halloran, William F., 'W. B. Yeats, William Sharp and Fiona Macleod: A Celtic Drama, 1887 to 1897', *Yeats Annual*, 13 (1998): 62–109.

— 'W. B. Yeats, William Sharp and Fiona Macleod: A Celtic Drama, 1897', *Yeats Annual*, 14 (2001): 159–208.

Hanham, H. J., *Scottish Nationalism* (London: Faber and Faber, 1969).

Hanna, Julian, 'Manifestoes at Dawn: Nation, City and Self in Patrick Geddes and William Sharp's *Evergreen*', *International Journal of Scottish Literature*, 8 (2011): 1–15.

Hannah, Rosemary, *The Grand Designer: Third Marquess of Bute* (Edinburgh: Birlinn, 2013).

Hardie, William, *Scottish Painting: 1837 to the Present* (Glasgow: Waverley, 2010).

Harris, Jason Marc, *Folklore and the Fantastic in Nineteenth-Century British Fiction* (Aldershot: Ashgate, 2008).

Hay, William J., 'Masque of Learning', *The Scotsman*, 16 March 1912, p. 11.

Helland, Janice, *The Studios of Frances and Margaret Macdonald* (Manchester: Manchester University Press, 1996).

Henderson, George, *The Norse Influence on Celtic Scotland* (Glasgow: James Maclehose and Sons, 1912).

Henderson, T. F., *Scottish Vernacular Literature* (London: David Nutt, 1898).

Henshaw, Peter, 'John Buchan from the "Borders" to the "Berg": Nature, Empire and White South African Identity, 1901–1910', *African Studies*, 62 (2003): 3–32.

'The Highland Society', *The Scotsman*, 27 March 1847, p. 2.

Hill, Richard J., 'Robert Louis Stevenson's Davos Studio: Author and Art in 1882', *Scottish Literary Review*, 2.2 (2010): 65–83.

Hobsbawm, Eric, 'Mass-Producing Traditions: Europe 1870–1914', in *The Invention of Tradition*, ed. Eric Hobsbawm and Terence Ranger (Cambridge: Cambridge University Press, 2007), pp. 263–307.

— *Nations and Nationalism Since 1780: Programme, Myth, Reality* (Cambridge: Cambridge University Press, 1997).

Hodd, Thomas, 'The Celtic Twilight in Canada: William Sharp's Early Occult Influence on Charles G. D. Roberts and Bliss Carman', *Canadian Poetry*, 54 (2004): 37–55.

Hofer, Matthew, and Gary Scharnhorst (eds), *Oscar Wilde in America: The Interviews* (Urbana: University of Illinois Press, 2010).

Holt, Ysanne '"The Veriest Poem of Art in Nature": E. A. Hornel's Japanese Garden in the Scottish Borders', *Tate Papers*, 2 (2004), available at <http://www.tate.org.uk/research/tateresearch/tatepapers/04autumn/holt.htm> (last accessed 24 January 2012).

Hornel, E. A., *Japan: Lecture by E. A. Hornel Delivered in the Corporation Art Galleries, Glasgow, 9th February, 1895* (Castle Douglas: J. H. Maxwell, 1895).

Howarth, Thomas, *Charles Rennie Mackintosh and the Modern Movement* (London: Routledge and Kegan Paul, 1952).

Howe, Marjory, *Yeats's Nations: Gender, Class, and Irishness* (Cambridge: Cambridge University Press, 1996).

Hubbard, Tom, 'The Unco Paon: The Long Fin de Siècle in Scottish Literature, Art and Music (1874–1914)', in *The Fantastic of the Fin de Siècle*, ed. Irena Grubica and Zdeněk Beran (Cambridge: Cambridge Scholars, 2016), pp. 261–81.

Hulme, Tom, '"A Nation of Town Criers": Civic Publicity and Historical Pageantry in Inter-War Britain', *Urban History*, 44 (2017): 270–92.

Hume, David, *The History of England: From the Invasion of Julius Caesar to the Revolution in 1688*, 6 vols (Indianapolis: Liberty Fund, 1983).

Hunter, James, 'The Gaelic Connection: The Highlands, Ireland and Nationalism, 1873–1922', *The Scottish Historical Review*, 54 (1975): 178–204.

Hutchinson, John, 'Cultural Nationalism and Moral Regeneration', in *Nationalism*, ed. John Hutchinson and Anthony D. Smith (Oxford: Oxford University Press, 1994), pp. 122–31.

Hyde, Douglas, 'The Necessity for De-Anglicising Ireland', in *The Handbook of the Irish Revival: An Anthology of Irish Cultural and Political Writings 1891–1922*, ed. Declan Kiberd and P. J. Matthews (Dublin: Abbey Theatre Press, 2015), pp. 42–6.

Hynd, Hazel, 'John Davidson and the Hidden Legacy of Burns', *Studies in Scottish Literature*, 33.1 (2004): 87–96.

'Inquiry – Into the Distress in the Highlands and Islands', *The Scotsman*, 3 February 1847, p. 3.

Interpretation of the Pictures in the Common Room of Ramsay Lodge (Edinburgh: Patrick Geddes and Colleagues, 1928).

'Introductory', *Occult, Scientific, and Literary Papers, Read at the Scottish Lodge*, 3.1 (1895): 1–2.

Jack, R. D. S., 'Barrie and the Extreme Heroine', in *Gendering the Nation: Studies in Modern Scottish Literature*, ed. Christopher Whyte (Edinburgh: Edinburgh University Press, 1995), pp. 137–67.

— *The Road to Neverland: A Reassessment of J. M. Barrie's Dramatic Art* (Aberdeen: Aberdeen University Press, 1991).

Jackson, Alvin, *The Two Unions: Ireland, Scotland and the Survival of the United Kingdom, 1707–2007* (Oxford: Oxford University Press, 2011).

Jackson, Holbrook, *The Eighteen Nineties: A Review of Art and Ideas at the Close of the Nineteenth Century* (Harmondsworth: Penguin, 1950).

Jacob, Violet, *Flemington and Tales from Angus*, ed. Carol Anderson (Edinburgh: Canongate: 1998).

Jarron, Matthew, *Independent & Individualist: Art in Dundee 1867–1924* (Dundee: Abertay Historical Society, 2015).

Jeffares, A. Norman, *W. B. Yeats, Man and Poet* (New York: Barnes & Noble, 1966).

Johnston, Alexandra F., and Margaret Dorrell, 'The Doomsday Pageant of the York Mercers, 1433', *Leeds Studies in English*, 5 (1971): 29–34.

Jolly, Roslyn, *Robert Louis Stevenson in the Pacific: Travel, Empire, and the Author's Profession* (Abingdon: Routledge, 2016).

Jones, Anthony, 'Introduction', in *Charles Rennie Mackintosh* (Tokyo: Japan Art and Culture Association, 1985) pp. 8–10.

'Justice to Scotland', *Examiner*, 2388 (1853): 712.
Keating, Geoffrey, *A General History of Ireland* (Dublin: James Duffy, 1861).
Keating, Michael, *The Independence of Scotland: Self-Government and the Shifting Politics of Union* (Oxford: Oxford University Press, 2009).
Kelly, Stuart, 'Scotland and Decadence', in *The Decadent Handbook*, ed. Rowan Pelling (Sawtry: Dedalus, 2006), pp. 54–7.
Kelman, John, *The Interpreter's House: The Ideals Embodied in the Outlook Tower* (Edinburgh and London: Oliphant, Anderson and Ferrier, 1905).
Kennedy, Howard Angus, *Professor Blackie, His Sayings and Doings: A Biographical Sketch* (London: J. Clarke, 1895).
Kent, Neil, *Helsinki: A Cultural and Literary History* (Oxford: Signal, 2004).
Khursheed, Anjam, *The Seven Candles of Unity: The Story of Abdu'l-Bahá in Edinburgh* (London: Bahá'í Publishing Trust, 1991).
Kidd, Colin, 'Teutonist Ethnology and the Scottish Nationalist Inhibition, 1780–1880', *The Scottish Historical Review*, 74 (1995): 45–68.
— *Union and Unionisms: Political Thought in Scotland, 1500–2000* (Cambridge: Cambridge University Press, 2008).
Kinchin, Juliet, 'Art and History into Life: Pageantry Revived in Scotland', *Journal of the Scottish Society for Art History*, 2 (1997): 42–51.
Kinchin, Pernilla, and Juliet Kinchin, *Glasgow's Great Exhibitions: 1880, 1901, 1911, 1938, 1988* (Wendlebury: White Cockade, 1988).
Kingston, Angela, *Oscar Wilde as a Character in Victorian Fiction* (Houndmills: Palgrave Macmillan, 2007).
Kooistra, Lorraine Janzen, 'The Politics of Ornament: Remediation and/in *The Evergreen*', *English Studies in Canada*, 41 (2015): 105–28.
'La Jeune Belgique', *La Jeune Belgique*, 1 (1881): 1.
Lang, Andrew, 'The Celtic Renascence', *Blackwood's Magazine*, 161 (1897): 181–91.
— *In the Wrong Paradise and Other Stories* (London: Kegan Paul, Trench, 1886).
— 'Realism and Romance', *The Contemporary Review*, 52 (1887): 683–93.
— *The Red True Story Book* (London: Longmans, Green, 1917).
Lawrence, D. H., 'Pan in America', in *Green History: A Reader in Environmental Literature, Philosophy and Politics*, ed. Derek Wall (London: Routledge, 1994), pp. 81–3.
Lawrence, Emmeline Pethink, 'A Man with Two Souls', *Votes for Women*, 6 January 1911, p. 226.
Le Gallienne, Richard, *The Romantic Nineties* (New York: Doubleday, Page, 1925).
'Lecture on Japan', *Glasgow Herald*, 2 May 1873, p. 4.
Ledger, Sally, *The New Woman: Fiction and Feminism at the Fin de Siècle* (Manchester: Manchester University Press, 1997).
Lellenberg, Jon, Daniel Stashower and Charles Foley (eds), *Arthur Conan Doyle: A Life in Letters* (London: Harper Perennial, 2008).

Lendrum, Lesley, *Neil Munro: The Biography* (Colonsay: House of Lochar, 2004).

Lennon, Joseph, *Irish Orientalism: A Literary and Intellectual History* (Syracuse, NY: Syracuse University Press, 2008).

Leonard, Sofia G., 'The Context and Legacy of Patrick Geddes in Europe', in *The City after Patrick Geddes*, ed. Volker M. Welter and James Lawson (Oxford: Peter Lang, 2000), pp. 71–87.

'Les Livres', *La Jeune Belgique*, 10 (1891): 226–8.

Lethaby, W. R., *Architecture, Mysticism and Myth* (New York: Cosimo Classics, 2005).

Lloyd-Jones, Naomi, 'Liberalism, Scottish Nationalism and the Home Rule Crisis, c.1886–93', *English Historical Review*, 129 (2014): 862–87.

Löffler, Marion, *A Book of Mad Celts: John Wickens and the Celtic Congress of Caernarfon 1904* (Llandysul: Gwasg Gomer, 2000).

Lovelace, Antonia, *The Glasgow Japan Exchange of 1878* (Glasgow: Glasgow Museums, 1991).

Luckhurst, Roger, *The Invention of Telepathy, 1870–1901* (Oxford: Oxford University Press, 2002).

Lumsden, Alison, 'Stevenson, Scott and Scottish History', in *The Edinburgh Companion to Robert Louis Stevenson*, ed. Penny Fielding (Edinburgh: Edinburgh University Press, 2010), pp. 70–85.

Lyall, Scott, *Hugh MacDiarmid's Poetry and the Politics of Place: Imagining a Scottish Republic* (Edinburgh: Edinburgh University Press, 2006).

— '"That Ancient Self": Scottish Modernism's Counter-Renaissance', *European Journal of English Studies*, 18.1 (2014): 73–85.

McCluskey, Raymond, and Linden Bicket, 'Two Neglected Poets of Late-Victorian Scotland: John Luby and James Lynch', *Scottish Literary Review*, 9 (2017): 59–81.

McCracken-Flesher, Caroline, 'Fin-de-Siècle Scotland', in *The Edinburgh Companion to Fin-de-Siècle Literature, Culture and the Arts*, ed. Josephine M. Guy (Edinburgh: Edinburgh University Press, 2018), pp. 181–95.

McCulloch, Margery Palmer, *Modernism and Nationalism: Literature and Society in Scotland 1918–1939* (Glasgow: Association for Scottish Studies, 2004).

— *Scottish Modernism and its Contexts 1918–1959: Literature, National Identity and Cultural Exchange* (Edinburgh: Edinburgh University Press, 2009).

MacDiarmid, Hugh, *Albyn*, ed. Alan Riach (Manchester: Carcanet, 1996).

— *The Company I've Kept* (London: Hutchinson, 1966).

— *Contemporary Scottish Studies* (Manchester: Carcanet, 1995).

— *Cunninghame Graham: A Centenary Study* (Glasgow: Caledonian Press, 1952).

— *Selected Essays of Hugh MacDiarmid* (Berkeley: University of California Press, 1969).

Macdonald, Catriona, 'Andrew Lang and Scottish Historiography: Taking on Tradition', *The Scottish Historical Review*, 94 (2015): 207–23.

Macdonald, Murdo '*Anima Celtica:* Embodying the Soul of the Nation in 1890s Edinburgh', in *Art, Nation and Gender: Ethnic Landscapes, Myths and Mother-Figures*, ed. Tricia Cusack and Síghle Bhreathnach-Lynch (Aldershot: Ashgate, 2003), pp. 29–37.

— 'Patrick Geddes's Generalism: From Edinburgh's Old Town to Paris's Universal Exhibition', in *Patrick Geddes: The French Connection*, ed. Frances Fowle and Belinda Thomson (Oxford: White Cockade, 2004), pp. 83–94.

— *Scottish Art* (London: Thames & Hudson, 2000).

— 'Visual Culture Japan – Scotland', <www.thenorthernmirror.com/pdf/Macdonald_Visual.pdf> (last accessed 28 August 2018).

McFarlan, Donald, 'Introduction', in *Kidnapped*, ed. Donald McFarlan (London: Penguin, 1994), pp. vii–xvi.

Machen, Arthur, *The Great God Pan and the Hill of Dreams* (Mineola, NY: Dover, 2006).

— *The White People and Other Weird Stories*, ed. S. T. Johsi (London: Penguin, 2011).

Mackintosh, Charles Rennie, 'Scotch Baronial Architecture (1891)', in *Charles Rennie Mackintosh: The Architectural Papers*, ed. Pamela Robertson (Wendlebury: White Cockade, 1990), pp. 49–63.

— 'Untitled Paper on Architecture (c. 1892)', in *Charles Rennie Mackintosh: The Architectural Papers*, ed. Pamela Robertson (Wendlebury: White Cockade, 1990), pp. 180–200.

Macleod, Kirsten, *Fictions of British Decadence: High Art, Popular Writing, and the* Fin de Siècle (Houndmills: Palgrave Macmillan, 2006).

MacMillan, Andrew, 'Charles Rennie Mackintosh: A Mainstream Forerunner', *Architectural Association Quarterly*, 12.3 (1980): 4–10.

MacRaild, Donald M., 'Irish Immigration and the "Condition of England" Question: The Roots of Historiographical Tradition', *Historical Studies in Ethnicity, Migration and Diaspora*, 14 (1995): 67–85.

Maeterlinck, Maurice, *The Blue Bird*, trans. Alexander Teixeira de Mattos (New York: Dodd, Mead, 1919).

— *The Plays of Maurice Maeterlinck*, trans. Richard Hovey, 2 vols (New York: Duffield, 1906).

— *Ruysbroeck and the Mystics: With Selections from Ruysbroeck*, trans. Jane T. Stoddart (London: Hodder and Stoughton, 1894).

— *The Treasure of the Humble*, trans. Alfred Sutro (London: George Allen, 1902).

Maley, Willy, 'Away with the Faeries (or, It's Grimm up North): Yeats and Scotland', *Journal of Irish Scottish Studies*, 1 (2007): 161–78.

Maloney, Paul, *Scotland and the Music Hall, 1850–1914* (Manchester: Manchester University Press, 2003).

Marsden, Richard, *Cosmo Innes and the Defence of Scotland's Past c.1825–1875* (Farnham: Ashgate, 2015).

Martin, Maureen M., *The Mighty Scot: Nation, Gender, and the Nineteenth-Century Mystique of Scottish Masculinity* (Albany: State University of New York Press, 2009).

'The Masque of Ancient Learning', *The Scots Pictorial*, 30 March 1912, p. 613.

Mathers, S. L. MacGregor, 'Concerning the Symbolism of Self-Sacrifice', in *Astral Projection, Ritual Magic and Alchemy*, ed. Francis King (Wellingborough: Aquarian Press, 1971), pp. 131–40.

— *The Kabbalah Unveiled* (London: Arkana, 1991).

Meier-Graefe, Julius, *Modern Art: Being a Contribution to a New System of Aesthetics* (London: William Heinemann, 1908).

Meller, Helen, *Patrick Geddes: Social Evolutionist and City Planner* (London: Routledge, 1990).

Menikoff, Barry, *Narrating Scotland: The Imagination of Robert Louis Stevenson* (Columbia: University of South Carolina Press, 2005).

Meyers, Terry L., *The Sexual Tensions of William Sharp: A Study of the Birth of Fiona Macleod, Incorporating Two Lost Works, Ariadne in Naxos and Beatrice* (New York: Peter Lang, 1996).

Miller, Mrs, 'As Seen in Passing', in *I Can Remember Robert Louis Stevenson*, ed. Rosaline Masson (Edinburgh: W. & R. Chambers, 1925), p. 159.

Milton, Colin, '"Half a trade and, half an art": Adult and Juvenile Fiction in the Victorian Period', in *The Edinburgh History of Scottish Literature*, ed. Ian Brown, Thomas Owen Clancy, Susan Manning and Murray Pittock, 3 vols (Edinburgh: Edinburgh University Press, 2007), II, pp. 286–300.

'Miscellaneous Books', *Glasgow Herald*, 15 November 1895, p. 4.

Moore, George, *Confessions of a Young Man* (London: William Heinemann, 1917).

Morris, David B., *Robert Louis Stevenson and the Scottish Highlands* (Stirling: Eneas Mackay, 1929).

Morris, William, *Hopes and Fears for Art* (Boston: Roberts Brothers, 1882).

Morrison, John, 'Nationalism and Nationhood: Late-Nineteenth-Century Painting in Scotland', in *Art, Culture and National Identity in Fin-de-Siècle Europe*, ed. Michelle Facos and Sharon L. Hirsh (Cambridge: Cambridge University Press, 2003), pp. 186–206.

— *Painting the Nation: Identity and Nationalism in Scottish Painting* (Edinburgh: Edinburgh University Press, 2003).

Morton, Graeme, 'Scotland is Britain: The Union and Unionist-Nationalism, 1807–1907', *Journal of Irish and Scottish Studies*, 1 (2008): 127–41.

— *Unionist Nationalism: Governing Urban Scotland, 1830–1860* (East Linton: Tuckwell Press, 1999).

Mosse, George L., 'Nationalism and Sexuality in Nineteenth Century Europe', *Society*, 20 (1983): 75–84.

'Mr. Louis N. Parker on Pageantry', *Review of Reviews*, 33 (1906): 598–9.

Muir, Edwin, 'Scotland's Winter', in *Scottish Literature in the Twentieth Century: An Anthology*, ed. David McCordick (Dalkeith: Scottish Cultural Press, 2002), p. 262.

— 'Scotland 1941', in *Scottish Literature in the Twentieth Century: An Anthology*, ed. David McCordick (Dalkeith: Scottish Cultural Press, 2002), p. 255.

Murdoch, W. G. Blaikie, *The Renaissance of the Nineties* (London: Alexander Moring, 1911).

— *The Royal Stuarts in their Connection with Art and Letters* (Edinburgh: J. & J. Gray, 1908).

Murray, Alex, 'Decadent Conservatism: Politics and Aesthetics in *The Senate*', *Journal of Victorian Culture*, 20.2 (2015): 186–211.

— *Landscapes of Decadence: Literature and Place at the* Fin de Siècle (Cambridge: Cambridge University Press, 2016).

Murray, Alex, and Jason David Hall, 'Introduction: Decadent Poetics', in *Decadent Poetics: Literature and Form at the British Fin de Siècle*, ed. Alex Murray and Jason David Hall (Houndmills: Palgrave Macmillan, 2013), pp. 1–25.

Mus, Francis, and Hans Vandevoorde, '"Streetscape of New Districts Permeated by the Fresh Scent of Cement": Brussels, the Avant-Garde, and Internationalism', in Peter Brooker Sascha Bru, Andrew Thacker and Christian Weikop, *The Oxford Critical and Cultural History of Modernist Magazines*, 3 vols (Oxford: Oxford University Press, 2013), III, pp. 336–60.

'Music and Maeterlinck', *The Outlook*, 5 (1900): 434.

Nairn, Tom, *The Break-Up of Britain: Crisis and Neo-Nationalism* (London: Verso, 1981).

Nally, Claire, *Envisioning Ireland: W. B. Yeats's Occult Nationalism* (Bern: Peter Lang, 2010).

Nash, Andrew, *Kailyard and Scottish Literature* (Amsterdam: Rodopi, 2007).

'National Exhibition: Scotland's Day', *The Scots Pictorial*, 4 (1908): 290.

Neat, Timothy, *Part Seen, Part Imagined: Meaning and Symbolism in the Work of Charles Rennie Mackintosh and Margaret Macdonald* (Edinburgh: Canongate, 1994).

'New Books', *The Scotsman*, 26 February 1894, p. 2.

Newbery, Fra, *The Birth and Growth of Art: A Symbolistic Masque in Five Ages and an Allegory* (Pamphlet, 1909).

Newby, Andrew, *Ireland, Radicalism and the Scottish Highlands, c. 1870–1912* (Edinburgh: Edinburgh University Press, 2007).

Nicholson, Robin, 'From Fever to Fresh Air: *The Evergreen, The Yellow Book* and the Threat of Decadence', *Journal of the Scottish Society for Art History*, 9 (2004): 63–8.

Nietzsche, Friedrich, *Thoughts out of Season*, trans. Adrian Collins, 2 vols (London: George Allen & Unwin, c.1910).

Nisbit, Robert A., *History of the Idea of Progress* (New Brunswick, NJ: Transaction, 1994).

Nordau, Max, *Degeneration* (New York: D. Appleton, 1897).

Norquay, Glenda, 'Geographies of Self: Scottish Women Writing Scotland', in *The History of British Women's Writing, 1880–1920*, ed. Holly A. Laird (Houndmills: Palgrave Macmillan, 2016), pp. 150–61.

— 'Squandering Names: Place, Nomenclature and Cultural Identity', *Journal of Stevenson Studies*, 7 (2010): 107–30.

Ono, Ayako, *Japonisme in Britain: Whistler, Menpes, Henry, Hornel and Nineteenth-Century Japan* (London: RoutledgeCurzon, 2003).

O'Toole, Fintan, *White Savage: William Johnson and the Invention of America* (London: Faber and Faber, 2005).

Ouida, *Frescoes* (London: Chatto & Windus, 1895).

Ovid, *Metamorphoses*, trans. David Raeburn (London: Penguin, 2004).

Owen, Alex, *The Place of Enchantment: British Occultism and the Culture of the Modern* (Chicago and London: University of Chicago Press, 2004).

'The Pageant and Masque', *The Scotsman*, 11 June 1908, p. 7.

Parker, Louis Napoleon, 'Historical Pageants', *Journal of the Society of the Arts*, 54 (1905): 142–6.

Parkins, Wendy, *Mobility and Modernity in Women's Novels 1850s-1930s: Women Moving Dangerously* (Houndmills: Palgrave Macmillan, 2008).

Pater, Walter, *Appreciations* (London: Macmillan, 1890).

— *Greek Studies* (London: Macmillan, 1920).

— *Imaginary Portraits* (London: Macmillan, 1890).

Pinkerton, John, *An Enquiry into the History of Scotland*, 2 vols (Edinburgh: Bell and Bradfute, 1814).

Pittock, Murray, *Celtic Identity and the British Image* (Manchester: Manchester University Press, 1999).

— *The Invention of Scotland: The Stuart Myth and the Scottish Identity, 1638 to the Present* (London: Routledge, 2014).

— *Material Culture and Sedition, 1688–1760: Treacherous Objects, Secret Places* (Houndmills: Palgrave Macmillan, 2013).

— *Poetry and Jacobite Politics in Eighteenth-Century Britain and Ireland* (Cambridge: Cambridge University Press, 1994).

— *Scottish and Irish Romanticism* (Oxford: Oxford University Press, 2008).

— 'Scottish Sovereignty and the Union of 1707: Then and Now', *National Identities*, 14 (2014): 11–21.

— 'Sir Walter Scott: Historiography Contested by Fiction', in *The Cambridge History of the English Novel*, ed. Robert L. Caserio and Clement Hawes (Cambridge: Cambridge University Press, 2012), pp. 277–91.

— *Spectrum of Decadence: The Literature of the 1890s* (London: Routledge, 1993).

Pittock, Murray, and Isla Jack, 'Patrick Geddes and the Celtic Revival', in *The Edinburgh History of Scottish Literature*, ed. Ian Brown, Thomas Owen Clancy, Susan Manning and Murray Pittock, 3 vols (Edinburgh: Edinburgh University Press, 2007), II, pp. 338–46.

Pittock, Murray, and Christopher A. Whatley, 'Poems and Festivals, Art and Artefact and the Commemoration of Robert Burns, c.1844–1896', *The Scottish Historical Review*, 93.1 (2014): 56–79.

Potolsky, Matthew, *The Decadent Republic of Letters: Taste, Politics, and Cosmopolitan Community from Baudelaire to Beardsley* (Philadelphia: University of Pennsylvania Press, 2013).

Quinault, Roland, 'The Cult of the Centenary c.1784–1914', *Historical Research*, 71 (1998): 303–23.

Raine, Kathleen, *Yeats the Initiate: Essays on Certain Themes in the Work of W. B. Yeats* (Mountrath: Dolmen Press, 1986).

Rapetti, Radolphe, *Symbolism*, trans. Deke Dusinberre (New York: Flammarion, 2005).

Readman, Paul, 'The Place of the Past in English Culture c.1890–1914', *Past and Present*, 186 (2005): 147–200.

Recently Published and Forthcoming Books Issued by Patrick Geddes and Colleagues (Edinburgh: Patrick Geddes and Colleagues, 1896).

'Recognition of War Services', *The Scotsman*, 19 November 1919, p. 7.

Regardie, Israel, *The Golden Dawn* (St Paul, MN: Llewellyn, 1986).

— *What You Should Know About the Golden Dawn* (Phoenix: Falcon Press, 1983).

Reid, Julia, '"King Romance" in *Longman's Magazine:* Andrew Lang and Literary Populism', *Victorian Periodicals Review*, 44 (2011): 354–76.

— *Robert Louis Stevenson, Science, and the Fin de Siècle* (Houndmills: Palgrave Macmillan, 2006).

Renan, Ernest, *What is a Nation? And Other Political Writings*, ed. M. F. N. Giglioli (New York: Columbia University Press, 1893).

'The Revival of Pageantry', *Manchester Guardian*, 21 June 1923, p. 6.

Reynolds, Sian, *Paris–Edinburgh: Cultural Connections in the* Belle Epoque (Aldershot: Ashgate, 2007).

Rhys, Ernest, *Everyman Remembers* (New York: Cosmopolitan Book Corporation, 1931).

— *The Fiddler of Carne: A North Sea Winter's Tale* (Edinburgh: Patrick Geddes & Colleagues, 1896).

Richardson, Elsa, *Second Sight in the Nineteenth Century: Prophecy, Imagination and Nationhood* (Houndmills: Palgrave Macmillan, 2017).

Rigney, Ann, 'Embodied Communities: Commemorating Robert Burns, 1859', *Representations*, 115 (2011): 71–101.

— 'Plenitude, Scarcity and the Circulation of Cultural Memory', *Journal of European Studies*, 35.1 (2005): 11–28.

— 'Portable Monuments: Literature, Cultural Memory, and the Case of Jeanie Deans', *Poetics Today*, 25.2 (2004): 361–96.

Robertson, Pamela, 'Margaret Macdonald Mackintosh: The Seven Princesses', in *A Thoroughly Modern Afternoon: Margaret Macdonald Mackintosh and the Salon Waerndorfer in Vienna*, ed. Hanna Egger, Pamela Robertson, Peter Vergo and Manfred Trummer (Vienna: Böhlau, 2000), pp. 41–78.

Robertson, Ritchie, 'Nietzsche in Glasgow: Alexander Tille, John Davidson and Edwin Muir', in *Scotland and the 19th-Century World*, ed. Gerard Carruthers, David Goldie and Alastair Renfrew (Amsterdam: Rodopi, 2012), pp. 213–30.

Robertson, Stewart Alan, *A Moray Loon* (Edinburgh: Moray Press, 1933).
Rolleston, T. W., *Celtic: Myths and Legends* (New York: Thomas Y. Crowell, 1911).
Rousseau, Jean-Jacques, *A Discourse on Inequality*, trans. Maurice Cranston (London: Penguin, 1984).
Rubinstein, David, 'Edith Lanchester', *Oxford Dictionary of National Biography* <https://doi.org/10.1093/ref:odnb/56471> (last accessed 8 December 2018).
Russell, George William, *Some Passages of the Letters from A.E. to W. B. Yeats* (Dublin: Cuala Press, 1936).
Sands, L., 'Survivals of Paganism in Foula', *Glasgow Herald*, 17 November 1884, p. 8.
Santucci, James A., 'Theosophy', in *The Cambridge Companion to New Religious Movements*, ed. Olav Hammer and Mikael Rothstein (Cambridge: Cambridge University Press, 2012), pp. 231–46.
Sartre, Jean-Paul, 'Preface', in *The Wretched of the Earth*, trans. Constance Farrington (London: Penguin, 1967), pp. 7–26.
Schimmerling, Andre, 'The Last Activity of Patrick Geddes's Life: The Scots College, Montpellier', in *The Outlook Tower: Essays on Urbanisation in Memory of Patrick Geddes*, ed. J. V. Ferreira and S. S. Jha (Bombay: Popular Prakashan Private, 1976), pp. 51–3.
Schreiner, Olive, *Woman and Labour* (London: T. Fisher Unwin, 1911).
'Scotland', *Lucifer*, 10 (1892): 520.
'Scotland and Ireland: Repeal of the Unions', *The Fiery Cross*, April (1902): 5.
Scott, John, and Ray Bromley, *Envisioning Sociology: Victor Branford, Patrick Geddes, and the Quest for Social Reconstruction* (Albany: State University of New York Press, 2013).
Scott, Paul H., *Towards Independence* (Edinburgh: Polygon, 1991).
Scott, Tania, 'The Fantasy of the Celtic Revival: Lord Dunsay, Fiona Macleod, and W. B. Yeats', in *Border Crossings: Narration, Nation and Imagination in Scots and Irish Literature and Culture*, ed. Colin Younger (Newcastle: Cambridge Scholars, 2013), pp. 127–41.
Scott, Walter, *Chronicles of the Canongate* (London: John C. Nimmo, 1894).
— *The Minstrelsy of the Scottish Border*, 4 vols (Edinburgh: Richard Cadell, 1849).
Scottish Children's League of Pity Pageant Handbook, 1908, Pamphlet (1908).
'The Scottish Exhibition', *The Scotsman*, 25 May 1911, p. 6.
'The Scottish Historical Pageant', *The Fiery Cross*, July 1908, p. 7.
'Scottish National Exhibition', *The Scots Pictorial*, 4 (1908): 235.
'Scottish National Exhibition', Scottish Screen Archive, <http://ssa.nls.uk/film/1699> (last accessed 12 June 2014).
'The Scottish National Pageant', *Linlithgowshire Gazette*, 19 June 1908, p. 3.
'The Scottish Review, 1882–1900', *The Wellesley Index to Victorian Periodicals 1824–1900*, ed. Walter E. Houghton, 2 vols (Toronto: University of Toronto Press, 1972), II, pp. 785–8.

Self Determination for Scotland (Glasgow: Scottish Home Rule Association, 1919).

Sharp, Elizabeth A., ed., *Lyra Celtica: An Anthology of Representative Celtic Poetry* (Edinburgh: Patrick Geddes and Colleagues, 1896).

— *William Sharp (Fiona Macleod)* (London: William Heinemann, 1910).

— ed., *Women Poets of the Victorian Era* (London: Walter Scott, 1890).

Sharp, William, *The Divine Adventure; Iona; Studies in Spiritual History* (London: William Heinemann, 1919).

— *Green Fire: A Romance* (New York: Harper & Brothers, 1896).

— *The House of Usna* (Portland: Thomas B. Mosher, 1903).

— 'Introduction', in *Lyra Celtica: An Anthology of Representative Celtic Poetry*, ed. Elizabeth A. Sharp (Edinburgh: Patrick Geddes and Colleagues, 1896), pp. xix–li.

— 'The Irish Muse – I', *The North American Review*, 179 (1904): 685–97.

— 'La Jeune Belgique', *The Nineteenth Century*, 34 (1893): 416–36.

— 'Marius the Epicurean', *Time*, 12 (1885): 341–54.

— 'A Note on the Belgian Renascence', *The Chap-Book*, 4 (1895): 149–57.

— 'Old World Japan: Legends of the Land of the Gods', *The Academy*, 1232 (1895): 516–17.

— *The Pagan Review*, 1 (1892).

— *Pharais: A Romance of the Isles* (New York: Duffield, 1907).

— '*The Princess Maleine* and *The Intruder*', *The Academy*, 41 (1892): 270–2.

— *The Sin-Eater and Other Tales* (Edinburgh: Patrick Geddes and Colleagues, 1895).

— *Vistas* (Chicago: Stone and Kimball, 1894).

— *The Washer of the Ford: And Other Legendary Moralities* (Edinburgh: Patrick Geddes and Colleagues, 1896).

— *The Winged Destiny: Studies in the Spiritual History of the Gael* (London: Chapman and Hall, 1904).

Shaw, Michael, 'Aestheticism and Decadence in Patrick Geddes's Socio-Economics', in *Victorian Sustainability in Literature and Culture*, ed. Wendy Parkins (Abingdon: Routledge, 2018), pp. 165–79.

— 'Theosophy in Scotland: Oriental Occultism and National Identity', in *The Occult Imagination in Britain, 1875–1947*, ed. Christine Ferguson and Andrew Radford (Abingdon: Routledge, 2018), pp. 23–40.

Shepherd, Gillian, 'The Kailyard', in *The History of Scottish Literature*, ed. Cairns Craig, 4 vols (Aberdeen: Aberdeen University Press, 1988), III, pp. 309–20.

Shimokusu, Masaya, 'True Poetic Comrades: Mineko Matsumura and the Reception of Fiona Macleod in Japan', in *Celtic Connections: Irish–Scottish Relations and the Politics of Culture*, ed. Willy Maley and Alison O'Malley-Younger (Bern: Peter Lang, 2012), pp. 115–32.

Showalter, Elaine, *Sexual Anarchy: Gender and Culture at the Fin de Siècle* (London: Virago, 2001).

Simpson, Roger, 'Arthurian Pageants in Twentieth-Century Britain', *Arthuriana*, 18.1 (2008): 63–87.

Sims-Williams, Patrick, 'The Invention of Celtic Nature Poetry', in *Celticism*, ed.Terence Brown (Amsterdam: Rodopi, 1996), pp. 97–124.

Sinclair, Marie, *A Midnight Visit to Holyrood* (London: C. L. H. Wallace, 1887).

Sisson, Elaine, *Pearse's Patriots: St Enda's and the Cult of Boyhood* (Cork: Cork University Press, 2004).

Sloan, John, *John Davidson: First of the Moderns* (Oxford: Clarendon Press, 1995).

Smailes, Helen E., 'Pride of Lions: Noel Paton and the National Wallace Monument', *Architectural Heritage*, 25 (2014): 85–106.

Smith, Anthony D., *Ethno-Symbolism and Nationalism: A Cultural Approach* (London: Routledge, 2009).

— *Myths and Memories of the Nation* (Oxford: Oxford University Press, 1999).

'Some Illustrated Books', *The Times*, 24 May 1895, p. 13.

Stashower, Daniel, *Teller of Tales: The Life of Arthur Conan Doyle* (London: Allen Lane, 1999).

Stephen, Walter, 'Patrick Geddes – the Life', in *Think Local, Act Global: The Life and Legacy of Patrick Geddes*, ed. Walter Stephen (Edinburgh: Luath Press, 2011), pp. 17–38.

Stephens, Riccardo, *The Cruciform Mark* (London: Chatto & Windus, 1896).

Stevenson, David, *The Origins of Freemasonry: Scotland's Century, 1590–1710* (Cambridge: Cambridge University Press, 1988).

Stevenson, Robert Louis, 'Byways of Book Illustration: Two Japanese Romances', *Magazine of Art*, 6 (1883): 8–15.

— *Catriona* (Edinburgh: Canongate, 1995).

— *Kidnapped* (Edinburgh: Canongate, 1989).

— *The Lantern-Bearers and Other Essays*, ed. Jeremy Treglown (New York: Farrar Straus Giroux, 1988).

— *The Letters of Robert Louis Stevenson*, ed. Bradford A. Booth and Ernest Mehew, 8 vols (New Haven, CT: Yale University Press, 1995).

— *The Master of Ballantrae* (Edinburgh: Canongate, 1992).

— *Memories and Portraits* (New York: Charles Scribner's Sons, 1902).

— *Pan's Pipes* (Boston: Houghton Mifflin, 1910).

— *Romances: Volume III* (Edinburgh: T. & A. Constable, 1897).

— *The Silverado Squatters* (Boston: Robert Brothers, 1884).

— *Travels with a Donkey in the Cévennes* (London: Chatto and Windus, 1912).

— *Weir of Hermiston* (Edinburgh: Canongate, 1995).

— 'Yoshida-Torajiro', *Cornhill Magazine*, 41 (1880): 327–34.

Stroh, Silke, *Gaelic Scotland in the Colonial Imagination: Anglophone Writing from 1600–1900* (Evanston: Northwestern University, 2017).

Sugg Ryan, Deborah, '"Pageantitis": Frank Lascelles' 1907 Oxford Historical Pageant, Visual Spectacle and Popular Memory', *Visual Culture in Britain*, 8.2 (2007): 63–82.

Sutherland, Douglas, 'Education as an Agent of Social Evolution: The Educational Projects of Patrick Geddes in Late-Victorian Scotland', *History of Education*, 38 (2009): 349–65.

Suzuki, Hiroyuki, 'From Glasgow to Japan: Background to Mackintosh', in *Charles Rennie Mackintosh* (Tokyo: Japan Art and Culture Association, 1985), pp. 11–15.

Swinburne, Algernon Charles, *Poems and Prose* (London: J. M. Dent & Sons, 1940).

Symonds, John, *The Beast 666: The Life of Aleister Crowley* (London: Pindar Press, 1997).

Symons, Arthur, 'In Praise of Gypsies', *Journal of the Gypsy Lore Society: New Series*, 1 (1907): 294–9.

— *The Symbolist Movement in Literature*, ed. Matthew Creasy (Manchester: Carcanet, 2014).

Talbott, Siobhan, 'British Commercial Interests on the French Atlantic Coast, c. 1560–1713', *Historical Research*, 85 (2012): 394–409.

Tanabe, Yukinobu, 'Robert Louis Stevenson's View of the Japanese' (1976) [chapter in unidentified book].

Tatarkowski, Maggie, 'Japanese Art and its Effect on the Art Nouveau Movement in Britain', in *The Anglo-Japanese Alliance, 1902–1922*, ed. Phillips Payson O'Brien (London: RoutledgeCurzon, 2004), pp. 208–21.

Thomas, Edward, *Beautiful Wales* (London: A. & C. Black, 1905).

Thompson, Catherine Ward, 'Patrick Geddes and the Edinburgh Zoological Garden: Expressing Universal Processes through Place', *Landscape History*, 25 (2006): 80–93.

Thuente, Mary Helen, *W. B. Yeats and Irish Folklore* (Totowa, NJ: Gill and Macmillan, 1980).

Townsend, J. Benjamin, *John Davidson: Poet of Armageddon* (New Haven, CT: Yale University Press, 1961).

Trotter, Mary, *Ireland's National Theatre: Political Performance and the Origins of the Irish Dramatic Movement* (Syracuse, NY: Syracuse University Press, 2001).

Tully, Caroline, 'Egyptosophy in the British Museum: Florence Farr, the Egyptian Adept and the *Ka*', in *The Occult Imagination in Britain 1875–1947*, ed. Christine Ferguson and Andrew Radford (London: Routledge, 2018), pp. 131–45.

'The Union with England and Scottish Nationality', *The North British Review*, 21 (1854): 69–100.

'University Hall Extension: Edinburgh', *The Builder*, 65 (1893): 140–1.

Vadillo, Ana Parejo, 'Another Renaissance: The Decadent Poetic Drama of A. C. Swinburne and Michael Field', in *Decadent Poetics: Literature and*

Form at the British Fin de Siècle, ed. Jason David Hall and Alex Murray (Houndmills: Palgrave Macmillan, 2013), pp. 116–40.
Vance, Norman, *The Victorians and Ancient Rome* (Oxford: Blackwell, 1997).
Vaninskaya, Anna, 'The Late-Victorian Romance Revival: A Generic Excursus', *English Literature in Transition*, 51 (2008): 57–79.
Varty, Anne, *A Preface to Oscar Wilde* (Harlow: Longman, 1998).
Vaughan, Dai, 'Secret Symbols and Hidden Meanings', *Journal of the Charles Rennie Mackintosh Society*, 84.1 (2003): 4–5.
Vergo, Peter, 'The Vanished Frieze', in *A Thoroughly Modern Afternoon: Margaret Macdonald Mackintosh and the Salon Waerndorfer in Vienna*, ed. Hanna Egger, Pamela Robertson, Peter Vergo and Manfred Trummer (Vienna: Böhlau, 2000), pp. 18–40.
Walker, Frank Arneil, 'Scottish Baronial Architecture', in *Charles Rennie Mackintosh: The Architectural Papers*, ed. Pamela Robertson (Wendlebury: White Cockade, 1990), pp. 29–48.
Walker, John, 'Introduction', in *The Scottish Sketches of R. B. Cunninghame Graham*, ed. John Walker (Edinburgh: Scottish Academic Press, 1982), pp. 1–15.
Wallace, Stuart, *John Stuart Blackie: Scottish Scholar and Patriot* (Edinburgh: Edinburgh University Press, 2006).
'The Wallace Monument', *The Aberdeen Journal*, 25 June 1856, p. 8.
'The Wallace Monument', *Glasgow Herald*, 13 June 1856, p. 4.
'The Wallace Monument', *The London Reader*, 130 (1865): 4.
Wanliss, T. D., *The Bars to British Unity: A Plea for National Sentiment* (Edinburgh: William Paterson, 1885).
'The Warwick Pageant', *The Saturday Review of Politics, Literature, Science and Art*, 102 (1906): 12–13.
Watanabe, Toshio, *High Victorian Japonisme* (Bern: Peter Lang, 1991).
Watson, Roderick, 'The Modern Scottish Literary Renaissance', in *The Edinburgh Companion to Twentieth-Century Scottish Literature*, ed. Ian Brown and Alan Riach (Edinburgh: Edinburgh University Press, 2009), pp. 75–87.
Watts, Cedric, 'Introduction', in *The Lost World & Other Stories* (Ware: Wordsworth, 2010), pp. vii–xxi.
Watts, Cedric, and Laurence Davies, *Cunninghame Graham: A Critical Biography* (Cambridge: Cambridge University Press, 1979).
Welter, Volker M., 'Arcades for Lucknow: Patrick Geddes, Charles Rennie Mackintosh and the Reconstruction of the City', *Architectural History*, 42 (1999): 316–32.
Westcott, Wynn, 'Alchemy', in *Astral Projection, Ritual Magic and Alchemy*, ed. Francis King (Wellingborough: Aquarian Press, 1971), pp. 179–91.
Westwood, Jennifer, and Sophia Kingshill, *The Lore of Scotland: A Guide to Scottish Legends* (London: Random House, 2009).
Whatley, Christopher, *Immortal Memory: Burns and the Scottish People* (Edinburgh: John Donald, 2016).

White, Joseph Gleeson, 'Some Glasgow Designers. Part I', *The Studio*, 11 (1897): 86–100.

Whyte, Iain Boyd, 'The Spirit of the City', in *The City after Patrick Geddes*, ed. Volker M. Welter and James Lawson (Oxford: Peter Lang, 2000), pp. 15–32.

Wilde, Oscar, *Complete Poetry*, ed. Isobel Murray (Oxford: Oxford University Press, 1997).

— *Plays, Prose Writings and Poems* (London: Everyman's Library, 1991).

Williams, Daniel G., 'Celticism', in *Late Victorian into Modern*, ed. Laura Marcus, Michèle Mendelssohn and Kirsten E. Shepherd-Barr (Oxford: Oxford University Press, 2016), pp. 67–82.

Williams, Mark, *Ireland's Immortals: A History of the Gods of Irish Myth* (Princeton, NJ: Princeton University Press, 2016).

Willsdon, Clare A. P., *Mural Painting in Britain 1840–1940: Image and Meaning* (Oxford: Oxford University Press, 2000).

Withington, Robert, *English Pageantry: An Historical Outline*, 2 vols (Cambridge, MA: Harvard University Press, 1920).

— 'Louis Napoleon Parker', *The New England Quarterly*, 12 (1939): 510–20.

Wittig, Kurt, *The Scottish Tradition in Literature* (Edinburgh: Mercat Press, 1978).

Wood, Christopher, *Olympian Dreamers: Victorian Classical Painters 1860–1914* (London: Constable, 1983).

Worth, Katharine, *The Irish Drama of Europe: From Yeats to Beckett* (London: Athlone Press, 1978).

— *Oscar Wilde* (Houndmills: Macmillan Education, 1983).

Yeats, W. B., *Memoirs*, ed. Denis Donoghue (London: Macmillan, 1972).

Young, Robert J. C., *The Idea of English Ethnicity* (Oxford: Blackwell, 2008).

Zangwill, Israel, 'Without Prejudice', *The Chap-Book*, 4 (1895): 230–6.

Zatlin, Linda Gertner, *Beardsley, Japonisme and the Perversion of the Victorian Ideal* (Cambridge: Cambridge University Press, 1997).

Index

A reference in *italics* shows a figure and references to plates are preceded by a P.